FIFTY GREAT THINKERS
ON HISTORY

FIFTY GREAT THINKERS ON HISTORY

Marnie Hughes-Warrington

London and New York

First published by Routledge
11 New Fetter Lane, London EC4P 4EE

Simultaneously published in the USA and Canada
by Routledge
29 West 35th Street, New York. NY 10001

Routledge is an imprint of the Taylor & Francis Group

© Marnie Hughes-Warrington

First Indian Reprint 2004

Typeset in Bembo by Keystroke, Jacaranda Lodge, Wolverhampton

Printed at Chennai Micro Print Pvt. Ltd. Export Division 100% EOU
No. 34, Nelson Manickam Road, Aminijikarai, Chennai 600 029, India

ISBN 0-415-16982-8 (pbk)

For Sale in South Asia only

ALPHABETICAL LIST OF CONTENTS

CHRONOLOGICAL LIST OF CONTENTS

PREFACE

These days, an invitation to write a book on 'fifty key thinkers' would make many people cringe. Works of this kind, and canons in general, are out of favour. And perhaps rightly so, for many writers have argued that canons are not objective and neutral descriptions of 'the good' of a subject. Rather, they are considered to be reflections of the ideas, values, hopes and experiences of a small segment of the population: white, middle-class, educated men. Canon compilers can be like the rules committee of a guild who, in Marc Bloch's words, 'codify the tasks permitted to the members of the trade, and who, with a list once and for all complete, unhesitatingly reserve their exercise to the licensed masters. . . . '[1] When they say that certain features or interpretations of a subject are important, they give them visibility and legitimacy. Conversely, ignoring or excluding interpretations of a subject can lead some people to feel that the subject has no relevance to their needs or interests. It can also damage their self-image. As Charles Taylor has written,

> a person or group of people can suffer real damage, real distortion, if the people or society around them mirror back to them a confining or demeaning or contemptible picture of themselves. Nonrecognition or misrecognition can inflict harm, can be a form of oppression, imprisoning someone in a false, distorted, and reduced mode of being.[2]

On the assumption that nonrecognition leads to poor self-image, it is a commonplace to argue that we ought to recognise and respect the ideas and interests of *all* persons. This argument is also often conjoined with the further assertion that there are deeply entrenched differences in the ways in which people view the world. A person's claims about a subject, it is suggested, are shaped and limited by his or her socio-historical context. There is no way to escape or rise above that context and write about a subject from a God's-eye point of view. As Donna Haraway puts it, both people and their knowledge claims are 'situated'.[3] Thus we should turn away from objective or universal claims about a subject, or 'metanarratives', because they entail talking for or over the top of other people. Rather, we should encourage people to talk for themselves. And indeed in recent years we have seen the fragmentation of historiography (discussion on historical writing and on the nature of history) into numerous situated conversations: conversations which acknowledge that they are of and for people of different gender, sexual orientation, economic, educational and/or professional status, race, religious affiliation, disability, age and so on.

At first sight, the case for the fragmentation of historiography appears compelling. It seems morally right that we should respect others and let them speak for themselves. Yet a number of problems arise. To begin with, in turning away from 'metanarratives', like canons, to 'situated discussions', we do not escape from questions about representation. For instance, do all women speak with the same historiographical voice? Do only women speak with that same voice? Would an economically disadvantaged or an illiterate woman see the features and methods of history in the same way that I do? That is, are situated feminist discussions simply reflections of the ideas and experiences of economically and educationally advantaged white women? As Maria Lugones and Elizabeth Spelman have written:

> The deck is stacked when one group takes it upon itself to develop the theory and then have others criticise it. Categories are quick to congeal, and the experiences of women whose lives do not fit the categories will appear as anomalous when in fact the theory should have grown out of them as much as others from the beginning.[4]

Lugones and Spelman are against the idea of an 'essential' concept of woman because they believe that it will lead to a hierarchy of categories of 'woman'. Those who do not conform to the ideal of 'true woman' will be viewed as inferior. For them, gender cannot be isolated from class and race and theorised separately. If we dispense with the idea of 'woman', however, we might also have to dispense with the idea of 'middle-class woman of colour', or 'economically disadvantaged white woman' or 'illiterate urban woman', and so on into infinite regress. The problem is that we have to, as Nancy Fraser puts it, 'navigate safely between the twin shoals of essentialism and nominalism, between reifying women's identity under stereotypes of femininity, on the one hand, and dissolving them into sheer nullity and oblivion on the other'.[5] It seems that if we are to discuss history at all, then we will at times have no choice but to talk for and over the top of other people.

Furthermore, we must face questions about the idea of 'difference'. Supporters of situated discussions have argued that an emphasis on the 'common' in discussions often masks the expectation of conformity to the ideas and ideals of a white male elite. In reaction to this, they have counter-emphasised 'difference'. But this should also be scrutinised: when people talk of 'difference', are they talking about the same thing? One person, for instance, may understand difference in terms of different kinds within a particular category (such as types of historical evidence, historical explanations and so on). Another may assume that difference means that two things have absolutely nothing in common. In addition, how do some differences come to be seen as significant and others not? Why, for instance, are differences in gender considered important but differences in handedness are not? There is also the thorny issue of identity history: whether discussions about a particular group's view of history ought only to be conducted by members of that group. If we conclude that women's history ought to be written only by women, do we unfairly silence men who identify strongly with feminist ideas? What is more, we have to ask whether we will have any authority to tell others that a group's voice is worth listening to or that it ought to be silenced. On what grounds, for instance, can I dismiss the claim that it is all right to fabricate evidence? Or that disputes in historiography ought to be settled in a boxing ring? Or that a student should ignore African-American perspectives on the American Civil War? We also have to question whether people will always benefit when traits they possess are highly valued. Advocates of situated discussions assume that all people will be better off if they are given the right to speak for themselves. This is not always the case, however, for accepting uncritically what an individual says may actually do them a disservice. Historians who spell badly, for example, might be better off in circumstances where poor spelling is not valued and where, as a consequence, others may help them to communicate more effectively.[6]

But most importantly, I believe that the idea of situated discussions is underpinned by an impoverished sense of what historiographical discussions can achieve. The promotion of discussion within different groups may come at the expense of communication *across* different groups. Some groups may emphasise differences so much that they lose sight of the fact that we do share ideas in common. Some may even use difference to foreclose discussion. Others may wonder whether inter-group discussion is worth the effort. The promotion of situated discussions may ultimately prove detrimental to the efforts of previously marginalised groups to bring about change. Situated discussions may thus simply stress those ideas and experiences that confirm one's identity in a community of essentially like-minded people. That leaves us, as Charles Altieri notes:

> precious little otherness, precious little ground for confronting our own self-satisfactions, for framing alternative views of our ends, for combating proposed moral reasons for a myopically narrow professionalism, or for understanding the past in a way that challenges the assumptions underlying competing contemporary theories.[7]

Although it is as slippery a concept as 'difference', 'otherness' is worth wrestling with because it has an important role to play in historiography. It can help us to understand what we hold in common with others and how and why we differ. But it can also lead us to reflect on and scrutinise our own hopes and interests. It can show us what we are and what we might be.

This dual aim of promoting exploration of ourselves and others through historiography underpins *Fifty Key Thinkers on History*.

Identifying fifty 'key thinkers on history' is no easy matter. It is apparent that no list that I can produce – even with the help of numerous other historians – will find universal agreement. Every historian will have different views about who ought to be included and why. But this doesn't trouble me, for two reasons. First, *Fifty Key Thinkers on History* is explicitly not a 'top fifty' of all-time greats on the basis of popularity. Many of the thinkers I have chosen would certainly make it on to such a list (for example, Gibbon, Ranke, Thucydides), but others are more likely to bring historians out in a rash. The list is not even a 'top fifty' on the basis of impact or significance alone, but rather of challenge, as I elaborate below. Second, and more importantly, universal agreement is not my goal. Indeed, if readers like every choice that I have made, then I will be disappointed, because universal agreement usually means the end of discussion. Nor would I dream of trying to convince readers that they should agree with and imitate every thinker they encounter. My choice of thinkers would make it impossible for anyone to do so. For example, try reconciling the views of Geoffrey Elton and Hayden White, or even those of Marc Bloch and Lucien Febvre. In my view, one of the hallmarks of a 'key thinker' is someone who inspires dispute. With Joan Wallach Scott, I endorse the idea that conflicts and disagreements about the content, uses and meanings of knowledge are an important part of 'history'.[8] Accordingly, I have tried to identify thinkers whose thought has come to be widely regarded in the historical community as a challenge to be reckoned with, requiring such reckoning if one is to earn the right to think similarly or otherwise, and rewarding the effort such a challenge involves. Thus for me, *Fifty Key Thinkers on History* is as much about provocation as it is about suggestion.

In line with my view of this work as suggestive, provocative and thus educational, I have tried to include a diverse range of views. To begin with, I have adopted a broad view of 'thinker on history': a person who offers us works of history (like Carr, Davis, Hobsbawm, Taylor, Thompson, Turner), works on history (such as Collingwood, Kuhn, Marx), more general works that have changed the shape of historical inquiry (for instance, Heidegger, Kant), the message that deeds can change the way we view the past (Woodson) or any of these in combination. My inclusion of the last reflects the belief that thought is not evidenced in print alone.

It is also important to note that the shape of history is not determined solely by historians, or even by those who believe the subject to be valuable. Kant, for instance, is no enthusiastic champion, but his writings on mind fundamentally changed the way in which we view the labours of historians. Furthermore, the forms of inquiry which make up history today, the kinds of issues addressed, the ways in which they are framed and dealt with, and the concepts that are drawn upon, have long genealogies.

It thus goes without saying that the study of history requires attention to the history of history writing. It is for this reason that my choice is not restricted to contemporary thinkers. We only have to imagine the absence of, say, Herodotus, Thucydides or Tacitus to realise how much our knowledge of ancient European history, as well as historiography, is dependent on them. Additionally, thinkers from the distant past may have much to contribute to ongoing inquiry; for instance, the works of the ancient Chinese historian Ssu-ma Ch'ien and the medieval French historian Froissart raise questions that are pertinent to postmodern historians. But I also believe that confronting a very different view of the world – such as that offered by Livy, Polybius, Bede or Gregory of Tours – may also help us to gain critical distance from our own views. Nor has the shaping of history from a Western perspective been the privilege of Europeans and North Americans alone. Ssu-ma Ch'ien, Ibn Khaldun, Cheikh Anta Diop and Manning Clark show us that that is not the case. In addition, I have excluded one thinker on the grounds that his ideas have been more than adequately explored by John Lechte in *Fifty Key Contemporary Thinkers*: Friedrich Nietzsche. His exclusion is more a comment on the quality of Lechte's writing than on his own. In all, the final justification of each choice is the content of the corresponding entry.

The variety in this work, however, is a variety within limits. It does not – indeed, cannot – include equally weighted contributions from all times and places or from people of different gender, sexual orientation, economic status, religious affiliation or disability. The majority of thinkers chosen are educated males from nineteenth- and twentieth-century Europe and North America. In part, this is a fair reflection of the emergence of history as a separate discipline in these areas in the nineteenth century and the subsequent explosion in the number of works of history and on history.

Furthermore, I do not believe that research into a particular group's history (and view of history) should be conducted only by members of that group. Michel Foucault's writings, for instance, have proved promising for those interested in women's history. But this predominance is also the regrettable but unavoidable result of the restriction of the *Fifty Key* series to the achievements of individuals. Historiography is not simply the sum of the deeds of great men. But standing out as an individual, as David Christian notes, has normally meant being literate and holding a prominent political or intellectual position in society.[9] Such conditions make it difficult to include individuals from communities without written languages, women, and the countless individuals who made it possible for the few to stand out. To get a clearer picture of historiography as more than the achievements of prominent individuals, I recommend that you explore such works as *The Companion to Historiography* (ed. M. Bentley, published by Routledge, 1997), Michael Stanford's *Introduction to the Philosophy of History* (published by Blackwell, 1998), Beverley Southgate's *History: What and Why?* (published by Routledge, 1996) and the ever-popular *The Nature of History* (by Arthur Marwick, published by Macmillan, 1989) and *The Pursuit of History* (by John Tosh, published by Longman, 1991). But I also invite you to use this work as a negative backdrop for reflection on the exclusions involved in past and present understandings of 'history'.[10]

Among the twentieth-century thinkers included are a number who challenge the traditional view of history formulated by male elites, that of an 'objective' account of the deeds of prominent individuals (such as Davis, Hobsbawm, Rowbotham, Scott, Thompson, White). But no thinker has been selected simply on the grounds of gender, ethnicity or economic status. It is important to stress that while I have aimed for diversity, my choices are underpinned by the unifying assumption that 'key thinkers' are those who are worth engaging with. For me, the bottom line is that they are worth taking seriously because they inspire discussion and even dispute about the content, uses and meanings of history; they have had a good deal to do with the genealogy of the discipline; and their questions and their ideas and ways of dealing with them suggest promising lines of inquiry.

The variety of thinkers included in *Fifty Key Thinkers on History* would make it difficult, I believe, to group them into 'schools of thought' or 'approaches to inquiry' as previous authors in this series have done. But I have also refrained from grouping them thus because I believe that it can lead us to consider thinkers in a one-dimensional way. Labelling a writer a 'Marxist', for instance, may lead to the neglect of ideas which he or she held that do not fit that mould. It also makes it difficult to deal with writers who combine more than one approach, change their views over time or do not draw on approaches in any systematic way. Questions can also be raised about who decides what 'labels' are legitimate and how their usage changes over time. That does not mean that I have avoided all mention of 'labels': where appropriate, I have mentioned them within particular entries. These cases are those in which, first, writers have applied a label to themselves, and second, a number of commentators have applied a label to a writer.

Given these concerns about groupings, I have opted instead for an alphabetical arrangement because it offers greatest ease of reference. I also believe that the strange bedfellows that result from this arrangement may stimulate critical reflection. So that you may consider the entries in historical context, however, a chronological table of contents is given.

As with other works in Routledge's *Fifty Key* series, each entry includes a short essay outlining biographical information and the key ideas of the thinker in focus. Each essay, I hope, will give you a taste of the thinker's interests and approach to the past and how others (myself included) have engaged with it. That I say 'taste' accords with my belief that this book offers points of departure, not points of arrival. Having read what I have to say, I hope that you will explore discussions on and by these thinkers in more depth for yourself. I have included details of each writer's major works and further resources. I call the latter further 'resources' rather than 'reading' because they include audio-visual materials and web addresses as well as printed materials. To help you explore connections between various writers, I have also cross-referenced each entry to other entries in this book and in the *Fifty Key* series.

These reflections, and my selection, are unlikely to satisfy either diehard defenders or bitter critics of canons, and I expect that people will ask me, 'Why didn't you include so-and-so?' for the rest of my life. If this work encourages more people to engage with historiography, however, then it will have been worth it.

Notes

1 M. Bloch, *The Historian's Craft*, trans. L. A. Manyon, Manchester: Manchester University Press, 1992, p. 18.
2 C. Taylor, *Multiculturalism and 'The Politics of Education'*, Princeton, NJ: Princeton University Press, 1992, p. 25.
3 D. J. Haraway, 'Situated Knowledges: the Science Question in Feminism and the Privilege of Partial Perspective', in *Simians, Cyborgs, and Women: the Reinvention of Nature*, London: Free Association Books, 1991, pp. 183–201. See also S. Harding, *The Science Question in Feminism*, Ithaca, NY: Cornell University Press, 1986; H. Longino, *Science as Social Knowledge*, Princeton, NJ: Princeton University Press, 1990; and A. M. Jaggar, *Feminist Politics and Human Nature*, Totowa, NJ: Rowman & Allanheld, 1983, p. 376.
4 M. Lugones and E. Spelman, 'Have We Got a Theory for You: Feminist Theory, Cultural Imperialism, and the Demand for "The Woman's Voice"', *Hypatia, a Special Issue of Women's Studies International Forum*, 1983, 6: 579; cf. E. Spelman, *Inessential Woman*, Boston, MA: Beacon Press, 1988.
5 N. Fraser, 'The Uses and Abuses of French Discourse Theory', in N. Fraser and S. Bartky (eds), *Revaluing French Feminism*, Bloomington, IN: Indiana University Press, 1991, p. 191.
6 H. Baber, 'The Market for Feminist Epistemology', *Monist*, 1994, 77(4): 405–6.
7 C. Altieri, 'Canons and Differences', in V. Nemoianu (ed.), *Canons and Consequences: Reflections on the Ethical Force of Imaginative Ideals*, Evanston, IL: Northwestern University Press, 1990, p. 59.
8 J. W. Scott, 'History in Crisis? The Others' Side of the Story', *American Historical Review*, 1989, 94(3): 680–92.
9 D. Christian, 'The Shapers', 'This Living Century: the Leaders', in *The Weekend Australian*, 12 June 1999, p. 20.
10 Elizabeth Fox-Genovese, 'The Feminist Challenge to the Canon', *National Forum*, Summer 1989, 33: 34.

ACKNOWLEDGEMENTS

A number of the thinkers in this work stress the importance of laying bare the ideas that shape human activities. Following their lead, I wish to offer some words of thanks to those people who have helped me to complete this project.

I would like to begin by acknowledging those individuals who read and commented on sections of the manuscript: David Boucher, Natalie Zemon Davis, Eric Hobsbawm, Trevor McClaughlin, Adrian Moore, Bob Purdie, Jill Roe, Mary Spongberg and Claudia Wagner. I am deeply appreciative of the advice they offered, though of course any errors are my own responsibility. In addition, I would like to thank Kieron Corless, Heather McCallum, Roger Thorp, the ten anonymous reviewers of the proposal and manuscript and Routledge for giving this kid from Oz a chance. I am also forever indebted to Bruce, who loved, honoured and proofread and pushed me to untangle a number of ideas and sentences. It is to him that this work is dedicated.

Setting was also very important. Living in different places helped me to appreciate the different ways people view the world. I am grateful to those who helped me with my research at the University of Oxford, the University of Washington and Macquarie University. In particular I would like to thank the Warden and Fellows of Merton College; the College of Education at Washington; the Department of Modern History at Macquarie; the staff of the Bodleian Library, especially Colin Harris and the staff of the Modern Manuscripts Reading Room; the staff of the Suzzallo and Allen Libraries; the staff of the Macquarie University Library and those library users who refrained from using mobile phones; and the R. G. Collingwood Society. I would also like to acknowledge the support of many friends, especially Susan Durber and the congregation of St Columba's in Oxford; Andrew Graydon; the ministers and folks at University Congregational in Seattle; Catherine Vickers; and Helen Verrier. A big thanks to Brad Portin, who kept me going with words of support and tater tots. I also welcome the opportunity to thank those people who helped me to set out on this historiographical journey: Mike Degenhardt, Mary Fearnley-Sander and the Tasmanian branch of the Australian Rhodes Scholars' Association.

Finally, I would like to thank the Hughes and Warrington families for their love, support and good humour.

ABBREVIATIONS

CT   Lechte, J., *Fifty Key Contemporary Thinkers: From Structuralism to Postmodernity*, London: Routledge, 1995.
IRT   Griffiths, M., *Fifty Key Thinkers in International Relations*, London: Routledge, 1999.
JT   Cohn-Sherbok, D., *Fifty Key Jewish Thinkers*, London: Routledge, 1997.
ME   Pressman, S., *Fifty Major Economists*, London: Routledge, 1999.
MP   Collinson, D., *Fifty Major Philosophers: A Reference Guide*, London: Routledge, 1989.

BEDE *c.* 673–735

Bede is often portrayed as a writer with a great fondness for miracles. And indeed, when one considers the work for which he is most remembered – *The Ecclesiastical History of the English People* (AD 731) – it is not hard to see why. In this one can read of the blind regaining their sight, the sick being cured, storms being quelled and cities being saved from destruction through the grace of God. Such things make for entertaining reading, but they also make it hard for modern readers to take him seriously as an historian. Yet he deserves to be taken seriously, for as Levison puts it, 'one only has to imagine [his] work as non-existent to realise how much of our knowledge of early English history, political as well as ecclesiastical, is dependent on him'.[1]

Nearly everything we know about the life of Bede derives from the last book of *The Ecclesiastical History of the English People* (5: §24; hereafter *History*).[2] He was born near the English monastery of Wearmouth around 673. When he was seven, his parents brought him to the monastery and gave him over to the care of the monks. Two years later, the founder of the monastery, Abbot Benedict Biscop, sent him and twenty other monks to the south bank of the River Tyne, where they established the community of Jarrow. He was ordained a deacon in 692 and a priest around 703. While Bede visited Lindisfarne Priory on Holy Island and possibly also York, he spent the rest of his life at Jarrow. There he took advantage of the impressive library that Biscop had amassed and wrote a number of works on scripture, Latin, saints' lives (hagiography), chronology and history. He died in 735. In the eleventh century his remains were removed to Durham for safekeeping. They were later dispersed, but his tomb may still be seen at Durham Cathedral.

Through his writings, Bede hoped to help people grow in Christian faith. In the preface to his *History*, for instance, he writes:

> if history records good things of good men, the thoughtful hearer is encouraged to imitate what is good: or if it records evil of wicked men, the devout, religious listener or reader is encouraged to avoid all that is sinful and perverse to follow what he knows to be good and pleasing to God.

And this meant, in the first instance, teaching his fellow monks the official language of the church: Latin. Bede drew on the works of Latin grammarians of late antiquity to compose a number of works on Latin grammar and spelling. Yet he also recognised the importance of the vernacular (Old English) in Christian instruction. Bede died, his pupil Cuthbert tells us, just after he dictated the last line in an Old English translation of the gospel of John.[3] Furthermore, in book 4 of his *History*, he introduces Caedmon, the first English poet known by name. In his account of Caedmon's life, Bede offers one of the earliest recorded observations concerning the difficulty of translating verse from one language to another. 'This is the general sense', he writes, 'but not the actual words that Caedmon sang in his dream; for verses, however masterly, cannot be translated literally from one language into another without losing much of their beauty and dignity' (4: §24). Proficiency in Latin made it possible for monks to study the Bible and works of theology by writers such as Ambrose, Jerome, Augustine of Hippo and Pope Gregory. It is clear that Bede wished to help with such study because over half of the works that he wrote were on the scriptures and the ideas of the 'church fathers' (5: §24).

Computus, the study of time and the calendar, also played an important part in monastic life during Bede's day. When the Anglo-Saxon invasions severed the ties between Ireland and the rest of Christendom, the means for calculating the date of Easter had not been universally established. As Roman Christianity re-established itself in Britain, it collided with the Christianity practised by Celtic missionaries from Iona and Lindisfarne. This led to arguments about the date of Easter. At the synod of Whitby (664) this dispute was settled in favour of the Roman side, but the decision applied only to the kingdom of Northumbria. In *De Temporibus* (trans. *On Time*, 703), Bede described and argued in favour of the rules and formulas used by Roman Christianity. Echoing the sixth-century monk Dionysius Exiguus, he also argued for a dating system centred on the birth of Christ. Previously, the Anglo-Saxons had usually dated by the regnal years of their kings, or by the indiction (fifteen-year fiscal period instituted by Constantine in 313). Both systems had their disadvantages, as the regnal years of one Anglo-Saxon kingdom were inapplicable to another and incomprehensible abroad, and as the indiction was only a cycle of fifteen years it was not always clear which cycle was intended.[4] Thus in the service of faith Bede solved a problem which had troubled earlier historians such as Gildas (who gave only one date in his writings) and Nennius (who used no fewer than twenty-eight different eras). It is due in no small part to Bede that the ideas of Roman Christianity were able to take root again in Britain and that many people still classify dates as either BC (Before Christ) or AD (Anno Domini, trans. 'in the year of our Lord').

De Temporibus and the later *De Temporum* (trans. *On the Reckoning of Time*, 725) also include chronicles of world history: lists of dates with corresponding events. These chronicles detail the intervention of God in human events and the lives of holy men and women. Out of these chronicles arose his celebrations of the deeds of a number of saints, of which the best known are his lives of the first three abbots of Wearmouth and Jarrow (Ceolfrid, Hwaetbet and Benedict Biscop) and *Two Lives of St Cuthbert*.

Bede's interest in chronology and hagiography are combined in his *History*. In this Bede offers us valuable insight into the ecclesiastical and political developments of a period – 597 to 731 – for which there are few other surviving sources. It is arranged in chronological order but this is broken up to some extent by saints' lives and descriptions of the phases in the Anglo-Saxon kingdoms. The first book of the *History* opens with a sketch of the historical and geographical background for the domination of the Anglo-Saxons over the British and the failure of the Celts to convert them to Christianity. He then writes of the persecution of Christians that became empire-wide and reached a new intensity under the rule of Diocletian. In Britain, it produced the land's first martyr, St Alban. Bede's account of Alban's execution is colourful, as this excerpt attests:

> Led out to execution, the saint came to a river which flowed swiftly between the town and the arena where he was to die. . . . [H]e approached the river, and as he raised his eyes to heaven in prayer, the river ran dry in its bed and left him a way to cross. When among others the appointed executioner himself saw this, he was so moved in spirit that he hurried to meet Alban at the place of execution, and throwing down his drawn sword, fell at his feet, begging that he might be thought worthy to die with the martyr if he could not die in his place. While . . . other executioners hesitated to pick up his sword from the ground, the most revered confessor of God ascended a hill about five hundred paces from the arena. . . . Here, then, the gallant martyr met his death, and received the crown of life which God has promised to those who love him. But the man whose impious hands struck off that pious head was not permitted to boast of his deed, for as the martyr's head fell off, the executioner's eyes dropped out on the ground.
>
> (1: §7)

For Bede, the Britons were like the Hebrews in their sojourn in Sinai on the way to the Promised Land. When they respected God's laws, they prospered; when they sinned, God permitted them to suffer the evil consequences of their misdeeds. Chief among their misdeeds was their failure to preach the faith to the Angles and Saxons who inhabited Britain with them. God, however, 'did not utterly abandon the people whom he had chosen; for he remembered them, and sent [Britain] more worthy preachers of truth to bring them to the faith' (1: §22). These 'more worthy preachers' were St Augustine of Canterbury and the band of monks sent with him to Britain in 597. Bede's description of Augustine's mission in Britain is notable for his inclusion of the purportedly verbatim responses of Gregory to Augustine's pastoral questions (1: §27).[5]

Book 2 focuses on the conversion of Edwin, King of Northumbria. God blessed Edwin and his realm so much, Bede claims, 'that the proverb still runs that a woman could carry her new-born babe across the island from sea to sea without any fear of harm' (2: §16). In this book, as with the previous one, political and ecclesiastical developments are intertwined. He records that in the year 633, for instance, Edwin became a victim of a revolt led in part by the pagan king Penda. He is happy to note in the opening of Book 3, however, that the army of King Oswald, 'small in numbers but strong in the faith of Christ', destroyed Penda and his army (3: §1). Later chapters of the third book document the growth of Christianity in Northumbria, concluding with the Celtic-Roman dispute over the calculation of the date of Easter. Given the importance that Bede attached to *computus*, he would have considered few events equal to the synod of Whitby. Though his sympathies were on the side of the Roman party, it must be said that he gives a fair account of the Celtic argument. Indeed here, as in other places in the *History*, Bede takes the opportunity to extol the virtues of the Celtic clergy and the devotion of their followers (3: §25).

In Book 4 Bede first recounts Archbishop Theodore's apostolate, which was of great importance because he was 'the first archbishop whom the whole Church of England obeyed'. Despite his age, we learn, Theodore energetically organised the church. He conducted official visits, encouraged students to go to Canterbury, arranged synods at Hertford and Hatfield and brought peace between the warring kings Egfrid and Ethelred (4: §§5, 17). This leads on to an account of the 'many proofs of holiness' at the convent at Barking and in the lives of Queen Etheldreda, St Hilda and St Cuthbert. The fifth and final book brings the *History* to mid-731. Bede's brief account of his own times reveals little of the unhappiness that he expressed in his *Letter to Egbert* about the ignorance, worldliness and corruption of contemporary clergymen. Rather, his criticisms are conveyed in his account of earlier events. In that account, one gets a pretty clear idea of what Bede sees as virtues and vices. Consider, for instance, his description of the life of Bishop Aidan:

> He never sought or cared for any worldly possessions, and loved to give away to the poor who chanced to meet him whatever he received from kings or wealthy folk. Whether in town or country, he always travelled on foot unless compelled by necessity to ride; and whatever people he met on his walks, whether high or low, he stopped and spoke to them. If they were heathen, he urged them to be baptised; and if they were Christians, he strengthened their faith, and inspired them by word and deed to live a good life and to be generous to others.
>
> His life is in marked contrast to the apathy of our times, for all who walked with him, whether monks or layfolk, were required to meditate, that is, either to read the scriptures or learn the Psalms.
>
> (3: §5)

The final chapter of the *History* consists primarily of a summary of events covered in the work, which Bede offers as 'an aid to the memory'. As the summary offered includes events not mentioned in the body of the work, it has been suggested that Bede began his *History* by generating a list of events from his several Easter-annals and chronological works. He then added entries from regnal and bishops' lists, and Irish records. Having composed an outline of dated events, he then expanded the narrative with undated material from saints' lives, legends, and accounts of battles that he thought would edify those who heard or read his book.[6]

In writing the *History*, Bede had to use the few sources available and was often chronologically distant from the events he described. He goes to great lengths, however, to assure us that he worked hard to verify the events detailed. For the first part of the work, covering the lead-up to the arrival of St Augustine of Canterbury in Britain in 597, he drew his material from 'the works of earlier writers gathered from various sources'. These have been identified chiefly as the works of Pliny the Elder, Eusebius, Orosius, Solinus, Gildas, Prosper of Aquitaine and Constantius. He also drew on the anonymous *Life of St Alban* and the *Liber Pontificalis*, the official record of the lives of the popes. For the years after 597, he cites as his principal authority Abbot Albinus. Albinus searched exhaustively for written records and verbal accounts of legends and traditions that pertained to Kent and surrounding regions. He passed

5

these on to Northelm, a priest of London, who in turn passed them on to Bede. Northelm also visited Rome, and gained permission from Pope Gregory II to examine the archives of the Roman church for letters and documents of Gregory the Great and later popes relating to Britain. Bede also acknowledges the help of Bishop Daniel of Winchester, Bishop Cynebert, Abbot Esi, the monks of Lashingham, and countless 'faithful witnesses' from Northumbria. These must have included monks from the communities of Wearmouth, Jarrow and Lindisfarne. Other sources include the community at Iona, Eddius's *Life of Wilfrid*, and the *Liber Pontificalis*. Unlike most medieval writers Bede meticulously named his sources, distinguished between indirect accounts of events and reports of witnesses (2: §16; 3: §15), and noted when he obtained a story by hearsay (1: §15; 2: §§5, 15). He was conscious of the uncertainty of rumour, and expressly requested that:

> [s]hould the reader discover any inaccuracies in what I have written, I humbly beg that he will not impute them to me, because, as the laws of history require, I have laboured honestly to transmit whatever I could ascertain from common report for the instruction of posterity.
>
> (preface)

Readers are unlikely to find such a denial of responsibility in present-day works of history.

Nor are they likely to find accounts of miracles. As suggested earlier, the miraculous element in the *History* tends to raise the eyebrows of many a present-day reader. Bede hoped that descriptions of miraculous demonstrations of God's power would encourage hearers and readers to 'follow what is good and pleasing to God' (1: §20; 2: §§7, 22; 4: §§25, 26). Being 'of God', he would have thought it wrong to tamper with descriptions of them. Occasionally, however, he does offer a rational explanation for a miracle. For example, he puts John of Beverly's cure of a dumb boy with a scabby head down to medical treatment and what we would now call speech therapy (5: §2).[7]

Bede's *History* was widely read and respected in the Middle Ages. More than 150 manuscripts still survive, the earliest of which were written at the monasteries of Wearmouth and Jarrow within a decade of his death. In the eighth century it was a great literary export, at first for Anglo-Saxon missionaries in Europe. Imitators and plagiarists soon appeared.[8] The *History* was translated into Old English during the reign of Alfred the Great and the first modern English translation was prepared by Thomas Stapleton. In the prefatory letter that Stapleton wrote to

Queen Elizabeth I, we get a sense of how the *History* could be used in disputes of faith:

> In this history your highness shall see in how many and weighty points the pretended refourmers of the Church in your grace's dominions have departed from the patern of that sounde and catholike faith planted first among Englishemen by holy St Augustine our Apostle.[9]

In subsequent years, the *History* was used to support the claims of Roman Catholics and Protestants alike. The first critical edition of the work was produced in 1722 by John and George Smith. Since then, studies of Bede's writings have been greatly boosted by the publication of Charles Plummer's *Operae Bedae* (1896), and numerous English translations of the *History*. There now exist a large number of essays and books treating Bede's ideas, and his ideas are commemorated annually in a lecture at Durham. Though in these secular times it may be difficult for the reader to understand the motivation behind Bede's works, there can be no doubt that he was, in the words of Schwartz: 'a brilliant example to all who, in dark ages, set themselves the task of handing on the glimmering torch of learning to coming generations.'[10]

Notes

1 W. Levison, 'Bede as Historian', in A. H. Thompson (ed.), *Bede: His Life, Times, and Writings*, Oxford: Oxford University Press, 1935, p. 146.
2 Citations refer to the book and section number of *The Ecclesiastical History of the English People*. Quotations derive from the Penguin edition.
3 Cuthbert's letter about Bede may be found in *Bede's Ecclesiastical History of the English People*, trans. B. Colgrave and R. A. B. Mynors, Oxford: Oxford University Press, 1969, p. 585.
4 R. L. Poole, *Chronicles and Annals*, Oxford: Oxford University Press, 1926, pp. 124–78.
5 P. Meyvaert, 'Bede's Text of the *Libellus responsionum* of Gregory the Great to Augustine of Canterbury', in P. Clemoes and K. Hughes (eds), *England before the Conquest: Studies in Primary Sources Presented to Dorothy Whitelock*, Cambridge: Cambridge University Press, 1971, pp. 15–33.
6 C. W. Jones, 'Bede the Medieval Historian', in *Bede, the Schools and the Computus*, Aldershot, Hampshire: Variorum, 1994, pp. 26–36.
7 C. Plummer, *Operae Bedae*, Oxford: Oxford University Press, 1896, vol. 2, pp. 17–18.
8 C. W. Jones, *Bedae Pseudepigrapha: Scientific Writings Falsely Attributed to Bede*, Ithaca, NY, Cornell University Press, 1939, p. 1.
9 J. E. King, *Thomas Stapleton's Edition of The Ecclesiastical History of the English People*, Loeb Classical Library, 2 vols, London: W. Heinemann, 1930, p. 32.
10 As quoted in Thompson (ed.), *Bede: Life, Times and Writings*, p. 151.

Bede's major works

The *Ecclesiastical History of the English People*, trans. J. McClure and R. Collins, Oxford: Oxford University Press, 1994. This also includes an excerpt from *De Temporum Ratione*.

The *Ecclesiastical History of the English People*, trans. L. Sherley-Price, Harmondsworth: Penguin, 1955.

Homilies on the Gospels, trans. L. T. Martin and D. Hurst, Kalamazoo, MI: Cistercian Publications, 1991.

Two Lives of St Cuthbert, trans. B. Colgrave, Cambridge: Cambridge University Press, 1940.

See also

Augustine (MP), Froissart, Gregory of Tours, Ssu-ma Ch'ien, Tacitus.

Further resources

Blair, P. H., *The World of Bede*, London: Secker and Warburg, 1970.

Bonner, G. (ed.), *Famulus Christi: Essays in Commemoration of the Thirteenth Century of the Birth of the Venerable Bede*, London: General Society for the Promotion of Christian Knowledge, 1976.

Brown, G. H., *Bede the Venerable*, Boston: Twayne Publications, 1987.

Goffart, W., *The Narrators of Barbarian History (AD 550–800): Jordanes, Gregory of Tours, Bede, and Paul the Deacon*, Princeton, NJ: Princeton University Press, 1988.

Gransden, A., *Historical Writing in England c. 550–c. 1307*, Ithaca, NY: Cornell University Press, 1974.

Hanning, R. W., *The Vision of History in Early Britain: From Gildas to Geoffrey of Monmouth*, New York: Columbia University Press, 1966.

Lapidge, M. (ed.), *Bede and His World: the Jarrow Lectures*, 2 vols, Aldershot: Brookfield, 1985.

Thompson, A. H., *Bede: His Life, Times, and Writings*, Oxford: Oxford University Press, 1935.

Wallace-Hadrill, J. M., *Bede's Ecclesiastical History of the English People: A Historical Commentary*, Oxford: Oxford University Press, 1988.

MARC BLOCH 1886–1944

There is much in the life and work of Marc Bloch to inspire anyone interested in history. Not only did he work tirelessly for a 'wider and more human history' but he also gave his life in the struggle to liberate France in the Second World War. The son of the distinguished Roman historian Gustave Bloch and Sarah Ebstein Bloch, Marc Bloch (1886–1944) saw himself as part of the 'last generation of the Dreyfus Affair' (*The Historian's Craft*, p. 158). While he was a student at the Lycée

Louis-le-Grand and the Ecole Normale Supérieure in Paris, public opinion was bitterly divided about whether Captain Alfred Dreyfus, a Jew, had sold military secrets to the Germans. The Dreyfus Affair made Bloch aware of anti-Semitism in contemporary France and fed his growing interest in the role and origins of rumour and misinformation in society. During his time at the Ecole Normale, Bloch was also made aware of the heated debate among French and Belgian historians about the nature of history. Some, such as Charles Seignobos and Charles-Victor Langlois, drew on German scholarship to establish the scientific principles of history. Others, such as Henri Hauser, Alphonse Aulard, Ferdinand Lot and Henri Pirenne, argued for a wider view of history that would embrace social, cultural, linguistic, geographical and economic factors.

When he began to formulate his own views of history, Bloch first compared history and science. Whilst chemistry and biology, he wrote in his notebook, involve analysis and classification, history largely involves description and narration. History and science also differ in the treatment of phenomena. Whereas the scientist deals with simple phenomena that pass only through his consciousness, the historian deals with 'psychosocial' phenomena that pass through both his and the historical agent's consciousness. This means, Bloch contends, that a myriad of interpretations of past events are possible. He still believed, however, that historians could aim for scientific validity.[1] It was only in later works that his 'wide' view of history would emerge.

After being turned down for a doctoral scholarship at the Fondation Thiers in Paris in 1908, Bloch left France to study in Berlin and Leipzig. His second application was successful, however, and a year later he returned to start work on a study of the disappearance of serfdom in the rural regions around Paris in the twelfth and thirteenth centuries. From an investigation of seigneurial and ecclesiastical records, Bloch hoped to produce a systematic account of the social, legal and economic aspects of a person's release from a feudal bond in a specific area. During his first year he made maps showing the disappearance of serfdom in the region of the Ile-de-France and examined the nature of serfdom. Themes echoed in his later work emerged: closed and open-fields in French rural society; land clearing around Paris in the eleventh and twelfth centuries; the clergy's role in society and the economy; the relationship between the monarchy and peasantry; the forms of feudal justice; the origins of tithes and the social and political aspects of medieval art, literature and architecture.

In his first published article, 'Blanche de Castille et les serfs du chapitre de Paris', Bloch argued that the royal ordinance of 1251–52, which freed several peasants imprisoned in the cloister of Notre Dame, was more the act of a weak monarchy trying to assert its control over the clergy and bourgeoisie than a victory for human freedom. In this paper, as with later works, Bloch subjected a wide range of evidence to critical scrutiny. In other early papers, such as 'Les formes de la rupture de l'hommage dans l'ancien droit féodal', he approached important historical problems from unusual angles. In that paper he argued that variations in the ceremony of the rending of a feudal bond supported the claim that the laws and practices of feudalism were not uniform.[2] Bloch's first major publication was a monograph on the Ile-de-France. Though this was part of the series 'Les régions de la France' that appeared in Henri Berr's *Revue de Synthèse Historique* between 1903 and 1913, Bloch denied that that Ile-de-France was a unified region. In looking for the features that characterise a distinct region, Bloch explored the factors that influence where people settle and the ways in which the physical features of the countryside reflect the ideas and actions of people (*L'Ile-de-France*, 1913, trans. *The Ile-de-France*).

At the end of his scholarship in 1912, Bloch accepted a teaching position at the lycée in Montpellier and then, a year later, at the lycée in Amiens. During his time at Amiens, Bloch wrote a critical review of his future collaborator, Lucien Febvre's *Histoire de Franche-Comté*, and gave a speech at the lycée's award ceremony on the importance of adopting a 'critical spirit'. In the latter he reiterated his claim that the historian, unlike the scientist, is doubly prone to the weakness and fragility of human memory. Much of the work of the historian therefore consists of identifying the true, the false and the probable. He or she cannot avoid judgement: 'If your neighbour on the left says two times two equals four, and the one the right says it is five, do not conclude that the answer is four and a half.'[3]

Shortly after Bloch delivered this speech, Germany declared war on France and invaded Belgium. Bloch was assigned as sergeant to the 272nd Reserve Regiment, and in taking part in battles along the French–Belgian border from 1914 to 1918, he was wounded twice, decorated four times and promoted to the rank of captain. Although impressed by the bravery of his fellow soldiers, Bloch had harsh words for the army leadership.[4] After the armistice, Bloch was appointed to an assistant lectureship at the newly established University of Strasbourg in the reclaimed region of Alsace. While at Strasbourg, Bloch married Simonne Vidal, raised a family and made the acquaintance of the modern historian Lucien Febvre. Bloch and Febvre shared many similar ideas about the nature of history, though Bloch was more interested in Durkheimian sociology and the use of comparison in historical research.

Together, they were to work for the reform of the ways in which history was written and taught in France. In order to secure a regular appointment, Bloch had to obtain his doctorate. To that end, he presented for examination a revised version of the 1912 paper 'Les formes de la rupture de l'hommage dans l'ancien droit féodal' and a new work, 'Rois et serfs'. 'Rois et serfs' was published immediately, and established Bloch's credentials as a medievalist. In it, Bloch argued that the two emancipation ordinances of Louis X in 1315 and Philip V in 1318 were not endorsements of human liberty but formulaic claims to power (*Rois et serfs*, 1920).

During this time, Bloch also penned the remarkable work *Les rois thaumaturges* (1924, trans. *The Royal Touch*). Drawing on insights from medicine, psychology, iconography and anthropology, Bloch analysed the origins, development and disappearance in England and France of the belief in the royal miracle of curing scrofula, a tuberculous inflammation of the neck glands. According to Bloch, around the year 1000 the French King Robert the Pious exercised this power in order to establish the legitimacy and hereditary right of his dynasty. Later, Henry I or II adopted the practice to keep the power of the clergy in check. For Bloch, their claims to power, combined with the Christian idea of the consecrated ruler, produced the royal touch. Thus in France and England, royal power was manifested not only in military, legal and institutional forms but also in miraculous ones. In this work, as with the earlier article 'Réflexions d'un historien sur les fausses nouvelles de la guerre', Bloch suggests that in order to discover how rumours and misconceptions gain credence, the historian must examine the 'collective consciousness' (assumptions and perceptions) of a people. For him, rumours and misconceptions are the glass by which we see *répresentations mentales* (collective consciousness) darkly.[5] Reviewers praised Bloch's ingenious use of the case of the royal touch to illuminate political history, but some noted that he did not examine the phenomenon in terms of ideology and assumed a consensus of belief.[6] In this work, Bloch shows us that there are many paths, some curious and unusual, which lead to the past.

Through his work on the royal touch Bloch was drawn into the discussion on the nature of feudalism. In his works on feudalism, Bloch took a middle course between those who believed that a uniform feudal system existed in Europe between the tenth and the thirteenth centuries and those who thought that the differences were too great from place to place to make any generalisations about feudalism. For him, the feudal system was an hierarchic and contractual regime based on reciprocal ties of dependence that existed in more or less similar forms throughout

Europe and other parts of the world. Furthermore, though it declined with the rise of the towns, money economies and national monarchies, it lived on in the notion of political contract.[7] He also wrote on the role of comparison in historical scholarship. Though Bloch did not pioneer the comparative method, he declared in 'Pour une histoire comparée des sociétés européenes' that the future of history as a discipline might depend on its use (trans. 'A Contribution towards a Comparative History of European Society', in *Land and Work in Medieval Europe*, pp. 44–81). There are, he suggests in this paper, two ways in which historians can compare. First, they can search for universal phenomena in cultures widely separated in time and/or space. Second, they can conduct a parallel study of neighbouring or contemporaneous societies. Bloch preferred the latter as he thought that it promised richer and more precise results (ibid., pp. 46–8). He did not, however, give a clear indication of the nature and limits of units of comparison. That is, is there any limit to how small or large a unit of comparison must be in order to be useful in history?[8]

In addition, Bloch was fascinated by the varieties of French field systems and the impact of the transformation of land into individual fenced holdings on rural life. This is clearly seen in his next major publication, *Les caractères originaux de l'histoire rurale française* (1931, trans. *French Rural History*), a work regarded by many scholars as Bloch's finest. In this he draws on a remarkably wide range of evidence, most notably maps, to describe the relationship between physical setting and social institutions from the early Middle Ages to the French Revolution. He also employs what he calls the 'regressive method' of 'reading history backwards', because he believed it wise to proceed from the known to the unknown.[9]

In 1929 Bloch and Febvre launched the journal *Annales d'Histoire Economique et Sociale*, which survives today under the title *Annales: Histoire, Sciences Sociales*.[10] In the first issue they outlined three aims: to provide a forum that would unite historians and social scientists in discussion; to question the division of history into ancient, medieval and modern and society into primitive and civilised; and to create a community of the human sciences.[11] Though tension arose between Bloch and Febvre about the scope and style of the journal, they managed to work together productively for quite a long time. Communication was particularly difficult after Febvre moved to Paris to take up a position at the prestigious Collège de France. Bloch too sought a position at the Collège de France, but was denied one, he believed because of his Jewish background and radical views about history. Disappointed, he turned his attention to the Sorbonne, where in 1936 he was offered a chair in economic history. There he cofounded the Institute of Economic and Social History with the sociologist Maurice Halbwachs, taught classes at the Ecoles Normale Supérieure and the Ecole Normales of Saint-Cloud and Fonteney, and served on national commissions on the history of law and the economic history of the French Revolution.

His primary preoccupation, however, was the composition of the last work that he would see into print: *La société féodale* (2 vols, 1939–40, trans. *Feudal Society*). In this Bloch sketched a masterful description of the social structure of Western and Central European society between the ninth and thirteenth centuries. He describes two feudal periods, one that grew out of invasion and devastation, and the other marked by economic expansion and intellectual revival. He not only examines the 'indigenous' feudal systems of France, Germany and Italy, but also compares these with imposed systems (such as England), places where feudalism did not gain acceptance (like Scotland, Scandinavia and Frisia) and systems outside of Europe (for example, Japan). The picture that Bloch paints of 'modes of feeling and thought' and social cohesion is broad in scope but rich in detail. For instance, the book contains fascinating accounts of the medieval understanding of the concept of time, the role of epics in society and the importance of the stirrup.

Due largely to the timing of its release, *La société féodale* received very little attention. Critics, including Lucien Febvre, complained about such things as Bloch's neglect of individuals, mistaken chronology of the development of feudal relationships, limitation of the main focus to the boundaries of the Carolingian world and overemphasis of the medieval roots of modern nationalism. Few, though, doubted that it was a landmark contribution to medieval history. Even today it is thought to have few equals.[12]

Just as Bloch completed *La société féodale*, the situation in Europe deteriorated and he was recalled to military service. With the disastrous capitulation of the army and government in mid-1940, two-thirds of France was brought under German control. Bloch and his family, fearing persecution because of their Jewish background, fled to Clermont-Ferrand in the 'free' or unoccupied zone. Bloch was able to work for a short time at the University of Strasbourg-in-exile (in Clermont-Ferrand) and the University of Montpellier, but increasing anti-Semitism led him to try to move his family to the United States and then to flee to Fourgères. Despite having to move around and being deprived of his notes and library, Bloch was still able to write. Shortly after moving to the unoccupied zone, he penned a critical assessment of France's collapse, which was published after his death under the title *L'étrange défaite* (1949, trans. *Strange Defeat*).

Bloch also recorded his reflections on history and historical method in what is probably his best-known work, *Apologie pour l'histoire ou métier d'historien* (1949, trans. *The Historian's Craft*). Here Bloch brings to the fore the ideas which underpin his works of history. *The Historian's Craft* offers a response to his son's question, 'What is the use of history?' Describing history as 'the science of men in time', Bloch attacks those who lose themselves in the study of politics and origins and erect barriers between the past and the present (*The Historian's Craft*, pp. 28ff., 150ff.). When studied rigorously, history not only feeds the imagination, but it also allows one to achieve an understanding of the human story. That entails: recognising the search for evidence as the pursuit of tracks through a variety of documents; interrogating evidence; interpreting evidence in the light of its context; comparing evidence; refraining from judging past events according to one's moral standards; and searching for a vocabulary that describes the 'precise outlines of the facts' but also preserves 'the necessary flexibility to adapt itself to further discoveries' (pp. 50–62, 91–119, 130).

The *Apologie pour l'histoire* was never completed, as Bloch was executed by German soldiers on 16 June 1944 for his part in the activities of the *Mouvements Unis de la Résistance* (MUR). Nevertheless, he hoped that his work would go on. As he wrote in his dedication to Lucien Febvre:

> Long have we worked together for a wider and more human history. Today our common task is threatened. Not by our fault. We are vanquished, for a moment, by an unjust destiny. But the time will come, I feel sure, when our collaboration can again be made public, and again be free. Meanwhile, it is in these pages filled with your presence that, for my part, our joint work goes on.

Through the work of subsequent writers in the *Annales* tradition, Bloch's work and his vision of a wider view of history do indeed live on.

Notes

1 Notebook, dated '1906' and 'Oct 07', described in C. Fink, *Marc Bloch: A Life in History*, Cambridge: Cambridge University Press, 1989, pp. 35–7.
2 'Blanche de Castille et les serfs du chapitre du Paris', *Mémoires de la Société de l'Histoire de Paris et de l'Ile-de-France*, 1911, vol. 38, pp. 224–72; 'Les formes de la rupture de l'hommage dans l'ancien droit féodal', *Nouvelle Revue Historique de Droit Français et Etranger*, 1912, vol. 36, pp. 141–77. Both are described in C. Fink, *Marc Bloch*, pp. 44–45.

3 'Critique historique et critique du temoignage', address delivered 13 July 1914, reprinted in *Annales: economies, sociétés, civilisations*, 1950, vol. 5, pp. 1–8; Review of *Histoire de Franche-Comté*, *Revue de Synthèse Historique*, 1914, vol. 28, pp. 354–6; described in C. Fink, *Marc Bloch*, pp. 23–4 and 51.

4 See *Memoirs of the War, 1914–15*, trans. with an introduction by C. Fink, Ithaca, NY: Cornell University Press, 1980.

5 'Réflexions d'un historien sur les fausses nouvelles de la guerre', *Revue Synthèse Historique*, 1921, 33: 41–57. See also 'Saint Martin de Tours: A propos d'une polémique', *Revue d'Histoire et de Littérature Religieuse*, 1921, 7: 44–57; 'La vie de saint Edouard le Confesseur, par Osbert de Clare, avec Introduction sur Osbert et les premières vies de saint Edouard', *Analecta Bollandiana*, 1923, 41: 5–31; and 'La vie d'outre-tombe du roi Salomon', *Revue Belge de Philologie et d'Histoire*, 1925, 4: 349–77.

6 See, for example, the reviews of *The Royal Touch* by E. F. Jacob, *English Historical Review*, 1925, 40(158): 267–70; and L. Thorndike, *American Historical Review*, 1925, 30(3): 584–5. See also H. Thurstin, 'Critical Commentary on the "Biographer" of St Edward the Confessor', *The Month*, 1923, no. 141: 448–51; R. W. Southern, 'The First Life of Edward the Confessor', *English Historical Review*, 1943, 58(232): 385–400; and G. H. Gerould, review of 'La vie d'outre-tombe du roi Salomon', *Speculum*, 1926, 1(2): 243.

7 'Feudalism: European', *Encyclopedia of the Social Sciences*, vol. 6, 1931, pp. 203–10.

8 For a discussion on Bloch's comparative method, see W. H. Sewell, Jr, 'Marc Bloch and the Logic of Comparative History', *History and Theory*, 1967, 6(2): 208–18; L. D. Walker, 'A Note on Historical Linguistics and Marc Bloch's Comparative Method', *History and Theory*, 1980, 19(2): 154–64; and A. O. Hill, B. H. Hill, Jr, W. H. Sewell, Jr, and S. Thrupp, 'AHR Forum: Marc Bloch and Comparative History', *American Historical Review*, 1980, 85(4): 828–57.

9 See F. M. Powicke, *History*, 1932, 17(66): 157–9; J. H. Clapham, *English Historical Review*, 1932, 47(188): 655–7; J. L. Cate, *Journal of Modern History*, 1933, 5(4): 517–18; C. H. Taylor, *American Historical Review*, 1931, 37(4): 736–7; and L. Febvre, *Revue Historique*, 1932, 169, pp. 189–95.

10 The journal kept its original title until 1938, was renamed *Annales d'Histoire Sociale* in 1939, *Mélanges d'Histoire Sociale* from 1942 to 1944, and *Annales d'Histoire Sociale* from 1945 to 1946.

11 'A nos lecteurs', *Annales d'Histoire Economique et Sociale*, 1929, 1: 1–2; described in C. Fink, *Marc Bloch*, p. 142.

12 See L. Febvre, *Annales d'Histoire Sociale*, 1940, vol. 2, pp. 39–43, 1941, vol. 3, pp. 125–30; W. A. Morris, *American Historical Review*, 1940, 45(4): 855–6; F. M. Powicke, *English Historical Review*, 1940, 55(219): 449–51; L. Walker, *History and Theory*, 1963, 3(2): 247–55; B. Lyon, 'The Feudalism of Marc Bloch', *Tijdshcrift voor Geschiedenis*, 1963, 76: 275–83; E. A. R. Brown, 'The Tyranny of a Construct: Feudalism and Historians of Medieval Europe', *American Historical Review*, 1974, 79(4): 1063–88; and C. B. Bouchard, 'The Origins of the French Nobility: a Reassessment', *American Historical Review*, 1981, 86(3): 501–32.

Bloch's major works

The Ile de France: the Country around Paris, trans. J. E. Anderson, Ithaca, NY: Cornell University Press, 1971.

The Royal Touch: Sacred Monarchy and Scrofula in England and France, trans. J. E. Anderson, London: Routledge & Kegan Paul, 1973.

French Rural History: an Essay on its Basic Characteristics, trans. J. Sondheimer, Berkeley: University of California Press, 1966.

Feudal Society, 2 vols, trans. L. A. Manyon, Chicago: University of Chicago Press, 1961.

Strange Defeat: a Statement of Evidence Written in 1940, trans. G. Hopkins, London: Oxford University Press, 1949.

The Historian's Craft, trans. L. A. Manyon, 1944, Manchester: Manchester University Press, 1992.

Slavery and Serfdom in the Middle Ages: Selected Essays, trans. W. R. Beer, Berkeley: University of California Press, 1975.

Land and Work in Medieval Europe: Selected Papers, trans. J. E. Anderson, Berkeley: University of California Press, 1967.

See also

Braudel, Davis, Febvre, Le Roy Ladurie.

Further resources

Brown, E. A. R., 'The Tyranny of a Construct: Feudalism and Historians of Medieval Europe', *American Historical Review*, 1974, 79(4): 1063–88.

Burke, P., 'Strengths and Weaknesses of the History of Mentalities', *History of European Ideas*, 1986, 7(5): 439–51.

——, *The French Historical Revolution: the Annales School 1929–89*, Cambridge: Polity, 1990.

Fink, C., *Marc Bloch: a Life in History*, Cambridge: Cambridge University Press, 1989.

Friedman, S. W., *Marc Bloch, Sociology and Geography: Encountering Changing Disciplines*, Cambridge: Cambridge University Press, 1996.

Hill, A. O., Hill, B. H., Jr, Sewell, W. H., Jr, and Thrupp, S., 'AHR Forum: Marc Bloch and Comparative History', *American Historical Review*, 1980, 85(4): 828–57.

Lyon, B., 'Marc Bloch: Did he Repudiate Annales History?' *Journal of Medieval History*, 1987, 11: 181–91.

Lyon, B., and Lyon, M. (eds), *The Birth of Annales History: the Letters of Lucien Febvre and Marc Bloch to Henri Pirenne, 1921–1935*, Brussels: Comm. Royale d'Histoire, 1991.

Sewell, W. H., Jr, 'Marc Bloch and the Logic of Comparative History', *History and Theory*, 1967, 6(2): 208–18.

Walker, L. D., 'A Note on Historical Linguistics and Marc Bloch's Comparative Method', *History and Theory*, 1980, 19(2): 154–64.

FERNAND BRAUDEL 1902–85

Fernand Braudel, historian of early modern Europe and heir to the *Annales* approach promoted by Marc Bloch and Lucien Febvre, was born in the small French village of Luméville-en-Ornois on 24 August 1902. After moving to Paris at the age of seven, he studied at the Lycée Voltaire and the Sorbonne, from which he graduated as an *agrégé* in history (1923). While teaching at the University of Algiers (1923–32), he published a paper on the Spaniards in North Africa in the sixteenth century and worked on his doctoral thesis, which started as a study of Philip II's foreign policy.[1] Between 1932 and 1935, he taught at the Lycée Condorcet and the Lycée Henri IV in Paris and at the University of São Paolo, Brazil. During the return voyage from Brazil, Braudel befriended Lucien Febvre, who encouraged him to embrace a wider vision of history.

Braudel took up an appointment at the Ecole Pratique des Hautes Etudes in 1938, but with the outbreak of the Second World War he was called up for military service and later taken prisoner. In camps at Mainz (1940–42) and Lübeck (1942–45), Braudel transformed his ideas on the policies of Philip II into a far-reaching study of the Mediterranean during Philip's reign. Tales of the origins of this study have taken on a legendary quality, encouraged in no small part by Braudel himself. As he claimed: 'It was in captivity that I wrote this enormous work that Lucien Febvre received, composition book by composition book. Only my memory allowed me this tour de force.'[2] Braudel's achievement was the remarkable product of his memory and years of thorough research. But as Gemelli points out, even when he was in the difficult environment of Lübeck, he was able to use books from the local municipal library. Furthermore, it is difficult to date the modifications made to the notebooks sent to Lucien Febvre: for example, it is not clear whether additions to the preface precede or postdate his captivity. Such doubts make it difficult to determine precisely when he formulated the threefold view of time that was to become the hallmark of his vision of history.[3]

Braudel's ideas on the Mediterranean were published as *La Méditerranée et le monde méditerranéen à l'époque de Philippe II* (1949, revised edition 1966; trans. *The Mediterranean and the Mediterranean World in the Age of Philip II*, 1972–73), a work that has been described as 'the first historical work of our time' and a 'majestic monument of twentieth century historiography'.[4] In 1947, with Lucien Febvre and Charles Morazé, he founded the Sixième Section for the social sciences at the Ecole Pratique des Hautes Etudes, and two years later he succeeded

Febvre as a professor in the Collège de France. Up to his death he edited the post-war version of the *Annales* journal and published a host of articles and books, including *Civilisation matérielle et capitalisme, XVe–XVIIIe siècle* (1967, reprinted as vol. 1 of *Civilisation matérielle, économique, et capitalisme: XVe–XVIIIe siècle*, 3 vols, 1979; trans. *Capitalism and Material Life, 1400–1800,* 1973; revised edn, *Civilisation and Capitalism 15th–18th Century,* 3 vols, 1981–92), *Ecrits sur histoire* (1969; trans. *On History,* 1980), *Afterthoughts on Material Civilisation* (1977) and *L'identité de la France* (1986–90, 2 vols; trans. *The Identity of France,* 1990–92).

For Braudel, history as it is traditionally written illuminates the past as fireflies do the night:

> I remember a night near Bahia, when I was enveloped in a firework display of phosphorescent fireflies; their pale lights glowed, went out, shone again, all without piercing the night with any true illumination. So it is with events; beyond their glow, darkness prevails.
>
> ('The Situation of History in 1950', *On History*, pp. 10–11)

History offers a 'gleam but no illumination; facts but no illumination', because historians tend to focus exclusively on events, individual actions and short-term developments and assume that each can be perceived discretely. History is thus reduced to *histoire événementielle* or the history of events, particularly political events. Renouncing the drama and 'breathless rush' of *histoire événementielle* is no easy matter, but we must do so if we are to achieve a better understanding of the world. In Braudel's view, the short term is not the centre of history; historians have only taken it to be such. Rather, history does not have a centre. Like other structuralists, he believes that meaning is *relational* rather than *substantial*: the meaning of objects, events and individual actions lies not in the things themselves, but in the relationships we construct between them. He writes:

> In the living world there are no individuals entirely sealed off by themselves; all individual enterprise is rooted in a more complex reality, an 'intermeshed' reality, as sociology calls it.
>
> (Ibid., p. 11)

These 'structures' of relations are extensive and operate according to rules people may not be aware of.

Apprehending structures, Braudel believes, requires broadening and deepening our gaze across and through time. That is, historians must not only consider the relations of coexisting elements (for example, cultural, geographic, economic and political developments) but also those over different periods of time (for instance, long-term and short-term developments). When we change our gaze, we can no longer maintain the fiction that time is homogeneous: 'time does not flow at one even rate, but goes at a thousand different paces, swift or slow, which bear almost no relation to the day-to-day rhythm of a chronicle or of traditional history' (ibid., p. 11). Plotting out the various paces of time is impossible, but Braudel detects three broad groupings in historical time: geographical time (*la longue durée* – the long term: periods that span at least one century), social time and individual time (*histoire événementielle*).

This threefold view of time underpins all of Braudel's writings, but it is most clearly in evidence in *The Mediterranean and the Mediterranean World in the Age of Philip II* (hereafter *The Mediterranean*). *The Mediterranean* is divided into three parts, corresponding to the three paces of time. In the first part, 'The Role of the Environment', Braudel explores the history of the relationship of people to the physical environment, or what he calls 'geo-history'. This is a history

> whose passage is almost imperceptible, that of man in his relationship to the environment, a history in which all change is slow, a history of constant repetition, ever-recurring cycles. I could not neglect this almost timeless history, the story of man's contact with the inanimate, neither could I be satisfied with the traditional geographical introduction to history that often figures to little purpose at the beginning of so many books, with its descriptions of the mineral deposits, types of agriculture, and typical flora, briefly listed and never mentioned again, as if the flowers did not come back every spring, the flocks of sheep migrate every year, or the ships sail on a real sea that changes with the seasons.
>
> (*The Mediterranean*, vol. 1, p. 20)[5]

This part of the work is clearly shaped by Braudel's interest in the geographical research of Vidal de la Blanche and Albert Demangeon but also by his love of the region (ibid., p. 17). His goal is to show us that landscape has an important part to play in history. For example, he claims that the ideas of the plains rarely catch on in the mountains and thus that, in the mountains, 'civilisation is never stable' (ibid., p. 36). The second part, 'Collective Destinies and General Trends', looks to the history of social structures or *conjonctures* (trends or connections between diverse simultaneous phenomena): a history of the rhythms and forces at work in economic systems, scientific and technological developments, political institutions, conceptual changes, states, societies, civilisations and forms of warfare (ibid., p. 21; see also 'History and the social sciences: the Longue Durée', in *On History*, p. 30).[6] For example, the period of economic growth during the fifteenth and sixteenth centuries favoured the emergence of the large Spanish and Turkish empires (ibid., vol. 2, pp. 657–703). The third part, 'Events, Politics and People'

> gives a hearing to traditional history – history, one might say, on the scale not of man, but of individual men, what Paul Lacombe and François Simiand called *'l'histoire événementielle'* that is, the history of events: surface disturbances, crests of foam that the tides of history carry on their strong backs. A history of brief, rapid, nervous fluctuations, by definition ultrasensitive; the least tremor sets all its antennae quivering.
>
> (Ibid., vol. 1, p. 21)

In this part, Braudel offers us lively portraits of figures such as Philip II, Don García de Toledo and Don John of Austria, and accounts of the wars and treaties of the second half of the sixteenth century. Though Braudel does not want to 'dissolve' (as Lévi-Strauss puts it) the history of individuals, he suspects that it might steal attention from geographical and social history.[7] He thus takes pains to make it clear that, while individuals sometimes instigate change, more often than not they are the prisoners of geographical and social structures.[8] 'Men make history' he writes, 'but history also makes men' ('The Situation of History in 1950', *On History*, p. 11; see also 'History and the Social Sciences: the Longue Durée', *On History*, p. 30). Braudel is thus interested in the deeds of individuals in so far as they reveal structures. He also resists the temptation to make any one individual or object the centre of his book. Even the Mediterranean is fragmented: 'it is a complex of seas; and these seas are broken up by islands, interrupted by peninsulas, ringed by intricate coastlines' (*The Mediterranean*, vol. 1, p. 17).

Braudel is a spatial thinker; he describes the world by describing the webs of relationships between objects and people. This form of spatial mapping also plays a role in his second major study, the three-volume *Civilization and Capitalism 15th–18th Century* (*The Structures of Everyday Life*, *The Wheels of Commerce* and *The Perspective of the World*). In *The Structures of Everyday Life*, he suggests that the constraints of pre-industrial

European economies – 'inadequate food supplies, a population that was too big or too small for its resources, low productivity of labour, and the as yet slow progress in controlling nature' – barely changed between the fifteenth and eighteenth centuries (*The Structures of Everyday Life*, p. 27). Volume 2, *The Wheels of Commerce*, looks to forms of economic trends (such as markets, exchanges, partnerships and paper money) and volume 3, *The Perspective of the World*, traces the dramatic rise of capitalism, from fifteenth-century Venice, through Antwerp, Genoa and Amsterdam, to Britain at the outset of the Industrial Revolution. Two other features of the work stand out as original. First, Braudel is adamant that the global phenomenon of capitalism must be explained in global terms. Descriptions of the role of religious minorities in international trade, for instance, include Indian Parsees as well as the French Huguenots (*The Wheels of Commerce*, pp. 165–7). Furthermore, the relative expense of labour in Europe compared to Asia, Africa and America is seen as having provided a stimulus to the development of machinery associated with the Industrial Revolution. Second, as Wallerstein has noted, Braudel inverts the view of capitalism shared by most liberals and Marxists. Where these see capitalism as involving the establishment of a free, competitive market, Braudel sees it as involving a high degree of monopolisation (*The Wheels of Commerce*, pp. 412–28). In addition, where liberals and Marxists see capitalists as practitioners of economic specialisation, Braudel pins the success of capitalism on the refusal to specialise (ibid., pp. 377–82).[9]

Braudel's vision of history requires the study of a broad range of historical evidence over *la longue durée*. But it also demands an openness to the methods and questions of the many kinds of historical research and the social sciences. Typically, however, history and the social sciences erect barriers against each other and present their conclusions as being a complete vision of humanity ('History and the Social Sciences: the Longue Durée', *On History*, p. 25; 'Unity and Diversity in the Social Sciences', *On History*, pp. 25–55; 'History and Sociology', *On History*, p. 64). Furthermore, they cast their methods and selection of research topics as immune to change. In Braudel's view this propensity for erecting barriers and permanent foundations is unfortunate, as it denies us the possibility of understanding both the present and the past. It is clear for Braudel that the study of the past makes greater self-understanding possible. He writes:

> Live in London for a year and you will not learn much about England, but you will learn a lot about France: you see because you have distanced yourself. Past and present illuminate one

another reciprocally. So history is as much about the present as it is about the past.

('History and the Social Sciences: the Longue Durée',
On History, p. 37)

That Braudel took such a message to heart is evident in his two-volume study of the shaping of present-day France (*The Identity of France*). This work exposes the ephemeral nature of the present when seen in the context of the long term, and offers the painful conclusion that France's 'vulnerable' position in Europe has long been 'irreversibly' determined (*The Identity of France*, vol. 1, pp. 11, 15, 114, 262, 281, 298; vol. 2, p. 149).[10]

Braudel's interest in the relationship between history and the social sciences, in taking historical research beyond a largely political focus and in historical developments over the long term locates him as the successor to Marc Bloch and Lucien Febvre and the 'father' to Jacques Le Goff, Emmanuel Le Roy Ladurie and Marc Ferro. His plural vision of time and the 'decentring' of humanity that it entails, however, sets him apart from the *Annales* milieu. For him, structures never enable; they always constrain. Consequently, the study of individuals is only a means to the end of revealing structures. Few *Annales* historians, or any other historians for that matter, accord people such a marginal status. Braudel's Mediterranean, writes Elliott, 'is a world unresponsive to human control', and by denying humanity the role of unifier, Bailyn complains, history becomes nothing more than 'an exhausting treadmill'.[11] As a consequence, Mattingly concludes, 'the sea itself is slighted'.[12] A few commentators, however, have more sympathetic views of the organisation of the work. Hexter, for instance, sees *The Mediterranean* as a picaresque work, best read by being sampled at random, and Kellner as an anatomy, or encyclopaedic satire of dominant views of history.[13] Perhaps, as they suggest, Braudel wants us to consider the 'deeper waters' of style as well as content.

Notes

1 F. Braudel, 'Les espagnols et l'Afrique du Nord', *Revue africaine*, 1928, 69: 184–233, 351–410.

2 F. Braudel, 'Personal Testimony', *Journal of Modern History*, 44(4): 453.

3 G. Gemelli, *Fernand Braudel*, trans. B. Pasquett and B. Propetto Marzi, Paris: Editions Odile Jacob, 1995, p. 78.

4 Anon., 'Historian of the Mediterranean', *Times Literary Supplement*, 15 Feb. 1968, no. 3442, p. 156; W. H. McNeill, 'History with a French Accent', *Journal of Modern History*, 1972, 44(2): 447.

5 See also p. 23; and 'History and the Social Sciences: the Longue Durée', in *On History*, pp. 31–3, and 'The Situation of History in 1950', *On History*, p. 12.
6 P. Burke, *The French Historical Revolution: The Annales School 1929–89*, Cambridge: Polity, 1990, p. 112.
7 C. Lévi-Strauss, *The Savage Mind*, trans. anon., London: Weidenfeld & Nicolson, 1966. .
8 Burke, *The French Historical Revolution*, p. 34.
9 I. Wallerstein, 'Braudel on Capitalism, or Everything Upside Down', *Journal of Modern History*, 1991, 63(2): 354–61.
10 S. Kaplan, 'Long-run Lamentations: Braudel on France', *Journal of Modern History*, 1991, 63(2): 341–53.
11 J. H. Elliott, 'Mediterranean Mysteries', *New York Review of Books*, 3 May 1973, 20(7): 28; and B. Bailyn, 'Braudel's Geohistory – a Reconsideration', *Journal of Economic History*, 1951, 11(3): 279.
12 G. Mattingly, 'Review of *La Méditerranée et le monde méditerranéen à l'époque de Philippe II*', *American Historical Review*, 1950, 55(2): 350.
13 J. H. Hexter, 'Fernand Braudel and the *Monde Braudellien . . .*', *Journal of Modern History*, 44(4): 480–539; and H. Kellner, 'Disorderly Conduct: Braudel's Mediterranean Satire', *History and Theory*, 1979, 18(2): 197–222.

Braudel's major works

'Personal Testimony', *Journal of Modern History*, 1972, 44: 448–67.
The Mediterranean and the Mediterranean World in the Age of Philip II, 2 vols, trans. S. Reynolds, Glasgow: William Collins, 1972–73.
Capitalism and Material Life 1400–1800, trans. M. Kochan, Glasgow: Fontana, 1974, revised edn, *Civilization and Capitalism 15th–18th Century*, 3 vols (*The Structures of Everyday Life, The Wheels of Commerce, The Perspective of the World*), trans. S. Reynolds, Glasgow: William Collins, 1981–92.
Afterthoughts on Material Civilisation, trans. P. M. Ranum, Baltimore, MD: Johns Hopkins University Press, 1977.
On History, trans. S. Matthews, Chicago, IL: University of Chicago Press, 1980.
The Identity of France, 2 vols (*History and Environment, People and Production*), trans. S. Reynolds, London: Harper Collins, 1990–92.

See also

Bloch, Braudel (CT), Diop, Febvre, Foucault, Le Roy Ladurie, Lévi-Strauss (CT).

Further resources

Bulhof, I. N., 'The Cosmopolitan Orientation to History and Fernand Braudel', *Clio*, 1981, 11(1): 49–63.
Burke, P., *The French Historical Revolution: the Annales School 1929–89*, Cambridge: Polity, 1990.
Gemelli, G., *Fernand Braudel*, trans. from Italian to French by B. Pasquett and B. Propetto Marzi, Paris: Editions Odile Jacob, 1995.

Hufton, O., 'Fernand Braudel', *Past and Present*, 1986, 112: 208–13.

Kaplan, S., 'Long-run Lamentations: Braudel on France', *Journal of Modern History*, 1991, 63(2): 341–53.

Kellner, H., 'Disorderly Conduct: Braudel's Mediterranean Satire', *History and Theory*, 1979, 18(2): 197–222.

Kinser, S., '*Annaliste* Paradigm? The Geohistorical Structuralism of Fernand Braudel', *American Historical Review*, 1981, 86(1): 63–105.

Lai, C.- C., 'Second Thoughts on Fernand Braudel's "Civilization and Capitalism"', *Journal of European Economic History*, 1995, 24(1): 177–93.

McNeill, W. H. (ed.), *Journal of Modern History*, 1972, 44(4): 447–539.

Morineau, M., 'A Fresh Look at Fernand Braudel: Response to Cheng-chung Lai', *Journal of European Economic History*, 1997, 26(3): 627–30.

Stoianovich, T., 'Theoretical Implications of Braudel's *Civilisation matérielle*', *Journal of Modern History*, 1969, 41(1): 68–81.

Wallerstein, I., 'Braudel on Capitalism, or Everything Upside Down', *Journal of Modern History*, 1991, 63(2): 354–61.

E. H. CARR 1892–1982

The writings of Edward Hallett Carr (1892–1982), international relations scholar, historian and historiographer, have aroused as much animosity and acclaim as the regime that he spent much of his career writing about: the Soviet Union. The eldest son in a North London family, Carr was educated at Merchant Taylor's School, London, and at Trinity College, Cambridge, where he was awarded a first class degree in classics in 1916. From 1916 to 1936 he served in the British Foreign Office. He attended the Paris Peace Conference and was later an adviser on League of Nations affairs. After being assigned to Riga in the 1920s, Carr became increasingly absorbed in Russian culture and literature. Between 1931 and 1937 he published works on Dostoevsky, Marx and Bakunin. In 1936 he was appointed Woodrow Wilson professor of international politics at the University College of Wales at Aberystwyth. During his time there he published *The Twenty Years Crisis, 1919–1939* (1939), *Conditions of Peace* (1942) and *Nationalism and After* (1945), works that gave much shape to the fledgling discipline of international relations.[1] He was also an assistant editor of *The Times* of London during the Second World War. After the war, Carr was a fellow of Balliol College, Oxford, and then Trinity College. He remained at Trinity College until his death. It was in Oxford that he penned the works that he is best known for: the monumental *A History of Soviet Russia* (14 vols, 1950–78) and *What is History?* (1961, revised edition 1986).

Russia's tenacity during the Second World War prompted Carr's decision in late 1944 to write a history of the political, social and economic order that emerged in Russia after the October (November, new style) 1917 revolution. In *A History of Soviet Russia* (see also the summary work *The Russian Revolution*, 1979), Carr traces the transformation of Russia from a peasant economy to a modern industrial power able both to compete with the major capitalist powers on equal terms and to withstand the 1929 world economic crisis. As he sees it, that period was dominated by three distinct attempts to raise capital for industrial development. In the first place there were the 'war communism' policies of the early 1920s. These policies, Carr suggests, were characterised by the concentration of economic power in large units of production, the supply of basic goods and services for free or at fixed prices, rationing and payments in kind. Their success was undermined by slow growth in the agricultural sector. The second attempt, the New Economic Policy (NEP), allowed peasants, after the delivery of a fixed proportion of their output to the state, to sell the rest on the market. At the same time, industrialists were encouraged to make things that peasants would buy. Agriculture and light consumer industry took off, but at the expense of heavy industry. The third attempt, which was part of Stalin's plan for 'socialism in one country', was characterised by centrally determined production figures and then five-year plans, the forced collectivisation of agriculture and policies favourable to heavy industry.

For Carr, the transformation of Soviet Russia during the period 1917–29 is personified by the transition from Lenin to Stalin. Lenin saw himself as one of a small group of committed revolutionaries who sought ways to give power to the masses and to promote revolution elsewhere in the world. Stalin, on the other hand, required total support for his decisions, treated his opponents ruthlessly, imposed policies from above by force, cared not for world revolution but for making Russia self-sufficient, reduced the policies of the Communist International (Comintern) to those of the USSR and conflated socialism with Russian nationalism (see also *The Twilight of the Comintern*). Yet it was Stalin, Carr reminds us, who shaped Russia into a great industrial power. At the time that Carr wrote his *History*, the policies of the Soviet regime excited both acclaim and abuse. This polarisation of opinion can be clearly discerned in reviews of Carr's work. While historians such as A. J. P. Taylor and Hugh Trevor-Roper hailed Carr's efforts as a landmark in modern history, and Soviet reviewers were cautiously favourable, others considered Carr to be an apologist for Stalin. Although there is still debate about Carr's treatment of Stalin, the *History* is generally characterised as detailed, perceptive and even-handed.[2]

Carr's most popular work, *What is History?*, has also triggered considerable debate. In responding to the question 'What is history?', Carr claims to steer a middle course between views of history he attributes to 'commonsense' and to R. G. Collingwood, or

> between the Scylla of an untenable theory of history as an objective compilation of facts, of the unqualified primacy of fact over interpretation, and of the Charybdis of an equally untenable theory of history as the subjective product of the mind of the historian who establishes the facts of history and masters them through the process of interpretation, between a view of history having the centre of gravity in the past and a view having the centre of gravity in the present.
>
> (*What is History?*, p. 29)[3]

Facts are not ascertained like sense impressions and do not 'speak for themselves'. Nor are they entirely the creation of historians. For Carr, facts exist apart from the historian, but they only become 'historical facts' when they are judged historically significant by selection and interpretation. He writes:

> The facts speak only when the historian calls on them: it is he who decides to which facts to give the floor, and in what order or context. . . . It is the historian who has decided for his own reasons that Caesar's crossing of that petty stream, the Rubicon, is a fact of history, whereas the crossings of the Rubicon by millions of other people . . . interests nobody at all.
>
> (Ibid., p. 11; see also pp. 12–13)

Historians select, interpret and present facts according to their interests and experiences, but the facts that they study may also lead them to change their views. Historians are thus engaged in what Carr calls 'an unending dialogue between the past and the present' (ibid., p. 30). This dialogue, Carr feels, is as worthy of study as the phenomena that historians write about.

Similarly, the individual and society are engaged in reciprocal dialogue. Language and the environment help to shape people's desires and actions, but they are also able to become aware of their own and other people's views. Echoing Hegel, Carr contends that great individuals can 'put into words the will of [their] age'.[4] Yet they also have the power and the freedom to change and shape (both consciously and unconsciously) the world and people's ideas (ibid., p. 55). Consequently,

Carr is not unduly worried by questions about the extent to which human beings are free. For him, discussions on free will by such writers as Karl Popper and Isaiah Berlin are no more than Cold War polemics levelled against the reputedly deterministic doctrines of Nazism and Sovietism.

Though 'determinism' is generally understood as the belief that historical events are controlled by factors other than the motives and volition of human beings, Carr opts for a less common view of it as

> the belief that everything that happens has a cause or causes, and could not have happened differently unless something in the cause or causes had also been different.

> (Ibid., p. 93)

Understood in this sense, Carr argues, determinism is essential both to the study of history and to our everyday lives. For example, if a friend of yours does something unexpected, you take it for granted that there must be some cause of their behaviour. This is what W. H. Dray calls 'scientific determinism': the view that events occur in accord with empirically demonstrable relations of cause and effect.[5]

Discussions on the role of chance in history are for Carr another 'red herring'. Those who emphasise the role of accidents in history, he claims, do so because they have not grasped the purpose of writing history or because they are part of a group or nation 'which is riding in the trough, not the crest, of historical events' (ibid., p. 101). Historians should instead look to 'rational' causes, by which he means those that can be generalised and applied to other periods and places, because they serve to broaden our understanding of the past in the light of the present and the present in the light of the past. Anything that fails to contribute to that purpose is to the historian 'irrational', 'dead' and 'barren' (ibid., p. 108).[6] Carr's account of the historian's selection of 'rational' causes suggests a *functional* or conventional view of objectivity, not sceptical relativism. For him, saying that an account is objective means not that it mirrors absolute truths about the past but that it conforms to socially acceptable ways of viewing the past. Some accounts of the past are thus more adequate or 'right' than others (ibid., p. 26). What counts as 'socially acceptable' for Carr is that which puts into words the will and the goals of the historian's age. If the will and goals of a society change, then what is considered to be objective will change also. The objective account thus serves society. Though Carr is not sure what goals our society is aiming for, he is prepared to say that we are progressing

towards goals which can be defined only as we advance towards
them, and the validity of which can be verified only in a process
of attaining them. Thus history is a dialogue not only between
past and present, but past, present and progressively emerging
goals.

(Ibid., p. 119)

In saying that the study of history reveals the progressive development
of human potentialities, Carr displays a mood of optimism rare among
historians in the latter half of the twentieth century. For the majority of
his contemporaries, the catastrophic events of the first half of the century
made belief in progress impossible. Even in the preface for the second
edition of *What is History?*, which Carr wrote a few months before his
death, he was still prepared to go against the current wave of scepticism
and despair and 'strike out a claim, if not for an optimistic, at any rate
for a saner and more balanced outlook on the future' (ibid., p. 6).

Carr was also more willing than his contemporaries to suggest that
history is a science. Of the five objections generally made against the
claim that history is a science – that it reveals no generalisations; that
it teaches no lessons; that it is unable to predict; that it is necessarily
subjective; and that it involves questions of religion and morality – Carr
believes that none stand up to scrutiny. In the first case, the historian's
use of language commits them to generalisation (ibid., pp. 63–6).
If historians want to be understood, they must employ shared concepts.
It would make no sense for a historian to write of a 'revolution', for
instance, if no one knows what that word means. Furthermore, it is
not unheard of for historians to treat specific historical events as
instances of 'revolutions', 'wars' and so on (ibid., pp. 63–6). Second,
Carr believes that when historians generalise they often (consciously
or unconsciously) consider events in the light of the lessons learned
from other events (ibid., pp. 66–8). Third, although historians cannot
predict specific events, they can make generalisations which both serve
as guides to future action and as keys to our understanding of how things
happen. Moreover, Carr believes that scientists themselves do not make
predictions because the laws of science are only 'statements of tendency,
statements of what will happen other things being equal or in laboratory
conditions' (ibid., pp. 68–74). Fourth, Carr considers that scientists and
historians alike engage in a reciprocal relationship with their subjects
(ibid., pp. 163–5). Finally, for Carr, there is no obligation for historians
and scientists to believe in deities or in absolute moral standards (ibid.,
pp. 74–84). Carr thus concludes that there is no harm in calling history
a science. Much of what Carr has to say about the relationship between

science and history is contentious, and is likely to raise the eyebrows (if not the hackles) of scientists and historians alike.

Carr's treatment of value judgements in history is equally contentious. There are, he claims, no universally valid standards by which human actions may be judged. For him, the search for such standards is 'unhistorical and contradicts the very essence of history'. If the historian is to judge the actions of an individual, they must do so according to the moral norms that prevailed at the time. Carr would prefer, however, that historians restrict their judgements to events, policies and institutions. This, he claims, allows judgements to be made about groups or societies which might otherwise be provided with alibis if moral condemnation were restricted to individuals. For example, he believes that 'Russians, Englishmen and Americans readily join in personal attacks on Stalin, Neville Chamberlain, or McCarthy as scapegoats for their collective misdeeds' (ibid., p. 78). This may explain why in *The Russian Revolution* he writes of Stalin:

> He revived and outdid the worst brutalities of the earlier Tsars; and his record excited revulsion in later generations of historians. Yet his achievement in borrowing from the West, in forcing on primitive Russia the material foundations of modern civilisation, and in giving Russia a place among the European powers, obliged them to concede, however reluctantly, his title to greatness. Stalin was the most ruthless despot Russia had known since Peter, and also a great westerniser.
>
> (*The Russian Revolution*, p. 112)

The aim of historians is to warn their readers against acting in ways which would help create the type of society that gave rise to such individuals. In doing so, however, Carr leaves us wondering whether individuals are the product of their society in such a way that they could not have acted otherwise. Is Stalin, for instance, personally responsible for any of his misdeeds? As the above example also shows us, the selection of facts and use of evaluative terms are a necessary part of the historian's discourse. So even though the historian claims to abstain from judgement, their selection of particular facts and use of words such as 'ruthless', 'forcing' and 'brutalities' tell us something about their view of an individual.[7]

Many historians think that Carr's answer to the question, 'What is history?' veers in the direction of the Charybdis of sceptical relativism.[8] Though his pronouncements on the nature of facts and moral judgements in history would seem to support such a conclusion, Carr did believe that historians can be objective in the functional sense. For him, objective historians move beyond the limited vision of their own situation and put into words the will and goals of their age. In Carr's optimistic view, they thereby foster the progress of society. The task of describing what those goals are, or ought to be, and to what extent they do and should shape historical accounts will always keep them busy.

Notes

1 For a more detailed account of these works, see Carr (IRT).
2 See, for example, H. R. Trevor-Roper, 'E. H. Carr's Success Story', *Encounter*, 1962, 81(104): 69–77; V. I. Salov, 'Sovremennaia Burzhuaznaïa Istoriografiia Velikoi Oktiabrskoi Sotsialisticheskoi Revoliutsii', *Voprosy Istorii*, 1967, 11: 192–201; and J. Halsam, 'E. H. Carr and the History of Soviet Russia', *Historical Journal*, 1983, 26(4): 1021–7.
3 Scylla and Charybdis were two monsters that Odysseus encountered in his journey through the Strait of Messina. For a critical discussion on whether Collingwood was in fact a relativist, see T. Madood, 'The Later Collingwood's Alleged Historicism and Relativism', *Journal of the History of Philosophy*, 1989, 27(1): 101–25.
4 Hegel, *Philosophy of Right*, p. 295; quoted in *What is History?*, p. 54.
5 W. H. Dray, 'Determinism in History', in P. Edwards (ed.), *Encyclopedia of Philosophy*, New York: Macmillan, 1967, pp. 373–6.
6 In his notes towards a second edition of *What is History?*, Carr reiterates that accidents are causes extraneous to history but he also admits that they can affect its course. See *What is History?*, pp. 166–70.
7 A. Oldfield, 'Moral Judgements in History', *History and Theory*, 1981, 20(3): 260–77.
8 See, for example, J. Tosh, *The Pursuit of History*, London: Longman, 2nd edition, 1991, pp. 29, 236, 148; G. McLennon, *Marxism and the Methodologies of History*, London: Verso, 1981, p. 103; and D. LaCapra, *History and Criticism*, London: Cornell University Press, 1985, p. 137.

Carr's major works

Dostoevsky (1821–1881): a New Biography, New York: Houghton Mifflin, 1931.
The Romantic Exiles: a Nineteenth Century Portrait Gallery, London: Gollancz, 1933.
Karl Marx: a Study in Fanaticism, London: Dent, 1934.
Michael Bakunin, London: Macmillan, 1937.
The Twenty Years Crisis, 1919–1939: an Introduction to the Study of International Relations, London: Macmillan, revised edition of 1936 text, 1946.
Conditions of Peace, London: Macmillan, 1942.
Nationalism and After, London: Macmillan, 1945.
A History of Soviet Russia, 14 vols, vols 1–3: *The Bolshevik Revolution*; vol. 4: *The Interregnum*; vols 5–8: *Socialism in One Country*; vols 9–14: *Foundations of a*

Planned Economy, vols 9 and 10 written with R. W. Davies, London: Macmillan, 1950–78.

What is History?, revised edition, (ed.) R. W. Davies, Harmondsworth: Penguin, 1986.

The Russian Revolution: From Lenin to Stalin (1917–1929), London: Macmillan, 1979.

From Napoleon to Stalin and Other Essays, New York: St Martin's Press, 1980.

The Twilight of the Comintern, 1930–1935, London: Macmillan, 1982.

See also

Carr (IRT), Collingwood, Popper (MP), Taylor.

Further resources

Abramsky, C. and Williams, B. J. (eds), *Essays in Honour of E. H. Carr*, London: Macmillan, 1974.

Davies, R. W., 'Edward Hallett Carr, 1892–1982', *Proceedings of the British Academy*, 1983, no. 69, pp. 473–511.

——, '"Drop the Glass Industry": Collaborating with E. H. Carr', *New Left Review*, 1984, 145: 56–70.

Deutscher, T., 'E. H. Carr – a Personal Memoir', *New Left Review*, 1983, 137: 78–86.

Haslam, J., 'We Need a Faith: E. H. Carr, 1892–1982', *History Today*, August 1983, 33: 36–9.

——, 'E. H. Carr and the History of Soviet Russia', *Historical Journal*, 1983, 26(4): 1021–7.

Howe, P., 'The Utopian Realism of E. H. Carr', *Review of International Studies*, 1994, 20(3): 277–97.

Jenkins, K., *On 'What is History?': From Carr and Elton to Rorty and White*, London: Routledge, 1995.

Labedz, L., 'E. H. Carr: an Historian Overtaken by History', *Survey*, 1988, 30(1–2): 94–111.

Oldfield, A., 'Moral Judgments in History', *History and Theory*, 1981, 20(3): 260–77.

Prince, J. R., Review of *What is History?*, *History and Theory*, 1963, 3(1): 136–45.

Trevor-Roper, H. R., 'E. H. Carr's Success Story', *Encounter*, 1962, 84(104): 69–77.

White, M. *Pragmatism and the American Mind: Essays and Reviews in Philosophy and Intellectual History*, New York: Oxford University Press, 1973.

CHARLES MANNING HOPE CLARK 1915–91

From the time of European settlement in the late eighteenth century, Australians tried to frame their experiences in the manner of Britons. Their history was simply a part of the history of the British Empire. In the mid-twentieth century, however, some Australians began to question the assumption that their history was made for them in Britain. Chief among the historians who looked for new ways in which to frame experiences was Manning Clark. In a career spanning over fifty years, Clark laboured to make Australians aware of the emptiness of many of the ideals they cherished and to build a new society in an 'age of ruins'.

The son of an Anglican minister and a woman from a leading family of colonial pastoralists, Charles Manning Hope Clark (b. 3 March 1915) believed that the conflicts he experienced in childhood mirrored those of Australian society at large:

> My mother came from the old patrician, landed magnificoes in Australia; my father from the working class first of London, then of Sydney. . . . In my veins, there was a conflict between 'immigrants' and the 'native born', between 'Australian Britons' and 'Australians', between making the country an echo of the old world, and cultivating an Australian national sentiment, between being an exile at heart, and being a 'dinkum Aussie'.
>
> (*A Discovery of Australia*, p. 10)[1]

He also claimed to have experienced the conflict between town and country, moving from Burwood, a suburb between Sydney and Parramatta, to Cowes, a rural settlement on Phillip Island, and then to Belgrave, a popular holiday spot in the Dandenong Ranges near Melbourne. In 1928 Clark won a scholarship to attend Melbourne Church of England Grammar, a prestigious school for the sons of local notables. During his years there (1928–33), Clark held three different scholarships. Under the guidance of the Headmaster, R. P. Franklin, Clark read works by Herodotus, Thucydides and Dostoevsky and was encouraged to study history.[2] Clark's interest in history can be clearly seen in a number of articles that he wrote for the school magazine, *The Melburnian*. In 'The Australian Aborigine', for instance, he argued that 'the Australian Aborigine is not the idiot and brainless man that some historians have made him out to be', and in a later article he claimed that Poland, an artificial creation of the Treaty of Versailles, was likely to trigger a war because it separated Germany from East Prussia.[3] In 1934 he won a scholarship to go to Trinity College, an Anglican residential college within the University of Melbourne. At Trinity he studied ancient, British and constitutional history and politics under Kenneth Bailey, W. MacMahon Ball and R. M. Crawford. During his four years at the University of Melbourne, his only work in Australian history was a short thesis on the electoral system of Victoria from 1842 to 1870. At that stage, Clark seemed to be more interested in the role of various ideologies in the international crises of the 1930s.

Scholastic success at the University of Melbourne gained Clark a scholarship to Balliol College, Oxford, in 1938. Under the supervision of Humphrey Sumne, an authority on nineteenth-century Russian history, Clark was to write a thesis on the ideals of the nineteenth-century political thinker Alexis de Tocqueville. Clark plunged into de Tocqueville's writings and visited the de Tocqueville family seat in Normandy. There he was granted access to many of de Tocqueville's manuscripts. Studying de Tocqueville allowed Clark to see Europe firsthand. It was at that time that he married Dymphna Lodewyckx, a skilled Dutch and German linguist. With the outbreak of the Second World War, Clark was forced to abandon his studies after only a year. After a short stint as a schoolmaster in Tiverton, he returned to Australia in 1940 to take up a teaching position at Geelong Church of England Grammar School.

Clark was a very popular and influential teacher at Geelong Grammar, but his sympathetic attitude towards Marxism and the Soviet Union raised a few eyebrows.[4] During his time at Geelong he gave talks for a number of school societies, conducted an adult education course on the reasons for the collapse of the Third Republic in 1940 and published two papers on the French and German intelligentsia. In the first of these, 'The Dilemma of the French Intelligentsia: a Reply to Professor Chisholm', Clark argued that French intellectuals such as Charles Maurras had been driven into supporting the Vichy regime by their dislike of middle-class conservatism and fear that the realisation of socialism by mass action might lead to a repeat of the terrors of 1794. Clark's paper brought a reply from L. J. Austin, who countered that the collaboration of Maurras and others was the result not of the French political situation but of a wider intellectual, moral and spiritual malaise.[5] In his second paper, 'France and Germany', Clark addressed the rise of Nazism. For him, the roots of Nazism could be traced back to the rejection of liberalism by German intellectuals after they learned of the apparently catastrophic results of post-revolutionary liberal rule in France.[6]

In 1941, Clark recommenced his research into de Tocqueville as a masters student at the University of Melbourne. In the resulting thesis, 'The Ideal of Alexis de Tocqueville', Clark argued that de Tocqueville's ignorance of the hardships faced by the masses and refusal to contemplate the use of compulsion to ensure good and just action fatally undermined his plans for a society based on liberty.[7] Not long after he completed his thesis, Clark was appointed as a lecturer in political science at the University of Melbourne. In preparing for his lectures, Clark sought information that would shed light on the nature of Australian society, politics and government. Although he found the works of historians and social scientists helpful, Clark later claimed that it was the works of novelists, poets and playwrights such as D. H. Lawrence, Joseph Furphy, Henry Lawson, James McAuley and Douglas Stewart that led to his 'discovery of Australia'. Like the early European explorers of Australia, however, what he 'discovered' disappointed and troubled him. Many writers, and the public, characterised 'dinkum' or genuine Australians as people who sought egalitarianism, 'mateship' and material well-being and were distrustful of political, economic, cultural and intellectual elites. For Clark, such 'dinkum' ideals are merely 'comforters' used to make life in a hostile land a little more bearable; they help people to forget about their failure to respect and adapt to the Australian environment.[8] They make the elite, who revere polite European culture, cringe, and are poor soil for a civilisation to grow in. Clark professed that he was unable to suggest ideals that would be more fertile, but thought that it was important for historians to make people aware of the ideas and conflicts that shape their lives.

Progress in such a task was bound to be difficult, however, because the entire scope of Australian history was only covered by a handful of scholarly books and many primary materials were held in Britain. Along with L. J. Pryor, Clark resolved to prepare two volumes of documents illustrating Australia's history. During 1946 he collected, from the Mitchell Library in Sydney and the Melbourne Public Library, materials relating to the foundation of the colony of New South Wales, squatters and the transportation of convicts. Volume 1 of *Select Documents in Australian History* (1950), which covered the period 1788–1850, was hailed as an important work in Australian history in many newspapers and academic journals.[9] In 1949 Clark was made a professor of history and assigned a chair at Canberra University College, an offshoot of the University of Melbourne in the Australian capital. Clark's academic success could not ease the disquiet he felt about contemporary political events such as the Chifley government's use of force to break strikes and its defeat in the 1949 federal election, the investigation of persons with 'suspect' political views, the escalation of hostilities in Indo-China, and the Communist Party Dissolution Bill introduced by Robert Menzies in 1950. Left-wing politicians, he believed, had shied away from the problem of building a new society in Australia.[10]

Determined to make people question the foundations of society, Clark used volume 2 of *Select Documents in Australian History* (1955) and his inaugural lecture at Canberra, 'Rewriting Australian History' (1956), to take aim at a number of popular 'comforters'. Historical evidence, he argued, did not support the common assumptions that Australia's past automatically condemned the country to cultural barbarism; that the convicts of early colonial Australia were simply victims of impersonal socio-economic change in the English countryside and the tyrannical political and legal system during George III's reign; that the gold diggers at the Eureka stockade were evangelists for Chartism; and that the Australian land and electoral reforms of the late nineteenth century diminished the power of old privileged groups. Such assumptions, he concluded, were not only escapist but also dangerous, because they encouraged anti-intellectualism, racism and sexism.[11] Clark was by now gaining a clearer picture of the historian's role in society:

> I think . . . of the historian as a prophet, by which I do not mean someone who can foretell or predict future events, but rather what the word means literally, namely someone who can speak for his generation. He does this by telling a story about the past. He tells the story by creating scenes which make some point about life, and help his readers or his listeners to understand what life is like. . . . All the great historians wrote like the prophets of the Old Testament.
>
> (*A Discovery of Australia*, p. 11)

At the end of 1955 Clark was given a grant by the Rockefeller Foundation to travel to Asia and Europe to collect primary materials concerning the discovery and foundation of Australia.[12] Clark hoped to use those materials and *Select Documents in Australian History* to write a textbook. In England his plans unravelled:

> It was going to be very academic, very careful, very much a 'Yes' and 'No' performance, with genuflexions in the direction of Mr 'Dry-as-Dust', and anxious looking back over the shoulder at people that I liked, hoping they were not as bored or lost as I was. It was all hopeless, lifeless, meaningless and false. I was in England, writing about Australia, writing about a country I did not really know, and about a country with which I had a love–hate relationship.
>
> (*A Discovery of Australia*, p. 46)

After further travelling he realised that what he wanted to do was to tell a story about the impact of European civilisation on the Australian continent and vice versa. In particular, he wanted to describe what happened when three different views of the nature of man and God – Catholic, Protestant and Enlightenment – confronted each in a new society (ibid., p. 47). These ideas were to be at the core of Clark's most ambitious and famous work: *A History of Australia* (6 vols, 1962–87; see also *A Short History of Australia*, 1986).

Ignoring those who believed that the field of Australian history was as barren as the interior of the continent, Clark set about telling the story of the conflicts that had shaped both Australian society and his life. In six volumes, published between 1962 and 1987, he explored such topics and events as the coming of civilisation to Australia in the last quarter of the eighteenth century; reasons for settlement; the foundation of the colony of New South Wales and then those of Tasmania, Victoria, South Australia, Western Australia and Queensland; attempts by the Protestant ascendancy to retain its dominance despite Irish Catholic resistance; the work of the elite to create a European society; the accumulation of wealth through farming, trade and, later, gold; the end of convict transportation; the linking of the colonies by rail and communication networks; the establishment of Australia as a federation of states and territories in 1901; the depressions of the late nineteenth century and twentieth century; the establishment of a public education system; attempts to eradicate Aboriginal culture; the exploration of the continent; the Allied battle for Gallipoli in the First World War and public resistance to conscription; Australian participation in battles in Europe, Africa and Asia during the Second World War; the measures taken to protect Australia from non-European immigration and communism; and the loss of control over resources to multinational companies. Clark's story tells not of a 'lucky country' blessed with increasing prosperity, but of the slump of a country of petit-bourgeois property owners into a 'kingdom of nothingness' in an 'age of ruins'. His fellow Australians were so obsessed with material gain as to render them spiritually and morally mute. He still had hope, however:

> Australians have liberated themselves from the fate of being second-rate Europeans and have begun to contribute to the neverending conversation of humanity on the meaning of life and the means of wisdom and understanding. So far no one has described the phoenix that will arise from the ashes of an age of ruins. No one has risked prophesying whether an age of ruins will be the prelude to the coming of the barbarians or to taking a seat at the great banquet of life. The life-deniers and the straiteners have been swept into the dustbin of human

history. Now is the time for the life affirmers and the enlargers
to show whether they have anything to say, whether they have
any food for the great hungers of humanity.

(*A Short History of Australia*, p. 292)

Clark's message is magnified by his distinctive writing style, particularly his use of apocalyptic images, Biblical allusions and language, and sketches of the inner struggles of humans.

Clark's very personal interpretation of Australian history made a number of academics wince. His writing style seemed far away from the ideal of scientific history and he made a number of factual errors. Criticisms arose soon after the publication of the first volume and continued with gusto after Peter Ryan's far-reaching complaints in 1993.[13] Clark himself was also critical about his efforts. This is especially clear in his treatment of the history of Australian Aborigines. Whereas in the first volume of the *History* he suggests that '[c]ivilisation did not begin in Australia until the last quarter of the eighteenth century', he later admitted that he wrote the work with a British clock in mind:

now I [want] to go on to persuade Australians to build their
own clock. That clock, I think, must start forty or fifty
thousand years ago with the migration of the Aborigines to
Australia. . . . I told only a part of what is possibly the greatest
human tragedy in the history of Australia – the confrontation
between the white man and the Aborigine.

(*A Discovery of Australia*, pp. 56–7)[14]

Few historians, however, doubted that the *History* was a landmark work.[15] The theatrical power of his writing also made the work immensely popular with the public. *A Short History of Australia*, which Clark updated and revised twice before his death in 1991, and the abridged version of *A History of Australia*, still enjoy healthy sales. During the 1988 bicentennial a musical version of the *History* was even produced. Though not a box-office success, 'Manning Clark's History of Australia – the Musical' fed the public's image of Clark as a 'shameless lover' of Australia:

For me Australia, and no other/ Mistress, harlot, goddess,
mother/ Whose first great native son I am.[16]

His pronouncements against the dismissal of Whitlam's Labour government in 1975 and in favour of republicanism also endeared him to the Labour Party. Paul Keating, a recent Prime Minister, drew on many of the positive themes of *A History of Australia* in order to promote his vision of an Asian-oriented, republican Australia. He, like the many other Australians who continue to struggle to define themselves, have found Clark's writings to be a great source of both inspiration and comfort.[17]

Notes

1 On Clark's childhood, see S. Holt, *Manning Clark and Australian History, 1915–1963*, St Lucia, Qld: University of Queensland Press, 1982; J. Hooton, 'Australian Autobiography and the Question of National Identity: Patrick White, Barry Humphries and Manning Clark', *Auto/biography Studies*, 1994, 9(1): 43–63; C. M. H. Clark, *Disquiet and Other Stories*, Sydney: Angus & Robertson, 1969; id., *The Puzzles of Childhood*, Ringwood, Vic.: Penguin, 1989; and id., *The Quest for Grace*, Ringwood, Vic.: Penguin, 1990.

2 'Manning Clark', in T. Lane (ed.), *As the Twig is Bent*, Melbourne: Dover, 1979, pp. 18–19.

3 'The Australian Aborigine', *Melburnian*, 1931, 56(2): 121; and 'A Retrospect', *Melburnian*, 1933, 58(1): 33–4. These papers are described in Holt, *Manning Clark and Australian History*, p. 21.

4 On Manning Clark as a teacher, see S. Davies, 'The Teacher', in C. Bridge (ed.), *Manning Clark: Essays on his Place in History*, Melbourne: Melbourne University Press, 1994, pp. 136–52. On Clark's interest in the Soviet Union, see C. M. H. Clark, *Meeting Soviet Man*, Sydney: Angus & Robertson, 1960; H. McQueen, *Suspect History: Manning Clark and the Future of Australia's Past*, Adelaide, SA: Wakefield, 1997; 'The Man who Rewrote Australia: Manning Clark and the Order of Lenin', *The Economist*, 25 January 1997, 342 (8001): 77–8.

5 'The Dilemma of the French Intelligentsia: a Reply to Professor Chisholm', *Australian Quarterly*, 1940, 12(4): 51–7. See also L. J. Austin, 'France: a Reply to Mr C. M. H. Clark', *Australian Quarterly*, 1941, 13(1): 94–101.

6 'France and Germany', *Australian Quarterly*, 1941, 13(2): 14–21.

7 'The Ideal of Alexis de Tocqueville', MA thesis, University of Melbourne, 1944. Described in Holt, *Manning Clark and Australian History*, pp. 82–6.

8 See 'Letter to Tom Collins', *Meanjin Papers*, 1943, 2(3): 40–1. Reprinted in I. Turner (ed.), *The Australian Dream*, Melbourne: Sun Books, 1968, pp. 345–7.

9 See the reviews in *The Age* (Melbourne), 27 May 1950, p. 8; *The Sydney Morning Herald*, 19 August 1950, p. 12; *Historical Studies*, 1949–50, 4: 286–8; *Canadian Historical Review*, 1951, 32: 146; and *Economic Record*, 1951, 27: 257–60.

10 'The Years of Unleavened Bread: December 1949 to December 1972', *Meanjin Quarterly*, 1973, 32: 245–50.

11 'Re-writing Australian History', in T. A. G. Hungerford (ed.), *Australian Signpost*, Melbourne: Cheshire, 1956, pp. 130–43.

12 See *Sources of Australian History*, London: Oxford University Press, 1957.

13 See M. H. Ellis, 'History without Facts', in Bridge (ed.), *Manning Clark*,

pp. 70–8; P. Ryan, *Lines of Fire: Manning Clark and Other Writings*, Binalong, NSW: Clarion, 1997, pp. 177–234; and P. Craven, 'The Ryan Affair', in Bridge (ed.), *Manning Clark*, pp. 165–87.

14 On Manning Clark's changing views of Aborigines, see J. Woolmington, 'I'm Sorry, Very Sorry . . .' in Bridge (ed.), *Manning Clark*, pp. 104–12. On the way that he wrote about women, see S. Pfisterer-Smith in ibid., pp. 78–93.

15 On the reception of volume 1, see Holt, *Manning Clark and Australian History*, chap. 8. For retrospective reviews, see Bridge (ed.), *Manning Clark: Essays on his Place in History; The Economist*, 11 June 1994, 331(7867): 90; and H. Bourke, 'History as Revelation: the Problem of Manning Clark', *Journal of Historical Geography*, 1983, 9(2): 196–9.

16 See P. Fitzpatrick, '"History – the Musical": a Review and a Retrospect', *Australian Historical Studies*, 1988, 23(91): 171–9.

17 On the political usefulness of Clark's views, see McQueen, *Suspect History*.

Clark's major works

Select Documents in Australian History, 2 vols, Sydney: Angus & Robertson, 1950–55.

'Re-writing Australian History', in T. A. G. Hungerford (ed.), *Australian Signpost*, Melbourne: Cheshire, 1956, pp. 130–43.

Sources of Australian History, London: Oxford University Press, 1957.

A History of Australia, 6 vols, Melbourne: Melbourne University Press, 1962–87.

A Discovery of Australia, 1976 Boyer Lectures, Sydney: Australian Broadcasting Commission, 1976, revised edition, 1991.

A Short History of Australia, 1963, 3rd revised edition, Melbourne: Macmillan, 1986.

See also

Michelet, Moody.

Further resources

Bourke, H., 'History as Revelation: the Problem of Manning Clark', *Journal of Historical Geography*, 1983, 9(2): 196–9.

Bridge, C. (ed.), *Manning Clark: Essays on his Place in History*, Melbourne: Melbourne University Press, 1994.

Davies, S. (ed.), *Dear Kathleen, Dear Manning: the Correspondence of Manning Clark and Kathleen Fitzpatrick*, Melbourne: Melbourne University Press, 1996.

Fitzpatrick, P., '"History – the Musical": a Review and a Retrospect', *Australian Historical Studies*, 1988, 23(91): 171–9.

Holt, S., *Manning Clark and Australian History, 1915–1963*, St Lucia: University of Queensland Press, 1982.

——, *A Short History of Manning Clark*, Melbourne: Allen Unwin, 1999.

Hooton, J., 'Australian Autobiography and the Question of National Identity:

Patrick White, Barry Humphries, and Manning Clark', *Auto/biography Studies*, 1994, 9(1): 43–63.

McQueen, H., *Suspect History: Manning Clark and the Future of Australia's Past*, Adelaide: Wakefield Press, 1997.

Rickard, J., 'Manning Clark and Patrick White: a Reflection', *Australian Historical Studies*, 1992, 25(98): 116–22.

Ryan, P., *Lines of Fire: Manning Clark and Other Writings*, Binalong, NSW: Clarion, 1997.

Shaw, G. P., 'Themes in Australian Historical Writing', *Australian Journal of Politics and History*, 1995, 41: 1–16.

Ward, R., *Manning Clark* [sound recording], Sydney: Australian Broadcasting Corporation, 1990.

R. G. COLLINGWOOD 1889–1943

Historians, R. G. Collingwood believes, have long known that history is about *res gestae* or past actions by human beings. Moreover, they are only interested in some human actions:

> What men have done and undergone simply in their capacity as animals, human animals but still animals, done under the stress of animal inclination and suffered under the compulsion of animal destiny is traditionally no part of their history. . . . On a foundation of animal life [man's] rationality builds a structure of free activities, free in the sense that although they are based on his animal nature they do not proceed from it but are invented by his reason on its own initiative, and serve not the purposes of animal life but the purposes of reason itself.

Res gestae are thus 'actions done by reasonable agents in pursuit of ends determined by their reason' (*The Principles of History*, p. 37; cf. §5, Epilegomena, *The Idea of History*).[1] And for Collingwood the key to gaining knowledge of *res gestae* is re-enactment. In re-enactment, he writes in an oft-quoted passage from *An Autobiography*:

> the historian must be able to think over again for himself the thought whose expression he is trying to interpret. If for any reason he is such a kind of man that he cannot do this, he had better leave the problem alone. The important point here is that the historian of a certain thought must think for himself that very same thought, not another like it.
>
> (P. 111; cf. *The Idea of History*, p. 218)

Collingwood's various pronouncements on re-enactment and the subject-matter of history have been subject to much criticism. For instance, W. H. Walsh talks of Collingwood's 'narrow, rational view' of history, Arnold Toynbee of a history that 'squeezes out the emotions', Louis Mink of 'epistemological individualism', in which history is no more than 'the sum of innumerable biographies', and Patrick Gardiner of re-enactment as an 'additional power of knowing' which 'allows [historians] to penetrate into the minds of their study and take, as it were, psychological x-ray photographs'.[2] In recent years, however, close examination of his unpublished and published works has led to a greater appreciation of the complexity and richness of his views.

Robin George Collingwood was born on 22 February 1889 at Gillhead, in the English Lake District. His father, William Gershom Collingwood, was an author, painter and archaeologist, while his mother, Edith Mary Isaac, was a painter and a musician. Collingwood's parents educated him at home until he was thirteen, after which he was sent to a grammar school, and a year later, Rugby School. It was during his early education that he developed a delight in ancient and modern languages, philosophy, archaeology, the writing and binding of books, art, music and sailing.[3] Although Collingwood's early education later provided him with an exemplar of what education ought to entail, he was deeply dissatisfied with his time at Rugby (see *An Autobiography*, pp. 6–12, and *The New Leviathan*, §§22.32, 23.6).[4] In 1908, he gained a classics scholarship at University College, Oxford. In 1912 he was awarded a first in Greats (*Literae Humaniores*, classics and philosophy) and elected to a fellowship in philosophy at Pembroke College. In 1934 he was elected a fellow of the British Academy, and in 1935 he was appointed Waynflete Professor of Metaphysical Philosophy at Magdalen College, Oxford. Collingwood resigned his chair in 1941 on the grounds of poor health and retired to Coniston, where he died on 9 January 1943.

Collingwood was a successful teacher and writer.[5] During his lifetime, he published books on religion (*Religion and Philosophy*, 1916), the nature of knowledge (*Speculum Mentis*, 1924), metaphysics (*An Essay on Philosophical Method*, 1933; *An Essay on Metaphysics*, 1940), art (*Outlines of a Philosophy of Art*, 1925; *The Principles of Art*, 1938), politics (*The New Leviathan*, 1940), archaeology (with J. N. L. Myres, *Roman Britain and the English Settlements*, 1937; *The Archaeology of Roman Britain*, 1930) and his travels around the Greek Islands (*The First Mate's Log of a Voyage to Greece in the Schooner Yacht 'Fleur de Lys' in 1939*, 1940). He also wrote scores of papers on topics ranging from Jane Austen to the gramophone. After his death, Malcolm Knox edited *The Idea of Nature* (1945) and the

work for which Collingwood is best known, *The Idea of History* (1946).[6]
Since 1978 many of Collingwood's manuscripts have been made
available at the Bodleian Library, Oxford, including the recently redis--
covered *The Principles of History* (1999). Many scholars consider *The
Principles of History* – most of which was left out of *The Idea of History*
by Knox – to be the most significant expression of Collingwood's ideas
on history.

If, Collingwood argues, we take the word 'science' to mean 'any
organised body of knowledge', then it is clear that history is a science.
It is a science, but a science of a special kind:

> It is a science whose business is to study events not accessible
> to our observation, and to study these events inferentially,
> arguing to them from something else which is accessible to
> our observation, and which the historian calls 'evidence' for
> the events in which he is interested.
>
> (*The Idea of History*, pp. 251–2)

It should not, however, be confused with what Collingwood calls a
'scissors-and-paste' view of history. The 'scissors-and-paste' theory of
history is dominated by the ideas of memory and authority. According
to this view, history is about believing someone when they say that
something is the case. The believer is the historian; the person believed
is called their authority (*The Idea of History*, pp. 234–5). For example, if
Cicero recorded that he met Caesar at a certain time and in a certain
place, then the historian must accept Cicero's recollections as true.[7] In
writing a work of history, the historian simply 'cuts' out the statements
of authorities and pastes them together. This view, Collingwood points
out, is riddled with problems. Historians must simply accept the
omissions, concealments, distortions or even lies on the part of their
authorities. Furthermore, they have no authority to select which pieces
of evidence are relevant or to judge their authorities when they
contradict each other (ibid., pp. 278–9). Though historians are bound
to their evidence, they are not subject to it. Collingwood writes:

> Throughout the course of his work the historian is selecting,
> constructing and criticising. . . . By explicitly realising this
> fact it is possible to effect what, borrowing a Kantian phrase,
> one might call a Kantian revolution in the theory of history:
> the discovery that, so far from relying on an authority other
> than himself, to whose statements his thought must conform,
> the historian is his own authority and his thought autonomous,

self-authorising, possessed of a criterion to which his so-called authorities must conform and by reference to which they are criticised.

(*The Idea of History*, p. 236)

Historians do not look at evidence and simply describe what they see: they 'read' it. Documents and artefacts are not in themselves evidence. Evidence consists of 'what they say'. I could, for instance, look at a triangular piece of clay discovered in an archaeological dig simply as a triangular piece of clay. But I could also 'read it' as a loom weight. The important thing here is that the historian assumes that the piece of clay is an expression of thought or language. Indeed, Collingwood argues that 'every action has the character of language' and that 'every action is an expression of thought' (*The Principles of History*, pp. 39–40, 52; cf. *The Principles of Art*, chap. 11). Thus he writes:

> The starting-point of any genuinely historical argument is, strictly speaking, not 'this person, or this printed book, or this set of footprints, says so-and-so', but 'I, knowing the language, read this person, or this book, or these footprints, as saying so-and-so'. This is why it could be insisted . . . that in respect of his evidence the historian was autonomous or dependent on his own authority: for . . . his evidence is always an experience of his own, an act which he has performed by his own powers and is conscious of having performed by his own powers: the aesthetic act of reading a certain text in a language he knows, and assigning to it a certain sense.
>
> (*The Principles of History*, pp. 43–4)

These ideas link up, as Jan van der Dussen has pointed out, with that of 're-enactment'.[8] The cornerstone of Collingwood's view of re-enactment is that language is essentially public and shared. Common concepts and the rules that bind them provide the intersubjective ground on which we respond to and evaluate another person's actions.[9] This 'conceptual' view of re-enactment can be clearly discerned in Collingwood's rejection of the copy-theory of identity in §4 ('History as Re-enactment of Past Experience') of the epilegomena of *The Idea of History*.[10] In re-enactment, the historian thinks *the same* thought as the historical agent. For the copy-theorist, however, the historian cannot think the same thought as the historical agent because acts of thought are numerically and temporally different when performed in different contexts by different persons. Thus the best that the historian can do is to re-enact a copy of the historical agent's thought. But, as Collingwood reminds us, according to our common usage of the concepts 'the same thought', numerical and temporal difference are not relevant if the thoughts are *identical in content* (see also *The Idea of History*, pp. 446, 450). Thus we have moved away from a view of re-enactment as a special power that allows historians to take x-rays of the private minds of historical agents and towards a conceptual view more in keeping with the writings of the philosopher Ludwig Wittgenstein.

So far, this description of 're-enactment' has focused on the historian and the historical agent sharing the same *thought*. Looking at the published writings of Collingwood, we get the impression that only thought, and reflective thought at that, can be re-enacted (see, for example, *The Idea of History*, pp. 302–5). In *The Principles of History*, however, he tries to correct that impression. On pages 38 and 54 he makes it clear that emotions and irrational thoughts are involved in the actions of historical agents and can thus be understood by the historian. However, thoughts – rational and irrational – and emotions are only considered by the historian when there is evidence of them and they have a bearing on the actions being studied. For instance, it would not be essential to know Hitler's thoughts and feelings about his socks.[11]

Given that re-enactment operates through the medium of language – a social, conventional and rule-governed activity – part of the historian's task will also be to elucidate the conventions or 'rules' that bind the historical agent's actions. This will be particularly important in cases where historical agents follow social conventions different from those of the historian. Thus history is clearly more than the 'sum of innumerable biographies'. Some of these assumptions may presuppose some prior assumptions. For example, my assumption that 'X is a brigand' rests on prior assumptions about what a 'brigand' is. These are what Collingwood calls 'relative presuppositions'. 'Absolute presuppositions', on the other hand, do not presuppose prior assumptions (*An Essay on Metaphysics*, pp. 29–33). Complexes or 'constellations' of absolute presuppositions govern our activities. These complexes do not form an atemporal, unchanging foundation for language and meaning. Rather, they are perpetually subject to strains and conflicts, the intensity of which varies, but when the strains become too great the structure collapses and is replaced by another (ibid., pp. 48n., 66–7, 75–7). A number of commentators have noted the similarity between these ideas and those of Thomas Kuhn. Absolute presuppositions are not arbitrary conventions to which there are clear and intelligible alternatives. We do not decide to reject or accept them at all, any more than we decide to be human beings as opposed to glow worms. They, as Rex Martin tells us, 'just are'.[12] Absolute presuppositions are at work in our lives, but they do their work in darkness (ibid., p. 43).[13] We must have some knowledge of them, otherwise we would not be able to talk of them at all. Bringing them out of darkness is no easy matter. While historians may not be able to spell out clearly the conventions that shape a historical agent's actions, they should be able to tell when that agent is following or violating a particular convention. Collingwood does not tell us, however, the extent to which presuppositions determine (if at all) the 'free activities' that historians are interested in.

Of course, historical study is also bound by rules or conventions. Collingwood says as much in 'The Limits of Historical Knowledge' when he describes historical thinking as a game.[14] It is possible, and, Collingwood believes, desirable, that in laying bare the assumptions of others we gain a better idea of our own. The development of self-knowledge is for Collingwood the fundamental aim of humanity. Through self-knowledge I realise both that my life is given shape by particular presuppositions and that it is imperative that I help others to achieve the same realisation (*The Idea of History*, p. 297; *The New Leviathan*, §21.76). Here Collingwood echoes the English philosopher T. H. Green's Hegelian dictate that 'man cannot contemplate himself as in a better state, or on the way to be best, without contemplating others, not merely as a means to that better state, but as sharing it with him'.[15] As we can achieve self-knowledge through the study of history, then it has a crucial part to play in education. Thus for Collingwood study of history is not a luxury, but a prime duty that everyone must discharge:

> When we think of history as merely a trade or profession, a craft or calling, we find it hard to justify our existence as historians. What can the historian do for people except turn them into historians like himself? And what is the good of doing that? It is not simply a vicious circle, whose tendency is to overcrowd the ranks of the profession and to produce an underpaid 'intellectual proletariat' of sweated teachers. This may be a valid argument against the multiplication of historians, if history is merely a profession, but it cannot be if history is a universal human interest; for in that case there are already as many historians as there are human beings, and the question is not 'Shall I be an historian or not?' but 'How good an historian shall I be?'[16]

Not everyone has the inclination or the ability to help others gain self-knowledge, but Collingwood's question is worth taking seriously.

Notes

1. At the time of writing, *The Principles of History* had not been published. Citations thus correspond to the manuscript page numbers.

2. P. Gardiner, *The Nature of Historical Explanation*, Oxford: Oxford University Press, 1952, pp. 28–31; W. H. Walsh, *An Introduction to the Philosophy of History*, London: Hutchinson, 1964, pp. 44, 48; L. J. Cohen, 'A Survey of Work Done in the Philosophy of History 1946–50', *Philosophical Quarterly*, 1957, 7(2): 177; H. White, 'Collingwood and Toynbee: Transitions in English Historical Work', *English Miscellany*, 8: 166; and A. Marwick, *The Nature of History*, London: Macmillan, 1989.

3. On Collingwood's early education, see W. M. Johnston, *The Formative Years of R. G. Collingwood*, The Hague: Martinus Nijhoff, 1967; and T. Smith, 'R. G. Collingwood: "This Ring of Thought": Notes on Early Influences', *Collingwood Studies*, 1994, 1: 27–43.

4. D. Boucher, *The Social and Political Thought of R. G. Collingwood*, Cambridge: Cambridge University Press, 1989, p. 4.

5. On the popularity of his lectures, see E. W. F. Tomlin, *R. G. Collingwood*, London: Longmans Green, 1961, p. 8.

6. For a discussion on Knox's editing of *The Idea of Nature* and *The Idea of History*, see D. Boucher, 'The Principles of History and the Cosmology Conclusion to the Idea of Nature', *Collingwood Studies*, 1995, 2: 140–74, and W. J. van der Dussen, 'Collingwood's "Lost" Manuscript of *The Principles of History*', *History and Theory*, 1997, 36(1): 32–62.

7. 'Inaugural 1935 Rough Notes', Ms Collingwood, Dep. 13(1), 1935, Bodleian Library, Oxford, p. 2. Reprinted in *The Principles of History and Other Writings in Philosophy of History*.

8. W. J. van der Dussen, 'Collingwood's "Lost" Manuscript of *The Principles of History*', p. 45.

9. R. G. Collingwood, 'Observations on Language', Ms Collingwood Dep. 16(3), n.d., Bodleian Library, Oxford, p. 4.

10. H. Saari, *Re-enactment: a Study in R. G. Collingwood's Philosophy of History*, Academiae Aboensis, ser. A, vol. 63, Abo, Abo Akademi, 1984; and id., 'R. G. Collingwood on the Identity of Thoughts', in *Dialogue*, 1989, 28(1): 77–89.

11. On the scope of re-enactment and *The Principles of History*, see W. H. Dray, 'Broadening the Historian's Subject-matter in *The Principles of History*', *Collingwood Studies*, 1997, 4: 2–33.

12. R. Martin, 'Editor's Introduction', *An Essay On Metaphysics*, p. xxviii.

13. G. Vanheeswijck, 'The Function of "Unconscious Thought" in R. G. Collingwood's Philosophy', *Collingwood Studies*, 1994, 1: 115. For a discussion on the similarities between Collingwood's and Wittgenstein's views of the a priori, see M. Hughes-Warrington, 'History Education and the Conversation of Mankind', *Collingwood Studies*, 1996, 3: 96–116.

14. R. G. Collingwood, 'The Limits of Historical Knowledge', 1928, in W. Debbins (ed.), *Essays in the Philosophy of History: R. G. Collingwood*, New York: McGraw Hill, 1965, pp. 97–8.

15 T. H. Green, *Prolegomena to Ethics*, (ed.) A. C. Bradley, Oxford: Oxford University Press, 1883, §99.

16 *The Philosophy of History*, Historical Association Leaflet no. 79, London: Bell, 1930, p. 3; cf. *The Idea of History*, pp. 227–8.

Collingwood's major works

Religion and Philosophy, 1916, Bristol: Thoemmes, 1995.

Speculum Mentis, Oxford: Oxford University Press, 1924.

Outlines of a Philosophy of Art, 1925, Bristol: Thoemmes, 1995.

An Essay on Philosophical Method, Oxford: Oxford University Press, 1933.

The Archaeology of Roman Britain, 1930, London: Bracken.

(With J. N. L. Myres) *Roman Britain and the English Settlements*, *Oxford History of England*, vol. 1, Oxford: Oxford University Press, 1936.

The Principles of Art, Oxford: Oxford University Press, 1938.

An Autobiography, Oxford: Oxford University Press, 1939.

An Essay on Metaphysics, 1940, revised edition (ed.) R. Martin, Oxford: Oxford University Press, 1998.

The New Leviathan, 1942, revised edition (ed.) D. Boucher, Oxford: Oxford University Press, 1992.

The Idea of Nature, 1945, (ed.) T. M. Knox, Oxford: Oxford University Press.

The Idea of History, 1946, revised edition (ed.) W. J. van der Dussen, Oxford: Oxford University Press, 1993.

Essays in the Philosophy of History: R. G. Collingwood, (ed.) W. Debbins, New York: McGraw Hill, 1967.

Essays in Political Philosophy, (ed.) D. Boucher, Oxford: Oxford University Press, 1989.

The Principles of History and Other Writings in Philosophy of History, (eds) W. H. Dray and W. J. van der Dussen, Oxford: Oxford University Press, 1999.

See also

Croce, Dilthey, Hegel, Kuhn, Vico, Walsh, Wittgenstein (MP).

Further resources

Boucher, D., *The Social and Political Thought of R. G. Collingwood*, Cambridge: Cambridge University Press, 1989.

Code, L., 'Collingwood's Epistemological Individualism', *Monist*, 1989, 72(4): 542–67.

Collingwood Studies, published annually by the University of Wales Press for the R. G. Collingwood Society, vol. 1, 1994–.

Donagan, A., *The Later Philosophy of R. G. Collingwood*, Oxford: Oxford University Press, 1962.

Dray, W. H., *History as Re-enactment: R. G. Collingwood's Idea of History*, Oxford: Oxford University Press, 1995.

Dussen, W. J. van der, *History as a Science: the Philosophy of R. G. Collingwood*, The Hague: Martinus Nijhoff, 1981.

——, 'Collingwood's "Lost" Manuscript of *The Principles of History*', *History and Theory*, 1997, 36(1): 32–62.

Johnson, D., *The Idea of History*, Bristol: Thoemmes, 1998.

Madood, T., 'The Later Collingwood's Alleged Historicism and Relativism', *Journal of the History of Philosophy*, 1989, 27(1): 101–25.

Neilson, M., 'Re-enactment and Reconstruction in Collingwood's Philosophy of History', in *History and Theory*, 1981, 20(1): 1–31.

R. G. Collingwood Society homepage: http://www.swan.ac.uk/poli/coll/coll.htm

Saari, H., *Re-enactment: a Study in R. G. Collingwood's Philosophy of History*, Academiae Aboensis, ser. A, vol. 63, Abo: Abo Akademi, 1984.

——, 'R. G. Collingwood on the Identity of Thoughts', *Dialogue*, 1989, 28(1): 77–89.

BENEDETTO CROCE 1866–1952

Benedetto Croce (1866–1952) was one of twentieth-century Italy's most innovative and radical thinkers. In an age that sought stability in ahistorical transcendental or foundational ideas, Croce dared to say that although there is no world but the one we have made for ourselves, there can still be moral action, true and useful knowledge, coherence and meaning.

Born in the village of Pescasseroli in the Abruzzi region of southern Italy, Benedetto Croce was part of a family of wealthy landowners. His father, Pasquale Croce, spent much of his time dealing with the administrative affairs of the family estates, while his mother, Luisa Sipari Croce, divided her time between raising a family and studying art, literature and classical monuments. At the age of nine, Croce commenced studies at the Collegio della Carità, a Catholic school in Naples. He was relatively happy at school, but as his passion for literature flourished, his faith waned. Croce completed the remainder of his studies at the Liceo Genovese in Naples. At this time he was intrigued by the ideas of Francisco De Sanctis and Giosué Carducci, writers who were to give much shape to his thoughts on literary criticism and art. On 28 June 1883, he was lucky to escape from an earthquake in Casamicciola (on the island of Ischia, near Naples) which claimed the lives of his parents and younger sister Maria. Being trapped in rubble for many hours and hearing his father's dying cries marked the beginning of a 'bad dream' from which he never completely recovered. He went to live with his uncle Silvio Spaventa (brother of the Hegelian philosopher Bertrando Spaventa) in Rome. While in Rome he attended university lectures by Antonio Labriola, a moral philosopher and former student of Bertrando Spaventa. Labriola introduced him to the ideas of

Johann Friedrich Herbart, a Kantian who believed that concepts and ideals were transcendent, and thus immune to historical change.

In 1885, before he had completed his university education, Croce returned to Naples to administer the family's estates. Between 1886 and 1891 (after which time his brother Alfonso took over) Croce was absorbed with administrative duties and research on the history and culture of Naples. He published a number of essays on local history and some were included in a book on the Neapolitan revolution of 1799. Although he received much praise for these publications he was not satisfied and resolved to write something more 'serious' and 'inward' (*Autobiography*, p. 51). He determined to write a history of the influence of Spanish culture on Italian life since the Renaissance. As he began to work out what such a history would entail, he decided that he needed to deepen his understanding of the nature of history and of knowledge. He read a number of German and Italian authors on these topics, including Giambattista Vico. His investigations culminated in his first philosophical essay, 'History Subsumed under the General Concept of Art' (1893).

The question of the status of historical knowledge had been given much attention by German writers such as Wilhelm Windelband, Heinrich Rickert and Wilhelm Dilthey. Historians, they thought, used a special 'scientific' method to understand particular and unique phenomena in the human world. Croce agreed with many of their ideas but refused to accept that history was a science. For him, history was an art. Whereas science, Croce argued, is knowledge of the general, art is intuition of the particular. Following De Sanctis, Croce regarded intuition as a nonconceptual form of knowledge; as the immediate awareness of a particular image either of inner sense (for example, an emotion, a mood) or of outer sense (such as a person or object). As history is concerned with particular, concrete phenomena, then it is a form of art. It is a peculiar form of art, however, because, rather than representing the possible, it represents the actual. That is, the historian, unlike the poet, has to assure himself that his accounts of the past are true.

In 1895 Labriola sought Croce's help for the publication of his essays on Marx. Croce agreed, and immediately delved into the central works of Marx, Engels and a number of economists. Croce liked much of what he read in Marx. Like Marx, he believed that thought develops from the needs of the practical life of the world and serves as an instrument for action in the world. He thought, however, that Marx had over-emphasised the influence of economics in human actions and was too much inclined to a Hegelian 'philosophy of history'. Out of his reflections on Marx arose *Materialismo storico ed economia marxista* (*Historical Materialism and the Economics of Karl Marx*, 1900). While working on this, Croce began correspondence with the philosopher Giovanni Gentile, and in 1902 they announced the publication of the bimonthly journal *La critica*. *La critica* was devoted to reviews of recent European books in the humanities and surveys of Italian thought and literature since unification.

In the same year that Croce started *La critica*, he also published his first major work on aesthetics, *Estetica come scienza dell'espressione e linguistica generale* (1902, trans. *Aesthetic as the Science of Expression and General Linguistic*). In this, Croce insists that art is the root of all knowledge. Drawing on Vico, Croce claims that language is the central human attribute and activity (*Aesthetic*, pp. 30 and 485).[1] As intuition is bound up with language, then art forms the basis for all knowledge (*Aesthetic*, pp. 11, 20–1, 26–7, 31).[2] Croce's vision of a world dominated by art was immediately popular with young intellectuals. Croce, however, was dissatisfied with his work and, in trying to come to grips with a number of questions, he was led to the ideas of Hegel. Though Croce thought that Hegel was wrong to force the particulars of history into a particular philosophical schema, he resolved none the less to separate out what was 'living' and what was 'dead' in his philosophy.

Hegel's logic of the dialectic was, Croce believed, both his claim to glory and his Achilles' heel (1907, *Ciò che è vivo e ciò che è morto nella filosofia di Hegel*, trans. *What is Living and What is Dead in the Philosophy of Hegel*). Hegel had argued that the negative and positive aspects of ideas are the wellspring of movement and change. But Croce felt that Hegel had got carried away and applied the dialectic indiscriminately to things that were not truly opposite but merely distinct.[3] For Croce, only universal concepts such as 'beauty' and 'ugliness' can be opposite and thus subject to the logic of the dialectic. Empirical phenomena, on the other hand, are merely distinct from one another. As history details empirical phenomena, then the dialectic is not at work in history. Nor did he believe, as Hegel did, that it entailed the gradual revelation of freedom. Hegel, Croce believed, only counted those things which he saw as revealing freedom to be history. In contrast, Croce claimed that *everything* is historical.

Absolute idealism links together Croce's four-volume 'philosophy of the spirit' (*Estetica come scienza dell'espressione e linguistica generale*, 1902, trans. *Aesthetic as the Science of Expression and General Linguistic*; *Logica come scienza del concetto puro*, 1905, trans. *Logic as the Science of the Pure Concept*; *Filosofia della pratica, economia ed etica*, 1909, trans. *Philosophy of the Practical: Economics and Ethic*; *Teoria e storia della storiografia*, 1917, trans.

History: Its Theory and Practice). This form of historicism, as D. D. Roberts has pointed out, has three main features: radical immanence, philosophical idealism and emphasis on the radical historicity of the human world.[4] In the *Logic*, Croce insists that there is no world but the human world (*Logic*, pp. 104–5). We are here alone and there is no external point of reference. Even nature, which is commonly understood as something independent of the human world, is swept away by Croce's radical immanence. The idea of an independent nature, Croce insists, has too long distracted us from seeing that when we look to nature, we find only human concepts and categories stemming from human designs. To describe this immanent world, Croce utilised the language of philosophical idealists like Hegel, including the term 'Spirit'. By 'Spirit', however, Croce did not mean some Hegelian entity that uses history to reveal itself. On the contrary, the 'Spirit' simply refers to us: concrete, historically bound individuals. We do no violence to our concrete individuality, Croce claims, if we recognise that we individuals are also a part of something larger. Thus the 'Spirit' is simply a way of characterising the larger whole of which the individual is a part, and which has its existence only in individuals (*Logic*, pp. 243–4).

For Croce, historical facts do not point to permanent truths, an unchanging human nature or a God (*Logic*, pp. 126–8, 136, 222, 266–7, 276; *History as the Story of Liberty*, pp. 103–4, 270–1). The way in which we communicate about life can never be exact, because we constantly encounter situations in which existing concepts and definitions need to be altered. For instance, different people will consider the same piece of historical evidence in different ways because of changes in the 'Spirit'. Thus every thought, work of art, science, philosophy and history is historically conditioned in the sense that it is a response to historically specific problems and reflects the preoccupations of a particular moment. Such a world of particulars, however, is not utterly chaotic because of the logic of what Croce calls, echoing Kant and Hegel, the 'concrete universal'. Croce argues that *every* definition is historically specific: it is made for a particular reason and in response to particular circumstances. Concepts and definitions are thus constantly changing. This need not lead to an 'anything goes' situation, however, because the concepts that we use are fundamentally social. That is, we share enough of an understanding of the 'rules' of using a concept to understand one another when we communicate. Our knowledge is therefore 'concrete' because it is historically bound, but also 'universal' because our concepts are fundamentally social.

In addition, Croce believed that there is a fairly stable 'circle' of the ways in which humans respond to and change the world (*Philosophy of the Practical*, pp. 211–13, 231–48). Humans first apprehend a situation in its particularity, through intuition and art; they then understand it by relating it to the rest of the world through concepts; and finally, on the basis of that understanding, they respond through forms of action that can either be based on the principle of utility ('economic action') or on the principal of morality ('moral action'). None of these forms is higher than another and none is found in a pure state in the world (*Philosophy of the Practical*, pp. 205–6). 'Concrete universals' and the 'circle of the Spirit' make understanding (including historical understanding) possible.[5]

Such a vision of the world has radical implications for the status of the various forms of knowledge. For Croce, the natural and the social sciences are parasitical on history, and philosophy is greatly humbled (*History as the Story of Liberty*, pp. 34–5, 280, 148). The sciences can do no more than provide mere 'pseudo concepts' (artificial summaries of actual aesthetic and historical experience), and philosophy simply elaborates and clarifies the concepts through which we understand history. This new humbled role for philosophy is implied in his controversial claim that philosophy is nothing more than the 'methodology of history' (*History as the Story of Liberty*, pp. 138–9).

Croce's 'philosophy of spirit' secured his reputation as an innovative philosopher and earned him a life senatorship in 1910. When Giovanni Giolitti became Prime Minister in 1920, he asked Croce to be his Minister of Education. Croce accepted the post, but his tenure was short-lived. In 1921 Giolitti was replaced by Mussolini, who selected Gentile to be his Minister of Education. Initially Croce had little to say about the rise of Mussolini, as he thought that fascism would give way to a liberal regime. His silence turned to opposition, however, when Mussolini established an overt dictatorship in his Chamber speech of 3 January 1925. In the same year, Mussolini asked Gentile to draft the 'fascist intellectual's manifesto'. In this, Gentile aimed to demonstrate the historical and cultural roots of fascism in Italy and to show that it was an innovative force in politics. Croce was horrified by Gentile's claims, and endeavoured to demolish them in a countermanifesto. Gentile thus became the intellectual spokesman for the fascist government and Croce was its most outspoken opponent. For instance, his was the only speech against the Lateran Pacts of 1929, which created the State of Vatican City, and affirmed the catholicity of the Italian state. Although Mussolini exercised tight control over the press for twenty years, *La critica* escaped censorship. Croce invited contributions from a number of well-known intellectuals, including Einstein, Thomas Mann, André Gide and Julius von Schlosser. He was also able to travel abroad freely. Though Mussolini could not have been happy with the things that Croce said, he was probably more worried about what would happen to his international reputation if he tried to hinder Croce's activities. Although Croce's works were not banned, they were moved to the back shelves of libraries and stores and were replaced by those of Gentile. Mussolini also kept him under constant police surveillance, but removed it after complaints about its cost.[6]

During the period of fascist rule, Croce wrote a large number of works. Increasingly, he stressed that history was the story of liberty. Here he seems to step back in the direction of Hegel's search for freedom in world history. This theme is evident in his four 'ethico-political' histories (*La storia del regno di Napoli*, 1925; *The History of the Baroque Era in Italy*, 1925; *Storia d'Italia dal 1871 al 1915*, 1928, trans. *The History of Italy 1871–1915*, 1927; *Storia d'Europa nel secolo XIX*, 1932, trans. *History of Europe in the Nineteenth Century*).

Upon the collapse of fascism in 1943 Croce participated in the formation of the new government. At Salerno during April 1944 Croce became Minister Without Portfolio of the new democratic government and in July he joined the cabinet formed by Ivanoe Bonomi. Even after he left government in 1947, he remained president of the Liberal Party, an office that he had assumed after the downfall of the fascist government. Though Croce played an active part in politics, many felt that he was really only a figurehead, because his ideas were too elitist, conservative and traditional to lead the way to a new Italy. One-time supporters, such as Guido de Ruggiero, began to question many of Croce's ideas. Ruggiero felt that Croce, by historicising virtually everything, fostered relativism and nihilism.[7] This was thought to be dangerous in the age of fascism and Nazism. Many young scholars were also attracted to the ideas of the communist Antonio Gramsci, whose posthumously published prison notebooks included a forceful critique of Croce. In comparison to Gramsci, Croce seemed to seek refuge in the past. It became fashionable to blame Croce and his influence for holding Italian culture back. Though he still commanded enormous respect, by the time of his death in 1952 he no longer dominated Italian thought. Even today there remains disagreement about the significance of his ideas.

Though writers such as Bernard Bosanquet, J. A. Smith, H. W. Carr, G. R. G. Mure, R. G. Collingwood, Joel Springarn, John Dewey, Charles Beard, Carl Becker and Maurice Mandelbaum have recognised the depth and innovation of Croce's thought, he remains virtually unknown in the Anglo-American world. To many contemporary scholars, Croce is simply a 'neo-idealist' or 'neo-Hegelian' and thus unworthy of serious study.[8] Characterisations of him as a relativist, romantic, expressionist, primitivist and partisan of the imagination also discourage scholarly engagement. Furthermore, many historians conflate Croce with Collingwood. As Collingwood is more accessible, he is taken to offer the definitive statement of 'their' combined position. The varying quality of translations of his works also make it difficult to get a sense of what he was saying. Perhaps the real problem, however, is that we, like the blind men confronting the elephant, cannot grasp the scope of Croce's intellectual enterprise.[9]

Notes

1 G. Vico, *The New Science of Giambattista Vico*, §§218–19, 375–84, 460, 779.
2 D. D. Roberts, *Benedetto Croce and the Uses of Historicism*, p. 47; M. E. Moss, *Benedetto Croce Reconsidered: Truth and Error in Theories of Art, Literature, and History*, Hanover, NH: University Press of New England, 1987, chaps 2 and 3.
3 See R. G. Collingwood, *An Essay on Philosophical Method*, Oxford: Oxford University Press, 1933; H. White, *Metahistory: the Historical Imagination in Nineteenth Century Europe*, Baltimore, MD: Johns Hopkins University Press, 1973, pp. 407–15.
4 Roberts, *Benedetto Croce and the Uses of Historicism*, p. 55.
5 Ibid., p. 83.
6 D. M. Smith, *Mussolini*, New York: Knopf, 1982, p. 147.
7 *Il ritorno alla ragione*, pp. 3–41; Roberts, *Benedetto Croce and the Uses of Historicism*, p. 120.
8 See F. Simoni, 'Benedetto Croce: a Case of International Misunderstanding', *The Journal of Aesthetics and Art Criticism*, 1952, 11(1): 7–14.
9 D. D. Roberts, 'Croce in America: Influence, Misunderstanding and Neglect', *Humanitas*, 1995, 8(2); online at: http://nhumanties.org/Roberts.htm

Croce's major works

Aesthetic as Science of Expression of General Linguistic, trans. D. Ainslie, London: Macmillan, 1909.
Benedetto Croce: an Autobiography, trans. R. G. Collingwood, Oxford: Oxford University Press, 1927.
Historical Materialism and the Economics of Karl Marx, trans. C. M. Meredith, New York: Russell & Russell, 1966.
History as the Story of Liberty, trans. S. Sprigge, New York: W. W. Norton, 1941.
History of Europe in the Nineteenth Century, trans. H. Furst, New York: Harcourt, Brace & World, 1963.
History of Italy 1871–1915, trans. C. M. Ady, Oxford: Oxford University Press, 1929.
History of the Kingdom of Naples, trans. and ed. F. Frenaye, with an introduction by H. S. Hughes, Chicago, IL: University of Chicago Press, 1970.
Logic as the Science of the Pure Concept, trans. D. Ainslie, London: Macmillan, 1917.

The Philosophy of Giambattista Vico, trans. R. G. Collingwood, Oxford: Oxford
University Press, 1913.
Philosophy of the Practical: Economic and Ethic, trans. D. Ainslie, New York: Biblo
& Tannen, 1967.
Philosophy Poetry History: an Anthology of Essays, trans. with an introduction by
C. Sprigge, London: Oxford University Press, 1966.
Theory and History of Historiography, trans. D. Ainslie, London: Harrap, 1921;
published in the USA under the title *History: its Theory and Practice*, New York:
Russell & Russell, 1921.
What is Living and What is Dead in the Philosophy of Hegel, trans. D. Ainslie, New
York: Russell & Russell, 1969.

See also

Collingwood, Dilthey, Hegel, Kant, Marx, Vico, White.

Further resources

Bellamy, R. P., *Modern Italian Social Theory: Ideology and Politics from Pareto to the
Present*, Cambridge: Polity, 1987.
Bosworth, R. J. B., *Explaining Auschwitz and Hiroshima: History Writing and the
Second World War 1945–1990*, London: Routledge, 1993.
Caponigri, A. R., *History and Liberty: the Historical Writings of Benedetto Croce*,
London: Routledge & Kegan Paul, 1955.
Carr, H. W., *The Philosophy of Benedetto Croce: the Problem of Art and History*, New
York: Russell & Russell, 1917.
Collingwood, R. G., *The Idea of History*, revised edition, ed. W. J. van der
Dussen, Oxford: Oxford University Press, 1993.
——, *An Essay on Philosophical Method*, Oxford: Oxford University Press, 1933.
Jacobitti, E. E., *Revolutionary Humanism and Historicism in Modern Italy*, New
Haven, CT: Yale University Press, 1981.
Moss, M. E., *Benedetto Croce Reconsidered: Truth and Error in Theories of Art,
Literature and History*, Hanover, NH: University Press of New England, 1987.
Palmer, L. M. and Harris, H. S. (eds), *Thought, Action and Intuition: a Symposium
on the Philosophy of Benedetto Croce*, University of Delaware, 1972, New York:
Hildesheim, 1975.
Roberts, D. D., *Benedetto Croce and the Uses of Historicism*, Berkeley, CA:
University of California Press, 1987.
Ward, D., *Antifascisms: Cultural Politics in Italy, 1943–1946: Benedetto Croce and the
Liberals, Carlo Levi and the 'Actionists'*, Madison, NJ: Fairleigh Dickinson
University Press, 1996.

NATALIE ZEMON DAVIS 1928–

For Natalie Ann Zemon Davis (1928–), an American historian of
France and early modern Europe, history arises from a conversation

between the historian and historical agents, other scholars and the consumers of history. Like any conversationalist, she has shown in her essays and books – *Society and Culture in Early Modern France: Eight Essays* (1975), *The Return of Martin Guerre* (1983), *Frauen und Gesellschaft am Beginn der Neuzeit* (1986), *Fiction in the Archives: Pardon Tales and their Tellers in Sixteenth Century France* (1987), *A History of Women in the West: Renaissance and Enlightenment Paradoxes* (ed. with A. Farge, 1993) and *Women on the Margins: Three Seventeenth-century Lives* (1995) – that she is willing to share her views. But she has also recognised that she is one voice among many, and has been prepared to listen to what others have to say.

That Davis is a good listener is clear from her commitment to seek out voices traditionally neglected by historians of early modern Europe: those of women, youth, illiterate artisans and peasants. Furthermore, she does not assume that context or any single feature of these people, whether it be their gender, their wealth or their social status, defines what they are. Rather, she writes,

> I have imagined these features of their lives as shaping their condition and their goals, as limiting or expanding their options; but I have seen them as actors, making use of what physical, social, and cultural resources they had in order to survive, to cope, or sometimes to change things.
>
> (*Society and Culture in Early Modern Europe*, p. xvii)

She tries to respect their views and choices, even when she does not agree with them, and sometimes even voices what their objections to her account might be. *Women on the Margins*, for instance, opens with an exchange between Davis and her subjects – Glikl bas Judah Leib, Marie de l'incarnation and Maria Sibylla Merian – and *Society and Culture in Early Modern Europe* concludes with a dialogue between Davis and Laurent Joubert, the author of a sixteenth-century book on popular errors. It is important to note, though, that Davis does not listen to such voices solely because they have been previously ignored. The voice of the nun, the beggar, the journeyman printer and the man dressed in women's clothing, and so on, she believes, can enhance our understanding of early modern society. Davis has shown us, for instance, that the Reformation, as experienced in Lyon, cut across rather than reflected class lines; that Protestantism had more than emotional appeal for women; that youth misrule groups behaved in ways that we would today call 'adolescent'; that the image of the disorderly woman widened behavioural options for women and sanctioned disobedience for women and men; that crowd uprisings were not necessarily for economic reasons; that printed books supplemented, rather than hindered, oral culture; that planning for a family's future required invention and effort rather than reliance on custom and providence; and that religion shaped what was possible in autobiography.[1]

In seeking out those voices, Davis has looked to a wide range of sources, including books, pamphlets, plays, poems, criminal and judicial records, welfare rolls, notarial contracts, and militia and financial lists. But she has also looked to scholars in other disciplines, especially literature, the history of art, ethnography and anthropology, for ideas on how to find the strange and surprising in the familiar. For example, Davis has argued in various places that anthropological writings have four features that make them useful for historians: 'close observation of living processes of social interaction; interesting ways of interpreting symbolic behaviour; suggestions about how the parts of a social system fit together; and material from cultures very different from those which historians are used to studying'.[2] She is aware, however, that the use of anthropological insights can also create problems. Historians, she argues, should 'consult anthropological writings not for prescriptions, but for suggestions; not for universal rules of human behaviour, but for relevant comparisons' and 'should also be prepared to offer advice about their own work and about anthropological theory'.[3]

Thus it is important to share one's ideas and commitments with other scholars. But history, Davis believes, is not just the property of scholars. There are many people who are interested in reading and constructing history. Davis thus prefers to talk of history not as something that can be owned, but as a gift that can be shared by all.[4] Davis's commitment to the idea of history being a gift is most clear in her work on the case of Martin Guerre, a sixteenth-century French peasant who left his village for eight years and returned to find that another man (Arnaud du Tilh) had impersonated him, lived with his wife (Betrande de Rols), and claimed his inheritance. When Davis read Jean de Coras's account of the case in *Arrest Memorable* (1561), she thought that it would make a good film. 'Rarely', she wrote later, 'does a historian find so perfect a narrative structure in the events of the past or one with such dramatic popular appeal' (*The Return of Martin Guerre*, p. vii). The same idea had also occurred to two French film makers, Daniel Vigne and Jean Claude Carrière, and in 1980 Davis was invited to be a historical consultant to *Le retour de Martin Guerre*. It is an engaging film. The recreation of sixteenth-century village life is vivid and the story is rendered in a suspenseful manner. As one commentator wrote (rather humorously):

Despite its medieval setting, the film deals with issues of identity and deception, the individual's role in society, and love and greed, all of which have a remarkable relevance to modern society.[5]

And indeed the film was a popular success. But there is another aspect of the film which makes it fascinating: the marks of Davis's influence. If Davis had not been involved with *Le retour de Martin Guerre*, would young Martin and Bertrande have been shown as the target of a *charivari*, or 'rough music', complete with men dressed in women's clothes? Would the villagers have used such proverbs as 'He carries water in one hand and fire in the other'? And would so much attention have been given to literacy and printing? (See 'The Reasons of Misrule', 'Women on Top', 'Printing and the People' and 'Proverbial Wisdom and Popular Errors' in *Society and Culture in Early Modern France*.)

Le retour de Martin Guerre, Davis believes, 'posed the problem of invention to the historian as surely as it was posed to the wife of Martin Guerre' (*The Return of Martin Guerre*, p. viii). Aspects of the story were sacrificed and altered. Such modifications, she writes:

> may have helped to give the film the powerful simplicity that had allowed the Martin Guerre story to become a legend in the first place, but they also made it hard to explain what actually happened. Where was there room in this beautiful and compelling cinematographic recreation of a village for the uncertainties, the 'perhapses', the 'may-have-beens', to which the historian has recourse when the evidence is inadequate or perplexing?
>
> (Ibid.)

She determined to find out 'what happened' in more detail and to present her findings in a manner accessible to a wide audience. The result was the book *The Return of Martin Guerre*, published in 1983. In this, Davis details the Basque background of the Guerres, Martin's service as a lackey in Burgos, Spain, and his injury during the 1557 battle against the French at Saint Quentin. But, more controversially, she also argues that the story must tell of the 'double game' of Bertrande de Rols, Arnaud du Tilh's 'self-refashioning', rural Protestantism, and the reasons for Jean de Coras's and her own interest in the case. Traditional accounts of the story portray Bertrande de Rols as a dupe. Davis's Bertrande, however, displays 'a concern for her reputation as a woman, a stubborn independence, and a shrewd realism about how she could manoeuvre within the constraints placed upon one of her sex' (ibid., p. 28). She knew that Arnaud du Tilh was not Martin, and 'by explicit or tacit agreement, she helped him become her husband' (ibid., p. 43). Arnaud du Tilh, Davis believes, was more than an impostor. Echoing the ideas of Stephen Greenblatt, she claims that he 're-fashioned' himself into Martin Guerre.[6] That is, he was interested in taking over Martin's life, not just his money. For Davis, Arnaud du Tilh's 'self-fashioning' was not an isolated form of behaviour, but was an extreme example of a 'sixteenth-century spectrum of personal change for purposes of play, of advantage, or of "attracting the benevolence of others"'.[7] The 'invented' marriage of Arnaud and Bertrande, Davis claims, can also be located in the spectrum of sixteenth-century practices. To legitimise their union, she suggests, they probably drew on the traditional custom of clandestine marriage, which required no more than the exchange of words and tokens, and the Protestant teaching that a wife deserted by her husband is free to remarry after a year. Thus Protestantism has a part to play in Davis's version of the story. Furthermore, Davis contends that Jean de Coras wrote an account of the case because it 'allowed him to condemn Arnaud again, but also to give him another chance' and to comment on legal and social issues such as evidence, torture, the nature of proof, marriage, impotence, desertion, adultery and blasphemy (ibid., pp. 103, 106). Davis, too, wants to use the case as an entry point for a discussion on the social and legal practices of the time. But she also wants to give both Arnaud *and* Bertrande another chance to tell *their* story.

Working on *Le retour de Martin Guerre* and *The Return of Martin Guerre* also made Davis acutely aware of the problem of invention in all historical films. In papers such as '"Any Resemblance to Persons Living or Dead": Film and the Challenge of Authenticity' (1987), Davis has explored some of the ways in which historical films can give 'more complex and dramatic indications of their truth status' than the poles of 'The characters and incidents portrayed and the names used herein are fictitious . . . ' and 'This is a true story . . . '.[8] Historians, Davis tells us, are generally open about their doubts and reasons. They qualify statements with words like 'perhaps' and 'possible' and with references. Film makers, she claims, can also convey ambiguity and give scope to the viewer to decide what they are seeing. They should aim for authenticity, or 'represent values, relations, and issues in a period; . . . animate props and locations by their connections with historical people; and . . . let the past have its distinctiveness before remaking it to resemble the present'.[9] But film also offers many possibilities for suggesting multiple tellings. For instance, film makers should, in their recreation of a 'period look', reflect 'the mixture of goods, clothes, and buildings found in documents from the past' and even play cultural artefacts off against one another.[10] *Le retour de Martin Guerre*, Davis tells us, was shaped not only by the art of Brueghel and La Tour, but also by popular woodcuts, documentary sources about favoured colours in the Pyrenees and Daniel Vigne's understanding of traditional French agriculture. Film makers could also, like Kurosawa in *Rashomon*, offer multiple accounts of the same event or, as in *Last Year at Marienbad*, use repeats and openly question the reliability of memory.[11] Furthermore, they could do more to show viewers where knowledge of the past comes from. The makers of *The French Lieutenant's Woman*, for instance, use a scene in which a twentieth-century character is reading and commenting on a history of London prostitution to lead into a nineteenth-century street scene. But they could also acknowledge their sources in the credits and fashion better openings.

Given the chance, Davis would love to remake the beginning of *Le retour de Martin Guerre*. At present, the film opens with the notary arriving in Artigat on horseback, moves to the marriage of young Martin and Bertrande, and then an anonymous voice says, 'You will not regret listening to this account, for it is not a tale of adventure or imaginary fable, but a pure, true story . . . '.[12] Viewers should be made aware, she argues, that these words come from a printer's blurb from an edition of de Coras's book about the case. She thus recommends another opening:

> Coras: I judged this case four months ago, and it is so strange,
>   I still wonder about it. Will readers ever believe my
>   book?
> Printer: With your name on it, they're sure to. And I'll say in
>   my preface: 'This is not a made-up fantastic tale, but
>   *une pure et vraie histoire*'.
>   [*Cut to the village of Artigat.*][13]

I admire Davis's openness to her own doubts and beliefs and to those of others. But I also have reservations about the results of her efforts. Sometimes I wonder whether Davis has imposed her own voice on those she is meant to be conversing with. For instance, although I would not go so far as to say, as Finlay has, that 'there is no warrant in the sources for introducing a religious dimension to the Martin Guerre story', I believe that the evidence she offers on that point is pretty thin.[14] I also think that it is important not to forget that few of the sources that she uses are testimonies of the previously silenced about themselves. For example, if Martin Guerre had been able to record 'his side of the story', how different from Jean de Coras's account might it be? Finally, in her keenness to show us that the study of individuals and small groups can serve as a bridge to an examination of the assumptions of wider society (past and present), I wonder whether she always remembers her aim to 'let the past be the past, strange before it is familiar, particular before it is universal'.[15]

Notes

1 See *Society and Culture in Early Modern France*; 'Ghosts, Kin and Progeny: Some Features of Family Life in Early Modern France', *Daedalus*, 1977, 106(2): 87–114; 'Fame and Secrecy: Leon Modena's Life as an Early Modern Autobiography', *History and Theory*, 1988, 27(4): 103–18; and *Women on the Margins*.
2 'Anthropology and History in the 1980s: the Possibilities of the Past', *Journal of Interdisciplinary History*, 1981, 12(2): 267. See also R. Harding and J. Coffin, 'Interview with Natalie Zemon Davis', in H. Abelove, B. Blackmar, P. Dimock and J. Schneer (eds), *Visions of History*, Manchester: Manchester University Press, 1984, pp. 110–13; and R. Adelson, 'Interview with Natalie Zemon Davis', *Historian*, 1991, 53(3): 414–15.
3 'Anthropology and History in the 1980s', pp. 274, 275.
4 'Who Owns History?', *Perspectives: the Newsletter of the American Historical Association*, 1996, 34(8): 1, 4–6.
5 M. E. Biggs, *French Films, 1945–1993*, Jefferson, NC: McFarland, 1993, p. 232.
6 S. J. Greenblatt, *Renaissance Self-fashioning: From More to Shakespeare*, Chicago, IL: University of Chicago Press, 1980.
7 'On the Lame', *American Historical Review*, 1988, 93(3): 590.
8 '"Any Resemblance to Persons Living or Dead": Film and the Challenge of Authenticity', *The Yale Review*, 1987, 76(4): 459.
9 Ibid., p. 476.
10 Ibid., pp. 461–2.
11 Ibid., p. 480.
12 This is Davis's translation. The subtitles supplied for the Embassy Pictures release of the film are: 'You will not regret having followed this story, for it is not a tale of adventure nor an imaginary tale. It is a true story.'
13 '"Any Resemblance to Persons Living or Dead"', p. 481.
14 R. Finlay, 'The Refashioning of Martin Guerre', *American Historical Review*, 1988, 93(3): 553–71. For Davis's reply to Finlay, see pp. 572–603 in the same volume. For more favourable reviews of *The Return of Martin Guerre*, see A. L. Moore, *American Historical Review*, 1985, 90(4): 943; D. R. Kelley, *Renaissance Quarterly*, 1984, 37(2): 252; E. Le Roy Ladurie, *New York Review of Books*, 30 December 1983, pp. 12–14; W. Monter, *Sixteenth Century Journal*, 1983, 14(4): 516; E. Benson, *French Review*, 1984, 57(5): 753–4; and R. J. Knecht, *History*, 1985, 70(1): 121.
15 '"Any Resemblance to Persons Living or Dead"', p. 460.

Davis's major works

Society and Culture in Early Modern France: Eight Essays, Stanford, CA: Stanford University Press, 1975.

'"Women's History" in Transition: the European Case', *Feminist Studies*, 1975, 3(3): 83–103.

'Ghosts, Kin and Progeny: Some Features of Family Life in Early Modern France', *Daedalus*, 1977, 106(2): 87–114.

'Gender and Genre: Women as Historical Writers, 1400–1820', *University of Ottowa Quarterly*, 1980, 50(1): 123–44.

'Anthropology and History in the 1980s: the Possibilities of the Past', *Journal of Interdisciplinary History*, 1981, 12(2): 267–75.

'The Sacred and the Body Social in Sixteenth-century Lyon', *Past and Present*, 1981, 90: 40–70.

'Women in the Crafts in Sixteenth-century Lyon', *Feminist Studies*, 1982, 8(1): 47–80.

'Beyond the Market: Books as Gifts in Sixteenth-century France', *Transactions of the Royal Historical Society*, 1983, 33: 69–88.

The Return of Martin Guerre, Cambridge, MA: Harvard University Press, 1983.

Frauen und Gesellschaft am Beginn der Nerzeit, trans. W. Kaiser, Berlin: Wagenbach, 1986.

'"Any Resemblance to Persons Living or Dead": Film and the Challenge of Authenticity', *The Yale Review*, 1987, 76(4): 457–82.

Fiction in the Archives: Pardon Tales and their Tellers in Sixteenth Century France, Stanford, CA: Stanford University Press, 1987.

'Fame and Secrecy: Leon Modena's Life as an Early Modern Autobiography', *History and Theory*, 1988, 27(4): 103–18.

'History's Two Bodies', *American Historical Review*, 1988, 93(1): 1–13.

'On the Lame', *American Historical Review*, 1988, 93(3): 572–603.

'Rabelais among the Censors (1940s, 1540s)', *Representations*, 1990, 32(1): 1–32.

'The Shapes of Social History', *Storia della Storiographia*, 1990, 17(1): 28–34.

'Women and the World of Annales', *History Workshop Journal*, 1992, 33: 121–37.

(Ed. with A. Farge) *Renaissance and Enlightenment Paradoxes*, vol. 3 of *A History of Women in the West*, Cambridge, MA: Belknap Press of Harvard University Press, 1993.

Women on the Margins: Three Seventeenth-century Lives, Cambridge, MA: Harvard University Press, 1995.

A Life of Learning: Charles Homer Haskins Lecture for 1997, New York: American Council of Learned Societies, 1997.

Remaking Imposters: From Martin Guerre to Sommersby, Hayes Robinson Lecture Series no. 1, Egham, Surrey: Royal Holloway Publications Unit, 1997.

'Beyond Evolution: Comparative History and its Goals', in W. Wrzoska (ed.), *Swiat historii*, Poznan: Instytut Historii UAM, 1998, pp. 149–58.

See also

Bloch, Febvre, Le Roy Ladurie, Scott.

Further resources

Adams, R. M., 'Review of *Fiction in the Archives*', *New York Review of Books*, 16 March 1989, 36(4): 35.

Adelson, R., 'Interview with Natalie Zemon Davis', *Historian*, 1991, 53(3): 405–22.

Benson, E., 'The Look of the Past: *Le Retour de Martin Guerre*', *Radical History Review*, 1984, 28–30: 125–35.

Bossy, J., 'As it Happened: Review of *Fiction in the Archives*', *Times Literary Supplement*, 7 April 1989, 4488: 359.

Coffin, J. and Harding, R. 'Interview with Natalie Zemon Davis', in H. Abelove, B. Blackmar, P. Dimock and J. Schneer (eds), *Visions of History*, Manchester: Manchester University Press, 1984, pp. 99–122.

Finlay, R., 'The Refashioning of Martin Guerre', *American Historical Review*, 1988, 93(3): 553–71.

Guneratne, A., 'Cinehistory and the Puzzling Case of Martin Guerre', *Film and History*, 1991, 21(1): 2–19.

Image as Artifact [video recording], Washington, DC: American Historical Association, 1987.

Le retour de Martin Guerre [video recording], director D. Vigne, SFP, Les Films Marcel Dassault FR3, released with English subtitles by Embassy Pictures, Los Angeles, 1984.

Le Roy Ladurie, E., 'Double Trouble: Review of *The Return of Martin Guerre*', *New York Review of Books*, 22 December 1983, 30(20): 12–14.

O'Connor, J. E. (ed.), *Image as Artifact: the Historical Analysis of Film and Television*, Malabar, FL: R. E. Krieger, 1990.

Orest, R., Review of *Women on the Margins*, *American Historical Review*, 1997, 102(3): 808–10.

Quinn, A., Review of *Women on the Margins*, *New York Times Review of Books*, 10 December 1995, p. 18.

Roelker, N. L., Review of *Fiction in the Archives*, *American Historical Review*, 1989, 94(5): 1392–3.

Roper, L., Review of *Women on the Margins*, *Times Literary Supplement*, 19 July 1996, 4868: 4–5.

WILHELM DILTHEY 1833–1911

Wilhelm Dilthey, one commentator has suggested, has cast 'an enormous shadow' over modern thought.[1] This is an apt description, as few people have more than a shadowy notion of how important his philosophy – an ambitious combination of the ideas of writers such as Vico, Kant, Hegel, Schleiermacher, Droysen and Ranke – has been for twentieth-century discussions on hermeneutics and the principles that govern the human sciences.

Wilhelm Dilthey was born on 19 November 1833, in Biebrich, near Wiesbaden in Germany. The son of a Reformed church clergyman, he went to the grammar school at Wiesbaden and from there to Heidelberg to study theology. In 1853 he transferred to the University of Berlin. At Berlin his theological interests were eclipsed by historical and philosophical projects which drew their shape from the ideas of August Boeckh, Leopold Ranke, Theodor Mommsen and Jakob Grimm. In 1860 he composed a prize-winning essay on Friedrich Schleiermacher's hermeneutics, and he was invited to edit Schleiermacher's correspondence and to write his biography. In 1861 he transferred from the theology to the philosophy faculty and three years later he completed his dissertation on Schleiermacher's ethics (in *Gesammelte Schriften*, vol. 6, pp. 1–55).

Around 1865, Dilthey began to explore the differences between the human and natural sciences (ibid., vol. 18, pp. 1–16). His first publication in this area was the essay 'On the Study of the History of Man, Society and the State' (ibid., vol. 5, pp. 31–73). This essay served as a stepping stone to his first major work, *Einleitung in die Geisteswissenschaften* (trans. *Introduction to the Human Sciences*), the first volume of which appeared in 1883. In this, Dilthey tried to establish a view of history based on strong philosophical principles. Although he wrote two drafts of volume 2 ('Breslau Draft', 1880; 'Berlin Draft', 1893), neither was published during his lifetime (ibid., vol. 1, pp. 243–492). This work was followed up by a series of essays, one of the most important of which was 'Ideas concerning a Descriptive and Analytic Psychology' (in *Descriptive Psychology and Historical Understanding*, pp. 23–120). In this, Dilthey argued that we can only understand ourselves and others through psychological descriptions. After 1896 Dilthey halted work related to the *Introduction to the Human Sciences* and never returned to it.

Between 1896 and 1905 Dilthey wrote historical studies of Leibniz and his age, Frederick the Great and the German Enlightenment, and the eighteenth century (*Gesammelte Schriften*, vol. 3). He also undertook a study of the development of Hegel's ideas (ibid., vol. 4), which helped him to develop his own ideas on meaning. In the middle of the period he published 'The Rise of Hermeneutics', in which he outlined the methodological approach that he would endorse for the rest of his life.[2] Understanding ourselves and others, Dilthey argued, begins not with psychological descriptions but with the interpretation of human expressions. During the last years of his life he explored the role played by socio-historical contexts in the shaping of meaning and experience. This culminated in *Der Aufbau der geschichtlichen Welt in den Geisteswissenschaften* (1910), which was unfinished at the time of his death in October 1911.

Although the subject-matter of his writings is diverse, Dilthey's main project was to establish the principles of the human sciences, much as Kant's critical philosophy had for the natural sciences. Dilthey concurred with Kant's suggestion that the world of experience is actively shaped by the mind but did not believe that the forms and categories of the mind are universal, unchanging and revealed through reason alone (*Introduction to the Human Sciences*, p. 192). Rather, for Dilthey, all values, emotions, ideas and actions are the products of particular individuals living in certain socio-historical contexts, influenced by the ideas around them and bound by the limits of their age. All knowledge is thus rooted in life as it is lived (ibid., pp. 162, 500–1). He writes: 'The "I" is not an onlooker who sits before the stage of the world but is itself action and reaction.'[3] His point is that we shape and respond to others and our world. As the actual conditions of life are always changing, then reason cannot be thought of as a timeless, changeless, fixed point of departure. Dilthey firmly believed that 'there is no absolute starting point' and that 'every beginning is arbitrary' (*Gesammelte Schriften*, vol. 5, p. cx; vol. 1, p. 419).[4]

Dilthey's view of Kant reflected the general mood of the post-Hegelian 'historical school'. Writers in this 'school', such as Leopold Ranke, Franz Bopp, Jakob Grimm, August Boekh, Theodor Mommsen, Johann Gustav Droysen and Friedrich Karl Savigny, denied that there is a body of absolute knowledge outside experience that can be reached by pure, detached reason. Dilthey praised the historical school's recognition of the historicity of humans as an 'emancipation of historical consciousness' but thought that their ideas were philosophically impoverished (*Gesammelte Schriften*, vol. 5, p. 11).[5] If one acknowledges the historicity of humanity, he pointed out, then how can I, from my limited socio-historical perspective, make valid knowledge and truth claims that apply to others? Can any knowledge be certain or true? Or as he puts it:

> How are we to overcome the difficulty that everywhere weighs upon the human sciences of deriving universally valid propositions from inner experiences that are so personally limited, so indeterminate, so compacted and resistant to analysis?
>
> (*Gesammelte Schriften*, vol. 6, p. 107)[6]

To answer this question, Dilthey tried to combine what he saw as the strengths of Kantianism, Hegelianism and the historical school (*Introduction to the Human Sciences*, p. 49).

Dilthey thought that the problem of finding certainty in the variety of human experiences should be viewed in light of a more general reflection on the nature of the human sciences (*Geisteswissenschaften*) as distinct from the natural sciences (*Naturwissenschaften*). Being active participants in the historical process, he claimed, we are able to identify with and understand our socio-historical contexts in a way that is impossible for those who study the natural environment. We can understand the human world with more certainty than the natural world because it is a product of our own making (*Gesammelte Schriften*, vol. 1, pp. 36–7).[7] For instance, from looking at our own experiences, we are able to understand what it is like to hope, loathe and fear as we can never know what it is like to be a planet orbiting the sun. While natural scientists must be satisfied by merely explaining (*Erklären*) experiences from the 'outside', human scientists can understand (*Verstehen*) their subject-matter from the 'inside'.

There has been much debate about what *Verstehen* means to Dilthey, and some commentators prefer to leave it untranslated. As Rickman suggests, however, I believe it is fair to describe it as the process of understanding in which we apprehend the meaning of gestures, words, actions and so on.[8] This form of understanding is common to humans and requires no special skill or ability. Understanding some communications may require extra effort or experience but that is due to the complexity of what is to be understood.

That task, however, can be greatly aided through the study of what Dilthey calls 'descriptive psychology'. Dilthey was unhappy with the traditional or 'explanatory' view of psychology that was popular at the time in Germany because it assumed that both individuals and mental phenomena, such as feelings, thoughts and desires, are discrete. Psychology should, he claimed, describe inner experiences in such a way as to take account of an individual's mental unity and socio-historical context. Like all humans, the descriptive psychologist employs principles for the organisation of his experience. These 'categories of life', as Dilthey calls them, which all contribute to our search for meaning and certainty, govern different aspects of our experience. Dilthey produced a list of categories, but he left it unfinished on the grounds that further categories could be revealed through empirical research. The most important category for Dilthey was that of 'temporality'. People are by nature 'temporal' beings because they experience it in terms of the connections between past, present and future. That is, they respond to the present by relating it to past experiences, and anticipate the future in terms of hopes and aims that have been formed over time. In order to understand how people live through time, the descriptive psychologist looks to biographies, eyewitness accounts of events and self-reflections and the 'objectifications of mind' that surround us. 'Objectifications of mind' describes the shape that areas of reality such as architecture, clothing styles, languages, arts and so on, have taken on as a result of particular thoughts, feelings and aspirations.[9]

Most of the time, understanding is straightforward and unproblematic. For instance, when a librarian puts her index finger on her lips, little effort is required on my part to see that she is telling me to be quiet. What makes this understanding possible are shared conventions. In other cases, however, achieving understanding is not so straightforward: expressions may arise from an historical or social background unfamiliar to us. For example, clasping another's hands may not signal homage, and research on 'creep behaviour' may not have anything to do with people we find socially unacceptable. These cases, Dilthey contends, require interpretation. Interpretation is the process of unravelling the meaning of something that is not immediately clear.

Interpretation, or hermeneutics as the ancient Greeks called it, traditionally focused on exegetical criticism of classical texts and the Bible. With Schleiermacher, however, it achieved broader application. He thought that hermeneutics could be logically extended to include such things as literary texts, codes of law and historical documents. Dilthey, who spent a considerable amount of his early career researching the ideas and intellectual background of Schleiermacher, recognised the importance of this broader account. However, he believed that the method could be further extended to the interpretation of life in general: that is, we can treat gestures, actions and so forth as if they were texts being interpreted. In this we lay bare both the conventions binding the subject of our study and our own conventions. That allows us to use shared conventions as a bridge to unfamiliar conventions. Dilthey is thus insistent that understanding others entails self-understanding. And understanding others, in turn, deepens self-understanding. He writes: 'Understanding is a rediscovery of the I in the Thou.'[10] This interrelation and unravelling of self and other is an example of Dilthey's idea of an 'hermeneutic circle'; the reciprocal relationship in which experience influences interpretation, and interpretation in turn influences experience. This circular movement is characteristic of all human sciences. For example, from knowledge of an historical agent's actions an understanding of a period or age grows, and this, in turn, enhances our understanding of that individual's actions, and so on.

Dilthey's ideas have been taken up and developed by a number of twentieth-century European thinkers such as Sartre, Heidegger, Gadamer, Ortega y Gasset, Mannheim, Aron, Horkheimer, Habermas and Ricoeur. General distrust of European ideas in the Anglo-American world, however, has meant that his ideas are largely unfamiliar to many scholars. Furthermore, the difficulty of his style and scattered nature of his writings has made unambiguous translation and illustrative selection difficult. A number of historians, for instance, believe that terms like *Verstehen* are too vague to be useful. *Verstehen* has been picked over thoroughly by generations of commentators, including Weber, Jaspers, Wach, Collingwood, Berlin, Martin and Gardiner, but little headway was made until the German edition of Dilthey's collected works was republished and expanded by seven volumes (*Gesammelte Schriften*, 1914–90). This edition of Dilthey's works, along with English selections by Hodges and Rickman, have given rise to a growing number of English publications on his thought. The publication by Makkreel and Rodi of a six-volume collection of selections (1985–) has fuelled the growing interest in Dilthey and opened up questions once thought to be resolved. It seems, as Ermath has noted, that the very thinker who drew attention to the problem of interpretation still poses himself a major problem of interpretation.[11]

Notes

1 H. P. Rickman, *Wilhelm Dilthey: Pioneer of the Human Studies*, London: Paul Elek, 1979, p. 165.
2 There has been quite a bit of discussion on the development and continuity of Dilthey's thought. H. N. Tuttle focuses primarily on his later ideas (*Wilhelm Dilthey's Philosophy of Historical Understanding: a Critical Analysis*, Leiden: E. J. Brill, 1969). T. Plantinga and H. Ineichen divide Dilthey's scholarship into three periods (*Historical Understanding in the Thought of Wilhelm Dilthey*, Toronto: University of Toronto Press, 1980; *Erkenntnistheorie und geschichtlichgesellschaftliche Welt: Diltheys Logik der Geisteswissenshaften*, Frankfurt am Main: Vittorio Klostermann, 1975). H. U. Lessing divides it into two periods (*Die Idee einer Kritik der historischen Vernunft: Wilhelm Diltheys erkenntnistheoretisch – logisch – methodologische Grundelgung der Geisteswissenshaften*, Munich: Verlag Karl Alber, 1984). And R. A. Makkreel (*Dilthey, Philosopher of the Human Studies*, Princeton, NJ: Princeton University Press, 1975); M. Ermath (*Wilhelm Dilthey: the Critique of Historical Reason*, Chicago, IL: University of Chicago Press, 1978); H. P. Rickman (*Dilthey Today: a Critical Appraisal of the Contemporary Relevance of his Work*, New York: Greenwood, 1988); and J. Owensby (*Dilthey and the Narrative of History*, Ithaca, NY: Cornell University Press, 1994) argue for the continuity of Dilthey's thought.
3 As quoted in Ermath, *Wilhelm Dilthey*, p. 119.
4 C. R. Bambach, *Heidegger, Dilthey and the Crisis of Historicism*, Ithaca, NY: Cornell University Press, 1995, p. 134.
5 Ibid., p. 138.
6 Ibid., p. 160.

7 Dilthey's suggestion that we can only really understand things that have been made by the human mind was probably inspired by Vico's famous dictum '*verum et factum convertuntur*'. See H. Tuttle, 'The Epistemological Status of the Cultural World in Vico and Dilthey', in G. Tagliacozzo and D. P. Verene (eds), *Giambattista Vico's Science of Humanity*, Baltimore, MD: Johns Hopkins University Press, 1976, pp. 241–50; H. A. Hodges, 'Vico and Dilthey', and H. P. Rickman, 'Vico and Dilthey's Methodology of the Human Studies', in G. Tagliacozzo (ed.), *Giambattista Vico: an International Symposium*, Baltimore, MD: Johns Hopkins University Press, 1969, pp. 439–56; and P. Gardiner, 'Interpretation in History: Collingwood and Historical Understanding', in A. O'Hear (ed.), *Verstehen and Humane Understanding*, Royal Institute of Philosophy, Supplement 41, Cambridge: Cambridge University Press, 1997, pp. 109–19.

8 Rickman, *Dilthey Today*, p. 108.

9 Although Dilthey borrowed the phrase 'objectifications of mind' from Hegel, he made no metaphysical claims for the reality of these entities. We only retain talk of 'societies', 'nations' and 'eras', for instance, because they are a convenient aid to understanding individuals in their socio-historical perspectives. See H. P. Rickman, *Pattern and Meaning in History*, New York: Harper & Brothers, 1961, introduction.

10 Quoted in Rickman, *Wilhelm Dilthey*, p. 208.

11 Ermath, *Wilhelm Dilthey*, p. 4.

Dilthey's major works

Gesammelte Schriften, 20 vols, Göttingen: Vandenhoech & Ruprecht, 1914–90.
Selected Works, 6 vols, trans. and ed. R. A. Makkreel and F. Rodi; vol. 1, *Introduction to the Human Sciences*; vol. 4, *Hermeneutics and the Study of History*; vol. 5, *Poetry and Experience*, Princeton, NJ: Princeton University Press, 1985– .
Pattern and Meaning in History, trans. and ed. H. P. Rickman, New York: Harper & Brothers, 1961.
Descriptive Psychology and Historical Understanding, trans. and ed. R. M. Zaner and K. L. Heiges, The Hague: Martinus Nijhoff, 1977.

See also

Collingwood, Habermas (CT), Hegel, Heidegger, Husserl (MP), Kant, Ranke, Ricoeur, Sartre (MP), Vico.

Further resources

Bambach, C. R., *Heidegger, Dilthey and the Crisis of Historicism*, Ithaca, NY: Cornell University Press, 1995.
Bulhof, I., *Wilhelm Dilthey: a Hermeneutic Approach to the Study of History and Culture*, The Hague: Martinus Nijhoff, 1980.
Collingwood, R. G., *The Idea of History*, revised edition (ed.) W. J. van der Dussen, Oxford: Oxford University Press, 1993.

Ermath, M., *Wilhelm Dilthey: the Critique of Historical Reason*, Chicago, IL: University of Chicago Press, 1978.

Hodges, H. A., *The Philosophy of Wilhelm Dilthey*, London: Routledge & Kegan Paul, 1952.

Makkreel, R. A., *Dilthey, Philosopher of the Human Studies*, Princeton, NJ: Princeton University Press, revised edition of 1975 text, 1987.

O'Hear, A., *Verstehen and Humane Understanding*, Royal Institute of Philosophy, Supplement 41, Cambridge: Cambridge University Press, 1997.

Owensby, J., *Dilthey and the Narrative of History*, Ithaca, NY: Cornell University Press, 1994.

Rickman, H. P., *Dilthey Today: a Critical Reappraisal of the Contemporary Relevance of his Work*, New York: Greenwood Press, 1988.

CHEIKH ANTA DIOP 1923–86

With his conception of *histoire non événementielle* – history free from the chronological description of events – Cheikh Anta Diop hoped to produce an African history that would lead to 'racial self-retrieval'.[1] Diop is not the only writer to have concerned himself with the 'decolonisation of African history', but his work is unusual in not being concerned with the modern period of interaction between Africans and Europeans. Rather, for Diop, the key to the struggle for African independence lies in demonstrating that contemporary Black Africans belong to the same race as that which ruled ancient Egypt.

Diop was born on 23 December 1923 in Diourbel, Senegal. He received his primary and secondary education in Senegal, and then moved to Paris to pursue university studies in mathematics, physics, archaeology, sociology, linguistics, ancient history and pre-history. While he was at university, 'Négritude' emerged: a cultural, literary and political movement, dedicated to the affirmation of the value of Negro culture, that had its roots in Jean-Paul Sartre and Leopold Senghor's *Orphée noire*. Diop was influenced greatly by Négritude, as evidenced both by his involvement in the Rassemblement Démocratique Africain, a pan-regional political group presenting the most radical anticolonial stance in France's African colonies, and by the work that he submitted to Présence Africaine, a publication house that was to be at the centre of the discussions that occupied French-speaking African intellectuals in the period during which a number of African nations gained independence.

While in Paris, Diop also began studies in Egyptology, the subject at the heart of the majority of his publications. Becoming established in the discipline was not easy, as Diop recalled in 1985:

I noticed that whenever a Black showed the slightest interest in things Egyptian, Whites would actually begin to tremble. . . . Not a single person in all of France ever encouraged me in my researches and the more I pursued them, the more uncomfortable and hostile they became, even issuing vague threats against my future teaching career. I didn't care. I was an angry young man and the more I was resisted the more determined and stubborn I became.[2]

Diop considered Egypt to be the source of African civilisation and wanted contemporary Africa to seek inspiration from ancient Egypt as the West seeks inspiration from ancient Greece. Diop set out to show that not only was Egypt a Black civilisation, but it was also the first civilisation. Nearly all of Diop's historical writings are concerned with establishing this ancient Egyptian connection. He is also known for having advanced a theory of African cultural unity, asserting that African civilisation is fundamentally matriarchal and European civilisation fundamentally patriarchal, and that these two civilisations were separate before fusing together in the Mediterranean and giving rise to ancient Greece.

The first published outline of his views on 'African anteriority' is to be found in the article 'Etude de linguistique oulove: Origine de la langue et de la race Wolof' (1948).[3] In this, Diop drew on his background to point to a number of Wolof (the language of the Cayor kingdom in Senegal) and ancient Egyptian cognates (related words from the same root). He continued to look for evidence for the Egyptian origin of African civilisation in his doctoral research, and although his thesis was rejected as too polemical, he published much of it under the title *Nations nègres et culture* (1955, trans. *The African Origin of Civilization: Myth or Reality?*). This work generated quite a stir among French-speaking African intellectuals and played a significant part in the development of post-war Africanist history.

Nations nègres et culture is divided into two parts; first, an argument for the African origins of Egyptian civilisation; and second, an examination of the issues central to the African struggle for independence in the 1950s. In the first part, Diop claims that a wide range of evidence points to the ancient Egyptian civilisation being Negroid. Furthermore, he suggests that it was the first civilisation, and that it shaped northern cultures. According to Diop, Pythagorean mathematics, Judaism, Islam and modern science all have their roots in Egyptian thought. This is not known to the Western world, he believes, because

The desire to legitimise colonisation and the slave trade – in other words, the social condition of the Negro in the modern world – engendered an entire literature to describe the so-called inferior traits of the Blacks.[4]

And Western scholarship continues to deny Black Africa its cultural heritage. Diop even goes so far as to suggest the destruction of skeletons to explain why there are so few pre-dynastic Negroid mummies. He does present more constructive arguments as well, however – for example, citing a large number of cultural and linguistic similarities between ancient Egyptian and present-day black African civilisations. These include closely related ideas about totems, circumcision, cosmology, monarchy and caste. In the second part Diop asserts that a reappraisal of the ancient past will not only boost the self-pride of Africans, but also help them to construct a unified culture that will benefit all of humanity. Diop does not tell us how such a unified African culture will benefit the world, but language, he believes, will play a crucial part in the struggle for unity. In order to foster unity, languages must be flexible enough to accommodate modern concepts. To demonstrate that African languages could embrace such concepts, Diop offers a Wolof translation of part of Einstein's theory of relativity.

Diop revisited many of the themes established in *Nations nègres et culture* in *L'unité culturelle de l'Afrique noire* (1959, trans. *The Cultural Unity of Black Africa*). He also offered what is probably the clearest statement of his 'two cradles' thesis. Western thinkers like Friedrich Engels, Diop tells us, have long argued that matriarchy is an intermediate stage in the history of the family. For Diop, this is a Eurocentric claim used to demean traditionally matriarchal African societies. He instead supports the idea of there being two family 'cradles'; he holds that

> instead of a universal transition from matriarchy to patriarchy, humanity has from the beginning been divided into two geographically distinct 'cradles', one of which was favourable to the flourishing of matriarchy and the other to that of patriarchy, and that these two systems encountered one another and even disputed with each other in different human societies, that in certain places they were superimposed on each other or even existed side by side.
>
> (*The Cultural Unity of Black Africa*, p. 26)

The northern Indo-European cradle possessed material conditions that encouraged a nomadic form of life, the southern African cradle a sedentary, agricultural form. These conditions led to one being patriarchal and the other being matriarchal. These forms of family organisation, in turn, played a large part in shaping particular cultures. For example, Diop suggests that these cradles fostered different views of marriage, child-rearing, property, inheritance and sin (ibid., chap. 5).

In 1960, Diop submitted a new thesis, and this time he was awarded his doctorat des lettres. A pared-down version of his thesis was published as *L'Afrique noire précoloniale* (trans. *Precolonial Black Africa*). In this book, Diop uses medieval Arabic sources to build up descriptions of the social, political and economic features of the precolonial West African kingdoms of Ghana, Mali and Songhai. Furthermore, he draws out parallels with the social, political and economic features of the Cayor kingdom of Senegal. His purpose is not so much to detail historical events or establish a chronology, but rather to demonstrate a shared historical heritage and continuity among the peoples of Sahelian West Africa (*Precolonial Black Africa*, pp. 147–8). Drawing on the ideas of '*Annales*' historians such as Ferdinand Braudel, he gives this approach to writing history the label *histoire non événementielle*: the 'eventless' description of the political and economic structures of societies over a long time-span. He writes:

> Up to the present day the history of Black Africa has been written with dates as dry as a grocer's invoice without hardly ever looking to find the key that opens the door to the intelligence, to the comprehension of African society.[5]
>
> (*Precolonial Black Africa*, p. 5)

Diop's point is that existing African scholars, in concentrating on events, tend to look to the modern period of interaction between Africans and Europeans. Such historians, he claims, can do no more than produce perfunctory chronicles that assume a single, European, perspective. For Diop the key to the comprehension of African society lies with the analysis of long-term social, economic and cultural changes. It is only when one looks to such changes over the course of many centuries that one gets an idea of the cultural richness to which Black Africa can lay claim. For instance, in *Civilisation ou barbarie* (1981, trans. *Civilisation or Barbarism*), Diop claims that his approach allows him to refute Marx's suggestion that Asian–African societies were stagnant and lacked the characteristics needed for revolutionary activity (chaps 8–11; see also *Antériorité des civilisations nègres: Mythe ou vérité historique?* 1967, partially trans. in *Soulbook*).

In 1961, Diop returned to Senegal, which was now independent. He immediately became involved in politics and formed an opposition party, the Bloc des Masses Sénégalaises (BMS). In 1962 he was arrested and imprisoned. In his absence, the BMS fell apart. He was released, and in 1965 he founded the Front National du Sénégal. This party was banned, along with other opposition parties. In 1973 the ban was lifted and he formed a third interest group, the Rassemblement National Démocratique. In 1981, the RND became a political party.

Alongside his political involvement, Diop also worked hard to establish a radio-carbon laboratory so that he could pursue research in archaeology and physics; ultimately a laboratory was opened at the Dakar-based Institut Fondemental d'Afrique Noire (IFAN) in 1971. Diop continued to publish his ideas on African anteriority and in 1971 he was elected vice-president of UNESCO's Scientific Committee for the writing of a history of Africa. In 1982, Diop accepted a history appointment at the University of Dakar, a position that he held until his death in 1986.

In the 1960s, the impact of Diop's works was limited to the French-speaking world; they were criticised by leading French Africanists such as Raymond Mauny, Jean Suret-Canale, Jean Devisse and Louis-Vincent Thomas. Although these and later critics noted the value of his works for the generation of a 'politically useful mythology'[6] that would promote African unity, concerns were raised about Diop's almost exclusive concentration on long-term cultural and social developments, his construction of an African history with European intellectual tools, and the polemical tone of his writing.

In the first instance, criticism has been levelled at Diop's sweeping aside of historical events in order to concentrate on long-term social, political and economic changes. Writers such as Diouf and Mbodj have pointed out that in writing a long-term history that excludes events, Diop risks offering work that assumes the homogeneity of time and a singularity of perspective.[7] History, as Braudel and other Annalists suggest, includes anything from the most fleeting events to the slowest of environmental changes and assumes a plurality of times and perspectives. Yet it is the Western obsession with *histoire événementielle*, Diop replied, that has led to a number of misunderstandings about his work:

> It is the difference in intellectual attitude between African and European researchers that is often the cause of these misunderstandings about the interpretation of facts and their relative importance. The scientific curiosity of the European

researcher toward African data is essentially analytical. Viewing things from the exterior, often not desiring to develop a synthesis, the European researcher essentially attaches himself to explosive micro-analysis that is more or less tendentious as regards the facts and indefinitely puts off the stage of synthesis. The African researcher mistrusts this 'scientific' activity whose goal seems to be to dissolve African collective, historical consciousness in the pettiness of details.

(*Antériorité des civilisations nègres*, in *Soulbook*, p. 26)

Diop wants African historians to avoid the extremes of both attitudes (ibid., n.1) but is clear that they must concern themselves with 'macro-history' in order to liberate African history from the distorted colonial version of events.

Though there has been a great deal of sympathy expressed by Western scholars for the idea of African history being written by Africans, some have pointed out that historians like Diop, in looking for the existence of state structures in the African past to support contemporary nation-building efforts, have drawn on ideas that are ultimately foreign to African historical experience, such as those supplied by Marx.[8] Diop has been criticised, as Duvignard points out, for using terms as contestable as 'feudalism', 'socialism' and 'matriarchy' as if they labelled universal realities.[9] Bernal sees this ironical problem as evidence of the control that Europe continues to exert over its former colonies:

Naturally, the institutional rise of Orientalism must – at least in England and France – be associated with the huge expansion of colonialism and other forms of domination over Asia and Africa taking place at the same time. Not only was a systematic understanding of non-European peoples and their spoken language needed to control these people but a knowledge of their civilisations, by seizing and categorising their cultures, ensured that the natives themselves could learn about their own civilisations only through European scholarship. This provided yet another rope to the colonial elites to the metropolitan countries, which has been an increasingly important factor in the retention of European cultural hegemony since the decline of direct colonisation in the second half of the twentieth century.[10]

Finally, for a number of Western scholars, Diop is thought to have created a nationalist or pan-African mythology at the expense of sound scholarship. Immanuel Geiss, for instance, has suggested that Diop's work is no more than a reaction to perceived inferiority in the face of European civilisation, and plays the same role as nineteenth-century European nationalist ideologies – that of contributing to the cultural readjustment needed to enter the modern world.[11] Mary Lefkowitz has a similar view:

> Afrocentrism not only teaches what is untrue; it encourages students to ignore known chronology, to forget about looking to material evidence, to select only those facts that are convenient, and to invent facts whenever useful or necessary. . . . In short, the Afrocentric myth of antiquity does not educate its adherents. Instead, it keeps them in a state of illusion, both about the true course of history and also of the ways in which people have always been able [to] learn from cultures other than their own.[12]

Diop's attempt to create a pan-African nationalism through the writing of African history has also been given a critical reception in Europe because of the suspicion and even fear with which nationalist sympathies have been viewed in the latter half of the twentieth century. Diop wanted dialogue with, and ultimately acceptance by, African and European academics, but was adamant that African historians should be polemical:

> One must, in the first phase, establish scientifically the facts, and in this domain not even the least complacency is permitted. The way in which unbiased scientific truth must be presented depends on the circumstances, because in the order of the human sciences, it is one thing to demonstrate the veracity and it is another to make this thing accepted right away. Consequently, in a second phase and without doing harm to the scientific value of the theory, *one has the right to make use of the polemic* to drive out the bad faith of men, to undermine the superstructures which have nothing but the appearance of science – finally to bringing the sleeping spirits out of their lethargy.[13]

Although Diop's works have generally been met with what he called a 'qualified silence'[14] in Europe, a good deal of enthusiasm has been shown for his ideas by French-speaking African historians and

Afro-American historians alike. Théophile Obenga, a Senegalese historian, has tried to refine and develop Diop's ideas, and a number of English translations of Diop's works have been prepared in the United States. In Africa and the United States, it appears that many historians have taken seriously Diop's suggestion that 'It is high time that we learn that other people cannot teach us about Africa anymore.'[15]

Notes

1 W. Soyinka, *Myth, Literature, and the African World*, Cambridge: Cambridge University Press, 1976, p. 105.
2 C. Finch, 'Further Conversations with the Pharoah', in I. van Sertima and L. Williams (eds), *Great African Thinkers: Cheikh Anta Diop*, New Brunswick, NJ: Transaction Books, 1986, p. 229.
3 *Présence Africaine*, 1948, 4: 672–84 and 5: 848–53.
4 Quoted in J. G. Spady, 'The Changing Perception of C. A. Diop and his Work: the Preeminence of a Scientific Spirit', in I. van Sertima and L. Williams (eds), *Great African Thinkers*, p. 97.
5 This was just a few years after K. O. Dike's and B. A. Ogot's attempts to establish a separate discipline of African history in Nigeria and Kenya. On this, see R. July, *An African Voice: the Role of Humanities in African Independence*, Durham, NC: Duke University Press, 1987, pp. 129–56, 177–97.
6 C. Gray, *Conceptions of History: Cheikh Anta Diop and Théophile Obenga*, London: Karnak Press, 1989, chap. 1.
7 See M. Diouf and M. Mbodj, 'Senegalese Historiography: Present Practices and Future Perspectives', in B. Jewsiewicki and D. Newbury (eds), *African Historiographies: What History for Which Africa?* London: Sage Publications, 1986, p. 212.
8 See C. Neale, *Writing 'Independent' History: African Historiography 1960–1980*, London: Greenwood Press, 1985, pp. 125–50.
9 J. Duvignard, 'Idéologies africaines: Critique de *L'Afrique Noire Précoloniale* et *L'Unité Culturelle*', *Preuves*, 1960, 113: 84–7.
10 M. Bernal, *Black Athena, the Afroasiatic Roots of Classical Civilization*, vol. 1, *The Fabrication of Ancient Greece 1785–1985*, New Brunswick, NJ: Rutgers University Press, 1987, p. 236.
11 I. Geiss, *The Pan-African Movement*, trans. A. Kemp, London: Methuen, 1974, pp. 318–19.
12 M. Lefkowitz, *Not Out of Africa: How Afrocentrism Became an Excuse to Teach Myth as History*, New York: Basic Books, 1996, pp. 157–8.
13 Quoted in J. Spady (1972) 'Negritude, Pan Banegritude and the Diopian Philosophy of History', in *A Current Bibliography on African Affairs*, p. 26.
14 C. Finch (1987) 'Meeting the Pharoah: Conversations with Cheikh Anta Diop', in *Cheikh Anta Diop: Great African Thinkers*, vol. 1, p. 30.
15 C. A. Diop (1987) 'Nile Valley Executive Committee Interviews Diop', in *Cheikh Anta Diop*, p. 291.

Diop's major writings

The African Origin of Civilisation: Myth or Reality?, trans. M. Cook, Westport, CT: Lawrence Hill, 1974.

The Cultural Unity of Black Africa: the Domains of Patriarchy and of Matriarchy in Classical Antiquity, trans. anon., Chicago, IL: Third World Press, 1978.

Precolonial Black Africa, trans. anon., Westport, CT: Lawrence Hill & Company, 1987.

Black Africa: the Economic and Cultural Basis for a Federated State, trans. H. J. Salemson, Westport, CT: Lawrence Hill & Company, 1978.

Antériorité des civilisations nègres: Mythe ou vérité historique? partially trans. in Soulbook: the Revolutionary Journal of the Black World, vol. 2(4), 1969.

Civilisation or Barbarism: Anthropology without Compromise, trans. Y.-L.M. Ngemi New York: Lawrence Hill, 1991.

'Origin of the Ancient Egyptians', in G. Mokhtar (ed.), General History of Africa II, Ancient Civilisations of Africa, Paris/Berkeley, CA: UNESCO/University of California Press, 1987, pp. 27–57.

See also

Braudel, Marx, Woodson.

Further resources

Bernal, M., Black Athena, the Afroasiatic Roots of Classical Civilisation, vol. 1, The Fabrication of Ancient Greece 1785–1985, New Brunswick, NJ: Rutgers University Press, 1987.

Collins, R. O., Problems in African History, Englewood Cliffs, NJ: Prentice-Hall, 1979.

Geiss, I., The Pan African Movement, trans. A. Kemp, London: Methuen, 1974.

Gray, C., Conceptions of History: Cheikh Anta Diop and Théophile Obenga, London: Karnak House, 1989.

Howe, S. Afrocentrism: Mythical Pasts and Imagined Homes, New York: Verso, 1998.

Jewsiewicki, B. and Newbury, D. (eds), African Historiographies, What History for Which Africa? London: Sage, 1986.

July, R., An African Voice: the Role of Humanities in African Independence, Durham, NC: Duke University Press, 1987.

Lefkowitz, M., Not Out of Africa: How Afrocentrism Became an Excuse to Teach History as Myth, New York: Basic Books, 1996.

Neale, C., Writing 'Independent' History: African Historiography 1960–1980, London: Greenwood, 1985.

Obenga, T., L'Afrique dans l'antiquité, Egypte pharaonique–Afrique noire, Paris: Présence Africaine, 1973.

Présence Africaine, 1989, nos 149–50.

Sartre, J.-P. and Senghor, L. S., Orphée noire: Anthologie de la nouvelle poésie nègre et malgache de langue française, Paris: Presses universitaires de France, 1948.

Soyinka, W., Myth, Literature and the African World, Cambridge: Cambridge University Press, 1976.

Van Sertima, I. and Williams, C. (eds), Great African Thinkers, vol. 1, Cheikh Anta Diop, New Brunswick, NJ: Transaction Books, 1987.

G. R. ELTON 1921–94

It is commonly thought that radical historical research requires radical historiographical principles. The writings of the English historian Geoffrey Rudolph Elton, however, show us that this is not necessarily true. In a career spanning over forty years, Elton articulated and applied many 'old-fashioned convictions and practices' and brought about a 'revolution' in Tudor history.

The elder son of Eva Dorothea Sommer and the ancient historian Victor Ehrenberg, Geoffrey Rudolph Ehrenberg (1921–94) lived first in Frankfurt and then in Prague. In 1939, the Ehrenberg family emigrated to Britain under a grant from the Society for the Protection of Science and Learning (SPSL). Geoffrey and his brother Lewis enrolled at Rydal School, a Methodist school in Colwyn Bay, North Wales. Though neither knew much English, they advanced rapidly and by 1941 Geoffrey was made an assistant master in history, German and mathematics.[1] When not teaching, he studied for an external degree in ancient history at the University of London. After being awarded a first class degree, Geoffrey joined the British Army and changed his name to Elton under Army Council instruction. Until 1946 he served in the East Surrey Regiment and the Intelligence Corps. After the war, Ehrenberg, now Elton, began research for a doctorate in English history at the University of London. Under the guidance of the eminent Tudor historian J. E. Neale, Elton began to investigate documents dealing with the administration of Thomas Cromwell, a minister of Henry VIII who held office from 1531 until his execution in 1540. The resulting thesis, 'Thomas Cromwell, Aspects of his Administrative Work', contained ideas that were to form the foundation of all of his subsequent historical work. When Elton completed his doctorate, he taught for a short time at the University of Glasgow before accepting a position at the University of Cambridge. Elton worked in Cambridge until his retirement in 1988, and rose from being an assistant lecturer to the Regius Professor of Modern History.

Central to Elton's historical work is the idea that Thomas Cromwell was the architect of a 'Tudor revolution in government'. The Tudor period, Elton argued in his first book, was not one of despotism:

> it was a time when men were ready to be governed, and when order and peace seemed more important than principles and rights. What distinguished the Tudors from their European contemporaries, who were facing similar problems, was just

that they provided peace and order without despotism –
certainly without the weapons of a despot.

> (*The Tudor Revolution in Government*, pp. 1–2)

It was a period in which Thomas Cromwell took advantage of Henry
VIII's plan to break with the church in Rome. He introduced so many
significant administrative changes that by 1603 'Elizabeth handed to her
successor a country administered on modern lines' (ibid., p. 71). Elton's
thesis was radical, because few historians located the roots of modern
government in the 1530s, and those who did considered Henry VIII to
be the architect of the reforms. As he wrote in a review of an earlier text
on Tudor history:

> What has to be grasped . . . is that there is no question of just
> correcting points of detail or of discovering a few new facts.
> A whole complex of underlying ideas, a whole frame of
> reference, is being discarded.
>
> ('Renaissance Monarchy?' in *Studies in Tudor and*
> *Stuart Politics and Government*, vol. 1, p. 39)

Elton elaborated on his thesis in a series of articles and two
best-selling textbooks, *England under the Tudors* (1956) and *The Tudor
Constitution* (1960), and before long he had convinced both scholars
and public alike that Cromwell's 'revolution' was the most important
British event of the sixteenth century. Even as Elton's ideas became
orthodox, however, criticism emerged. For instance, Penry Williams
and G. L. Harris argued that Elton had neglected medieval precedents
for Cromwell's policies, and J. J. Scarisbrick, a former student of Elton's,
continued to argue that Henry VIII was the principal architect of the
administrative changes.[2]

Undeterred, Elton argued in the 1972 Ford Lectures at the University
of Oxford that the rule of law prevailed in the 1530s because Cromwell's
leadership assured that there was 'neither holocaust nor reign of terror'
in response to popular unrest (*Policy and Police*, 1972, pp. 399–400). His
next book, *Reform and Renewal* (1973), considered the reforms initiated
by Cromwell in Parliament, especially the Sheep and Enclosure Act,
a new Poor Law, and statutes which radically altered land law. Though
the core of Elton's thesis remained the same, his portrayal of Cromwell
changed slightly. Cromwell, he wrote, 'was less determinedly secular and
less ruthlessly radical than I once supposed'; his plans for the reformation
of the English church were seen to be underpinned by Protestant and
humanist ideas (*Reform and Renewal*, pp. vii–viii). This view of Cromwell

as a Protestant humanist is even clearer in the later work *Reform and Reformation* (1977). In this, Elton also reconsiders his evaluation of Cromwell's achievements as a 'revolution'. Cromwell's reforms, he admits, were not without precedents. They were, however, still significant. Thus in *Reform and Reformation* the 'Tudor revolution' is recast as an age of radical *reform*. Elton did not consider this new view to be a recantation. Rather, he considered it to be the result of a different 'air and approach' than earlier 'forecasts' (*Reform and Reformation*, p. v).

Writers such as Brendan Bradshaw and J. A. Guy welcomed Elton's revision of the revolution thesis but still expressed doubts about his portrayals of Cromwell, Henry VIII, Cardinal Wolsey and Thomas More. In 1986 six writers, including former Elton students, published *Revolution Reassessed: Revisions in the History of Tudor Government and Administration*.[3] In this they questioned Elton's research on the court, the Privy Council, and government finance, and his emphasis on Cromwell. Elton refused to bow to his critics, and maintained until his death that the financial reforms of the 1530s heralded the beginning of modern government. As J. A. Guy has commented, it seems that Elton considered his most influential critic to be himself.[4] Elton was severe with himself and with those who held ideas different from his own (for an example of self-criticism, see *Reform and Reformation*). His writings are peppered with aggressive attacks on a wide range of writers, including Lawrence Stone, Christopher Hill, G. M. Trevelyan, R. H. Tawney, J. E. Neale, E. H. Carr, Arnold Toynbee, Heidegger, Adorno, Saussure, Barthes, Gadamer, Derrida, Foucault, Hayden White, Dominick La Capra and David Harlan. It is through these attacks that we obtain a clear idea of Elton's views on the nature of history.

The study of history, Elton argues passionately in his historiographical works, must be reclaimed from at least seven groups of people. First, there are amateurs, who view the past from the 'outside, through a veil woven out of strangeness, and wonderment' (*The Practice of History*, 1967, p. 18). Such people see the exceptional in the ordinary and vice versa, are unable to formulate significant questions about the past and judge it on its own terms, and are prone to sentimentality. Second, there are those who adopt ideas and methods from neighbouring disciplines without critical consideration. While Elton is not opposed to the endeavour of opening up new lines of inquiry in history, he believes that '[w]hen the externally obtained scheme becomes doctrine, as it too often does, it stultifies the study of history by reducing history to a repository of examples selected or distorted to buttress the scheme' (ibid., pp. 35–7). Sometimes, also, historians may latch onto ideas that have been discredited in the discipline from which they originated (see *Which Road to the Past?*, 1983). Third, there are those who seek law-like generalisations in the past in the hope that they will be able to make predictions about the future. Historians, Elton acknowledges, do make generalisations. Without them, they would not be able to describe the past to others. But events and people are *individual* and *particular*: '*like* other entities of a similar kind, but never entirely identical with them' (*The Practice of History*, p. 11). The search for laws that explain our actions, he claims, gives us an excuse to say that we cannot avoid our misdeeds. In his estimation it also contradicts the 'essence of the historical enterprise' because it involves reasoning from 'what is' to 'what may come of it', not from 'what is' to 'how it came about'. Attempts at finding laws will be frustrated, however, because history demonstrates the unpredictability of what humans may think and do:

> There are no human beings who do not feel the influence of the setting within which they move, but all of them also transcend their setting and in their turn affect it: what they do both within and to it remains explicable but unpredictable.
>
> (*Return to Essentials*, 1991, p. 8)

Fourth, there are those who 'seek salvation' in theoretical frameworks. Whilst such theories allow for the construction of 'imposing looking edifices', they tell us more about the present than the past. For Elton there is no question that theories are imposed on the past: they do not arise out of it. Furthermore, in his view '[a]ll questions are so framed as to produce support for the theory, and all answers are predetermined by it' (ibid., p. 16). Those who fall for theories cling to them with blind faith:

> It takes a mental revolution equal to a spiritual conversion to separate a devotee from his theory, and the chances are that that will happen only if another theory stands by to catch the convert.
>
> (Ibid., p. 23)

For example, Marxist historians cling to the view that seventeenth-century England saw the rise of capitalist principles despite evidence to the contrary (ibid., pp. 17–18; *The Practice of History*, pp. 36–7, 43–7). We should also be wary, he instructs us, of philosophers and theoreticians who write confidently about history but have never undertaken historical research.

Fifth, there are those who write 'present-centred' history. Such people select from the past those details that match present-day concerns. Any use of the past in such a way, Elton believes, is 'suspect and dangerous'. If the past is to be understood, it must be done so on its own terms from the 'inside'. At best, the study of the past affords us 'with a much wider and deeper acquaintance with the possibilities open to human thought and action than [we] can ever gather from [our] own limited experience' (*Return to Essentials*, p. 8).

Sixth, there are those who use history to support myths. While such myths may offer us comfort, arguments about the revision of Irish and Nazi history show us that they can also be dangerous. Historians, Elton tells us, must relentlessly pursue truth, even if they gain no solace from doing so (*Return to Essentials*, pp. 44–9).

Finally, there are those who have

> absorbed the apparently widespread conviction that certain extravagances current among students of literature render all forms of objective study impossible and therefore disable the historian from ever achieving what for a long time now he has stated as his ambition.
>
> (*Return to Essentials*, p. 26)

For Elton, if historians accept the belief that the past cannot be 'really known', then the study of the past will become either a case of 'anything goes', where all accounts are considered to be acceptable and meaning is determined by the reader, or nothing more than the study of the manner in which historians write about the past. Elton is clearly horrified by these possibilities:

> we are fighting for the lives of innocent young people beset by devilish tempters who claim to offer higher forms of thought and deeper truths and insights – the intellectual equivalent of crack, in fact.
>
> (*Return to Essentials*, p. 41)

Though Elton does not believe that historians can rid themselves entirely of presuppositions and prejudices, he still thinks that objective knowledge is possible. This is because the historian's subject-matter has a 'dead reality independent of the inquiry'. Historians cannot know everything that happened in the past, but there is 'truth to be discovered if only we can find it' (*The Practice of History*, pp. 73–4).

It is upon this cornerstone of certainty that Elton builds his view of history. 'Professional' historians, he claims, can get at the truth of the past, the 'inside' of it, through the meticulous study of historical sources (see, for example, *Return to Essentials*, pp. 52–3). In doing so, they are guided by four principles. First, they try to ensure that the questions they put to the evidence are not biased towards an answer already in mind. Second, they remember that the people of the past did not have the benefit of hindsight. Third, they keep an open mind and allow further study to modify their ideas. Fourth, they try to present their ideas to others in an intelligible form (ibid., pp. 66–9; *The Practice of History*, pp. 88–141). These aims and principles, Elton claims, ought to be inculcated in students of history. This can best be done, he argues in the last chapter of *The Practice of History*, in activities that require problem solving, reasoning, wide reading and the assessment of evidence. Though he believes that it matters little what content is taught, he declares a preference for basing university courses in England on the study of English political history. This is because much has been written about it and it deals with problems that, in Elton's estimation, require little specialised knowledge (*The Practice of History*, p. 151; see also *Political History*, 1970, and 'The Future of the Past' and 'The History of England', in *Return to Essentials*, pp. 7–12).

Elton's historiographical ideas clearly beg many questions. At the least, Keith Jenkins is right to claim, for instance, that Elton's ideas are undermined by the fact that he fails to meet philosophical points by articulating his own ideas philosophically.[5] But if we dismiss Elton upon such grounds, we miss the point of what he was trying to do. Elton did not express his ideas philosophically because he believed that history could be talked about in a different way. It was his aim to give voice to the beliefs of many professional historians and to make sure that they are not excluded from discussions on the nature of history.

Notes

1   B. L. Beer, 'G. R. Elton: Tudor Champion', in W. L. Arnstein (ed.), *Recent Historians of Great Britain*, Ames, IA: Iowa State University Press, 1990, p. 15.
2   P. Williams and G. L. Harriss, 'A Revolution in Tudor History?', *Past and Present*, 1963, 25: 3–58; and J. J. Scarisbrick, *Henry VIII*, Berkeley, CA: University of California Press, 1968. See also L. Stone, 'How Nasty was Thomas Cromwell?' *New York Review of Books*, 22 March 1973, 20(4): 31–2; C. Russell, *The Crisis of Parliaments: English History 1509–1660*, London: Oxford University Press, 1971; and C. S. L. Davies, *Peace, Print and Protestantism, 1450–1558*, London: Hart-Davis McGibbon, 1976, pp. 226–32.
3   B. Bradshaw, 'The Tudor Commonwealth: Reform and Revision', *Historical Journal*, 1979, 22(2): 455–76; J. A. Guy, 'The Tudor Commonwealth: Revising

Thomas Cromwell', *Historical Journal*, 1980, 23(3): 681–5; and C. Coleman and
D. Starkey (eds), *Revolution Reassessed: Revisions in the History of Tudor Government
and Administration*, Oxford: Oxford University Press, 1986.
4   Guy, 'The Tudor Commonwealth'.
5   K. Jenkins, *On 'What is History?' From Carr to Elton to Rorty and White*,
London: Routledge, 1995, p. 92.

Elton's major works

*The Tudor Revolution in Government: Administrative Changes in the Reign of Henry
VIII*, Cambridge: Cambridge University Press, 1953.
England under the Tudors, London: Methuen, 1956.
(ed.) *The Reformation*, New Cambridge Modern History, vol. 2, Cambridge:
Cambridge University Press, 1958.
Star Chamber Stories, London: Methuen, 1958.
The Tudor Constitution: Documents and Commentary, Cambridge: Cambridge
University Press, 1960.
The Practice of History, London: Fontana, 1967.
Modern Historians on British History, 1485–1945, London: Methuen, 1970.
Political History: Principles and Practice, London: Penguin, 1970.
Policy and Police: the Enforcement of the Reformation in the Age of Thomas Cromwell,
Cambridge: Cambridge University Press, 1972.
Reform and Renewal: Thomas Cromwell and the Common Weal, Cambridge:
Cambridge University Press, 1973.
Reform and Reformation: England 1509–1558, London: Arnold, 1977.
(with R. W. Fogel) *Which Road to the Past? Two Views of History*, New Haven,
CT: Yale University Press, 1983.
Return to Essentials: Some Reflections on the Present State of Historical Study,
Cambridge: Cambridge University Press, 1991.
Studies in Tudor and Stuart Politics and Government: Papers and Reviews, 1946–1972,
4 vols, London: Cambridge University Press, 1974–92.

See also

Carr, White.

Further resources

Bradshaw, B., 'The Tudor Commonwealth: Reform and Revision', *Historical
Journal*, 1979, 22(2): 455–76.
Coleman, C. and Starkey, D. (eds), *Revolution Reassessed: Revisions in the History of
Tudor Government and Administration*, Oxford: Oxford University Press, 1986.
Cross, M. C., Loades, D. M. and Scarisbrick, J. J. (eds), *Law and Government under
the Tudors: Essays Presented to Sir Geoffrey Elton, Regius Professor of Modern
History in the University of Cambridge on the Occasion of his Retirement*,
Cambridge: Cambridge University Press, 1988.
Guth, D. J. and McKenna, J. W. (eds), *Tudor Rule and Revolution: Essays for G. R.
Elton from his American Friends*, New York: Cambridge University Press, 1982.

Guy, J. A., 'The Tudor Commonwealth: Revising Thomas Cromwell', *Historical Journal*, 1980, 23(3): 681–5.

Horowitz, M. R., 'Which Road to the Past?', *History Today*, January 1984, 34: 5–10.

Jenkins, K., *On 'What is History?' From Carr to Elton to Rorty and White*, London: Routledge, 1995.

Kenyon, J., *The History Men*, London: Weidenfeld & Nicolson, 1983.

Kouri, E. I. and Scott, T. (eds), *Politics and Society in Reformation Europe: Essays for Sir Geoffrey Elton on his Sixty-fifth Birthday*, London: Macmillan, 1986.

Schlatter, R., *Recent Views on British History: Essays on Historical Writing since 1966*, New Brunswick, NJ: Rutgers University Press, 1984.

Slavin, A. J., 'Telling the Story: G. R. Elton and the Tudor Age', *Sixteenth Century Journal*, 1990, 21(2): 151–69.

Transactions of the Royal Historical Society, 1997, 7: 177–336.

Williams, P. and Harriss, G. L., 'A Revolution in Tudor History?' *Past and Present*, 1963, 25: 3–58.

LUCIEN FEBVRE 1878–1956

It is ironic that Lucien Febvre, a modern historian who worked with Marc Bloch to foster international exchange through the writing of problem-orientated histories of the whole range of human experiences, is relatively unknown beyond the mental frontiers of France.

The son of a grammar teacher, Lucien Febvre (1878–1956) spent his childhood in Lorraine. After studying at the Lycée Louis-le-Grand and performing his military service, Febvre won a place at the prestigious Ecole Normale Supérieure in Paris. Between 1898 and 1902 he attended seminars by the philosophers Henri Bergson and Lucien Lévy-Bruhl, the geographer Paul Vidal de la Blanche, art historian Emile Mâle, literary critic Henri Bremond and linguist Antoine Meillet. While Febvre learned much from these seminars, he also gained a great deal from reading works by historians and political thinkers such as Jules Michelet, Jacob Burkhardt, Fustel de Coulanges, Louis Courajod and Jean Jaurès. From early on in his studies, Febvre rejected the dominant Germanic view of history as the scientific study of political and military events. Rather, he favoured a wider view of history informed by the ideas of social theorists such as geographers, anthropologists, sociologists, economists and philologists.

Such a view of history underpins his doctoral thesis, a study of the Franche-Comté region when it was ruled by Philip II of Spain in the sixteenth century. In this, Febvre describes the revolt of the Netherlands against Philip II and the approach of the Reformation. He also presents a vivid account of the socio-geographical features of the region and the bitter economic, political and emotional struggle between a nobility falling into debt and an increasingly wealthy bourgeoisie (*Philippe II et la Franche-Comté: Etude d'histoire politique, religieuse et sociale*, 1912). With the support of Henri Berr, the founder of the journal *Revue de synthèse historique*, Febvre planned to write a more general study of the relationship between history and geography. His plans, however, were interrupted by the outbreak of the First World War. During the war, Febvre served in a machine-gun company. He was wounded once, received five citations and was promoted to the rank of captain.

In October 1919, Febvre was offered a lectureship in modern history at the University of Strasbourg in the newly reclaimed region of Alsace. In his inaugural lecture, Febvre outlined the function of history in a 'world in ruins'. When historians, he argued, free themselves from idle fact gathering, writing accounts to serve political, ideological and nationalistic ends, and subsuming events under artificial or false laws, they can be the 'best and surest safeguard for our national ideal, for our civilisation, for our independence and our will to peace and freedom'.[1]

At Strasbourg he turned back to his study of the relationship between geography and history, which was published as *La terre et l'évolution humaine* (1922, trans. *A Geographical Introduction to History*). This book takes as its point of departure Friedrich Ratzel's contention that the physical environment 'serves as a fixed foundation for the moods and changing aspirations of men, and governs the destinies of peoples with blind brutality' (*A Geographical Introduction to History*, p. 18). Echoing Vidal de la Blanche, Febvre presents two objections to the Ratzelian view. First, he stresses the variety of responses that can be given to a particular environment; for example, mountain ranges may or may not act as a boundary. Second, the influence of the environment on people is always mediated through social structures and ideas; so, for instance, a river may be considered by one group to be a barrier and by another to be a valuable trade route. Thus society plays an important role in shaping each individual's views of the world.

These two points are further explored in his study of the Rhine with Albert Demangeon, *Le Rhin: problèmes d'histoire et d'économie* (1935). In this work, Febvre argues that people's perceptions of the Rhine are not naturally given but are the product of human experiences. The case of the Rhine demonstrates the point that a 'frontier' exists when

> you find yourself in a different world, among a set of ideas, feelings and enthusiasms surprising and disconcerting to the foreigner. In other words, what 'engraves' a frontier powerfully

in the earth is not policemen or customs men or cannons drawn up behind ramparts. It is feelings, and exalted passions – and hatreds.[2]

Febvre hoped that critical discussion on the mental frontiers of the Rhine would help people to disarm contemporary nationalist myths.

Not long after he started work at the University of Strasbourg, Febvre struck up what would be a lifelong friendship with the medievalist Marc Bloch. Febvre and Bloch shared the vision of a 'wider and more human' view of history. In 1929 they founded the journal *Annales d'Histoire Economique et Sociale*, which survives today under the title *Annales: Histoire, Sciences Sociales*, to promote their 'new kind of history'.[3] Through *Annales*, Febvre and Bloch hoped first to foster the unity of the human sciences and, second, to question the division of history into ancient, medieval and modern periods and societies into 'primitive' or 'civilised' types. Febvre wrote a number of polemical reviews and articles directed against views of history that were not 'ours', especially those which idolised facts and specialisation.

After finishing *A Geographical Introduction to History*, Febvre turned to the study of French views of the Renaissance and Reformation. In a number of articles and lectures Febvre argued that Michelet's concept of the 'Renaissance' or 'rebirth' had led historians to ignore the connections between the Middle Ages and the Renaissance. For instance, Febvre claims that the emergence of the bourgeoisie straddled both periods (see, for instance, 'Amiens' and 'How Jules Michelet Invented the Renaissance' in *A New Kind of History*, pp. 193–207, 258–67). In other writings and lectures, such as 'The Origins of the French Reformation: a Badly Put Question?', Febvre challenged the orthodox view of the Reformation as a revolt led by Luther against the abuses of the Catholic church. The history of religion, he contends, should not only involve the history of particular church institutions, but also take into account people's religious ideas, emotions, tendencies and responses (see also 'Religious Practice and the History of France', in *A New Kind of History*, pp. 268–75). For Febvre, the Reformation came about largely because of the emerging bourgeoisie's search for a 'clear, reasonably human and gently fraternal church' in which the Bible could be studied by all men and a direct dialogue between believer and God was possible ('The Origins of the French Reformation', in *A New Kind of History*, pp. 66, 69–80). The bourgeoisie are also accorded an important role in Febvre's biography of Luther, *Un destin: Martin Luther* (1928, trans. *Martin Luther: a Destiny*). The bourgeoisie, Febvre claims, were a willing audience for Luther's ideas. He is careful to note, however, that Luther's ideas cannot be reduced to those of the bourgeoisie. Some of the bourgeoisie, for instance, rejected Luther's ideas when he denounced the Dutch reformer Erasmus and the 'robbing and murderous' peasants. In these papers, the Reformation is not dominated by any one individual.

In 1933 Febvre left Strasbourg to take up a chair in history at the Collège de France in Paris. Not long after, he was appointed president of the committee organising the *Encyclopédie française*, an interdisciplinary project focused on a number of particular topics. Febvre's influence can be clearly discerned in the dedication of a volume to the topic of '*outillage mental*': the mental or conceptual 'apparatus' of individuals and societies. Febvre also had to take on more of the work associated with *Annales* when the anti-Semitic policies of occupied and Vichy France made it impossible for Bloch, a Jew, to co-direct. *Annales* and the *Encyclopédie* left Febvre little time to pursue his own writing projects. The outbreak of the Second World War changed that. At sixty-two, Febvre was too old to fight, so he spent most of the war gardening and writing at his country cottage in Franche-Comté. He wrote three books: *Le problème de l'incroyance au XVIe siècle: la Religion de Rabelais* (1942, trans. *The Problem of Unbelief in the Sixteenth Century*), *Origène et Des Périers: ou, l'énigme du 'cymbalum mundi'* (1942), and *Autour de l'Heptaméron: amour sacré, amour profane* (1944).

The Problem of Unbelief in the Sixteenth Century is Febvre's most important and controversial work. In this book, Febvre sets out to show that Abel Lefranc's portrayal of François Rabelais's *Gargantua and Pantagruel* (1532–34) as an attack on Christianity is unfounded. Febvre begins by scrutinising the accusations of atheism supposedly levelled at Rabelais by his contemporaries. Drawing on the ideas of minor publishers, theologians, controversialists and poets, he shows that a number of the denunciations assumed by historians to be levelled at Rabelais are ambiguous and could have been addressed to other people. He also claims 'atheist' was a common term of abuse or a 'kind of obscenity meant to cause a shudder in an audience of the faithful' (*The Problem of Unbelief in the Sixteenth Century*, p. 135). He writes:

> Let us be suspicious of the words of the past. They generally have two meanings, one absolute, the other relative. Even the first is often difficult to define. To say that atheism is the act of denying the deity is not to say anything precise. But on top of that the relative meaning of the word has changed considerably. In the sixteenth century it implied the most terrible scandal one

could decry. This is apparent in a rather general way. What is
less apparent is how much the very modes of reasoning were
transformed from generation to generation.

(Ibid., p. 146)

Because of such imprecision, we cannot either affirm or deny that
Rabelais was an atheist. A stronger case for denial, Febvre believes,
can be achieved by interrogating Rabelais through *Gargantua and
Pantagruel*. Where Lefranc sees the work of an atheist, Febvre sees the
work of a man influenced by the widespread medieval tradition of
the parody of the sacred. For example, in chapter 5 Febvre shows us
that the tale of how Epistemon's head was reattached by Panurge
(*Gargantua and Pantagruel*, 2:30) is more of a copy of the medieval
romance *The Four Sons of Aymon* than a blasphemous commentary on
the accounts of the resurrection of Lazarus and Jairus's daughter in the
Gospels.[4] In Febvre's estimation, Rabelais, like the Dutch reformer
Erasmus, was critical of some of the practices and ideas of the late
medieval church, but he still hoped to renew the church through
reason and toleration. Febvre's analysis of the links between Erasmus
and Rabelais opens the way for a more general discussion on the
possibility of 'absolute' atheism in the sixteenth century. In this he claims
that the ideas of Christianity so permeated sixteenth-century life as
to make atheism all but impossible. Even philosophy and the sciences,
which might be seen as a possible support for unbelief, lacked the
distinction between the natural and the supernatural and concepts
such as 'absolute' and 'relative', 'abstract' and 'concrete', 'causality' and
'regularity' that would feed the rationalism of thinkers like Descartes
a century later.[5] The lack of concepts such as these, along with an
imprecise understanding of space and time and a lack of a sense of beauty
in nature, Febvre concludes, show us just how far away the *outillage
mental* of the sixteenth century is from our own.

The Problem of Unbelief in the Sixteenth Century offers us a vivid account
of a very different mental 'apparatus'. Furthermore, the style of the work
allows us to glimpse something of Febvre's own mental 'apparatus'.
History, his words show us, can be like a lively conversation. *The Problem
of Unbelief* is widely recognised as one of the most significant historical
works of the twentieth century but it has also been subjected to much
criticism. Numerous historians have pointed out that Rabelais may have
had more sympathy for Luther's ideas than Febvre allows; that records
of the Spanish and Italian inquisitions show that some individuals were
sceptics; and that there was a greater plurality of thought and belief in
the sixteenth century. Many have also taken issue with Febvre's claims

about sixteenth-century man's underdeveloped sense of time, space and beauty.[6]

After Bloch's execution by German soldiers in 1944, Febvre was entrusted with the task of bringing the unfinished *Apologie pour l'histoire ou métier d'historien* to publication (1949, trans. *The Historian's Craft*).[7] He was also invited to assist with the reorganisation of the Ecole des Hautes Etudes and to serve as the president of its 'sixième section' (dedicated to the social sciences). Febvre had little time to write, but he still managed to establish his and Bloch's '*Annales*' view of history as the dominant one in France.[8] Though the '*Annales*' view survives as an international milieu dedicated to the writing of history without boundaries, few people outside of France are aware that Bloch was not its sole founder.

Notes

1 'L'histoire dans le monde en ruines: la Leçon d'ouverture du cours d'histoire moderne de l'Université de Strasbourg', *Revue Synthèse Historique*, 1920, 30(1): 1–15; quoted in C. Fink, *Marc Bloch: a Life in History*, Cambridge: Cambridge University Press, 1989, p. 138.

2 *Le Rhin: Problèmes d'histoire et d'économie*, with A. Demangeon, Paris: Colin, 1935. Quotation from P. Schöttler, 'The Rhine as an Object of Historical Controversy in the Inter-war Years: Towards a History of Frontier Mentalities', trans. C. Turner, *History Workshop Journal*, 1995, 39: 15.

3 The journal kept its original title until 1938, was renamed *Annales d'Histoire Sociale* in 1939, *Mélanges d'Histoire Sociale* from 1942 to 1944, and *Annales d'Histoire Sociale* from 1945 to 1946.

4 F. Rabelais, *Gargantua and Pantagruel*, trans. J. M. Cohen, Harmondsworth, Penguin, 1955, pp. 264–70.

5 On the lack of a distinction between the natural and supernatural, see also 'Witchcraft: Nonsense or a Mental Revolution?', in *A New Kind of History*, pp. 185–92.

6 See C. Ginzburg, *The Cheese and the Worms: the Cosmos of a Sixteenth Century Miller*, trans. J. and A. Tedeschi, Baltimore, MD: Johns Hopkins University Press, 1980; J. Edwards, 'Religious Faith and Doubt in Late Medieval Spain: Soria *circa* 1450–1500', *Past and Present*, 1988, 120: 3–25; C. J. Sommerville and J. Edwards, 'Debate: Religious Fate, Doubt and Atheism', *Past and Present*, 1990, 128: 152–61; D. Wootton, 'Lucien Febvre and the Problem of Unbelief in the Early Modern Period', *Journal of Modern History*, 1988, 60(4): 695–730; S. Kinser, 'The Problem of Belief', in D. Hollier (ed.), *A New History of French Literature*, Cambridge, MA: Harvard University Press, 1989, pp. 958–66.

7 For Febvre's response to *The Historian's Craft*, see 'A New Kind of History', in *A New Kind of History*, pp. 27–43.

8 For example, *L'apparition du livre* (1958, translated as *The Coming of the Book*) was largely written by Henri-Jean Martin, and the *Introduction à la France moderne* (1961, translated as *Introduction to Modern France*) was written from lecture notes taken by Febvre's pupil Robert Mandrou.

Febvre's major works

Philippe II et la Franche-Comté: étude d'histoire politique, religieuse et sociale, Paris: Champion, 1912.
A Geographical Introduction to History, London: Routledge & Kegan Paul, 1924.
Martin Luther: a Destiny, New York: Dutton, 1929.
The Problem of Unbelief in the Sixteenth Century: the Religion of Rabelais, Cambridge, MA: Harvard University Press, 1983.
Combats pour l'histoire, Paris: Colin, 1953.
A New Kind of History: from the Writings of Febvre, ed. P. Burke, trans. K. Folca, London: Routledge & Kegan Paul, 1973.
Life in Renaissance France, trans. and ed. M. Rothstein, Cambridge, MA: Harvard University Press.

See also

Bakhtin (CT), Bloch, Braudel, Davis, Hobsbawm, Le Roy Ladurie, Michelet.

Further resources

Berti, S., 'At the Roots of Unbelief', *Journal of the History of Ideas*, 1995, 56(4): 555–75.
Braudel, F., 'Lucien Febvre', in *Encyclopedia of the Social Sciences*, 1968, vol. 5, pp. 348–50.
Burguière, A., 'The Fate of the History of Mentalities in the *Annales*', *Comparative Studies in Society and History*, 1982, 24(3): 424–37.
Burke, P., *The French Historical Revolution: the Annales School, 1929–1989*, Cambridge: Polity, 1990.
Clark, S., 'French Historians and Early Modern Popular Culture', *Past and Present*, 1983, 100: 67–9.
Davis, N. Z., 'Rabelais among the Censors (1940s, 1540s)', *Representations*, 1990, 32(1): 1–32.
Fink, C., *Marc Bloch: a Life in History*, Cambridge: Cambridge University Press, 1989.
Hughes, H. S., *The Obstructed Path: French Social Thought in the Years of Desperation 1930–1960*, New York, Harper & Row, 1969.
Hutton, P. H., 'The History of Mentalities: the New Map of Cultural History', *History and Theory*, 1981, 20(3): 237–59.
Lyon, B. and Lyon, M., *The Birth of Annales History: the Letters of Lucien Febvre and Marc Bloch to Henri Pirenne*, Brussels: Comm. Royale d'Histoire, 1991.
Schöttler, P., 'Lucie Varga: a Central European Refugee in the Circle of the French "Annales", 1934–41', *History Workshop Journal*, 1992, 33: 100–20.
——, 'The Rhine as an Object of Historical Controversy in the Inter-war Years: Towards a History of Frontier Mentalities', *History Workshop Journal*, 1995, 39: 1–21.
Wootton, D., 'Lucien Febvre and the Problem of Unbelief in the Early Modern Period', *Journal of Modern History*, 1988, 60(4): 695–730.

MICHEL FOUCAULT 1926–84

Social features such as madness, gender and sexuality are generally assumed to be 'natural' and unchanging. Past views of 'sexuality', for instance, are thought to equate with our own views. For the French philosopher and historian Michel Foucault, however, our views of these social features are not the only ones possible. Rather, for him, such features are cultural constructions that vary throughout time and space, and thus they are worthy of historical exploration.

The son of a physician, Foucault was born on 15 June 1926 in Poitiers. After studying philosophy and psychology at the Ecole Normale Supérieure, he held a number of academic posts in Sweden, Poland and Germany. During that time he completed his doctorat dès lettres with a thesis on the origins of modern psychiatry. This was published in 1961 as *Folie et déraison: histoire de la folie à l'âge classique* (1961, trans. and abr. *Madness and Civilization: a History of Insanity in the Age of Reason*). Foucault returned to France, and in 1969 he was made Professor of the History of Systems of Thought at the Collège de France. Foucault held that post until his death from an AIDS-related illness on 25 June 1984.

Foucault's interest in the history of social features may be traced back to his early explorations of psychiatry and madness. Our equation of 'madness' with 'mental illness', he believes, 'is much more *historical* than is usually believed, and much *younger* too' (*Mental Illness and Psychology*, p. 69). This can be shown, he tells us in *Madness and Civilization*, through an historical analysis of views of madness in Europe from the Middle Ages to the late nineteenth century. Prior to the seventeenth century, madness was viewed as the rejection of the framework of rationality that shapes society's norms. Mad people chose unreason over reason. Though on the margins of society, they were thought to be capable of laying bare people's hopes and follies. This attitude towards madness, Foucault claims, is conveyed in the writings of Erasmus, Shakespeare, Cervantes and Sebastian Brant. With the advent of the 'classical age' (1650–1800), however, madness came to be seen as *deviation* from society's norms. Foucault writes: 'the classical age was to reduce to silence the madness whose voices the Renaissance had just liberated, but whose violence it had already tamed' (*Madness and Civilization*, p. 38). The mad were considered 'ill' and a threat to the rationality and morality of others. Thus they were confined and given the same brutal treatment as paupers and criminals. This attitude, Foucault claims, can be clearly discerned in such things as Descartes's rejection of madness as grounds for doubting his discovery of the self through the 'Cogito argument' ('I am thinking, therefore I exist').

Many people, Foucault argues, believe that the advent of asylums in the nineteenth century ushered in more humane treatment of the mad. By contrast, in his opinion, asylums are more brutal because they are accompanied by the view of the mad as morally responsible for their illness:

> The madman . . . must feel morally responsible for everything within him that may disturb morality and society and must hold no one but himself responsible for the punishment he receives.
>
> (Ibid., p. 246)

With the incorporation of responsibility in madness, '[t]he asylum sets itself the task of the homogenous rule of morality, its rigorous extension to all those who tend to escape from it' (ibid., p. 258). This is achieved not through overt acts of repression but through more subtle forms of control such as continuous surveillance and systems of punishment and reward. In this way they are reduced to silence and are kept prisoner by those who 'do not listen to madness in its own being' (ibid., p. 278).

Seeing social features like madness as Foucault does requires a transformation of historiographical perception. This transformation parallels the transformation in medical perception that Foucault details in *Naissance de la clinique: une archéologie de regard médical* (1963, trans. *The Birth of the Clinic: an Archaeology of Medical Perception*). Prior to the end of the eighteenth century diseases were considered to be different species of entities that had no necessary connection to the human body. The individual patient had no positive role to play in diagnosis; indeed, their symptoms might obscure the true nature of the disease. With the advent of the nineteenth century, disease was recognised to be localised in the human body. Doctors realised that in order to understand the nature of diseases they had to explore the body through autopsy. Typologies of diseases thus gave way to pathological anatomy. The medical gaze became three dimensional, travelling from surface symptoms to hidden tissues (*The Birth of the Clinic*, p. 136). The historian's gaze, Foucault contends, should also be three dimensional. Historians must abandon the surface-level study of the ideas of individuals (*connaissance*) in favour of an analysis of deeper or more fundamental structures of thought (*savoir*). This transformation of historiographical gaze forms the cornerstone of the 'archaeological method' Foucault describes in *Les mots et les choses: une archéologie des sciences humaines* (1966, trans. *The Order of Things: an Archaeology of the Human Sciences*) and *L'Archéologie du savoir* (1969, trans. *The Archaeology of Knowledge*). The 'archaeologist', he suggests, tries to uncover *epistêmês*; sets of 'rules' which are not consciously grasped that shape what can be thought and said (*The Order of Things*, p. xxi).

In *The Order of Things*, Foucault suggests that the archaeological method differs from traditional forms of intellectual history in two important ways. First, it raises questions about our understanding of chronology. Traditional intellectual histories, he claims, explicitly or implicitly regard the present as the culmination of the process of thought sparked by the Enlightenment. Foucault is troubled by the obsession with continuity and progress that emerges from such a view. For him, history is not the tale of continuous development of rational man from the Renaissance to the present. Echoing Gaston Bachelard's writings on 'epistemic breaks', Foucault argues that Western thought is divided into three discrete and discontinuous *epistêmês*.[1] Until the end of the sixteenth century discourse was shaped by the belief that everything in the world was related and that these relations could be discerned in the hidden 'signatures' that God marked on the world. This principle of 'resemblance' was abruptly overthrown by the classical principle of 'representation'. Classical thinkers believed that language could be used to represent accurately the true nature of the social and natural worlds. This belief was in turn replaced at the beginning of the nineteenth century by the idea that people and the discourses they use are finite and context bound (*The Order of Things*, p. 251).

Second, the archaeological method makes it possible for historians to move beyond the idea that people are rational and reflexive beings that have sovereignty over their lives (ibid., p. xiv). For Foucault, people's thoughts are in the main shaped by rules or regularities that they are unaware of. Our notion of reflexive man, he believes, is a social construction that can be dated to the beginning of the nineteenth century. As he writes in an oft-quoted passage:

> As the archaeology of our thought easily shows, man is an invention of recent date. And one perhaps nearing its end. If those arrangements were to disappear as they appeared, if some event of which we can at the moment do no more than sense the possibility . . . were to cause them to crumble, as the ground of classical thought did . . . then one can certainly wager that man would be erased, like a face drawn in sand at the edge of the sea.
>
> (Ibid., p. 387)

In *The Archaeology of Knowledge*, Foucault recasts his concept of the *epistêmê* into that of the *archive*. Like the *epistêmê*, the *archive* is a system of rules or regularities which determines what can and cannot be thought and said at a particular time. The *archive*, however, governs both linguistic *and* material practices ('words and things'), such as the movement of the body (*The Archaeology of Knowledge*, pp. 48–9). Furthermore, the 'rules' that constitute the *archive* are different from those of the *epistêmê*. The *epistêmê* is a set of rules 'whose jurisdiction extends without contingence'. The *archive*, on the other hand, is a set of rules that are themselves historically determined and are therefore subject to change. In shifting his position thus, Foucault takes 'account of the fact that discourse has not only a meaning or truth, but a . . . specific history' (ibid., p. 127).[2]

Importantly, Foucault also notes that what can and cannot be said and done at a particular time is related to issues of power. Discourse, he writes:

> appears as an asset – finite, limited, desirable, useful – that has its own rules of appearance, but also its own conditions of appropriation and operation; an asset that consequently, from the moment of its existence poses the question of power; an asset that is, by nature, the object of a struggle, a political struggle.
>
> (Ibid., p. 120)

The relationship between power and discourse is at the forefront of *L'ordre du discours: leçon inaugurale au Collège de France prononcée le 2 décembre 1970* (1971, trans. 'The Order of Discourse'),[3] 'Nietzsche, Genealogy, History' (1977),[4] and *Surveiller et punir: naissance de la prison* (1975, trans. *Discipline and Punish: the Birth of the Prison*).[5] It is interesting, Foucault notes in 'The Order of Discourse', that despite our potential for the production of meaning, what it is possible for us to think and do at a particular time is actually quite limited. This is because the rules that shape what we think and do are in large part the product of power relations in society.[6] This idea leads Foucault to a historical method that is different from 'archaeology'. It is both critical and, echoing Nietzsche, 'genealogical'. The aim of the 'genealogist' is to illuminate a society's 'will to truth': repressive and permissive procedures that determine how knowledge is applied, distributed, valued and rejected. History tells of a constant struggle between different powers which try to impose their own 'will to truth':

Humanity does not gradually progress from combat to combat until it arrives at universal reciprocity, where the rule of law finally replaces warfare; humanity installs each of its violences in a system of rules and thus proceeds from domination to domination.

('Nietzsche, Genealogy, History', in *The Foucault Reader*, p. 85)

At the centre of this struggle for domination is the human body. This idea underpins *Discipline and Punish*. In this, Foucault explores in gory detail the shift from a system of justice characterised by public executions to one characterised by incarceration. This shift, Foucault tells us, has generally been attributed to the advent of the Enlightenment, when claims for more humane punishments prevailed. He believes, however, that the shift can be explained in terms of a search for more efficient and (economically and politically) less costly forms of social control (*Discipline and Punish*, p. 78). These reforms herald a new way of organising social relations: 'disciplinary power'. Disciplinary power, Foucault tells us, seeks 'docile bodies': human bodies organised and disciplined in such a way that they provide a submissive, productive and trained source of labour power (ibid., pp. 25–6, 220–1). The production of 'docile bodies' is ensured in prisons and prison-like institutions such as schools, hospitals and factories through such strategies as the designation of individuals to particular places, detailed scheduling of activities and the installation of intense forms of surveillance. These strategies culminate in Jeremy Bentham's Panopticon, a circular building in which cells are arranged around a central observation tower (ibid., pp. 169–70). Our society, Foucault claims, is riddled with the marks of 'panopticism'. 'Panopticism' embraces the ideas of permanent surveillance and control through normalisation. People's activities are scrutinised and regulated in such a way as to ensure that they are subject to covert and overt standards and values associated with 'normality'.

That power can be a normalising rather than a repressive force shows Foucault that it can be a positive as well as a negative. Foucault explores the positive aspects of power in more detail in the first volume of his *Histoire de la sexualité: la volonté de savoir* (1976, trans. *The History of Sexuality: an Introduction*). In this, he looks at the emergence of modern understandings of sexuality in the nineteenth century. For him, the Victorian era marks the culmination of an obsessive interest, beginning in the eighteenth century, with sex as a social and political problem (ibid., p. 18). This interest took the form principally of medical and psychiatric discourses on female fecundity, infantile sexuality, 'deviant' sexualities and sex crimes. The chief aim of such discourse was to identify and exclude forms of sexuality that 'were not amenable to the strict economy of reproduction' (ibid., p. 36). Sexuality came to be seen as the key to understanding the individual. Both society and individuals demanded that sex 'tell us our truth' through religious and secular forms of confession (ibid., pp. 61–2, 69, 129–30). Such an obsession with disclosure, which remains with us, does not lead to self-knowledge. Rather, Foucault suggests, it further entangles us in a web of disciplinary power relations:

> The obligation to confess is now relayed through so many different points, is so deeply engrained in us, that we no longer perceive it as the effect of a power that constrains us; on the contrary, it seems to us that truth, lodged in our most secret nature, demands only to surface.
>
> (Ibid., p. 60)

Control in society is thus achieved through direct repression by others and our own desire for 'normality'.

Foucault's suggestion that individuals are entangled in an invisible web of power relations seems bleak. In the second and third volumes of *The History of Sexuality* (*L'usage des plaisirs*, 1984, trans. *The Use of Pleasure* and *Le Souci de soi*, 1984, trans. *The Care of the Self*) and the essay 'What is Enlightenment?' (in *The Foucault Reader*, pp. 32–50), however, he balances his picture with an account of how individuals can resist normalising forces. Central to an individual's 'ethics' – their 'real behaviour' in response to the rules and values pressed on them – is an attitude of critical self-awareness similar to that described in Kant's essay 'What is Enlightenment?' Foucault wants no part of Kant's linking of moral codes to a notion of universally valid rationality. He believes that there are multiple and historically specific forms of rationality. But he does want us to interrogate what seems to be natural in our identity and our world ('What is Enlightenment?', pp. 49–50). And, as Foucault's various works show us, history can play an important part in that interrogation.

Foucault has opened up new perspectives on clinical medicine, madness, punishment and sexuality, and shown us that many of our 'enlightened practices' restrict the freedom of individuals. That we have unmasked such social features as changing rather than immutable may be his most important legacy. He invites us to lay bare the chains that bind us. But for all the promise of his work, it is plagued by problems. Foucault's use of evidence is selective, and it often seems as if he has forced his interpretation on his materials. He also tends to favour the idea that an argument can be made convincing if it is delivered forcefully. Critics have responded to his work with a raft of questions concerning such issues as whether there was a 'dialogue' between reason and unreason in the Middle Ages and Renaissance; whether Enlightenment rationality is firmly connected to the desire for social control; whether a history of madness can be written within the language of reason and order; whether changes in *epistêmês* are always sudden and complete; whether power relations can be differentiated with regard to gender; and whether power relations in prisons are the same as those in other institutions.

Notes

1 G. Gutting, *Michel Foucault's Archaeology of Scientific Reason*, Cambridge: Cambridge University Press, 1989, pp. 9–32.
2 For an account of Foucault's relationship with structuralism and post-structuralism, see Foucault (CT).
3 'The Order of Discourse', in R. Young, trans. and ed., *Untying the Text: a Poststructuralist Reader*, London: Routledge, 1981, pp. 55–68.
4 'Nietzsche, Genealogy, History', in P. Rabinow (ed.), *The Foucault Reader*, Harmondsworth: Penguin, 1984, pp. 76–100.
5 See also *Power/Knowledge: Selected Interviews and Other Writings, 1972–77*, C. Gordon (ed.), Brighton: Harvester, 1980.
6 'The Order of Discourse', in Young (ed.), *Untying the Text*, pp. 55–68.

Foucault's major works

Madness and Civilization: a History of Insanity in the Age of Reason, trans. and abr. R. Howard, London: Tavistock, 1965.

The Order of Things: an Archaeology of the Human Sciences, trans. anon., London: Tavistock, 1970.

The Archaeology of Knowledge, trans. A. M. Sheridan-Smith, London: Tavistock, 1972.

The Birth of the Clinic: an Archaeology of Medical Perception, trans. A. M. Sheridan-Smith, London: Tavistock, 1973.

Mental Illness and Psychology, trans. A. M. Sheridan-Smith, New York: Harper & Row, 1976.

Discipline and Punish: the Birth of the Prison, trans. A. M. Sheridan-Smith, Harmondsworth: Penguin, 1977.

Language, Counter-memory, Practice: Selected Interviews and Essays, ed. and trans. D. F. Bouchard, Ithaca, NY: Cornell University Press, 1977.

The History of Sexuality, 3 vols, *An Introduction, The Use of Pleasure* and *The Care of the Self*, trans. R. Hurley and R. McDougall, Harmondsworth: Penguin, 1978–86.

Power/Knowledge: Selected Interviews and Other Writings, 1972–77, ed. and trans. C. Gordon, Brighton: Harvester Press, 1980.

The Foucault Reader, ed. P. Rabinow, Harmondsworth: Penguin, 1984.
Politics, Philosophy, Culture: Interviews and Other Writings, 1977–84, ed. and trans. L. Kritzman, London: Routledge, 1988.
Foucault Live: Interviews 1966–84, ed. S. Lotringer, trans. J. Johnston, New York: Semiotext(e), 1989.

See also

Bachelard (CT), Braudel, Derrida (CT), Descartes (MP), Foucault (CT), Kant, Nietzsche (MP and CT), Scott.

Further resources

Bernauer, J. and Rasmussen, D. (eds), *The Final Foucault*, Cambridge, MA: MIT Press, 1988.
Burke, P. (ed.), *Critical Essays on Michel Foucault*, Cambridge: Scolar Press, 1992.
Clark, M., *Michel Foucault: an Annotated Bibliography: Tool Kit for a New Age*, New York: Garland, 1983.
Derrida, J., 'Cogito and the History of Madness', in *Writing and Difference*, London: Routledge & Kegan Paul, 1978, pp. 31–63.
Diamond, I. and Quinby, L. (eds), *Feminism and Foucault: Reflections on Resistance*, Boston, MA: Northwestern University Press, 1988.
Dreyfus, H. and Rabinow, P., *Michel Foucault: Beyond Structuralism and Hermeneutics*, Chicago, IL: Chicago University Press, 1982.
Goldstein, J. (ed.), *Foucault and the Writing of History*, Oxford: Basil Blackwell, 1994.
Gutting, G., *Michel Foucault's Archaeology of Scientific Reason*, Cambridge: Cambridge University Press, 1989.
——, (ed.), *The Cambridge Companion to Foucault*, Cambridge: Cambridge University Press, 1994.
Huppert, G., 'Divinatio et Eruditio: Thoughts on Foucault', *History and Theory*, 1974, 13(3): 191–207.
Leland, D., 'On Reading and Writing the World: Foucault's History of Thought', *Clio*, 1975, 4(2): 225–43.
McNay, L., *Foucault: a Critical Introduction*, Cambridge: Polity Press, 1994.
Midelfort, H. C. E., 'Madness and Civilization in Early Modern Europe: a Reappraisal of Michel Foucault', in B. Malament (ed.), *After the Reformation: Essays in Honor of J. H. Hexter*, Philadelphia, PA: University of Philadelphia Press, 1980, pp. 247–65.
O'Brien, P., 'Crime and Punishment as Historical Problems', *Journal of Social History*, 1978, 11(4): 508–20.
O'Farrell, C., *Foucault: Historian or Philosopher?* London: Macmillan, 1989.
Roth, M. S., 'Foucault's "History of the Present"', *History and Theory*, 1981, 20(1): 32–46.
Rousseau, G. S., 'Whose Enlightenment? Not Man's: the Case of Michel Foucault', *Eighteenth Century Studies*, 1972, 6(2): 238–56.
Still, A. and Velody, I., *Rewriting the History of Madness: Studies in Foucault's 'Histoire de la folie'*, London: Routledge, 1992.
Stone, L., 'Madness', *New York Review of Books*, 16 December 1982, 29(20): 28–36.

White, H., *The Tropics of Discourse: Essays in Cultural Criticism*, Baltimore, MD: Johns Hopkins University Press, 1973.

Wilson, T. H., 'Foucault, Genealogy, History', *Philosophy Today*, 1995, 39(2): 157–70.

JEAN FROISSART *c.* 1337–*c.* 1410

Jean Froissart, French poet, romance writer[1] and historian of chivalry, was born around 1337. He received a clerical education and probably entered the service of the counts of Hainaut at an early age. In 1361 he travelled to England and secured the patronage of Queen Philippa. While in her service, he travelled to Scotland (1365), Gascony (1366–67) and Milan (1368). After Philippa's death (1369), he went to the Netherlands. He took holy orders and in 1373 was given a parish in Les Estinnes (near Mons). In 1384 he became a canon at Chimay. Froissart began writing the work for which he is best known – *Les chroniques de France, d'Angleterre, et des païs voisins* (trans. *Froissart, Chronicles*, hereafter *Chroniques*) – around 1356, and continued revising it until shortly before his death, which is traditionally fixed at about 1410.

Froissart is credited with about 200 poems, most of which celebrate courtly love. 'Courtly love' refers to a paradoxical view of love that emerged in the courts of southern France at the end of the eleventh century. It is love that is both 'illicit and morally elevating, passionate and self-disciplined, humiliating and exalting, human and transcendent'.[2] The longest and the best-known of Froissart's poems is *Méliador*, in which a highly idealised Arthurian knight, Méliador, wins Hermondine, daughter of the king of Scotland, and the Scottish kingdom. As a young writer, Froissart also apparently tried his hand at capturing the chivalrous deeds of his contemporaries in verse. In the *Chroniques*, Froissart tells us that when he travelled to London, he presented to Queen Philippa an account of 'wars and adventure' from the Battle of Poitiers (1356) to around 1359.[3] This work, however, which is now lost, seems to have been his only chronicle in verse. It seems that, like other contemporary writers, he realised that historical works were more likely to be privately read than publicly performed, so there was no longer any need for the memory and performance devices of poems such as repetition or formulaic expressions.

Froissart's *Chroniques* is a history of the deeds of many Western European nobles – especially those engaged in the Hundred Years War between England and France – from the period just prior to the accession of Edward III (1325) to around the death of Richard II (1400). It is divided into four books. Book 1, of which at least five different versions survive, describes events up to 1350–78 (termination dates vary from version to version). For the period up to the mid-1360s, Froissart relied heavily on the works of two historians: the *Les Vrayes Chroniques* of Jean le Bel and the *Vie du Prince Noir* of Chandos Herald (for example, 1: 37–8).[4] As both of these works survive, historians have been able to study how Froissart made use of them.[5] After the mid-1360s, Froissart shaped his *Chroniques* out of his own observations, interviews and some documents. Book 2 was initially a separate work, *Chronique de Flandre*. It describes the Flemish troubles of 1378–87. Book 3 narrates the period 1386–88, including Charles VI's attempts to invade England, and book 4 the downfall of Richard II and the accession of Henry IV (1389–1400).

Clues to Froissart's methods of collecting information may be found scattered throughout the *Chroniques*. For Froissart, the preliminary task of documentation consisted of voyages for information throughout Western Europe, recollections of earlier visits to places like England and Scotland, interviews, writing up notes and collecting texts and documents. When travelling, he tried to write down what he had heard and seen as soon as he could. Sometimes he was able to dictate interviews; on other occasions he had to rely on his memory until he reached lodgings. How he later used such information to compose the *Chroniques* is harder to assess. Once he had collected information on a period or event, he may have sketched a chronological framework. After that, he may have dictated to scribes the version of the text that we have preserved in manuscripts. On occasion, he may have given his scribes general instructions and left them with the task of filling out the text. It is also possible that he may have written down parts of the final version of the text himself. It is clear, however, that he had plenty of opportunity to summarise, edit, synthesise and recast the evidence he collected. It cannot be said, therefore, that Froissart is merely a cipher for fourteenth-century nobility, as some have charged.[6]

Froissart thought of his work more as a 'history' than a 'chronicle' or 'annal' because he offered more than a bald chronological outline. In his view, the historian tries to provide a comprehensive, detailed and impartial account of events. For example, he tells us that he interviewed parties on both sides of the Hundred Years War and their respective allies. But he also tries to describe events in such a way that the moral truth he finds will be evident to the reader. History thus serves ethics.[7] In the prologue to book 1, for instance, he tells us that

In order that the honourable enterprises, noble adventures and deeds of arms which took place during the wars waged by France and England should be fittingly related and preserved for posterity, so that brave men should be inspired thereby to follow such examples, I wish to place on record these matters of great renown.

(1: 37)

Primarily, Froissart is interested in preserving the memory of those knights whose deeds expressed *Proece* or chivalrous valour; indeed it has been suggested that his work is the literary equivalent of funerary monuments.[8] Froissart believed that his words would provide a means of moral instruction, a sentiment that belongs to a tradition that can be traced back to the writings of ancient historians such as Tacitus and Livy. For Froissart, as for other fourteenth-century writers, *Proece* is characterised by the virtues of military prowess, honour, loyalty, fidelity and courtesy.[9] But Froissart also believes that the chivalrous seize opportunities, hence his interest in knights of modest lineage who performed great deeds. He is also concerned about the fragility of the ideals of *Proece* and of good government. For Froissart, 'good government' requires the maintenance of public order and social distinctions.[10] Consequently, the vices given most attention in the *Chroniques* are those of acquisitiveness, tyranny and factiousness. Froissart also warns his readers that knights are vulnerable to attack at the hands of the masses. Froissart shows little sympathy towards the poor. Events that must have loomed large in their world, such as the 'Black Death' of 1348–49, barely rate a mention and he scarcely disguises his disgust when writing of revolts (for instance, 1: 111–12, 151–5; 2: 211–30). Even when he examines cases of aristocratic oppression or violence against the masses, he is interested not so much in telling the story of the victims as he is in underscoring the lack of discipline on the part of the noble (for example, Charles VI's exploitation of the people of Flanders to pay for his projected invasion of England in 1386, 3: 303–8). The poor are no more than an out-of-focus backdrop. Froissart also criticises the clergy whenever they are seen by him as contributing to social disorder. On the other hand, however, he is not slow to praise saintly figures and warrior bishops (such as the Bishop of Norwich, 1: 91–2).

Ethics, however, is not the sole ingredient of the *Chroniques*. Froissart also delights in interesting stories, and brings all of his powers as a writer to bear in conveying their colour to the reader. His account of Richard II's loss of power, for instance, is every bit as engaging as Shakespeare's play on the same topic (4: 421–71).[11] As a number of writers have noted, the *Voyage en Béarn* sequence in book 3 (3: 263–94) marks a turning point in Froissart's awareness of his writing skills. Diverres writes that, at that point,

> Froissart expresses literary preoccupations: to record what he has learnt in 'fine language'. He is concerned with writing in an attractive manner, and . . . in order to do so he is prepared to take liberties with his material. While continuing to respect the facts which he has received he embroiders upon them and abandons to a certain extent the annalistic approach. Digression is more common, and so are the author's reminiscences, many of which have little to do with the main subject and would, at one time, have been considered by him unworthy of inclusion.[12]

That there are no fewer that five versions of book 1 – three of which differ substantially from one another – has both delighted and troubled Froissart scholars. No other part of his writings has stimulated such a lively discussion on his views of history and methods of composition.[13] As Ainsworth has argued,

> The historical tapestry that Froissart weaves is more than fascinating, and is sometimes even reliable as a record, but ultimately it is the weaving of the fabric itself, and the quality of the workmanship, that arrests one's attention – and this has been true for a good six hundred years.[14]

Traditionally, the order of composition has been thought to be:

1 first edition ('A' manuscript);
2 revised first edition ('B' manuscript);
3 second edition ('Amiens' manuscript);
4 epitome ('B6' manuscript); and
5 third edition ('Rome' manuscript).

As Palmer has pointed out, calling each of these manuscripts an 'edition' of book 1 would be misleading, for the extent of Froissart's revisions vary greatly. The B6 manuscript, for instance, is thought to be of minor interest because it is about one-sixth of the length of the A manuscript and lacks a great many of its analytical passages. Nor are the changes from the A manuscript to the B manuscript radical; they differ in detail rather than interpretation. The line of development from the A manuscript through Amiens to Rome, however, has been subject to much study. Studying this series of radical revisions, many scholars believe, will enable us to lay bare Froissart's development as an historian in a way that is not possible for most other medieval writers. The Rome manuscript differs considerably from the A manuscript in both detail and interpretation. It appears to be a later manuscript, as Froissart acknowledges that society is no longer as straightforward in terms of its composition and ideals as he suggested in the A and B manuscripts. He is no longer sure that society will see the realisation of *Proece*.[15] The Rome manuscript, however, only deals with the period in which Froissart relied heavily on le Bel (1325–50), so a thorough comparison is not possible. The only other version of book 1 which deals with the period 1325–78 and differs in detail and interpretation from the A and B manuscripts is the Amiens manuscript. However this is the only version of book 1 whose place in the order of composition is uncertain. From the nineteenth century onwards, there has been intense debate on whether A or Amiens claim precedence.[16] As Palmer shows, however, there is plenty of evidence to support *both* claims. This leads him to the conclusion that

> The Amiens [manuscript] is neither first nor second edition but both simultaneously. It also follows, of course, that the A and B [manuscripts] are also both first and second editions simultaneously. And it naturally follows from these two conclusions that there is no first or second edition of Book one at all in any meaningful sense of those terms, only a large number of [manuscripts] which combine elements of the two editions in different manners and different proportions.[17]

Palmer's point is that the various versions of book 1 were not written one after the other; some may have been written at the same time.

One way to counter this conclusion is to question whether the Amiens manuscript is the work of Froissart at all. It is possible that Froissart's scribes – and later copyists – may have played an important role in the development or 'mobility' of book 1.[18] There are three reasons to suspect their involvement. First, the Amiens and Rome manuscripts have very little in common. The author of the Rome manuscript never copied from the Amiens manuscript, as he did from the A and B manuscripts. Second, many of the details in the Rome manuscript are contradicted in the Amiens manuscript. Third, the Amiens manuscript shows evidence of French bias. On the other hand, it has long been acknowledged that Froissart often presents his readers with conflicting versions of the same events. For instance, in book 3 he describes Castilian and Portuguese views of the battle of Aljubarrota (1385) and makes no attempt to reconcile them.[19] Examples like these suggest that Amiens may be the work of Froissart after all. Palmer acknowledges that conclusion, but admits that he is troubled by it:

> We are forced to conclude that he did not see his revisions as superseding his earlier efforts but simply as an alternative – and equally valid – version of events. Such an attitude must appear to us as methodologically deplorable and fundamentally unhistorical. It suggests that we have a very long way to go indeed before we can penetrate and comprehend the mind of even the most fully documented of medieval historians.[20]

For some, this finding may cast doubt on Froissart's long-standing reputation as a priceless source for fourteenth-century history.[21] Historians of a more postmodern persuasion, however, might be delighted by it.

Notes

1 In this context, 'romance' refers to a medieval tale embodying the adventures of a hero of chivalry.

2 F. X. Newman (ed.), *The Meaning of Courtly Love*, Albany, NY: State University of New York Press, 1968, p. vii.

3 See N. R. Cartier, 'The Lost Chronicle', *Speculum*, 1961, 36(3): 424–34.

4 Citations refer to the book and page number of Brereton's translation of the *Chroniques*.

5 See, for example, J. J. N. Palmer, 'Book 1 (1325–78) and its Sources' in id. (ed.), *Froissart: Historian*, Totowa, NJ: Rowman & Littlefield, 1981, pp. 7–24.

6 G. T. Diller, 'Froissart: Patrons and Texts', in Palmer (ed.), *Froissart: Historian*, pp. 145–60; and P. F. Ainsworth, *Jean Froissart and the Fabric of History: Truth, Myth, and Fiction in the Chroniques*, Oxford: Oxford University Press, 1990, pp. 145–9.

7 J. Coleman, 'Late Scholastic Memoria et Reminiscentia: its Uses and Abuses' in P. Boitani and A. Torti (eds), *Intellectuals and Writers in Fourteenth Century Europe*, Cambridge: Cambridge University Press, 1986, p. 43.

8 Ainsworth, *Jean Froissart and the Fabric of History*, p. 70.

9 S. Painter, *French Chivalry: Chivalric Ideas and Practices in Medieval France*, Baltimore, MD: Johns Hopkins University Press, 1940, pp. 29–43.

10 J. van Herwaarden, 'The War in the Low Countries', in Palmer (ed.), *Froissart: Historian*, pp. 115–16.

11 See also Froissart's treatment of the brigand Mérigot Marchès, as described in Ainsworth, *Jean Froissart and the Fabric of History*, pp. 125–39.

12 J. Froissart, *Voyage en Béarn*, ed. A. H. Diverres, Manchester: Manchester University Press, 1953, pp. xx–xxi.
13 Palmer, 'Book I (1325–78) and its Sources'; Diller, 'Froissart: Patrons and Texts'; Ainsworth, *Jean Froissart and the Fabric of History*, pp. 217–302; and F. S. Shears, *Froissart, Chronicler and Poet*, London: G. Routledge & Sons, 1930, p. 82.
14 Ainsworth, *Jean Froissart and the Fabric of History*, p. 308.
15 Ibid., pp. 217–302.
16 J. Froissart, *Chroniques*, eds S. Luce, G. Raynaud, L. and A. Mirot, vol. 1, vi ff.; id. *Oeuvres*, ed. K. de Lettenhove, Académie Royale de Belgique, vol. 1, introduction; P. Saenger, 'A Lost Manuscript of Froissart Refound: Newberry Library Manuscript f37', *Manuscripta*, 1975, 19(1): 15–26; R. Barber, 'Jean Froissart and Edward the Black Prince', in Palmer (ed.), *Froissart*, pp. 25–35; and G. T. Diller, *Attitudes chevaleresques et réalités politiques chez Froissart*, Geneva, 1984.
17 Palmer, 'Book 1 (1325–78) and its Sources', p. 18; see also Ainsworth, *Jean Froissart and the Fabric of History*, p. 224.
18 G. T. Diller, 'Froissart: Patrons and Texts', p. 152.
19 P. E. Russell, 'The War in Spain and Portugal', in Palmer (ed.), *Froissart: Historian*, pp. 84–6; see also the discussion on Froissart's account of Edward III's invasion of Normandy in 1346 in Palmer, 'Book 1 (1325–78) and its Sources', p. 23.
20 Palmer, 'Book 1 (1325–78) and its Sources', p. 24.
21 On the history of the reception of Froissart's *Chroniques*, see J. J. N. Palmer, 'Introduction', in id. (ed.), *Froissart: Historian*, pp. 1–6.

Froissart's major works

Chroniques de Jean Froissart, eds S. Luce, G. Raynaud, L. and A. Mirot, 15 vols, Paris: Société de l'Histoire de France, 1869–1975.
Froissart, Chronicles, trans. and abr. G. Brereton, Harmondsworth: Penguin, 1968.
Méliador, ed. A. Longnon, 3 vols, Paris: Société des Anciens Textes Français, 1895–99.

See also

Bede, Gregory of Tours, Ibn Khaldun, Livy, Ssu-ma Ch'ien, Tacitus.

Further resources

Ainsworth, P. F., *Jean Froissart and the Fabric of History: Truth, Myth, and Fiction in the Chroniques*, Oxford: Oxford University Press, 1990.
Archambault, P., *Seven French Chroniclers: Witness to History*, Syracuse, NY: University of Syracuse Press, 1974.
Calin, W., 'Narrative Technique in Fourteenth-century France: Froissart and his *Chroniques*', in R. T. Pickens (ed.), *Studies in Honor of Hans-Erich Keller: Medieval French and Occitan Literature and Romance Linguistics*, Kalamazoo, MI: Medieval Institute Press, 1993, pp. 227–36.

De Looze, L., *Pseudo-Autobiography in the Fourteenth Century: Jean Ruiz, Guillaume de Machaut, Jean Froissart and Geoffrey Chaucer*, Miami, FL: University Press of Florida, 1997.

Dembowski, P. F., *Jean Froissart and his Méliador: Context, Craft and Sense*, Edward C. Armstrong Monographs on Medieval Literature no. 2, Lexington, KY: French Forum, 1983.

Diller, G., 'Froissart, Historiography, the University Curriculum and Isabeau of Bavière', *Romance Quarterly*, 1994, 41(3): 148–55.

Palmer, J. J. N., *Froissart: Historian*, Totowa, NJ: Rowman & Littlefield, 1981.

Schmolke-Hasselmann, B., *The Evolution of Arthurian Romance: the Verse Tradition from Chrétien to Froissart*, Studies in Medieval Literature no. 35, Cambridge: Cambridge University Press, 1998.

Shears, F. C., *Froissart: Chronicler and Poet*, London: G. Routledge & Sons, 1930.

FRANCIS FUKUYAMA 1952–

Francis Fukuyama, author of 'The End of History' (1989) and *The End of History and the Last Man* (1992), is unpopular among historians. Some, who are not well acquainted with his writings, dismiss the idea that history has come to an end as ludicrous. They look around and see no shortage of events for future historians to write about. Others, who are more familiar, understand that by 'History' he means a universal history of human society; however, they might still be lukewarm as to whether such a single narrative exists.

Fukuyama was born on 27 October 1952 in Chicago. After studying classics at Cornell University (1974), he completed a doctorate at Harvard University with a thesis on Soviet foreign policy in the Middle East (1981). During the 1980s, Fukuyama worked in policy planning for the US State Department and as a social science consultant for the Rand Corporation, a conservative think-tank devoted to foreign policy and defence issues. After the publication of 'The End of History', he worked full-time for the Rand Corporation. Between 1994 and 1996 he was a fellow in foreign policy at Johns Hopkins University. Currently he is Hirst Professor of Public Policy at George Mason University, Virginia.

People have long searched for a meaningful pattern in the course of human events. Fukuyama, however, is interested in 'serious' 'Universal Histories', beginning with Immanuel Kant's essay 'An Idea for a Universal History from a Cosmopolitan Point of View' (1784) (*End of History and the Last Man*, p. 57). In this, Kant notes that at first glance, historical developments can appear chaotic. On closer inspection, however, he believes that progress is being made towards the realisation of a 'perfect civil constitution': a state in which the fundamental human right to maximum freedom is balanced with the rights of others. The mechanism that makes such progress possible is 'antagonism' or the 'unsocial sociability of men'. People like to associate with others, but they also like to isolate themselves because they want to have everything go according to their wishes.[1] Historians should document human progress towards a civil constitution, Kant believes, in order to make people aware of the goal that they are working towards. If they are aware of that goal, then they might work harder to realise it. The task of writing such a 'Universal History', Fukuyama reminds us, was adopted by the nineteenth-century German philosopher Hegel. Hegel looked to the early and modern civilisations of Europe and Asia to support his contention that '[t]he history of the world is none other than the progress of the consciousness of freedom'.[2] For Hegel, freedom will be fully realised in a world in which individuals govern themselves according to their own conscience and convictions and all social and political institutions are organised rationally. Hegel believed that the mechanism for that progress was 'the cunning of reason': conflict brought about by the interplay of unconscious desires. Both Hegel and Kant believed that 'History' would end when people had achieved freedom or a civil constitution.

One of Hegel's best-known and most provocative interpreters, Alexandre Kojève, argued in a series of lectures in the 1930s that Hegel had been right to say that 'History' had ended in 1806.[3] For at that time Hegel saw in Napoleon's defeat of the Prussian monarchy at Jena the realisation of the principles of liberty and equality. Although there had been much conflict since 1806, the basic principles of liberty and equality could not be improved upon. Those principles were fully realised, Kojève believed, in capitalist societies that had achieved material abundance and political stability.

Like 'Hegel-Kojève' (Hegel as interpreted by Kojève), Fukuyama also believes that we have reached the end of a 'History of Mankind'. Looking back at the last quarter of the twentieth century he sees the emergence of liberal democracy as the only universal and coherent political aspiration (ibid., p. xiii). Fukuyama understands 'liberal' and 'democracy' to be 'a rule of law that recognises certain individual rights or freedoms from government control' and 'the right of all citizens to vote and participate in politics', respectively (ibid., pp. 42, 43). So why has liberal democracy emerged as the only apparently viable political aspiration? Fukuyama believes that the move towards liberal democracy was made possible by two 'mechanisms'. First, there is the 'mechanism of desire' (ibid., pp. 177, 189, 204). The almost constant threat of war encourages societies to develop, produce and deploy technology effectively. Furthermore, technological development makes possible the accumulation of wealth and the satisfaction of an ever-growing list of human desires. The desire for greater security and wealth encourages people to work for national unity, a strong centralised state authority, greater educational provision and an awareness of developments in other places. All of these developments lead towards a global economy dominated by large-scale multinational institutions and a universal consumer culture (ibid., pp. 73–81). While this economic 'mechanism of desire' accounts for many historical developments, it does not explain the emergence of liberal democracy. One can, as Fukuyama does, think of places such as Meiji Japan and present-day Singapore where technologically advanced capitalism has and does still coexist with political authoritarianism. Economic interpretations of History, such as that provided by Marx, are incomplete because humans are more than economic animals. In light of this, Fukuyama suggests that there is a second mechanism at work: the 'mechanism of recognition' (ibid., pp. 144, 174–80, 189, 198, 204).

The first systematic account of man's desire for recognition, Fukuyama claims, can be found in Plato's *Republic*. In book four of that work, Socrates suggests that the soul is driven by three things: desire, reason and *thymos*. Fukuyama translates *thymos* as 'spiritedness'.[4] Desire and reason shape many human actions. But people also seek a 'spirited' recognition of their own worth, or the people, things or principles that they value (ibid., p. xvii). The individual's desire for recognition is, Fukuyama points out, at the heart of Hegel-Kojève's 'History'. We tend to think that mutual recognition can be achieved peacefully. Hegel tells us in his *Phenomenology of Mind*, however, that we seek recognition that is not dependent on material objects such as our own body and the bodies of others. The way to achieve recognition and to prove that one is not attached to material objects is to engage in a life-and-death struggle with another person. That is, in risking one's life to kill another person, an individual shows that they are not attached to either their body or that of the other person. Killing the other person, however, destroys the source of recognition that the individual needs to confirm their own worth as a person. The individual thus spares the other person's life and becomes their master. Initially it seems that the master is in a better position than their slave. The master has the recognition of the slave, but because they consider the slave to be a mere thing, their demand for recognition is not satisfied. Meanwhile, the slave learns through work to value their own efforts (ibid., 143–61).

The internal 'contradiction' of the master–slave relationship was overcome, Fukuyama suggests, as a result of the French and American revolutions. These revolutions gave rise to liberal democratic states in which every person recognises the worth and dignity of other persons, and is recognised in turn by the state through the granting of rights (ibid., pp. 200–8). Thus liberal democracy substitutes the desire to be recognised as greater than others (what Fukuyama calls *megalothymia*) with a desire to be recognised as equal (*isothymia*). When all people become conscious of their common humanity, and are satisfied with the understanding of human worth promoted in liberal democracy, then 'History' is at an end. Thus the mechanism of recognition accounts for the developments left unexplained by the technological mechanism. If people wanted material wealth alone, Fukuyama suggests, then they

> would be content to live in market-oriented authoritarian states like Franco's Spain, or a South Korea or Brazil under military rule. But they also have a thymotic pride in their own self-worth, and this leads them to demand democratic governments that treat them like adults rather than children, recognising their autonomy as free individuals.
>
> (Ibid., pp. xviii–xix)

Even if it is granted that we have reached the 'end of History', the question still remains whether liberal democracy adequately satisfies people's desire for recognition. The possibility that it does not, Fukuyama points out, has been raised by critics both on the Left and the Right. Critics from the Left argue that the economic inequality fostered by capitalism implies unequal recognition (ibid., pp. 289–99). Critics from the Right, on the other hand, suggest that liberal democracy is flawed because the goal of equal recognition is itself flawed. For writers like Nietzsche, for instance, liberal democracy represents not the synthesis of the master and slave but the victory of the slave. As such, it is likely to lead to the rise of the 'last man':

> And thus spoke Zarathustra to the people: 'The time has come for man to set himself a goal. The time has come for man to plant the seed of his highest hope. His soil is still rich enough. But one day this soil will be poor and domesticated, and no tall tree will be able to grow in it. Alas, the time is coming when man will no longer shoot the arrow of his longing beyond man, and the string of his bow will have forgotten how to whir! I say unto you: one must still have chaos in oneself to be able to give birth to a dancing star. I say unto you: you still have

111

chaos in yourselves. Alas, the time is coming when man will no longer give birth to a star. Alas, the time of the most despicable man is coming, he that is no longer able to despise himself. Behold, I show you the *last man*.'[5]

The last man gives up belief in his superior worth in favour of self-preservation. He seeks comfort, security, and the fulfilment of petty desires. He consumes rather than creates. He feels no shame at being unable to rise above his desires. As Nietzsche writes, 'No shepherd and one herd! Everybody wants the same, everybody is the same: whoever feels different goes voluntarily into a madhouse.'[6] Freedom, creativity and excellence, Nietzsche argues, can only arise out of the desire to be recognised as better than others. Man seeks struggle, chaos and sacrifice in order to prove that he is more than a mass animal.

Fukuyama, like many other modern writers, shares Nietzsche's concern about the 'last man'. He does not go so far, however, as to accept Nietzsche's call for a new morality that favours the strong over the weak. Rather, he believes that liberal democracies can stay healthy and stable by offering their citizens a number of outlets for *megalothymia*. They can, for instance, encourage individual and group participation in experimental economic ventures, scientific and technological research, politics, sports and 'perfectly contentless' formal arts (ibid., pp. 313–21). Thus a healthy society balances *isothymia* with *megalothymia*.

Given the way that events have unfolded and continue to unfold, Fukuyama believes that it makes sense to speak of a 'Universal History' leading to liberal democracy. Mankind, he concludes, is like a long wagon train pulling into town:

> enough wagons would pull into town such that any reasonable person looking at the situation would be forced to agree that there had been only one journey and one destination. It is doubtful that we are at that point now, for despite the recent worldwide liberal revolution, the evidence available to us now concerning the direction of the wagons' wanderings must remain provisionally inconclusive. Nor can we in the final analysis know, provided a majority of the wagons eventually reach the same town, whether their occupants, having looked around a bit at their new surroundings, will not find them inadequate and set their eyes on a new and more distant journey.
>
> (Ibid., pp. 338–9)

In the last part of this excerpt, Fukuyama seems to be hedging his bets about whether history has really ended; as in all good Hollywood movies, he wants to leave open the possibility of a sequel.

Fukuyama's claims about the 'end of History' raise more questions than they answer. To begin with, numerous writers have taken issue with his interpretation of Plato, Kant, Hegel, Kojève and Nietzsche. Mark Tunick, for instance, has pointed out that Hegel was much more ambivalent about the liberal state than Fukuyama suggests.[7] Furthermore, a number of writers have argued that Fukuyama does not present enough empirical evidence to support his claim that there is such a thing as 'History', let alone that we are at the end of it. Fukuyama's definition of 'liberal democracy' is so broad as to be practically devoid of substance. His list of 'liberal democracies' around the world masks some pretty fundamental differences between states. Can we say, for instance, that the United Kingdom and the United States are part of the same story, let alone Brazil and the United States? Nor does he adequately account for the recent rise of tribalism, nationalism and Islamic fundamentalism. In addition, critics have questioned the universality of Fukuyama's claims. Some, for example, argue that Fukuyama's 'universal History' entails a privileging of Western economic and political history. What grounds can we offer (if any) to justify the claim that liberal democracy is 'satisfying' or that we *all* seek recognition? For these reasons, a number of critics have concluded that Fukuyama has not offered us the last word in history.

Notes

1 'An Idea for a Universal History from a Cosmopolitan Point of View', in I. Kant, *On History*, (ed.) L. W. Beck, Indianapolis, IN: Bobbs-Merrill, 1963, pp. 11–26.

2 G. W. F. Hegel, *Philosophy of History*, trans. J. Sibree, Buffalo, NY: Prometheus, 1991, p. 19.

3 A. Kojève, *Introduction to the Reading of Hegel*, trans. J. Nichols, New York: Basic Books, 1969.

4 Plato, *The Republic*, trans. D. Lee, Harmondsworth: Penguin, 1974, 435c–441c.

5 F. Nietzsche, *Thus Spoke Zarathustra*, in W. Kaufmann, trans. and ed., *The Portable Nietzsche*, New York: Viking Penguin, 1954, p. 129.

6 Ibid., p. 130.

7 M. Tunick, 'Hegel against Fukuyama's Hegel', *Clio*, 1993, 22(4): 383–9.

Fukuyama's major works

'The End of History? After the Battle of Jena', *The National Interest*, 1989, 16: 3–18.

The End of History and the Last Man, New York: Free Press, 1992.

'Interview with Francis Fukuyama', by Brian Lamb of 'Booknotes', 17 January 1992, transcript at http://www.booknotes.org.

'Reflections on the End of History, Five Years Later', in T. Burns (ed.), *After History? Fukuyama and his Critics*, Lanham, MD: Rowman & Littlefield, 1994, pp. 239–58.

See also

Fukuyama (IRT), Hegel, Kant, Marx, Nietzsche (MP and CT). Plato (MP).

Further resources

Anon., 'Time to Call History a Day', *The Economist*, 16 September 1989, 312(7620): 48.

Bertram, C. and Chitty, A. (eds), *Has History Ended? Fukuyama, Marx, Modernity*, Aldershot, Hants: Avebury, 1994.

Burns, T. (ed.), *After History? Fukuyama and his Critics*, Lanham, MD: Rowman & Littlefield, 1994.

Cooper, B., 'The End of History: Déjà-Vu All Over Again', *History of European Ideas*, 1994, 19(1–3): 377–83.

Dunn, J., Review of *The End of History and the Last Man*, *Times Literary Supplement*, 24 April 1992, 4647: 6.

Elson, J., 'Has History Come to an End?', *Time*, 4 September 1989, 134(10): 57.

Gourevitch, V., 'The End of History?', *Interpretation*, 1994, 21(2): 215–31.

Grumley, J., 'Fukuyama's Hegelianism: Historical Exhaustion or Philosophical Closure?', *History of European Ideas*, 1995, 21(3): 379–92.

Harris, H. S., 'The End of History in Hegel', *Bulletin of the Hegel Society of Great Britain*, 1991, 23–4: 1–14.

McCarney, J., 'Shaping Ends: Reflections on Fukuyama', *New Left Review*, 1993, 202: 37–53.

Roth, M. S., 'Review Essay: *The End of History and the Last Man*', *History and Theory*, 1993, 32(2): 188–96.

Tunick, M., 'Hegel against Fukuyama's Hegel', *Clio*, 1993, 22(4): 383–9.

PIETER GEYL 1887–1966

When Pieter Catharinus Arie Geyl (1887–1966), one of the Netherlands' foremost historians, was interned in a concentration camp because of his 'suspect general mentality', he wrote the following poem:

> The stars are fright'ning. The cold universe,/ Boundless and silent, goes revolving on,/ Worlds without end. The Grace of God is gone./ A vast indifference, deadlier than a curse,/ Chills

our poor globe, which Heaven seemed to nurse/ So fondly.
'Twas God's rainbow when it shone,/ Until we searched. Now,
as we count and con/ Gusts of infinity, our hopes disperse./
Well, if it's so, then turn your eyes away/ From Heav'n. Look
at the earth, in its array/ Of life and beauty. – Transitory?
Maybe,/ But so are you. Let stark eternity/ Heed its own self,
and you, enjoy your day,/ And when death calls, then quietly
obey.[1]

In this, and in his many writings on historiography and the history of
the Netherlands, Geyl explores the implications of his vision of people
as transitory creatures.

As a child, Geyl believed that he could realise his desire for self-
expression through poetry and fiction. After a lukewarm review of his
writing by the notable critic Albert Vermey, however, he turned to the
study of history ('Looking Back', in *Encounters in History*, p. 356). Geyl
was captivated by the subject, and by 1913 he had completed a doctorate
at the University of Leiden with a thesis on Christofforo Suriano, a
representative of the Venetian Republic at the Hague from 1616 to 1623
(*Christofforo Suriano, resident van de Serenissime Republiek van Venetië in Den
Haag*). In this, Geyl explored Suriano's understanding of contemporary
political opinions in great detail.[2] After a short stint as a schoolmaster at
the small *gymnasium* in Schiedam (1912–13), Geyl moved to London as
a correspondent for the Dutch newspaper *Nieuwe Rotterdamsche Courant*.
This position afforded him contact with many people in political and
academic circles, and before long he gained the reputation of being an
astute commentator on contemporary events. In 1919 he was appointed
reader, then professor, of Dutch history and institutions at the University
of London, where he remained until 1935.

Many of Geyl's writings from this period are dominated by an
issue that he was made aware of at Leiden: Flemish nationalism. At that
time, writers such as Henri Pirenne argued that as Belgium had long
been a separate country from Holland, the Dutch had no real ties to
the Dutch-speaking Flemings in north Belgium. Geyl rejected that
view as inaccurate, and argued in a series of books and papers for
the 'Great Netherlands idea' (see *De Groot-Nederlandsche Gedachte*,
1925; and *Geschiedenis van der Nederlandsche Stam*, 1930–37, revised
edition 1961–62, trans. and abr. *The Revolt of the Netherlands, 1555–
1609* and *The Netherlands in the Seventeenth Century*). For Geyl,
the 'Great Netherlands' is a unified linguistic–cultural community in
Holland and Flanders. This idea underpins Geyl's account of Dutch
history up to the nineteenth century, but it is especially clear in his novel

interpretation of the revolt against Spanish rule in 1567. The fact that the revolt was only successful in northern provinces such as Holland, Geyl argues, stemmed not from cultural or political differences. Indeed, Geyl considers the Dutch-speaking areas south of the Dutch state to have been the source of many of the earliest and most significant developments in Dutch literature and culture. Nor was the outcome due to religious differences. According to Geyl, Protestantism and Catholicism only took root in the north and the south respectively after the revolt. For him, the revolt was successful in the north because of its geographical features and position. It was a long way away from the central government in Brussels and was inaccessible to the Spanish Army because of its many rivers, lakes and bogs. Thus Holland came to be separated from Flanders simply because of its geography. While Geyl's reinterpretation of the sixteenth-century revolt was so persuasive that it is now taken for granted, critics complained when it was first proposed that he had imposed an unhistorical linguistic–cultural concept on the past to support his political beliefs.

In 1935, Geyl was appointed, against the recommendation of the faculty, to the chair of history at the University of Utrecht. At Utrecht, Geyl began to explore the role of the house of Orange in Dutch history. As he saw it, the dynastic ambitions of many of the house had often brought them into conflict with the Dutch people. For instance, in *Revolutiedagen te Amsterdam, Augustus–September 1748* (1936), Geyl explores the role of the Doelisten, a party of Amsterdam burghers hostile to the ruling patriciate, in the defeat of the Republican ('States') party and the establishment of the hereditary stadholdership[3] in 1747. Once William IV of Orange had used the uprising by the Doelisten to usurp the power of the magistracy and governing councils of Amsterdam, he had no intention of relinquishing power. This led to conflict between the house of Orange and the people, which culminated in the Patriot movement and the Batavian revolution of 1795.[4] The first gave voice to criticisms of the established government and the second triggered the political modernisation of the Netherlands. Geyl also examines seventeenth-century conflicts between the state and the house of Orange in *Oranje en Stuart, 1641–1672* (1939, trans. *Orange and Stuart, 1641–1672*). In this work he traces the consequences of the marriage of Prince William of Orange (later William II) to Princess Mary Stuart of England. This marriage, Geyl argues, led to disputes between the house and the Dutch Republic over trade with Cromwell's supporters during the English Civil War (1642–51). (See also 'Orange and Stuart, 1641–1650', in *Encounters in History*, pp. 152–205.) Although not as dramatic as his reinterpretation of the sixteenth-century revolt,

Geyl's writings on Orangeism offer a more finely shaded account of political developments in the history of the Netherlands.

After the outbreak of the Second World War, Geyl penned an article on the variety of interpretations of Napoleon's aims, character and achievements. This article was scheduled to appear in print in June 1940, but when Hitler seized Holland in May, the manuscript was returned to Geyl. Although no explanation was offered for why the manuscript had been returned, Geyl saw that many parallels could be drawn between Hitler and Napoleon. Ignoring warnings, he used the article as the basis of a series of lectures at the Rotterdam School of Economics in September 1940. One month later he was taken hostage along with 113 others by the German security police, in reprisal for the alleged maltreatment of German internees in the Dutch East Indies. After thirteen months in Buchenwald, Geyl and many of his fellow hostages were sent back to the Netherlands for continued internment. Up until his release on medical grounds in February 1944, Geyl gave lectures to the other internees and wrote sonnets and a detective novel. When released, he harboured members of the resistance in his home and tried to pursue historical research even though he had been dismissed from his professorship on the grounds that 'his general mentality [did] not hold out any guarantee for loyal co-operation' ('Looking Back', in *Encounters in History*, p. 367).

He returned to his article on Napoleon, and decided to rewrite it as a book. The result was *Napoleon For and Against*, a work that lays bare many of Geyl's fundamental beliefs about the nature of history. From the nineteenth century to Geyl's day, French historians had depicted Napoleon either as a son of France and the Revolution who brought liberty and stability to Europe or as a foreigner whose thirst for power and glory dragged France into disaster. These waves 'for' and 'against' Napoleon, Geyl claims, demonstrate that historical accounts are coloured by the ideological and political concerns of historians:

> History can reach no unchallengeable conclusions on so many-sided a character, on a life so dominated, so profoundly agitated, by the circumstances of the time. . . . To expect from history those final conclusions, which may perhaps be obtained in other disciplines, is, in my opinion, to misunderstand its nature. . . . Every historical narrative is dependent upon explanation, interpretation, appreciation. In other words we cannot see the past in a single, communicable picture except from a point of view, which implies a choice, a personal perspective.
>
> (*Napoleon For and Against*, p. 15)

There can be no 'God's-eye' or overarching view of historical developments because all histories arise from particular socio-historical contexts. Whether historians like it or not, or are even aware of it, their words are shaped by their ideas and hopes. For Geyl, good works of history result when historians reflect critically on their ideas and commitments and encourage their readers to do the same. This need not lead to an 'anything goes' situation though, for Geyl believes that history's 'argument without end' can make us aware of 'truths' that we share with others (see also *The Use and Abuse of History*).

After the liberation of Holland in 1945, Geyl was reinstated to the chair of history at Utrecht. In his opening lecture, he argued that historians must use 'criticism, again criticism and criticism once more' to shatter dangerous cultural and political myths. Furthermore, he asked his students to refrain from the mass condemnation of particular peoples ('Opening Lecture', in *Encounters in History*, pp. 269–75). That Geyl believed in such a principle is clear from his eloquent defence of Ranke against the charge that his writings paved the way for National Socialism ('Ranke in the Light of the Catastrophe', in *Debates with Historians*, pp. 9–29). He also took great pains to distinguish the leaders of the Batavian Republic, who realised Patriot principles with the assistance of a French army of occupation, from the NSBers (the Dutch Nazis), who he thought had turned their back on their country and its history (*Patriotten en NSBers*, 1946).[5]

Geyl also grew increasingly fond of defining himself by argument with other historians. This is seen most clearly in his fierce criticism of the writings of the English historian Arnold Toynbee. In *A Study of History* (1934–61), Toynbee claims that empirical study of the past reveals the existence of fewer than twenty-one civilisations. For him the rise and fall of those civilisations is determined by how people responded to challenges. Geyl found much to upset him in Toynbee's vision of history, and engaged in a prolonged debate with Toynbee both in print and on the radio (see *Can we Know the Pattern of the Past?*, *The Pattern of the Past*, and *Debates with Historians*, pp. 109–202). According to Geyl, Toynbee's 'empirical method' amounted to no more than the selective use of historical phenomena to demonstrate his preconceived ideas about the patterns of the past. Not only did Toynbee ignore counterexamples, but he also failed to see that the examples he cited were open to various interpretations. Nor was Geyl satisfied with Toynbee's claim that historical changes can be explained solely in terms of 'challenge and response'. Many factors, Geyl argued, determine historical change, and isolating one of them would be unhistorical. Furthermore, Geyl considered Toynbee's usage of 'challenge' and 'response' to be so loose that they could be made to fit just about any situation. Nor had Toynbee done a good job of explaining when a challenge is too small and too severe to stimulate the growth of civilisation. In addition, Geyl objected to Toynbee's suggestion that Western civilisation had reached a nadir and that salvation could be found in the love of God. He thought that Toynbee's plan for salvation was cold comfort for people who did not ascribe to his view of Christianity and that his view of Western civilisation in decline would encourage pessimism and apathy. Geyl saw much in Western civilisation to encourage him. Overall, Geyl's complaints were not just directed against Toynbee, but against anyone who sees a pattern or system in the past (see, for instance, 'Jan Romein, or Bowing to the Spirit of the Age', in *Encounters in History*, pp. 321–7). What we need to realise about history, he writes:

> is its infinite complexity, and, when I say infinite, I do mean that not only the number of the phenomena and incidents but their often shadowy and changing nature is such that the attempt to reduce them to a fixed relationship and to a scheme of absolute validity can never lead to anything but disappointment.
>
> (*Can we Know the Pattern of the Past?* p. 47)

Geyl's debates with Toynbee, like *The Study of History* itself, now appear dated. It is hard for readers today to understand what all the fuss was about, because 'grand narratives' of historical events are out of favour. What they might find more intriguing is Geyl's claim that even though we are transitory, context-bound beings, we can still find 'truths' in history's 'argument without end'.

Notes

1 Quoted in V. Mehta, *Fly and the Fly Bottle: Encounters with British Intellectuals*, London: Weidenfeld & Nicolson, 1962, pp. 156–7; and in R. J. B. Bosworth, *Explaining Auschwitz and Hiroshima: History Writing and the Second World War, 1945–1990*, London: Routledge, 1993, pp. 11–12.

2 *Christofforo Suriano, resident van de Serenissime Republiek van Venetië in Den Haag, 1616–1623*, The Hague: Martinus Nijhoff, 1913. For a description of the work, see H. H. Rowen, 'The Historical Work of Pieter Geyl', *Journal of Modern History*, 1965, 37(1): 36–7.

3 'Stateholders', appointed by the provinces, were drawn almost exclusively from the house of Orange.

4 *Revolutiedagen te Amsterdam, Augustus–September 1748: Willem IV en de*

Doelistenbeweging, The Hague: Martinus Nijhoff, 1936. For a description of the work, see Rowen, 'The Historical Work of Pieter Geyl', p. 42.
5   *Patriotten en NSBers*, Amsterdam: J. van Campen, 1946.

Geyl's major works

The Revolt of the Netherlands, 1555–1609, New York: Barnes & Noble, 1966.
The Netherlands in the Seventeenth Century, 2 vols, New York: Barnes & Noble, 1961–64.
Orange and Stuart, 1641–72, trans. A. Pomerans, New York: Scribner, 1970.
Napoleon, For and Against, trans. O. Renier, New Haven, CT: Yale University Press, 1949.
(with A. Toynbee) *Can we Know the Pattern of the Past? Discussion between P. Geyl and A. Toynbee concerning Toynbee's Book 'A Study of History'*, Bossum: F. G. Kroonder, 1948.
(with A. Toynbee and P. Sorokin) *The Pattern of the Past: Can we Determine it?*, New York: Greenwood, 1949.
Use and Abuse of History, New Haven, CT: Yale University Press, 1955.
Debates with Historians, Cleveland, OH: Meridian, 1958.
Encounters in History, Cleveland, OH: Meridian, 1961.

See also

Ranke, Taylor, Toynbee.

Further resources

Bark, W., 'Review of *Encounters in History*', *History and Theory*, 1964, 4(1): 107–23.
Bosworth, R. J. B., *Explaining Auschwitz and Hiroshima: History Writing and the Second World War, 1945–1990*, London: Routledge, 1993.
Duke, A. C. and Tamse, C. A. (eds), *Clio's Mirror: Historiography in Britain and the Netherlands*, Zutphen: De Walburg Pers, 1985.
Mehta, V., *Fly and the Fly Bottle: Encounters with British Intellectuals*, London: Weidenfeld & Nicolson, 1962.
Rogier, L. J., *Herdenking van P. Geyl*, Amsterdam: Noord-Hollandsche Uitgevers Maatschappij, 1967.
Rowen, H. H., 'The Historical Work of Pieter Geyl', *Journal of Modern History*, 1965, 37(1): 35–49.

EDWARD GIBBON 1737–94

Edward Gibbon, author of one of the world's most enduring works of history – *The History of the Decline and Fall of the Roman Empire* – was born in Surrey, England, in 1737. Gibbon's childhood was marked by frequent illness and patchy schooling. After attending a day school in Putney and studying with a private tutor, he went to a boarding school in Kingston. It was at Kingston, he tells us in his memoirs, that '[b]y the common methods of discipline, at the expense of many tears and some blood, I purchased the knowledge of Latin syntax' (*Memoirs of my Life and Writings*, p. 38). After a short stint at Westminster School, Gibbon went to Magdalen College, Oxford, at the young age of fifteen. Finding no intellectual or spiritual guidance there, he read himself into the Roman Catholic faith via Conyer Middleton's controversial book *A Free Inquiry into the Miraculous Powers Which are Supposed to Have Existed in the Christian Church* (1748). In rejecting Middleton's criticisms of the miracles of the early church, Gibbon found himself allied with Catholicism and in breach of the then requirement that members of Oxford subscribe to the Thirty-Nine Articles of the Church of England.[1] His father quickly intervened and sent Gibbon to live with the Calvinist minister Monsieur Pavillard, in Lausanne, Switzerland. The years that Gibbon spent in Lausanne were for him a 'fortunate banishment' (ibid., p. 209). Under Pavillard's guidance, Gibbon returned to Protestantism and learned to read with more discipline and focus. He mastered a great deal of Latin literature and studied logic, philosophy, mathematics, Greek, history and law. He also became fluent in French, which allowed him to explore the ideas of writers such as Montesquieu, Bayle and Voltaire.

In 1758, Gibbon was called home to help release his father from financial difficulties. For the next two years, he lived in London or at Buriton, the family estate in Hampshire. He penned a number of short essays in French, the most notable of which is *Essai sur l'étude de la littérature* (1761, trans. *An Essay on the Study of Literature*). Though ostensibly a defence of the study of ancient texts, or 'belles-lettres', Gibbon's *Essai* also introduces us to the view of history that shapes his later writings. For many of Gibbon's contemporaries, rational cogitation on the present world, not historical knowledge, was thought to be the primary source of truth. Gibbon, however, believed that the careful study of the past could assist philosophers in the search for both the underlying causes of things and an explanation of the development of civilisation. In order to do this, though, historians have to go past the traditional study of politics, battles and great men. This is because those things which 'give motion to the springs of action' are usually hidden (*An Essay on the Study of Literature*, p. 100). They can, however, be divined in the many trivial actions recorded by classical writers and modern antiquarians or *érudits*, because minutiae are more likely to be spontaneous:

There is no preparatory disguise to trivial actions. We undress only when we imagine we are not seen; but the curious will endeavour to penetrate the most secret retirement. Should I undertake to determine, whether virtue prevailed in the character of a certain age, or people, I should examine into their actions rather than their discourse.

(Ibid., pp. 102–3)

Thus historians aim to go beyond appearances to explain why things happened as they did.[2]

During the time that Gibbon wrote his *Essai*, Britain was at war with France. In 1762 Gibbon was called up to serve as a captain in the Hampshire militia. Military service disrupted Gibbon's studies, but he still managed to read works by Hume, Voltaire, Swift and Addison. He also studied works of military history such as Charles Théophile Guischardt's *Mémoires militaires sur les grecs et sur les romains*, which led him to compare his experience of modern methods of warfare with classical methods.[3] Within weeks of the end of the war, Gibbon left the militia and set out on a tour of France, Switzerland and Italy. In Paris, he met Diderot, Jean Le Rond D'Alembert, Claude Adrien Helvétius, Paul Henri D'Holbach and the Abbé de la Bléterie. He also looked at manuscript collections in a number of public libraries and took exhaustive notes on the history and geography of ancient Rome. It was in Rome, he later wrote:

on the fifteenth of October 1764, as I sat musing amidst the ruins of the Capitol while the barefooted friars were singing Vespers in the temple of Jupiter, that the idea of writing the decline and fall of the City first started to my mind.

(*Memoirs of my Life and Writings*, p. 134, n. 4)

Though it is likely that Gibbon's plan to write a history of the city took shape earlier than that, his experience of Rome might have inspired him to undertake the more ambitious project of tracing the fortunes of the Roman Empire.[4]

In 1765, Gibbon again returned to England to help manage his father's financial problems. Though struck by his experiences in Rome, he toyed with writing histories on Richard I and the Crusades, the invasion of Italy by Charles VIII of France, Edward the Black Prince, Henry V, Sir Walter Raleigh and Florence. He even wrote a history of the Swiss struggle for independence in the later Middle Ages and presented it anonymously to a literary society in London. The responses it attracted were sufficiently critical that Gibbon decided to leave the work unpublished and to write his next work in English.

Casting about for a new topic, Gibbon recalled Rome. He then started to examine both literary and non-literary artefacts:

> I insensibly plunged into the Ocean of the Augustan history, and in descending series I investigated, with my pen almost always in my hand, the original record, both Greek and Latin, from Dion Cassius to Ammianus Marcellinus, from the reign of Trajan to the last age of the western Caesars. The subsidiary rays of Medals and inscriptions, of Geography and Chronology were all thrown on their proper objects: and I applied the collections of Tillemont, whose inimitable accuracy almost assumes the character of Genius, to fix and arrange within my reach the loose and scattered atoms of historical information. Through the darkness of the middle ages I explored my way in the Annals and Antiquities of Italy of the learned Muratori . . . till I almost grasped the ruins of Rome in the fourteenth century, without suspecting that this final chapter must be by the labour of six quartos and twenty years.
>
> (*Memoirs of my Life and Writings*, pp. 146–7)

By 1773 he had begun to build a history that he hoped would edify his readers (*The History of the Decline and Fall of the Roman Empire*, 1776, hereafter *Decline and Fall*).[5] Financial insecurity, however, led him to seek employment. With the assistance of his cousin, Lord Eliot, Gibbon was able to take up the parliamentary seat of Liskeard in 1774. Although a poor orator, Gibbon's steadfast support for Lord North's government led to his appointment as a Lord Commissioner of Trade and Plantations. Shortly thereafter he composed *Mémoire justicatif* (1779), a response to Continental criticism of the British government's policy in America. In 1781 he published the second and third volumes of *Decline and Fall*, but before he could commence work on the fourth, Lord North's government fell. Gibbon lost his commission, and in order to economise, he moved to Lausanne to share a house with long-time friend Georges Deyverdun. There he completed the three final volumes of *Decline and Fall*, which were published in May 1788. What satisfaction Gibbon derived from having completed the *Decline and Fall* was diminished by the death of Deyverdun and the French Revolution. He proposed to write a seventh volume of *Decline and Fall*, which would include additional notes, a map and a critical review of his authorities, but never started it. He did, however, find time to write about the position of the meridional line and the supposed circumnavigation of Africa by the ancients, which was probably the result of his re-reading Herodotus' *Histories*. He also penned no fewer than six versions of an autobiography.[6] Escalating tensions in Europe brought him back to England in 1793. On his return he sought medical attention for a long-neglected condition, but died in 1794 after numerous failed operations.

When Gibbon began to write *Decline and Fall*, he planned to divide thirteen centuries of Roman history into three periods which he would treat at similar length: the age of Trajan and the Antonines to the capture of Rome by the Goths (*c.* AD 100–*c.* 500); the reign of Justinian and the restoration of the Eastern Empire to the emergence of Mohammed and Charlemagne (*c.* 500–814); and the revival of the Western Empire to the capture of Constantinople by the Turks (815–1453). Though the published work covers the same ground, three of the six volumes are dedicated to the first of these periods. The work is thus composed of two parts, divided in the middle by the collapse of the Western Empire. What binds such an ambitious survey of history together, as is suggested by the title, is Gibbon's focus on the disintegration of the Roman Empire.

For Gibbon, two dispositions prompted Rome's decline. The first of these, corruption brought on by enervation and luxury, was also closely associated with decline in the ancient writings of Livy, Tacitus and Herodotus. In their view, a people softened by the spoils of conquest become reluctant to govern and so call upon despots and mercenaries to assist them. In so doing, they lose their liberty, and are open to conquest by those mercenaries. The mercenaries, in turn, are prone to corruption, and so on. This pattern of events dominates the first half of *Decline and Fall*. In Gibbon's view, corruption led to the rise of despotic emperors and the degeneration of the Roman legions into an unstable body of hired barbarians. Those barbarians eventually took over the Emperor's Praetorian Guard, and exercised power over those who held the imperial title. When the legions in the provinces attempted to usurp this power, civil war ensued. The uprisings were eventually quashed by strong rulers such as Diocletian and Constantine in the third and fourth centuries, but at the cost of shifting the capital of the Empire to Constantinople. When this happened, the Empire was given an oriental religion and the politically corrupt character of an 'oriental monarchy'. Gibbon was unsympathetic towards Byzantine civilisation because, like many of his contemporaries, he believed that 'oriental monarchy' was the very antithesis of the 'mixed' polities (ruler and government) of ancient Rome and modern Britain. Constitutional monarchies like that of Britain, Gibbon believed, were most likely to guarantee the liberty and rights of their subjects. In oriental regimes, all subjects were reduced to the same state of servile dependence on the absolute will of the ruler.[7]

The second disposition is excessive enthusiasm or zeal. In *Decline and Fall*, these accompany the rise of Christianity (chapters 15 and 16). Before the appearance of Christianity in the Roman world, different kinds and intensities of religious observance were tolerated. Early Christianity was, by contrast, exclusive, dogmatic, zealous and ascetic. These characteristics, in addition to the 'convincing evidence of the doctrine itself', the promise of an afterlife and reports of miracles, helped the Christian church to form an independent state which soon swamped the Empire. While the intense single-mindedness of the early Christians was the chief cause of its success, it was also a source of internal division. Such divisions, Gibbon believed, gave rise to the violent sectarian disputes that remained in his day. At the heart of Gibbon's account of the rise of Christianity is a distaste for enthusiasm and zeal, which like his contemporaries, he believed undermined more civilised approaches to belief offered by reason and reflection. He is thus not disgusted by religion itself, but by the corruption of religion due to human weakness:

> The theologian may indulge the pleasing task of describing Religion as she descended from Heaven, arrayed in her native purity. A more melancholy duty is imposed on the historian. He must discover the inevitable mixture of error and corruption which she contracted in a long residence upon earth among a weak and degenerate race of beings.
>
> (*Decline and Fall*, vol. 2, p. 2)

Many contemporary readers took offence at Gibbon's portrayal of the early Christians. Others objected to his treatment of the history of religion as a part of general history. Gibbon was shocked by the criticism that chapters 15 and 16 attracted, and vigorously defended his portrayal of events in *A Vindication of Some Passages in the Fifteenth and Sixteenth Chapters of the Decline and Fall of the Roman Empire* (1779, in *The English Essays of Edward Gibbon*, pp. 229–331). After Gibbon died and his memoirs were published, numerous writers suggested that his treatment of Christianity arose from his disastrous early flirtation with Catholicism. They hoped that interest in *Decline and Fall* would soon wane. It did not, however, and by the nineteenth century a number of polemically annotated and abridged editions were published. Opinion was still divided as to whether Gibbon's treatment of Christianity was malicious, but most commentators agreed that his accounts of other subjects were generally well researched and well balanced.

More recently, church historians have recognised the complexity of Gibbon's views of early Christianity, and at the same time have sought to move beyond them with the assistance of evidence not considered by or available to Gibbon. Recent scholarship has also focused on Gibbon's understanding of the nature of history and the literary quality of his work. In particular, scholars have praised Gibbon's synthesis of classical and modern approaches to the writing of history, interest in the idea of a balance of power in Europe, account of Roman law and use of ethnographical digressions. Today, *Decline and Fall* survives in print unabridged and still acts as a stimulus for discussions on religion, law, history, historiography, politics and international relations.[8]

In the third volume, Gibbon recounts the old legend of the seven sleepers of Ephesus. According to that legend, seven young Christians who sought to escape the persecution of the Emperor Decius fell into a charmed sleep of 200 years. Upon waking, they encountered a world that had undergone an extraordinary transformation:

> During this period, the seat of the governor had been transported from Rome to a new city on the banks of the Thracian Bosphorus; and the abuse of military spirit had been suppressed by an artificial system of tame and ceremonious servitude. The throne of the persecuting Decius was filled by a succession of Christian and orthodox princes, who had extirpated the fabulous gods of antiquity; and the public devotion of the age was impatient to exalt the saints and martyrs of the Catholic Church on the altars of Diana and Hercules. The union of the Roman Empire was dissolved; its genius was humbled in the dust; and armies of unknown Barbarians, issuing from the frozen reigns of the North, had established their victorious reign over the fairest provinces of Europe and Africa.
>
> (*Decline and Fall*, vol. 3, p. 415)

If Gibbon was himself to wake from a charmed sleep in the present day, what would he think of the changes in our understanding of historiography and Roman history over the last 200 years?

Notes

1 On Gibbon's experiences of Catholicism, see E. J. Oliver, *Gibbon and Rome*, London: Sheed & Ward, 1958.

2 M. W. Brownley, 'Appearance and Reality in Gibbon's History', *Journal of the History of Ideas*, 1977, 38(4): 651–66; J. W. Burrow, *Gibbon*, Oxford: Oxford University Press, 1985, chap. 3; C. Hartog, 'Time and Metaphor in Gibbon's History', *Clio*, 1983, 12(2): 153–68; and A. Momgliano, 'Gibbon's Contribution to Historical Method', in *Studies in Historiography*, London: Weidenfeld & Nicolson, 1966, pp. 40–55.
3 R. Woodall, 'Captain Gibbon of the Militia', *Army Quarterly and Defence Journal*, 1992, 122(1): 88–92.
4 P. Ghosh, 'The Conception of Gibbon's *History*', in R. McKitterick and R. Quinault (eds), *Edward Gibbon and Empire*, Cambridge: Cambridge University Press, 1997, pp. 280–2.
5 On synthesising sources, see Gibbon's *Vindication*, in P. B. Craddock, *The English Essays of Edward Gibbon*, Oxford: Oxford University Press, 1972, esp. p. 264.
6 On Gibbon's autobiographies, see J. Gawthrop, 'Edward Gibbon's Autobiographical Intentions: a Bicentennial View', *Durham University Journal*, 1994, 86(1): 67–71; and J. H. Pearson, 'Reading the Writing in the Drafts of Edward Gibbon's Memoirs', *Biography*, 1991, 14(3): 222–42.
7 For a similar view of oriental monarchies, see the entry on Hegel in this book.
8 For a history of the reception of *Decline and Fall*, see P. B. Craddock, *Edward Gibbon: a Reference Guide*, Boston: G. K. Hall, 1987, preface.

Gibbon's major works

Essai sur l'étude de la littérature and *An Essay on the Study of Literature*, ed. J. V. Price, London: Thoemmes, 1994.
The History of the Decline and Fall of the Roman Empire, 3 vols, ed. D. Womersley, London: Allen Lane, 1994.
Memoirs of my Life and Writings, ed. G. A. Bonnard, London: Nelson, 1966.
The Miscellaneous Works of Edward Gibbon, ed. Lord Sheffield, London: J. Murray, 1814.
The English Essays of Edward Gibbon, ed. P. B. Craddock, Oxford: Oxford University Press, 1972.

See also

Herodotus, Hume (MP), Livy, Tacitus.

Further resources

Black, J., 'Empire and Enlightenment in Edward Gibbon's Treatment of International Relations', *International History Review*, 1995, 17(3): 441–58.
Bowerstock, G. N., Clive, J. and Graubard, S. R. (eds), 'Edward Gibbon and the Decline and Fall of the Roman Empire', in *Daedalus*, 1977, 105(3).
Brownley, M. W., 'Appearance and Reality in Gibbon's History', *Journal of the History of Ideas*, 1977, 38(4): 651–66.
Burrow, J. W., *Gibbon*, Oxford: Oxford University Press, 1985.
Carnochan, W. B., *Gibbon's Solitude: the Inward World of the Historian*, Stanford, CA: Stanford University Press, 1987.

Cartledge, P., 'The "Tacitism" of Gibbon Two Hundred Years On', *Mediterranean Historical Review*, 1989, 4(2): 251–70.

Craddock, P. B., *Edward Gibbon: a Reference Guide*, Boston: G. K. Hall, 1987.

——, *Edward Gibbon, Luminous Historian*, Baltimore, MD: Johns Hopkins University Press, 1989.

Gossman, L., *The Empire Unpossess'd*, Cambridge: Cambridge University Press, 1981.

Hartog, C., 'Time and Metaphor in Gibbon's History', *Clio*, 1983, 12(1): 153–68.

McKitterick, R. and Quinault, R. (eds) *Edward Gibbon and Empire*, Cambridge: Cambridge University Press, 1997.

White, L., Jnr, (ed.) *The Transformation of the Roman World: Gibbon's Problem after Two Centuries*, Berkeley: University of California Press, 1966.

Womersley, D., 'Gibbon's Unfinished History: the French Revolution and English Political Vocabularies', *Historical Journal*, 1992, 35(1): 63–89.

Wootton, D., 'Narrative, Irony, and Faith in Gibbon's *Decline and Fall*', *History and Theory*, 1994, 33(4): 77–105.

GREGORY OF TOURS *c. 539–c. 594*

Georgius Florentius, the writer we know as Gregory of Tours, was born around 539 in the Gaulish city-territory of Auvergne. Both his parents, Florentius and Armentaria, belonged to wealthy families who had occupied the rank of senators under the late Roman Empire and had strong ecclesiastical connections.[1] As a youth, he was sent to live with his great-uncle Nicetius (later Bishop of Lyons) and then Archdeacon Avitus (later Bishop of Clermont). By 565 he had been ordained a deacon.[2] In 573, Gregory was elected to succeed his mother's cousin Eufronius as the nineteenth bishop of the see of Tours. Up until that point, Gregory tells us, all but five of the Bishops of Tours had been relatives (*The History of the Franks*, 5.49).[3] Being Bishop of Tours was no easy matter. Tours was not only the site of the shrine of its fourth-century bishop St Martin, a popular destination for pilgrims and those seeking sanctuary, but also important territory in disputes between Frankish kings such as Chilperic and Sigibert. By the time of his death around 594, Gregory had rebuilt Tours cathedral, improved its collection of relics and written a number of books. Gregory himself tells us that he wrote:

> ten books of Histories, seven books of Miracles, and one on the life of the Fathers; I have commented on the Psalms, in one book; I have also written a book on the times of the ecclesiastical offices.
>
> (Ibid., 10.31)

A precise description of the order of composition is not possible, as he seems to have constantly revised his writings.[4] Gregory also had more minor writings to his credit than he chose to list, but none of them survives.[5] Elsewhere, he describes the *Life of the Fathers* as one of his eight books of *Miracles* (*Glory of the Confessors*, preface). These books are traditionally distributed among five titles: *Liber in Gloria Martyrum* (trans. *The Glory of the Martyrs*, book 1); *Liber de Passione et Virtutibus Sancti Iuliani Martyris* ('The Passion and Miracles of St Julian', book 2); *Libri I–IV de Virtutibus Sancti Martini Episcopi* ('The Miracles of St Martin', books 3–6); *Liber Vitae Patrum* (trans. *The Life of the Fathers*, book 7); and *Liber in Gloria Confessorum* (trans. *Glory of the Confessors*, book 8).

Gregory of Tours is best known for his *Decem Libri Historiarum*, translated misleadingly since the eighth century as the *History of the Franks* (hereafter *Histories*). This translated title is misleading for two reasons. First, it creates the impression that the work's central organising principle is the expansion of the Frankish or Merovingian kingdom under Clovis (*c.* 465–511) and his successors. Topics included, however, range in diversity from Clovis's attempts to eliminate rival Frankish kings, through a nuns' revolt at St Radegund's convent of Poitiers, to accounts of cataclysmic floods. The earliest manuscripts of Gregory's works do include an abridged version (books 1–6, minus 68 chapters) of the *Histories*, which more closely resembles a 'history of the Franks'. This is evidently the work of a seventh-century editor, however, as Gregory believed that those who did not keep his works intact would be 'condemned with the Devil' (*Histories*, 10.31). Moreover, Goffart has argued persuasively that Gregory saw secular and ecclesiastical history as intertwined.[6] It seems that he had no intention of writing a political history alone.

Second, the word 'History' fails to convey the sense in which Gregory understood the nature of his research. For Gregory, as for ancient writers like Herodotus, the word *Historiae* ('Histories') suggests a record of contemporary events that he witnessed, rather than just read or heard about. This is borne out by the fact that six of the ten books that make up the text concern Gregory's own times. Book 1 begins with Adam and Eve, hurries through selected episodes in the Old Testament, and ends with the death of Martin of Tours in 397. Book 2 looks to the quarrels of the early Frankish kings, and ends with the death of Clovis in 511. Book 3 traces the fortunes of the sons of Clovis, and book 4 brings events up to Gregory's election as bishop. In line with Goffart, I would thus argue in favour of the title *Ten Books of Histories*.[7]

If Gregory's work is not simply a 'history of the Franks', then what more is it? Until quite recently, most commentators portrayed him as an artless amateur who wrote about events willy-nilly.[8] He was thought to be a mirror of Merovingian society: disorderly, barbaric and chaotic. Looking at the list of chapter headings, that seems a fair judgement. How else are we to explain a work whose contents appear to ramble all over the place? Consequently, some historians have assumed that Gregory's work provides an accurate picture of Merovingian society, and have relied on him heavily in their own works. Closer analysis of the text, however, reveals a more conscious craftsman who interpreted the events he recorded. In the general preface to the text, for instance, Gregory writes:

> A great many things keep happening, some of them good, some of them bad. The inhabitants of different countries keep quarrelling fiercely with each other and kings go on losing their temper in the most furious way. Our churches are attacked by the heretics and then protected by the Catholics; the faith of Christ burns bright in many men, but it remains lukewarm in others. . . . However, no writer has come to the fore who has been sufficiently skilled in setting things down in an orderly fashion to be able to describe these events in prose or in verse. In fact in the towns of Gaul the writing of literature has declined to the point where it has virtually disappeared altogether. . . . I have written this work to keep alive the memory of those dead and gone, and to bring them to the notice of future generations. My style is not very polished, and I have had to devote much space to the quarrels between the wicked and the righteous. All the same I have been greatly encouraged by certain kind remarks . . . to the effect that few people understand a rhetorical speechifier, whereas many can follow a blunt speaker.
>
> (cf. *Life of the Fathers*, preface; *Glory of the Confessors*, preface; and *Glory of the Martyrs*, preface)

He thus spells out clearly for us that his work is to be a vehicle for Christian instruction. As a spokesman for his age, he will describe events and people that merit attention for the religious instruction they afford. That means, he reaffirms in the preface to book 2, describing both the 'blessed lives of the Saints together with the disasters of the unfortunate' (ibid., 2, preface). His view is that good coexists with bad, and that both are worthy of attention. Gregory evidently stuck to this plan in the text, for what we have is an account of what he saw as the highs and lows of the Merovingian age. He is no man of the middle; experiences or events that are neither spectacularly good nor bad rarely rate a mention.[9]

Gregory's fascination with miracles and disasters in the *Histories* – as well as in the *Miracles* – is usually deemed an embarrassment. Historians, we assume, are not meant to believe in dragons or that God can strike people down with jaundice (ibid., 10.1; 5.4). But in dismissing such aspects of his work, we throw away a valuable clue to Gregory's identity as a writer.[10] Miracles and disasters, Gregory believes, are a regular feature of our world. As Kurth explains:

> Wonders, to Gregory's way of thinking, are not extraordinary and exceptional acts of Providence momentarily suspending the course of natural laws. . . . They are, on the contrary, regular and daily manifestations of divine power. . . . One may say that Gregory knows nothing more natural than the super-natural; he is so imbued [with this belief] that he would be unable to conceive of the world otherwise than as a machine whose maker comes at every moment to correct, suspend, or change its workings.[11]

Kurth's point is that in Gregory's view God does not make the world, set it running and then leave it alone but is with us at many times and in many ways.[12] He changes the seasons, strikes the wicked down and works through his saints to cure even the smallest of ailments (for example, *Glory of the Confessors*, 6; 109; *Life of the Fathers*, 4.5; 7; 7.5; 8.12; 14.4).[13] Nor does Gregory differentiate between lesser and greater relics; stones, lamp oil, candle wax and wooden staffs are just as powerful as saints' bodies. In the *Glory of the Confessors*, for instance, he celebrates miracles by a stone on which St Martin sat, a tree that he moved, a chapel at which he prayed, and a grape from a vine that he planted (4; 6; 7; 8; 10). In documenting miracles and disasters of his time, Gregory reminds us that God is not an absent landlord.

In his accounts of various wonders, though, he tends to favour those of the present because they are easier to verify. In the *Life of the Fathers*, for instance, he makes this comment on St Illidius:

> since, as we believe, the deeds done by St Illidius before his death have been forgotten and have not come to our knowledge, we will tell what we have seen with our own eyes, what we have experienced, or what we have learnt from trustworthy people.
>
> (2.2)

For information about the events of his own times, Gregory relied in the main upon his own experiences and oral informants such as his mother, various bishops and clerics and people who had experienced miracles and misfortunes (see, for example, *Histories*, books 5–10 *passim* and *Glory of the Confessors*, 3; 29; 40; 77; 82; 85; 101). On the whole, the style and contents of the *Histories* are hard to derive from the small number of written sources he cites – such as the Bible, the Treaty of Andelot (588), a letter to St Radegund, the Eusebius-Jerome *Chronicle*, Rufinus's version of *Eusebius's Ecclesiastical History*, Orosius's *History Against the Pagans* and the *Chronicle* of Sulpicius Severus – because they would have offered little to guide a writer trying to report on his own age (*Histories* 1.1, 6, 7, 41; 2, preface, 8; 5, preface; 9.20, 39).

Gregory believes that within his own times, there were many divine truths for all to see. Moreover, he believes that immediate experience is more persuasive than knowledge of past deeds gained through the written word. On a number of occasions – as with the extract from the general preface of the *Histories* above – Gregory apologises for his defective Latin. A number of commentators agree that in his works we find 'grammatically confused, syntactically impoverished, and almost sophomoric Latin'.[14] As de Nie and Goffart have argued, however, his way of writing may have been a conscious expression of contempt for fine language.[15] Ever since 'the Word was made flesh' (John 1:14), words had become the playthings of those with purely worldly concerns. Words could no longer be trusted as concrete, divine manifestations seen by one's eyes could be. As Gregory himself says, 'few people understand a rhetorical speechifier, whereas many can follow a blunt speaker' (*Histories*, preface). That still leaves unanswered, however, the question of why Gregory chose to communicate through words rather than through word of mouth, carvings or a collection of relics.

It is also unclear how much control Gregory had over his materials. Drawing on Gregory's stories of Jews, Arians, the poor, holy men and women, for instance, Keely has argued that the *Histories* is united by an attempt to define and set the limits of *ecclesia* ('the people of God'), which unites past and present, heaven and earth.[16] Unfortunately, the relatively small number of examples she draws from what is a large pool diminishes the force of her claims. Goffart argues, on the other hand, that if we take plot to mean 'a series of events which constitutes change', then the *Histories* seems to lack one.[17] He writes: 'All sorts of crimes and miracles happen; kings and bishops die, naturally or not, and are replaced; but nothing ever changes.'[18] He thus concludes that in the *Histories* there is no discernible pattern 'except the common one of good and evil visible in the Bible, Eusebius and Orosius', and that'

Gregory probably thought that the sheer quantity of stories, rather than the quality of his argument, would turn people to God.[19] If we were to hold up histories written in our own times against the same definition of plot, however, how many of them would also be found lacking?

Notes

1 For a family tree of Gregory of Tours, see E. James, 'Introduction', in *Life of the Fathers*, p. xxvi.
2 *Libri de Virtutibus Sancti Martini Episcopi*, 1.32; cited in ibid., p. x.
3 Citations refer to the book and chapter number in Gregory's works.
4 R. Van Dam, 'Introduction', in *Glory of the Martyrs*, p. 4.
5 For a description of these minor writings, see R. Van Dam, 'Introduction', in *Glory of the Confessors*, pp. 2–3.
6 W. Goffart, *The Narrators of Barbarian History (AD 550–800): Jordanes, Gregory of Tours, Bede, and Paul the Deacon*, Princeton, NJ: Princeton University Press, 1988, pp. 119–27.
7 Ibid., p. 121.
8 See, for example, C. M. Radding, *A World Made by Men: Cognition and Society, 400–1200*, Chapel Hill, NC: University of North Carolina Press, 1985, pp. 58–64; and R. A. Markus, 'Bede and the Tradition of Ecclesiastical History', Jarrow Lecture 1975, Jarrow: University of Durham Press, 1976, pp. 5–6.
9 W. Goffart, *The Narrators of Barbarian History*, p. 229.
10 Ibid., pp. 168–83. See also P. Brown, *The Cult of the Saints: its Rise and Function in Latin Christianity*, London: SCM Press, 1981; and R. Van Dam, *Leadership and Community in Late Antique Gaul*, Berkeley, CA: University of California Press, 1985.
11 G. Kurth, 'De l'autorité de Grégoire de Tours', *Etudes franques II*, p. 122, as quoted in W. Goffart, *The Narrators of Barbarian History*, p. 132.
12 My description of God as masculine is a reflection of Gregory's view.
13 On Gregory's view of vengeance, see J. M. Wallace-Hadrill, 'The Bloodfeud of the Franks', in *The Long-haired Kings and other Studies of Frankish History*, Oxford: Oxford University Press, 1962, p. 127; and W. Goffart, *The Narrators of Barbarian History*, pp. 174–83.
14 E. Auerbach, *Mimesis: the Representation of Reality in Western Literature*, trans. W. Trask, Princeton, NJ: Princeton University Press, 1953, p. 78. Auerbach later recognised that Gregory's style may have been deliberate. See *Literary Language and its Public in Late Latin Antiquity and in the Middle Ages*, trans. R. Mannheim, London: Routledge & Kegan Paul, 1965, p. 107.
15 G. de Nie, 'Roses in January: a Neglected Dimension of Gregory of Tours', *Journal of Medieval History*, 1979, 5(2): 259–89; and W. Goffart, *The Narrators of Barbarian History*, pp. 143–53.
16 A. A. Keely, ' "*In sinu matris eclesiae*": the Concept of Eclesiae as a Unifying Principle in the Histories of Gregory of Tours', PhD thesis, Macquarie University, Sydney, 1993.
17 W. Goffart, *The Narrators of Barbarian History*, p. 183. Goffart's definition of 'plot' derives from A. B. Kernan, 'A Theory of Satire', in B. Fabian (ed.), *Satura: Ein Kompendium moderner Studien zur Satire*, Hildesheim: G. Olms, 1975, p. 271.

18 Ibid.
19 Ibid., p. 197.

Gregory of Tours' major works

Historiarum Libri X, trans. B. Krusch and W. Levinson, Hanover, 1951.
The History of the Franks, trans. L. Thorpe, Harmondsworth: Penguin, 1974.
The Glory of the Martyrs, trans. R. Van Dam, Liverpool: Liverpool University Press, 1988.
The Life of the Fathers, trans. E. James, Liverpool: Liverpool University Press, second edition, 1991.
The Glory of the Confessors, trans. R. Van Dam, Liverpool: Liverpool University Press, 1988.

See also

Bede, Froissart, Herodotus, Ibn Khaldun.

Further resources

Auerbach, E., *Mimesis: the Representation of Reality in Western Literature*, trans. W. Trask, Princeton, NJ: Princeton University Press, 1953.
——, *Literary Language and its Public in Late Latin Antiquity and in the Middle Ages*, trans. R. Mannheim, London: Routledge & Kegan Paul, 1965.
Breukelaar, A., *Historiography and Episcopal Power in Sixth-century Gaul: Histories of Gregory of Tours Interpreted in their Historical Context*, Berlin: Vandenhoeck & Ruprecht, 1993.
Cameron, A., *Christianity and the Rhetoric of Empire: the Development of Christian Discourse*, Berkeley, CA: University of California Press, 1991.
de Nie, G., *Views from a Many-windowed Tower: Studies of Imagination in the Works of Gregory of Tours*, Amsterdam: Rodopi B. V. Editions, 1987.
Fouracre, P., 'Merovingian History and Merovingian Hagiography', *Past and Present*, 1990, 127: 3–38.
Goffart, W., *The Narrators of Barbarian History (AD 550–800): Jordanes, Gregory of Tours, Bede and Paul the Deacon*, Princeton, NJ: Princeton University Press, 1988.
Keely, A. A., '"*In sinu matris eclesiae*": the Concept of Eclesiae as a Unifying Principle in the Histories of Gregory of Tours', PhD thesis, Macquarie University, Sydney, 1993.
Wallace-Hadrill, J. M., *The Long-haired Kings and other Studies of Frankish History*, Oxford: Oxford University Press, 1962.
——, *The Frankish Church*, Oxford: Oxford University Press, 1983.
Wood, I. N., 'Gregory of Tours and Clovis', *Revue Belge de Philologie et de l'Histoire*, 1985, 63(2): 250–72.

G. W. F. HEGEL 1770–1831

All of Georg Wilhelm Friedrich Hegel's writings bear the imprint of his fundamental interest in history. In the preface to the *Elements of the Philosophy of Right*, for instance, he writes:

> When philosophy paints grey on grey, then is a form of life grown old, and with grey on grey it does not allow itself to rejuvenate it, but only to know it; the Owl of Minerva begins its flight at the falling of the dusk.
>
> (*Elements of the Philosophy of Right*, pp. 12–13)[1]

The role of philosophy as the 'Owl of Minerva' is purely to look back and describe the ideas that have emerged in society. As he puts it, the 'business of philosophy is just to bring expressly to consciousness what men have believed about thinking for ages' (*Encyclopedia of the Philosophical Sciences*, 1.222).[2] Yet he also says in the Preface to the *Elements of the Philosophy of Right* that philosophy is 'its own time raised to the level of thought'. This suggests that philosophers can produce eternal truths out of historical events. In these statements, we see some of the tension between history and philosophy that is inherent in Hegel's view of the world. This tension has led to Hegel being viewed in very different ways by different readers. Whereas some have dismissed him on the grounds that he manipulated historical data in order to fit in with his philosophical ideas, others have praised him for introducing an historical dimension into philosophy. Both groups of readers agree, however, that Hegel's impact on nineteenth- and twentieth-century thought (including philosophy of history) alone makes it important to understand what he has to say.

Hegel was born in Stuttgart on 27 August 1770. He studied theology at Tübingen, where he formed friendships with the poet Friedrich Hölderlin and the philosopher F. D. E. Schelling. After working as a tutor in Bern and Frankfurt, Hegel was a lecturer and then professor at the University of Jena. He completed his first work, *System der Wissenschaft. Erster Theil, die Phänomenologie des Geistes*, on the eve of Napoleon's invasion of Jena (1807, trans. *The Phenomenology of Spirit*). The occupation of Jena by Napoleon's troops closed the university and Hegel was forced to leave. He worked as an editor of a newspaper in Bamberg (1808) and then as the headmaster and philosophy teacher at a school in Nuremberg (1808–16). During this time he completed his *Wissenschaft der Logik* (1812–16, trans. *Science of Logic*). In 1816 he took up a chair in philosophy at the University of Heidelberg, and then in 1818 was appointed to the prestigious chair of philosophy at the University of Berlin. While at Heidelberg he published the *Enzyklopädie der philosophischen Wissenschaften in Grundrisse* (1817, trans. partly as *The Encyclopedia of Logic, Philosophy of Nature* and *Philosophy of Subjective Spirit*). In Berlin Hegel expanded and revised the *Philosophy of Subjective Spirit*, which he released under the title *Naturrecht und Staatswissenschaft im Grundrisse. Grundlinien der Philosophie des Rechts* (1821, trans. *Elements of the Philosophy of Right*). Up to his death from cholera in 1831 he continued to teach at Berlin, and published revised editions of the *Encyclopedia* (1827 and 1830). After his death a number of his lectures on the philosophy of history, history of philosophy, philosophy of religion and aesthetics were published.[3]

For Hegel, every historian, even the one who claims to let the 'facts speak for themselves',

> brings his categories with him and sees the data through them.
> In everything that is supposed to be scientific, Reason must be
> awake and reflection applied.
>
> (*Philosophy of History*, p. 11)

Some categories are better than others, and historians who claim to be merely receptive are open to the danger of accepting poor ideas or falsehoods. They must, therefore, give due thought to the way in which they approach the past and keep up the search for more adequate categories. In the Introduction to the *Philosophy of History*, Hegel details what he sees as the history of the search for more adequate categories in historical research. This history has three stages – original, critical and philosophical – which may be viewed as a hierarchy of forms. Each of the forms in the hierarchy embodies the idea of history but the higher forms embody it more completely. Each form is the culmination of the idea of history at a particular point; that is, each is thought to represent the best embodiment of the idea of history until it is revealed as inadequate. When that inadequacy is exposed, historians are compelled to adopt a new idea of history.

According to Hegel, *Original* historians 'primarily [describe] the actions, events, and conditions which they [have] before their own eyes and whose spirit they [share]' (*Philosophy of History*, pp. 1–3). Original histories thus describe contemporary or near-contemporary events from the point of view of the historian. Such a view of history, Hegel suggests, can be seen in the works of Herodotus and Thucydides. This view of history is no longer the dominant one because historians realise that their own views and those of the people they write about may not be in accord. Nor do historians restrict themselves to the description of recent events. The original view of history, Hegel tells us, gave way to a universal view. *Universal* historians offer surveys of the history of a people, a country or even the world. Two problems trouble them. First, they find it hard to justify the limitation of the scope of their works. That is, what grounds do historians have to justify limiting their accounts to a particular time, people or place? Second, they are troubled by the problem of doing justice to points of view other than their own. Are they capturing the spirit of other ages or merely using historical data to express their own views? In responding to these concerns, Hegel believes, universal historians usually end up writing pragmatic, critical or fragmentary histories. Critical historians restrict their research to the ideas that have given shape to past history writing. Fragmentary historians are also interested in ideas, but they aim to go beyond the 'accidental peculiarities of a people, merely external relations' to the 'internal guiding soul of events and actions' (*Philosophy of History*, p. 8); that is, they try to identify what guides the history of a people. For Hegel, the histories of art, religion and law may afford clues to what guides the development of a people, but only philosophy, by being aware of its own methods and those of art, religion and law, can make *the* guiding force of history explicit.

Philosophical historians, Hegel tells us, realise that seemingly independent historical ideas and events are all part of the one reality that is 'Mind', and that this Mind is seeking unification and actualisation. 'Mind' is universal and cannot be identified with any particular person. Rather, each mind is a part of this World Mind (*Weltgeist*) and the development of rationality in individuals contributes to the development of Mind.[4] Hence reality emerges through rationality. To understand the development of reality, the philosophical historian must thus reason about the history of reason (*Philosophy of History*, p. 9). In Hegel's opinion, the development of reason is most clearly seen in the development of freedom. Thus 'the history of the world is none other than the progress of the consciousness of freedom' (ibid., p. 19).

In the main part of the *Philosophy of History*, Hegel aims to trace the unfolding of freedom in history. He begins with an account of the 'Oriental World', which covers the early civilisations of China, India and Persia. China and India are described as 'stationary' civilisations that are 'outside the World's History' because they have ceased developing (p. 116). World history only really begins with the Persian Empire (p. 173). What links these 'oriental' societies together is that law and morality are a matter of external regulation. According to Hegel, there is simply no sense in which 'oriental' individuals form their own moral judgements about right and wrong. This lack of individual morality takes different forms in the three societies surveyed, but they all produce the same result. In China, government is based on the paternal rule of the emperor, and all others see themselves as children of his state. Thus the basis of the Chinese civilisation is the extension of natural family obedience to the entire state (pp. 116–38). The ruling power in India is not a human despot, but the despotism of a caste system that is viewed as natural and therefore unchangeable (pp. 139–66). Although on first sight the Persian Emperor seems to be of the same ilk as the Chinese emperor, the basis of the Persian empire can be found in a general principle or law which regulates the ruler as well as the subject. This, Hegel believes, was because Persia was a theocratic monarchy, based on the religion of Zoroaster.[5] Although Persia was far from egalitarian, the fact that the general principle was not viewed as natural made development possible in principle. The idea of rule being based on a rationally devised principle signals the emergence of the consciousness of freedom (pp. 187–222). In its efforts to expand, the Persian Empire came into contact with Sparta and a number of the city-states of Greece. Drawing on Herodotus, Hegel notes that the eventual conflict between these groups was a contest between a despot who sought a world united under one leader, and the separate states who ruled by group decision.[6] With the victory of the Greeks, the story of the unfolding of freedom passes to Greece (pp. 256–7).

Though the Greeks possessed freedom to a greater degree than the Persians, Hegel claims that their freedom was limited for two main reasons. First, Greek democracy required slavery in order to work, because participation in the public assembly left no time to attend to everyday chores. Thus *some* people, not all, were free. Second, the Greeks did not distinguish between their individual interests and the interests of those in their community. In Hegel's view, because they acted from social convention they were still subject to external control. For example, genuinely free people would not allow their most important decisions to be determined by oracles; they would make their own decisions. Reason, Hegel contends, lifts people from external control and enables them to reflect critically upon their situation (pp. 258–68). The rise of critical reflection, Hegel contends, is seen in the philosophy of Socrates (pp. 269–70). Through dialogues with a number of Athenians, Socrates revealed that those who claimed to know the nature of, say, goodness or justice were simply parroting ideas that society had inculcated in them. For him, reason, not social custom, was the final judge of right and wrong. Given the radical nature of Socrates' ideas, Hegel is not surprised that he was put to death. Yet, though he was killed his ideas took root and were, Hegel argues, the ultimate cause of the downfall of Athens.

With the decline of Greek civilisation comes the rise of Roman civilisation. While the Greeks were united by 'conventional morality', the Romans, who were composed of a collection of diverse peoples, needed strict rules to keep themselves together. Though in Rome the idea of individual freedom did not disappear, it was 'abstract'. I am free in the abstract sense if others do not interfere with what I want to do.[7] In the *Elements of the Philosophy of Right* Hegel argues that this is not a genuine form of freedom because it accepts the preferences of the individual in an uncritical manner. Many of these unquestioned preferences are simply echoes of society's preferences. Thus abstract freedom, for Hegel, is the freedom to be manipulated by others (*Elements of the Philosophy of Right*, §15). The real freedom that allows people to embrace a diversity of ideas and ways of living was brutally crushed by the Roman government. Faced with the state's demands for outer conformity, individuals sought escape in Stoicism, Epicureanism and Scepticism. These movements aim to make their adherents indifferent to affairs in the world. Retreat into these philosophies, Hegel argues, is nothing more than escapism. For freedom to unfold further, he contends, a positive response was required (*Philosophy of History*, pp. 278–332).

Hegel believes that Christianity offered that positive response. In 'religious self-consciousness', humans recognise that the spiritual world is their true home. To achieve this consciousness, humans have to break the grip that material existence holds over them. This requires not just inner piety, but also the transformation of the material world into a place that acknowledges and fosters the spiritual development of people (*Philosophy of History*, p. 333). For Hegel, such a requirement was only just capable of being met in his own time. Christianity came to the fore when Constantine ruled Rome. Though the Western empire fell to the Barbarians, the Byzantine Empire remained Christian for more than a thousand years. Yet this was a stagnant branch of Christianity, Hegel claims, for it attempted to put a Christian veneer over institutions that were thoroughly corrupt (pp. 336–41). The Catholic church during the Middle Ages also did little to advance the spiritual development of man. It came between man and the spiritual world, embodied the Deity in the material world, focused worship on 'external' ceremonies and rituals and insisted on slavish obedience from its followers. The Middle Ages was a 'long eventful and terrible night' that was only ended by the Renaissance, 'that blush of dawn which after long storms first betokens the return of a bright and glorious day' and the Reformation, 'the all-enlightening Sun' (*Philosophy of History*, pp. 411–12). The Reformation, which was led by the Germanic people (Germany, Scandinavia, Britain, Italy and France), stripped away the power of the Catholic church and spread the idea that each individual has a direct spiritual relationship with Christ. No outside authority is needed to interpret the scriptures, perform ceremonies and grant salvation. In the Reformation the individual conscience became the arbiter of truth and people everywhere realised that 'Man in his very nature is destined to be free' (*Philosophy of History*, p. 417).

Putting this principle into practice is no easy matter, however, for it requires that individuals and institutions embrace rationality. Hegel agrees with Kant that we are not free when we act from socially conditioned desires and that freedom is to be found in reason. Hegel is not satisfied with Kant's ethical theory, however, because it does not detail what we ought to do (*Elements of the Philosophy of Right*, part 2). Hegel firmly believes that freedom can only be fully realised in a constitutional monarchy. A monarchy is needed because somewhere there must be the power of ultimate decision. If the legislature (two houses of parliament, the upper consisting of the landed class and the lower of the business class) and executive (civil servants, appointed on merit) are stable and well organised, however, the monarch often has nothing more to do than sign their name. He is just as firm in his belief that universal suffrage will not work because it would amount to people voting in accordance with their material interests, or even whimsical likes and dislikes they may form for one candidate or another. In a constitutional monarchy individual interests and the interests of the community are in harmony (ibid., §§291–2).

The unfolding of freedom in the *Philosophy of History* embodies Hegel's logic of the dialectic. In the dialectic, as we explore an idea (*thesis*) we arrive at its limits and are *necessarily* drawn to a consideration of a diametrically opposed idea (*antithesis*). The ensuing conflict between the thesis and antithesis leads to the contemplation of a new idea, or *synthesis*, which in turn may be taken as a thesis of another dialectical triad. For example, in *The Philosophy of History*, the customary morality of the Greeks forms the starting point of a dialectical movement. The inadequacy of this 'thesis' was demonstrated by Socrates, who encouraged the Greeks to embrace independent thought. Customary morality collapsed, and individual freedom triumphed. Individual freedom is the 'antithesis' of customary morality. But this freedom is too abstract. Thus we can see that customary morality and individual freedom are too one-sided. They must be united in a manner that preserves the strong points of each. Hegel believed that the constitutional monarchy in the

Germany of his day was a 'synthesis' because he thought that the community and individual were in harmony. Even though the synthesis present in the German society of Hegel's time is the end-point of the *Philosophy of History*, it may turn out to be one-sided in some other respect. It will then serve as the thesis for a new dialectical movement. For instance, in the introduction to the *Philosophy of History*, Hegel hints that America (and possibly even Australia) might see the further unfolding of freedom (pp. 81–91).

After Hegel's death his followers divided into old and new factions; out of the latter Karl Marx was to develop a theory of society and history that incorporated many Hegelian concepts. He argued, however, that it is the material life of people, not mind, that determines the unfolding of freedom. In France, Hegelianism gave shape to the thought of writers such as Sartre, Lacan and Kojève.[8] In Germany, Hegelian ideas were taken up by Theodor Adorno, Jürgen Habermas and H. G. Gadamer. Hegel's ideas were also very popular in Great Britain and the United States towards the end of the nineteenth century. Around the turn of the century, however, Hegel became one of the main targets of attack by 'analytic' philosophers such as Bertrand Russell and G. E. Moore. G. R. G. Mure, F. H. Bradley, William Wallace, R. G. Collingwood and T. M. Knox tried to revive interest in Hegel but they could not turn the analytic tide. For most of the twentieth century, Anglo-American interest in Hegel was mostly limited to his social and political thought. In the 1960s, however, the philosopher Klaus Hartmann developed a new interpretation of Hegel that has played an important role in the recent revival of interest in his philosophy.[9] There is now a great deal of debate on whether some works such as the *Phenomenology of Spirit*, or, more controversially, all of his writings, can be understood independently of the idea of 'Mind' outlined above ('metaphysics'). In addition, since 1989 Hegel scholars have been engaged in a debate about Francis Fukuyama's various pronouncements about 'the end of History'. Drawing on Hegel, Fukuyama claimed that 'History' culminates with liberal democracy. A number of Hegel scholars, however, were quick to point out that Fukuyama's argument depends upon Kojève's contentious *Introduction to Hegel's Philosophy*.[10] Such a conflation of Kojève's and Hegel's ideas, they point out, demonstrates the importance of reading Hegel. These recent debates have shown that, whether he be a metaphysical monster or a historicist hero, Hegel's writings still have the power to captivate those interested in history.

Notes

1 In Roman mythology Minerva was the goddess of wisdom, of the arts and of war. Many of her qualities correspond to those of the Greek goddess Athena. The owl is sacred to Athena. A journal devoted to Hegel's ideas bears the title *The Owl of Minerva*.
2 Quoted in M. Inwood, *Hegel*, The Arguments of the Philosophers Series, London: Routledge & Kegan Paul, 1983, p. 111.
3 For a more general account of Hegel's ideas, see Hegel (MP).
4 *Geist* is more commonly translated as 'Spirit'. That translation, a number of commentators have suggested, makes it hard for modern readers to grasp what Hegel is talking about. In consequence, I have opted for 'Mind'. The role and nature of God in Hegel's system has also been subject to much debate. See Hegel (MP).
5 Zoroaster (or Zarathusthra *c.* 628–551 BC) was a prophet who transformed the ancient polytheistic religion of the Iranians. The rituals of Zoroastrianism revolve around devotion to the good and the battle against the forces of evil. Adopted as the faith of the Persian kings, Zoroastrianism flourished under the Achaemenid, Parthian and Sassanian empires.
6 See Herodotus, *The Histories*, trans. A. de Selincourt, revised A. R. Burn, Penguin Classics, Harmondsworth, Penguin, 1973, books 7–9.
7 P. Singer, *Hegel*, Past Masters Series, Oxford: Oxford University Press, 1983, chap. 2. See also I. Berlin, *Four Essays on Liberty*, London: Oxford University Press, 1969.
8 T. Rockmore, 'Aspects of French Hegelianism', *Owl of Minerva*, 1993, 24(2): 191–206.
9 H. S. Harris, 'The Hegel Renaissance in the Anglo-Saxon World since 1945', *Owl of Minerva*, 1983, 15(1): 77–106.
10 See, for instance, J. C. Flay, 'Essence and Time in Hegel', *Owl of Minerva*, 1989, 20(2): 183–92; P. T. Grier, 'The End of History, and the Return of History', *Owl of Minerva*, 1990, 21(2): 131–44; H. S. Harris, 'The End of History in Hegel', *Bulletin of the Hegel Society of Great Britain*, 1991, 23–24: 1–14; R. Bubner, 'Hegel and the End of History', *Bulletin of the Hegel Society of Great Britain*, 1991, 23–24: 15–23; L. Pompa, 'Philosophical History and the End of History', *Bulletin of the Hegel Society of Great Britain*, 1991, 23–24: 24–38.

Hegel's major works

Werke in zwanzig Bänden, 20 vols, eds E. Moldenhauer and K. M. Michel, Frankfurt am Main: Suhrkamp Verlag, 1969–71.
Elements of the Philosophy of Right, trans. H. B. Nisbet, ed. A. Wood, Cambridge: Cambridge University Press, 1991.
Hegel's Science of Logic, trans. A. V. Miller, London: Allen & Unwin, 1969.
Lectures on the History of Philosophy: the Lectures of 1825–26, 3 vols, ed. R. F. Brown, trans. R. F. Brown, J. M. Stewart and H. S. Harris, Berkeley and Los Angeles: University of California Press, 1990.
Lectures on the Philosophy of History, trans. J. Sibree, New York: Dover, 1956.
The Phenomenology of Spirit, trans. A. V. Miller, Oxford: Oxford University Press, 1970.

See also

Adorno (CT), Bradley (MP), Collingwood, Croce, Fukuyama, Habermas (CT), Kant, Lacan (CT), Marx, Popper (MP), Sartre (MP).

Further resources

Beiser, F. C., *The Cambridge Companion to Hegel*, Cambridge: Cambridge University Press, 1993.

Bulletin of the Hegel Society of Great Britain.

Hegel Society of America homepage: http://www.hegel.org

Houlgate, S., *Truth and History: an Introduction to Hegel's Philosophy*, New York: Routledge, 1991.

Inwood, M. J., *A Hegel Dictionary*, Oxford: Blackwell, 1992.

O'Brien, G. D., *Hegel on Reason and History*, Chicago, IL: University of Chicago Press, 1975.

Perkins, R. L., *History and System: Hegel's Philosophy of History: Proceedings of the 1982 Sessions of the Hegel Society of America Conference*, SUNY Series in Hegelian Studies, Albany, NY: State University of New York Press, 1984.

Pompa, L., *Human Nature and Historical Knowledge: Hume, Hegel and Vico*, Cambridge: Cambridge University Press, 1990.

Singer, P., *Hegel*, Past Masters Series, Oxford: Oxford University Press, 1983.

The Owl of Minerva, the journal of the Hegel Society of America.

Wilkins, B. T., *Hegel's Philosophy of History*, Ithaca, NY: Cornell University Press, 1974.

MARTIN HEIDEGGER 1889–1976

Early on in his life, Martin Heidegger (1889–1976) planned to become a Roman Catholic priest. After starting theological studies at the University of Freiburg, however, he turned to the study of mathematics, the natural sciences, and then philosophy. In 1913 he was awarded his doctorate with a thesis on psychologism and in 1915 he earned his university teaching qualification with a lecture on the historical sciences and a monograph on Duns Scotus' views on meaning. In these he argued, first, that the historical-cultural disciplines may be distinguished from the natural sciences because they are concerned with the individual rather than with general laws, and second, that it is possible to take a systematic approach to the problems of philosophy because of the constancy of human nature.[1] In these writings, and in later works, one can detect the influence of the ideas of Aristotle, St Paul, Augustine of Hippo, Meister Eckhart, Thomas Aquinas, Kierkegaard, Dilthey, Nietzsche, Rickert and Husserl. He taught at Freiburg until 1923, at Marburg University between 1923 and 1928, and returned to Freiburg to occupy the chair in philosophy left vacant after Edmund Husserl's retirement (1928–45).

His first major work, *Sein und Zeit* (1927, trans. *Being and Time*) brought him international attention, and later works such as *Kant und des Problem der Metaphysik* (1929, trans. *Kant and the Problem of Metaphysics*) and *Was ist Metaphysik?* (1929, trans. 'What is Metaphysics?' in *Pathmarks*) confirmed his reputation as an innovative thinker.[2] His open support for the Nazi regime led to his suspension from teaching between 1945 and 1950. In 1950 he was allowed to resume teaching, and from then until his death he lectured and published numerous works. His *Gesamtausgabe* (collected works) is expected to take up more than eighty volumes.

For Heidegger, it is astonishing that all things *are*. Take this book, for example. You can measure it, study the typeface, note the colour of the cover and list the contents. But where, Heidegger would ask us, is its *being*? Can we say that the being of this text consists in the printed marks on its pages? You and I would not hesitate to say that 'it *is*', but we would have a hard time articulating where its existence is to be found. We are confident that there *is* something more to it than the sum of its physical attributes, but it seems to be just out of reach of our grasp. Similarly, we talk confidently of symphonies, cultures, thermal underwear and chocolate bars, but when we are asked to explain what they *are* we become lost for words. That we stumble, Heidegger argues, is because we have forgotten the question of the meaning of 'Being' (*Being and Time*, §1:21). In questioning Being, we question what *is* in all entities. And so, Heidegger suggests, if we clarify what *is* in one entity, then we may gain some insight into the meaning of Being. In *Being and Time* Heidegger argues that the study of ourselves, or *Dasein* ('there-being'), is the key to the question of the meaning of Being. This is because we are the only entity for which Being is an issue. We, unlike prunes and prawns, are able consciously to choose how we want to be or whether we want to be at all. The context in which we live may set limits on the choices that we make, but we still have to choose. It is through our choices that our idea, whether hazily or explicitly understood, of what it is to be a human being is made manifest. Furthermore, our everyday activities in the world are shaped by our ability to grasp the fact that all entities *are* entities. We thus have a capacity for *ontological* understanding (see ibid., §4).

In order to throw into relief the essential ideas about what it is for a human being to *be* we must, Heidegger insists, study *Dasein* 'in its *average everydayness*' (ibid., §5:37–8). Here Heidegger departs from the philosophical tradition, as seen in the works of Kant, Descartes and

Hume, of treating human beings as detached spectators of the world. What is wrongly assumed here, he suggests, is that we can extract ourselves from the spectacle without affecting it or ourselves. We are not located in the world as water is in a glass or a table is in a room. Human existence is inconceivable apart from the world. *Dasein* is 'there-being', and 'there' is the world. Thus the being of *Dasein* is necessarily 'being-in-the-world'. We interact with entities and accord them meaning or significance in the light of our needs, interests and goals. Take, for example, the need to make clothes to keep warm. Some animals become significant because of their coats, some plants because of their suitability as feed and some tools because of their usefulness in trimming and spinning the coats of the animals. The significance of entities varies according to the variation in human needs and goals. For example, a stick may be used as a fence post, a truncheon or a didgeridoo. In our everyday interaction with entities, we are aware of them *as being for* or 'ready-to-hand' rather than *as being* that or 'present-to-hand' (ibid., §15:98). While philosophers, scientists and other academics favour studying entities as 'present-to-hand', the above point shows us that even when we are aware of objects as 'ready-to-hand', we have some understanding of the being of things. Furthermore, considering entities as being 'ready-to-hand' brings to light the web of activities and concepts that make up a society (ibid., §§14–24).

The use of the word 'society' highlights that it is with other human beings that we meet needs, interests and goals. Consequently, *Dasein's* Being is also 'Being-with'. With others, we can win or lose ourselves. Heidegger writes:

> [B]ecause Dasein is in each case essentially its own possibility, it can, in its very Being, 'choose' itself and win itself; it can also lose itself and never win itself; or only 'seem' to do so. But only insofar as it is essentially something which can be *authentic* – that is, something of its own – can it have lost itself and not yet won itself. As modes of Being, *authenticity* and *inauthenticity* . . . are both grounded in the fact that any Dasein whatsoever is characterised by mineness.
>
> (Ibid., §9:68)[3]

We are 'thrown' into the world, as Heidegger puts it, without personal choice or previous knowledge, much as a potter throws clay onto the wheel. Unlike the analogy, however, we shape ourselves, not the potter. We are able to choose what we want to be. We can be ourselves or not ourselves. When we are 'inauthentic' or not ourselves, we live on the terms of 'others' or 'they'; we follow the herd. The 'others' or 'they' are not a group of particular individuals who dictate what we will think and do. The 'they' is rather a 'nobody' in which we offload responsibility for our choices (ibid., §27:165–6). Heidegger's point is not hard to understand: you may, as I do, recall blaming 'Mr nobody' for things that you did wrong as a child. In following the herd, Heidegger claims, we seek the stimulation afforded by novelty and drift from idea to idea.

In everyday life, we are unaware that our existence is inauthentic. One state of mind, however, can help us to see what we are: anxiety (*Angst*) (§40:235). Echoing Kierkegaard, Heidegger suggests that anxiety is not fear of anything in particular, such as spiders or what others will think of us. Rather, it is the realisation that we are thrown into the world and that our existence is finite. We see that it is possible that each moment may be our last and that each of us must die for ourselves. Nobody else can die for me and I cannot choose not to die. By threatening to obliterate me, death highlights that I am what I do and that I am free to make something of my life (ibid., §26:155). I see that the life choices open to me are as contingent as my life. This may lead me to acknowledge that my life is something for which I am responsible, that my life is my own to live. In coming face to face with the possibility of death I see that I am 'guilty' of following the herd and that I am capable of altering that fact (§53:311; §54–60). This does not isolate me from others, Heidegger believes, but makes me more inclined to help others to become aware of their freedom. I may also choose to flee from this knowledge, and seek refuge in the 'they'. In fleeing from authenticity, I try not to let myself be troubled by the thought of death: '*The "they" does not permit us the courage for anxiety in the face of death*' (ibid., §51:298). For the 'they', death is something that happens to someone else. Authenticity thus entails making life choices in the knowledge of one's finitude. It is important to note that Heidegger does not think of inauthentic existence as something less than authentic existence. He is not making a value judgement about the way we ought to be. Indeed he suggests that *Dasein* in its average everydayness is by default inauthentic.

Authenticity also entails the realisation that we are temporal beings: our present experiences are shaped by our expectations and prior experiences. Past experiences are also given meaning by present experiences and expectations. It is the interrelation of past, present, and future, Heidegger claims, that binds our experiences into a single life. A key feature of the Being of *Dasein* is thus temporality. Heidegger writes: 'only as long as *Dasein* is, *can* it *be* as having been' (ibid., §65:373).

Being and time are thus interrelated. The principal manifestation of this temporality is history. The present and the future are only meaningful if they are an 'inheritance' and we are heirs. That is because in history, we find insights as to what we can accomplish as individuals and as a community.[4] As Heidegger puts it, *Dasein's* past 'is not something that *follows along after Dasein*, but something which already goes ahead of it' (ibid., §6:41). We look to history for 'heroes' and 'heroines' who can show us what is possible (ibid., §74:437; §76:448). History, for Heidegger, is a synthesis of what Nietzsche calls in *The Use and Abuse of History for Life* the 'monumental', 'antiquarian' and 'critical'. 'Monumental' history, Nietzsche suggests, shows us that 'the great which once existed was at least *possible* once and may well again be possible sometime'.[5] 'Antiquarian' history entails revering and preserving 'the existence that has been there, in which the possibility one is seizing upon became manifest' (§76:448), and 'Critical' history involves 'judging and annihilating a past'.[6] For Heidegger, though, critical history is about detaching ourselves from the 'they' (ibid., §75:444). It seems that authentic existence requires authentic history. Consequently, the historian must work to draw out the potential of the past. And this means that that historian must be aware of their own finitude (ibid., §76:447). History thus has a vital role to play in the quest for authenticity.

Despite the complexity, and often obscurity, of Heidegger's writings, works by philosophers, psychotherapists, literary theorists and theologians such as Jean-Paul Sartre, Maurice Merleau Ponty, Hans-Georg Gadamer, Ludwig Binswanger, Jacques Derrida, Rudolf Bultmann, Paul Tillich and Karl Rahner bear the imprint of his thought. To many historians and philosophers, however, it is not so much Heidegger's thought as his role in German history that is of interest. In 1933, Heidegger was elected rector of the University of Freiburg and joined the Nazi Party. In his inaugural address, *Die Selbstbehauptung der deutschen Universität* (27 May 1933; 'The Self-assertion of the German University'), and in shorter pronouncements made during his rectorship (until 23 April 1934), he argued that Adolf Hitler was leading the German people to authenticity.[7] Even after he resigned the rectorship, he continued to support Hitler. In his *Einführung in die Metaphysik* (lecture course from 1935, printed in 1953; translated as *An Introduction to Metaphysics*), for instance, he writes:

> The works that are being peddled about nowadays as the philosophy of National Socialism but have nothing whatever to do with the inner truth and greatness of this movement have

all been written by men fishing in the troubled waters of 'values' and 'totalities'.[8]

In an article published posthumously in *Der Spiegel* Heidegger responded to accusations made against him and acknowledged that compromises in stance were required for the survival of higher education and Germany itself during the 1930s.[9] However, many writers remain confused and angered about Heidegger's stance on National Socialism. For them, two important issues remain. First, can the ideas of *Being and Time* be firmly linked to those of Nazism? If so, what shall we do with the work? Second, is it possible to account for Heidegger's silence on the Third Reich and the Holocaust after 1945? Such questions require us to consider for ourselves an idea which lies at the heart of Heidegger's writings: responsibility.[10]

Notes

1 On Heidegger's early writings, see J. A. Barash, *Martin Heidegger and the Problem of Historical Meaning*, The Hague: Martinus Nijhoff, 1988.

2 All references to *Being and Time* correspond to the standard translation by Macquarrie and Robinson (1962). There is also a 1996 translation by J. Stambaugh, published by the State University of New York Press.

3 As quoted in S. Mulhall, *Heidegger and Being and Time*, London: Routledge, 1996, p. 37.

4 C. Guignon, 'History and Commitment in the Early Heidegger', in H. Dreyfus and H. Hall (eds) *Heidegger: a Critical Reader*, Oxford: Basil Blackwell, 1992, p. 136.·

5 F. Nietzsche, *On the Advantage and Disadvantage of History for Life*, trans. P. Preuss, Indianapolis, IN: Hackett Publishing, 1980, p. 16.

6 Ibid., p. 22.

7 Heidegger's inaugural address has been translated into English by K. Harries. This translation appears in the *Review of Metaphysics*, 1985, 38: 470–80.

8 As quoted in G. Steiner, *Martin Heidegger*, London: Fontana, 1994, p. 120.

9 'Nur noch ein Gott kann uns retten', *Der Spiegel*, 1976, 23: 193–219; trans. W. J. Richardson as 'Only a God can Save Us: the *Spiegel* Interview', in T. Sheehan (ed.), *Heidegger, the Man and the Thinker*, New Brunswick, NJ: Rutgers University Press, 1981.

10 On Heidegger's stance regarding National Socialism, see V. Farias, *Heidegger and Nazism*, Philadelphia, PA: Temple University Press, 1989; H. Ott, *Martin Heidegger: a Political Life*, New York: Basic Books, 1993; R. Wolin (ed.), *The Heidegger Controversy: a Critical Reader*, New York: Columbia University Press, 1991; T. Rockmore and J. Margolis (eds), *The Heidegger Case: on Philosophy and Politics*, Philadelphia, PA: Temple University Press, 1992; G. Neske and E. Kettering (eds), *Martin Heidegger and National Socialism: Questions and Answers*, New York: Paragon House, 1990; T. Rockmore, *On Heidegger's Nazism and Philosophy*, Berkeley, CA: University of California Press, 1992; J. Derrida, *Of Spirit: Heidegger and the Question*, Chicago, IL:

University of Chicago Press, 1989; P. Lacoue-Labarthe, *Heidegger, Art and Politics: the Fiction of the Political*, Oxford: Basil Blackwell, 1990; *Critical Inquiry*, 1989, 15(2); J.-F. Lyotard, *Heidegger and 'the Jews'*, trans. A. Michel and M. S. Roberts, Minneapolis, MN: University of Minneapolis Press, 1990; and A. Milchman and A. Rosenberg (eds), *Martin Heidegger and the Holocaust*, Atlantic Highlands, NJ: Humanities Press, 1996.

Heidegger's major works

Being and Time, trans. J. Macquarrie and E. Robinson, New York: Harper & Row, 1962.

See also

Arendt (CT), Derrida (CT), Heidegger (MP), Husserl (MP), Kierkegaard (MP), Nietzsche (MP and CT), Sartre (MP).

Further resources

Bambach, C. R., *Heidegger, Dilthey and the Crisis of Historicism*, Ithaca, NY: Cornell University Press, 1995.
Barash, J. A., *Martin Heidegger and the Problem of Historical Meaning*, The Hague: Martinus Nijhoff, 1988.
Congdon, L., 'Nietzsche, Heidegger and History', *Journal of European Studies*, 1973, 3(3): 211–17.
Cooper, D., *Thinkers of our Time: Heidegger*, London: Claridge Press, 1996.
Gillespie, M., *Hegel, Heidegger and the Ground of History*, Chicago, IL: University of Chicago Press, 1984.
Guignon, C. (ed.), *The Cambridge Companion to Heidegger*, Cambridge: Cambridge University Press, 1993.
Henning, E. M., 'Destruction and Repetition: Heidegger's Philosophy of History', *Journal of European Studies*, 1982, 12(4): 260–82.
Hoy, D. C., 'History, Historicity and Historiography', in M. Murray (ed.), *Heidegger and Modern Philosophy*, New Haven, CT: Yale University Press, 1978, pp. 329–53.
Mulhall, S., *Heidegger and Being and Time*, London: Routledge, 1996.
Murray, M., *Modern Philosophy of History: its Origin and Destination*, The Hague: Martinus Nijhoff, 1970.
Poggeler, O., *The Paths of Heidegger's Life and Thought*, Atlantic Highlands, NJ: Humanities Press, 1997.
Sass, H.-M., *Martin Heidegger: Bibliography and Glossary*, Bowling Green, OH: Philosophy Documentation Centre, 1982.
Steiner, G., *Martin Heidegger*, revised edition, London: Fontana, 1994.
Taylor, C., *Sources of the Self*, Cambridge: Cambridge University Press, 1989.
Wren, T., 'Heidegger's Philosophy of History', *Journal of the British Society for Phenomenology*, 1972, 3(2): 111–26.

CARL GUSTAV HEMPEL 1905–97

For most of the mid- to the late-twentieth century, debates in historiography centred on the relationship between history and science. Hempel was not the first writer to suggest that historians should employ scientific methods, but his 1942 *Journal of Philosophy* paper, 'The Function of General Laws in History', became the classic statement of the deductive-nomological or 'covering law' model of historical explanation.

Carl Gustav ('Peter') Hempel was born on 8 January 1905 in Oranienburg, Germany, and studied at the universities of Göttingen, Heidelberg, Vienna and Berlin. Though originally trained in physics and mathematics, he turned to philosophy and came under the influence of Hans Reichenbach, Moritz Schlick and Rudolf Carnap. He joined the 'Berlin Society of Empirical Philosophy', which held in common with the 'Vienna Circle' the belief that all knowledge claims should be justified by scientific methods. Hempel left Germany for Brussels in 1934 and was employed by Paul Oppenheim as a philosophical tutor and researcher. When the threat of a German invasion led Oppenheim to leave Brussels, Carnap secured a research grant for Hempel to move to the University of Chicago. Hempel stayed at Chicago until 1939 and then taught at City College and Queen's College in New York (1939–48) and Yale (1948–55). His ideas on how theories and hypotheses are confirmed, scientific explanation and the content of assumptions about the world became widely known through a stream of publications, and he was awarded professorships at Columbia (1950), Harvard (1953–54), Princeton (1955–73), Hebrew University in Jerusalem (1974), Berkeley (1975 and 1977) and Pittsburgh (1976–85). Hempel retired to Princeton in 1985 and died on 9 November 1997.

In Hempel's deductive-nomological model of explanation, the occurrence of an event (E) is explained when a statement describing that event (*Explanandum*) is logically deduced from general laws (L) and conditions that preceded the event (C) (*Explanans*). A general law is a universal claim that is capable of being confirmed or refuted by suitable empirical evidence. This may be represented in the schema shown on p. 151 (*Philosophy of Natural Science*, p. 50).

For example, in trying to explain why the egg I cooked in the microwave exploded (E), I can logically deduce from the antecedent conditions (C, I put a complete egg in the microwave; the eggshell did not have any visible cracks; the egg was cooked for x minutes and the temperature of its contents increased by y degrees before it exploded;

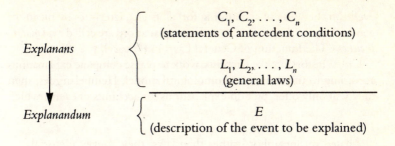

$$C_1, C_2, \ldots, C_n$$
(statements of antecedent conditions)

Explanans

$$L_1, L_2, \ldots, L_n$$
(general laws)

Explanandum

$$E$$
(description of the event to be explained)

the air pressure was normal) and general laws (*L*, the pressure of a constant mass of egg contents increases with increasing temperature) that the build-up of pressure in the contents of the egg caused its shell to explode. Here the conclusion is related to the antecedent conditions and general laws in such a manner that if they are true then the conclusion cannot fail to be true as well (*Philosophy of Science*, p. 10). If, on the other hand, I try to explain the phenomenon of the exploding egg *inductively*, I conclude, as all the eggs that I have tried to cook in the microwave have exploded, that *all* eggs cooked in a microwave will explode. Here the premises only imply the conclusion with higher or lower probability: they do not guarantee it. It is thus the *deductive* relation between the premises and the conclusion which in Hempel's view accounts for the explanatory power of the deductive–nomological model.

In seeking to explain an event, the investigator should not aim to consider all antecedent conditions and general laws, but only those deemed to be relevant to a tentative hypothesis. Therefore a tentative hypothesis is needed to give shape to an investigation. While hypotheses may be 'freely invented and proposed', they must withstand critical scrutiny. The confirmation of a tentative hypothesis depends not only on the quantity of supportive evidence available, but also on its variety. For instance, it would better to seek confirmation of a hypothesis concerning the explosion of eggs in the microwave through a number of experiments in which I alter particular variables (such as eggs with or without shells; punctured and unpunctured shells; a conventional rather than a microwave oven; different temperatures and cooking times) rather than simply repeating the same experiment over and over again. When experimental control is impossible, however, the investigator must seek or wait for 'cases where the specified conditions are realised by nature, and then [determine] out whether *x* does occur' (*Philosophy of Science*, p. 20). Through experiment and logical deduction, the investigator aims to build up *as complete an explanation* of an individual event (in the sense of accounting for *all* its characteristics by means of general laws) as they can. Incomplete explanations are called *explanatory sketches* ('The Function of General Laws in History', p. 238).

Unless historians, like scientists, work to realise complete explanations according to the deductive-nomological model, Hempel argues, then they will only offer 'pseudo explanations' or accounts of events which are

> based on metaphors rather than laws; they convey pictorial and emotional appeals instead of insight into factual connections; they substitute vague analogies and intuitive 'plausibility' for deduction from testable statements and are therefore unacceptable as scientific explanations.
>
> (Ibid., p. 234)

This is especially true of explanations built upon 'empathetic understanding'. For Hempel, when the historian 'imagines himself in the place of persons involved in the events which he wants to explain', he resorts to an unnecessary heuristic device that does not guarantee the soundness of the explanation generated:

> In history as anywhere else in empirical science, the explanation of a phenomenon consists in subsuming it under general laws; and the criterion of its soundness is not whether it appeals to our imagination, whether it is presented in terms of suggestive analogies or is otherwise made to appear plausible – all this may occur in pseudo-explanations as well – but exclusively whether it rests on empirically well-confirmed assumptions concerning initial conditions and general laws.
>
> (Ibid., p. 240)

The deductive-nomological model should also be at work when historians are 'interpreting', ascertaining the 'meaning' or tracing the development of historical events (ibid., pp. 241–2). In his later writings, however, Hempel backs off a little from this claim and admits that 'inductive probabilistic' arguments are also a legitimate form of scientific explanation. The crucial change here is that the deductive connection between the explanans and the explanandum is surrendered: the explanans only implies the explanandum with near-certainty or high probability. For example, it is highly probable that persons exposed to measles who have not had it before will contract the disease (ibid., p. 237; *Philosophy of Science*, p. 58).

There are two main reasons, Hempel claims, why historians fail to see that general laws have a function to play in historical explanation. First, many of the laws which relate to individual or social human behaviour are so well known that they are taken for granted. Second, it is usually difficult to formulate general laws 'with sufficient precision and at the same time in such a way that they are in agreement with all the relevant empirical evidence available' ('The Function of General Laws in History', p. 236). Despite this difficulty, however, Hempel believes that historians should try to reveal the laws which cover their explanations.

Hempel's 'The Function of General Laws in History' had a mixed reception among historians, historiographers and philosophers of history. Some saw it as a welcome step towards the establishment of a more rigorous, testable methodology. For example, though Hempel was neutral to the question of whether there are 'specifically historical laws' (ibid., p. 242), Morton White argued in 'Historical Explanation' that historians apply laws provided by social scientists.[1] Others tried to modify the deductive-nomological model to make it more palatable to historians. In *The Nature of Historical Explanation* (1952), for instance, Patrick Gardiner argues that the deductive-nomological model does have a part to play in historical research, but he also allows for a second type of explanation ('dispositional explanation') in cases where historians are trying to explain human conduct that is of a purposive kind. Here, the historian considers the behaviour of historical agents in the light of 'the pattern of [their] normal behaviour' (pp. 124–5). Gardiner also argues that, as historians use ordinary language, they formulate 'loose and porous' laws. In *Introduction to the Philosophy of History* (1951), W. H. Walsh also argues for a compromise. For Walsh, while historians make at least implicit reference to general truths in interpreting historical evidence, these truths derive from a non-technical knowledge of human nature. This knowledge is a kind of 'common sense', which is hard to see as being arrived at through any scientific research.[2]

Many, however, saw Hempel's ideas as irrelevant to the practice of historical research. It was pointed out, for instance, that historians do not in practice advance covering law explanations, or at least that they do not do so explicitly. To accept the deductive-nomological model we either have to discount nearly all claims made by historians as 'pseudo-explanations', or argue that historians really do follow the model but do not usually make the laws they draw upon explicit. To many historians these options seemed implausible.[3] Even firm adherents of the deductive-nomological model had difficulty thinking of examples of historical statements that explicitly included general laws.

Others argued that the model *ought* not to be applied in history. For instance, Alan Donagan complained in 'Historical Explanation' (1964–65)[4] that the deductive-nomological model 'mutilated research into human affairs', and W. H. Dray argued in *Laws and Explanation in History* (1957) that general laws are neither implied by or necessary for historical explanations.[5] For Dray, as history is about human actions, actions are best explained in terms of the reasons for which they were done. For example, in trying to explain why A did B, the historian should argue:

> Agent A was in a situation of kind X.
> When in a situation of type X, the thing to do is B.
> Therefore A did B.

The historian's aim is to show that the action was a reasonable thing to have done – from the agent's perspective – in the circumstances. A modified version of Dray's 'rational-action model' of explanation is at the heart of Rex Martin's *Historical Explanation: Re-enactment and Practical Inference* (1977). For Martin, the 'basic schema' of rational actions is this:

> If (1) any person x is in a particular situation which he proposes to deal with in a certain way, and (2) one of the courses of action he might take is A, although alternatively he might take courses B, C, and D, and (3) his purpose is to handle the situation by accomplishing such-and-so thing, and (4) this purpose, or end in view, is not overidden by any other purpose that he has, and (5) he does not prefer any of the alternative courses of action – B, C, or D – to doing A, and (6) doing A is judged by him to be a means to, or a part of accomplishing, his purpose, and (7) he is able, personally and situationally, to do A, then x does A.[6]

For Martin, any behaviour which does not fit in with this schema is not an action, and since the schema can only be disproved by finding an action which does not fit in with it, it can never be refuted.

Some writers even disagreed that the 'rational-action model' applied to history, and went on to claim that the narrative form of most written histories constituted a distinct type of explanation. Works on the role of narrative in history such as Danto's *Analytical Philosophy of History* (1965) and Gallie's *Philosophy and the Historical Understanding* (1964) became increasingly popular in the late 1970s. Although these works led many historians to question Hempel's ideas, changing views of the nature of science – stimulated in the main by Kuhn's *The Structure of Scientific Revolutions* – were to reduce the deductive-nomological model to tatters.

Notes

1 M. G. White, 'Historical Explanation', *Mind*, 1943, 52(207): 212–29. See also R. W. Fogel, 'The New Economic History', *The Economic History Review*, 1966, 19(3): 642–56; and J. R. Hollingsworth, 'Theory Construction for Historical Analysis', *Historical Methods Newsletter*, 1974, 7(3): 225–48.
2 See also A. C. Danto, *Analytical Philosophy of History*, Cambridge: Cambridge University Press, 1964; and P. Munz, 'The Skeleton and the Mollusc: Reflections on the Nature of Historical Narratives', *New Zealand Journal of History*, 1967, 1(1): 107–23.
3 See, for example, D. F. Fischer, *Historian's Fallacies: Towards a Logic of Historical Thought*, London: Routledge & Kegan Paul, 1971; J. H. Hexter, *The History Primer*, London: Penguin, 1971; and G. Leff, *History and Social Theory*, Montgomery, AL: University of Alabama Press, 1969.
4 A. Donagan, 'Historical Explanation: the Popper–Hempel Theory Reconsidered', *History and Theory*, 1964, 4(1): 25.
5 See also L. Goldstein, *Historical Knowing*, Austin, TX: University of Texas Press, 1976.
6 R. Martin, *Historical Explanation: Re-enactment and Practical Inference*, Ithaca, NY: Cornell University Press, pp. 158–9.

Hempel's major works

'The Function of General Laws in History', *The Journal of Philosophy*, 1942, 39(1): 35–48.
Aspects of Scientific Explanation and Other Essays in the Philosophy of Science, New York: The Free Press, 1965.
Philosophy of Natural Science, Englewood Cliffs, NJ: Prentice-Hall, 1966.

See also

Carnap (MP), Collingwood, Dilthey, Hume (MP), Kuhn, Oakeshott, Schlick (MP), Walsh.

Further resources

Danto, A. C., *Analytical Philosophy of History*, Cambridge: Cambridge University Press, 1965.
Donagan, A., 'Historical Explanation: the Popper–Hempel Theory Reconsidered', *History and Theory*, 1964, 4(1): 3–26.
Dray, W. H., *Laws and Explanation in History*, London: Oxford University Press, 1957.

—— (ed.), *Philosophical Analysis and History*, New York: Harper & Row, 1966.

Gallie, W. B., *Philosophy and the Historical Understanding*, London: Chatto & Windus, 1964.

Gardiner, P., *The Nature of Historical Explanation*, London: Oxford University Press, 1952.

Jeffrey, R., 'A Brief Guide to the Work of Carl Gustav Hempel', *Erkenntnis*, 1995, 42(1): 1–14.

Kuhn, T. S., *The Structure of Scientific Revolutions*, third edition, Chicago, IL: University of Chicago Press, 1996.

McCullagh, C. B., *Justifying Historical Descriptions*, Cambridge: Cambridge University Press, 1984.

——, *The Truth of History*, London: Routledge, 1998.

Mandelbaum, M., *The Anatomy of Historical Knowledge*, Baltimore, MD: Johns Hopkins University Press, 1977.

Martin, R., *Historical Explanation: Re-enactment and Practical Inference*, Ithaca, NY: Cornell University Press, 1977.

Murphey, M. G., 'Explanation, Causes, and Covering Laws', *History and Theory*, 1986, 13(1): 43–57.

Porter, D. H., 'History as Process', *History and Theory*, 1987, 14(3): 297–313.

Walsh, W. H., *Introduction to Philosophy of History*, London: Hutchinson University Library, 1951.

White, M. G., *The Foundations of Historical Knowledge*, New York: Harper & Row, 1965.

HERODOTUS *c.* 484–*c.* 424 BC

Father of history or father of lies?[1] This question sums up much of the debate on Herodotus' *Histories* that has raged since ancient times. Though Herodotus is credited with the production of the first narrative history, he has been accused of deliberate falsehood, inconsistency, errors of fact and judgement, undue credulity and easy acceptance of unreliable sources of information. It is only recently that scholars have begun to appreciate fully his remarkable fusion of chronology, ethnology, geography and poetry into a work that is both very readable and an important source of information on the ancient world.

Herodotus was born probably around 484 BC in Halicarnassus, now Bodrum on the Aegean coast of Turkey. He was possibly of mixed Carian-Greek origin, for his father's name was Carian. Carians lived in the hinterland of Halicarnassus. Herodotus' only known work, the *Histories*, suggests that he travelled widely, visiting Egypt, Cyrene, Babylon, Italy, the Ukraine, the Black Sea and the north Aegean area. There is good reason to believe that he wrote the *Histories* during the Peloponnesian War (431–404 BC) and that his work was published between 430 and 424 BC. The date of his death is uncertain.

The *Histories* consists of two parts. The second part outlines the struggles between the Persians and Greeks, from the Ionian Revolt of 499 BC to the defeat of Xerxes' invasion in 479 BC (5.28–9).[2] This is preceded by an account of these struggles and the growth of the Persian Empire and of the Greek states of Athens and Sparta (1–5.27). The work was divided by Aldus in 1511 into nine books named after the Muses and further divided into chapters by Jungerman in 1608.

In the preface, Herodotus writes of his project:

> Herodotus of Halicarnassus, his *Researches* are here set down to preserve the memory of the past by putting on record the astonishing achievements both of our own and of other peoples; and more particularly, to show how they came into conflict.
>
> (1.1.1)

With these words, Herodotus embarks upon the 'demonstration of his research' (*apodexis histories*) in order to preserve the essential facts and causes of recent events, a demonstration unparalleled in the ancient world. Herodotus had his predecessors in prose writing, but they wrote either histories of particular groups or cities or accounts of travel over the known world. No one until Herodotus, as Dionysius of Halicarnassus pointed out, had put together the many varied events of Asia and Europe and a description of their peoples and lands in a single work.[3]

The prologue (1.1–6), which states the aims of the work, leads directly to an account of the history of Lydia and its conquest by the Persians (1.7–94). In this, King Croesus of Lydia is fated to pay for the murder of King Candaules by his ancestor Gyges. This is followed by an account of the life of the Persian ruler Cyrus (*c.* 559–529 BC): his defeat of the Medes (1.95–130), second conquest of Ionia after the Revolt of Pactyas (1.141–76), conquest of Babylon (1.111–201) and war with Massagetae, which claimed his life (1.201–216). Book 2 looks to the rule of Cyrus' son, Cambyses (529–521 BC), and his plans to attack Egypt. This leads to a long digression on the geography, history and ethnology of Egypt. Book 3 describes Cambyses' conquest of Egypt, the failure of his invasions to the south (Ethiopia) and west, and his madness and death (3.1–25). Cambyses' madness, Herodotus claims, is clearly seen in his ridicule of Persian religious practices, for,

> if someone were to propose to each man to choose the best

customs of all that are, he would look them over and choose
his own.

(3.38.1)

Cambyses' death sparks off struggles over the succession in Persia,
ending with the enthroning of Darius (521–486 BC). The remainder
of book 3 is taken up mostly with an account of how Darius organised
the Persian Empire, what some of the distant provinces in the empire
were like (such as India, 3.98–105) and how he suppressed internal
revolts (3.61–158). This book also contains a description of three events
in the history of the Samians because these people, Herodotus claims,
were responsible for three of the greatest building and engineering
feats in the Greek world: a mile-long tunnel through a mountain; a
harbour created by a breakwater; and the largest temple in the Greek
world. Book 4 offers a description of the customs and history of the
Scythians of southern Russia (4.1–82) and an account of Darius' attempt
to conquer them (4.83–144). Book 4 also details the Persian attack
from Egypt on Libya, and the history and geography of that country
(4.168–205). This concludes the background history to the conflict
between the Greeks and the Persians.

In the Ionian Revolt (5.28), ill-feeling between the Persians and the
Greeks erupts into violence. The suppression of the Ionian Revolt is
described in the first half of book 6 (1–98), as is the nature of the
relationship between Athens and Sparta during the reign of Cleomenes
(6.49–66) and Leotychides (6.67–93). The Campaign of Marathon (490
BC), in which the Persians are defeated by the Athenians, takes up the
remainder of book 6 (94–120). Darius died not long after this battle and
his successor, Xerxes (485–465 BC), vowed to reverse its outcome. The
last three books (7–9) – those most highly regarded among historians –
look to the Persian and Greek preparations (7.20–138, 138–174), land
fights at Thermopylae (7.198–233), Plataea (9.12–88) and Mycale
(9.96–106) and the corresponding sea-fights at Artemisium (7.179–195;
8.1–23) and Salamis (8.40–113). The Persians are defeated and retreat.

History, Herodotus suggests, shows patterns of growth and decline:

> I will proceed with my history, telling the story as I go along
> of small cities no less than of great. For most of those which
> were great once are small today; and those which used to be
> small were great in my own time. Knowing, therefore, that
> human prosperity never abides long in the same place, I shall
> pay attention to both alike.
>
> (1.5)

Phases of growth and decline, he believes, can be explained in two ways. First, continual good fortune breeds arrogance. Arrogant people, Herodotus tells us, are liable to ignore warnings. Once they overstep their mortal limits, punishment is visited upon them in the form of Justice (*Dike*) or Retribution (*Nemesis*). This point may be seen in the account of the rise and fall of Cyrus in book 1 (1.108–204). Second, the rise and fall of states may be explained in terms of 'hard' and 'soft' cultures.[4] 'Hard' cultures are underdeveloped, lacking in central government and fiercely independent. Soft cultures are wealthy, often ruled by absolute monarchs and open to conquest by outsiders. *political?* Hard cultures, Herodotus suggests, are likely to conquer soft cultures. When they do so, they tend to become soft and thus liable to invasion. Persia demonstrates this cycle. At the beginning of the period Herodotus details, Persia is poor and backward (1.71). By book 7, however, all Persians look to Xerxes to maintain their safety and lavish lifestyles. Herodotus leaves us in no doubt that Xerxes is a harsh and megalomaniacal ruler. The softness or weakness of Persia is thrown into relief when Xerxes confronts the Greeks. The Greeks, in Herodotus' estimation, are a hard people who work together to keep poverty and invaders at bay (7.102). This difference between 'hardness' and 'softness' explains the success of the Greeks.

In the *Histories*, Herodotus only mentions one predecessor, Hecataeus of Miletus, who wrote a work on historical geography, *Periodos*. Hecataeus, Herodotus tells us, lived through the Ionian Revolt of 499 BC and twice gave the rebels advice that they rejected (5.36.2; 5.125). Herodotus also reports with thinly disguised glee the dismissal of Hecataeus' claim to have a deity as his ancestor by Egyptian priests (2.143). Herodotus had read what Hecataeus wrote about Egypt, but too little of *Periodos* survives to measure how dependent he was on it. It seems that the two had very similar ideas about the Ionian Revolt but that Herodotus had more developed ideas about cartography. He is dismissive, for instance, of maps that showed the world as a disc encircled by a river called Ocean. Other intellectual influences on Herodotus are more difficult to trace. He might have seen Charon of Campsaus' *On Persia*, Xanthus of Lydia's *On Lydia* and even perhaps works by Dionysius of Miletus, Hellanicus of Cesbo and Pherekydes of Athens.[5]

Whereas he fails to mention any prose writer except Hecataeus, he *poets* frequently cites poets such as Homer and Hesiod. Though he denounces *as* poets for preferring the suitable to the accurate, one can see the influence *precursors* of poetry on both the structure of the work (for example, 3.14; 5.11; 17, 106; 7.10, 159; 9.21ff.) and on his choice of particular phrases (such as 7.10, 103; 9.50). For instance, Herodotus' work is characterised by 'ring composition', a return at the end of a section to the subject announced at the beginning.[6] This is seen clearly in books 2 and 3, where the announcement of Cambyses' intention to invade Egypt leads to a digression on the geography and ethnology of Egypt and then returns to the details of the invasion. This was a common feature of epics at the time. Digressions were also not uncommon in epic narrative. There are more than 200 digressions in the *Histories*, ranging from single lines to twenty-eight *logoi*, or detailed expositions of 'what is said'. In the *logoi*, Herodotus considers the geography, climate, flora and fauna, customs and history of particular regions. 'Analysts' of the late nineteenth century and early twentieth century thought that the twenty-eight main *logoi* were originally published separately, but more recently 'unitarians' have stressed the continuity of themes in all parts of the work.[7]

Most of the *Histories* is constructed from oral evidence that Herodotus collected in his travels. In four places he mentions oral informants by name (3.55.2; 4.76.6; 8.65; 9.16.1). More frequently, he prefaces reports with phrases such as 'the Spartans say', 'the Greeks say' and the 'the Persians say'. When Herodotus cites ethnic groups as sources, it is implied that he is conveying their official traditions. For example, Sparta, Cyrene and Thera all had official accounts of the founding of Cyrene (4.150–151, 154.1).

When one considers Herodotus' accounts of giant ants, the gathering of the gum ledanon from the beards of billy goats, sheep with giant tails and flying snakes, it is not hard to see why many people think of him as a credulous writer who had a taste for the fantastic (3.102–113). In a number of places, however, Herodotus shows us that he did not accept everything that he was told. Sometimes he casts doubt on reports of an incident, indicates his scepticism about particular claims, reports what he heard without believing it himself and dismisses accounts outright (for instance, 2.123; 4.195.2; 6.105.3; 7.37.3; 152.3). He also offers alternative versions of events on more than 125 occasions. Instances where he offers alternatives include those where there are conflicting accounts and where he offers his own thoughts on an event. Some alternatives are posed only to be dismissed immediately (such as 3.9.2) but others are left open to the reader's judgement (for example, 3.122.1; 5.45.2). Generally, however, he tries to choose intelligently (like 2.146.1; 4.11.1; 8.94.1–4, 19). Subsequent archaeological and historical research has shown that he is reasonably accurate. Herodotus thus considers many accounts of events to be discussable, his own account to be the best working explanation and others' accounts to be worthy of more than dismissal. These features, Denniston believes, give his work a 'winning fallibility'.[8]

Herodotus probably also used oral information to construct the speeches in his *Histories*. In the work, we can distinguish between speeches given in *oratio recta* and those given in *oratio obliqua*.[9] The former are his own reconstruction of events and are used to present themes, while the latter are more likely to represent accurately the gist of the actual words. An example of speeches in *oratio recta* can be found in the debate in book 3 among Otanes, Megabyzus and Darius on the forms of government. This debate is clearly Herodotus' own composition, as it refers to the contemporary Greek division of forms of government into three types: democracy, oligarchy and monarchy. In inserting speeches by the leading figures into his narrative, Herodotus began a practice that would persist in later works of history.

The *Histories* also contains more than eighty references to oracular evidence. These range from single lines to the dozen lines of each of the pronouncements offered to the Athenians before the battle at Salamis (7.64). Delphi, as the foremost shrine of the time, predominates. The number of oracular references in the work may lead the modern reader to conclude that he was of a superstitious nature. For example, he writes in 8.77:

> Now I cannot deny that there is truth in prophecies, and I have no wish to discredit them when they are expressed in unambiguous language.

He does not simply accept this source of evidence as infallible, however, as he offers examples where oracles are unreliable, where some oracles are found to be better than others and where oracle-keepers have been corrupted (for instance, 1.46ff.; 2.152; 5.63; 6.66). Herodotus also refers to twenty-four inscriptions, half of which are Greek. Some he copied, for he gives the texts, but one at least, an inscription on the Great Pyramid at Gizah, he paraphrased from memory (2.156.6). His use of the above types of evidence, combined with much material evidence (such as descriptions of buildings, bridges, sculptures) make his work an invaluable source of information on the ancient world.

Herodotus' *Histories* have long been viewed with ambivalence. This ambivalence is typified in Cicero's suggestion that in history

> everything is meant to lead to the truth, but in poetry, a great deal is intended for pleasure – although in Herodotus, the father of history . . . there are countless numbers of myth and legends.[10]

[handwritten marginal note: Herodotus in between myth and history as science?]

161

His ideas had much influence on historians of the ancient world, but it was the style of the *Histories*, not the content, that elicited the praise of writers such as Cicero and Quintilian. Herodotus' work was not thought to stand up to the historian's aim of telling the truth. After all, historians tend not to write about flying snakes. He acquired the reputation of being biased and unreliable. Thucydides, for instance, never mentions Herodotus by name in his *History of the Peloponnesian War*, but the work carries the implied message that Herodotus' work will not last because it was designed to please the ear (1.22.4). Thucydides claimed to set a standard of research that was thought to be lacking in the *Histories*. Ctesias of Cnidus labelled Herodotus a liar and a storyteller in his account of Persia and the Wars and a number of pamphlets directed against Herodotus were produced down to the end of the Roman Empire. Of these, the only one that survives is Plutarch's 'On the Malice of Herodotus'. In this, Plutarch argues that Herodotus favoured what was discreditable to the Greeks.[11]

Herodotus' work continued to be viewed with ambivalence in the Renaissance. The *Histories* were fairly popular as there were forty-four editions or translations produced in Europe between 1450 and 1700, but much scepticism was also expressed about them. His rehabilitation, Momigliano has suggested, began in 1566 when Henri Estienne prefaced Lorenzo Vallas's Latin translation of the *Histories* (1479) with his *Apologia pro Herodoto*.[12] The *Apologia* was reproduced by Thomas Gale in London (1679), Gronovius in Leiden (1715) and Wesseling in Amsterdam (1763). Estienne expanded his defence of Herodotus in *Introduction au traité de la conformité des merveilles anciennes avec les modernes* (Geneva, 1566). Though his reputation was largely open to question in the eighteenth century, as the archaeology of Egypt, Persia and Assyria became better known in the nineteenth century, people began to see that many of his 'marvellous tales' had foundation. The twentieth century saw a growth in respect among scholars for Herodotus' attempts to get at the causes of events, his acknowledgement of fallibility and his skill in drawing readers into the text. With the release of the film of Michael Ondaatje's *The English Patient* (1996), in which Herodotus is frequently mentioned, the *Histories* even became for a time *the* book to read in trendy cafés.

Notes

1 J. A. S. Evans, 'The Reputation of Herodotus', *Classical Journal*, 1968, 64(1): 11–17.
2 Book, chapter and section citations correspond to the Loeb edition of the *Histories* translated by A. D. Godley.

3 W. K. Pritchett, *Dionysius of Halicarnassus: On Thucydides*, Berkeley, CA: University of California Press, 1975, pp. 50–7. See also A. Momigliano, 'Greek Historiography', *History and Theory*, 1978, 17(1): 1–28.
4 T. J. Luce, *The Greek Historians*, London: Routledge, 1997, p. 57.
5 Ibid., pp. 10, 13, 20, 36.
6 Ibid., p. 13.
7 S. Cagnazzi, 'Tavola dei 28 Logoi di Erodoto', *Hermes*, 1975, 103(385): 62; K. H. Waters, *Herodotos the Historian: his Problems, Method and Originality*, Sydney: Croom Helm, 1985; D. Lateiner, *The Historical Method of Herodotus*, Phoenix suppl. vol. 23, Toronto, University of Toronto Press, 1989, introduction.
8 J. D. Denniston, *The Greek Particles*, Oxford: Oxford University Press, 1934, p. 23.
9 J. E. Powell, *The History of Herodotus*, Cambridge: Cambridge University Press, 1939.
10 *Laws*, 1.5. See J. A. S. Evans, *Herodotus*, conclusion.
11 Plutarch, 'On the Malice of Herodotus', *Plutarch's Moralia*, trans. L. Pearson and F. H. Sandbach, Loeb Classical Library, London: Heinemann, 1970, vol. 11, pp. 9–129.
12 A. Momigliano, 'The Place of Herodotus in the History of Historiography', *History*, 1958, 43(1): 1–13. See also P. Burke, 'A Survey of the Popularity of Ancient Historians', *History and Theory*, 1966, 5(1): 135–52.

Herodotus' major works

Herodotus: The Histories, 4 vols, trans. A. D. Godley, Loeb Classical Series, London: W. Heinemann, 1926. Online at: http://www.perseus.tufts.edu/Texts.html
The Histories, trans. A. de Selincourt, rev. A. R. Burn, Penguin Classics, Harmondsworth: Penguin, 1972.

See also

Gregory of Tours, Livy, Polybius, Protagoras (MP), Tacitus, Thucydides.

Further resources

Bengston, H., *The Greeks and the Persians: the Defence of the West*, London: Weidenfeld & Nicolson, 1969.
Evans, J. A. S., *Herodotus*, Boston, MA: Twayne Publishers, 1985.
Fontenrose, J., *The Delphic Oracle*, Berkeley, CA: University of California Press, 1978.
Fornara, C. W., *The Nature of History in Ancient Greece and Rome*, Berkeley, CA: University of California Press, 1983.
Gould, J., *Herodotus*, New York: St Martin's Press, 1989.
Hornblower, S. (ed.), *Greek Historiography*, Oxford: Oxford University Press, 1994.
How, W. and Wells, J. A., *A Commentary on Herodotus*, 2 vols, Oxford: Oxford University Press, 1928.

Hunter, V., *Past and Process in Herodotus and Thucydides*, Princeton, NJ: Princeton University Press, 1982.

Lateiner, D., *The Historical Method of Herodotos*, Phoenix suppl. vol. 23, Toronto: University of Toronto Press, 1989.

Luce, T. J., *The Greek Historians*, London: Routledge, 1997.

Momigliano, A., *Studies in Historiography*, London: Weidenfeld & Nicolson, 1966.

The English Patient [video recording] directed by Anthony Minghella, Miramax Films, 1996.

Waters, K. H., *Herodotos, the Historian: his Problems, Method and Originality*, Sydney: Croom Helm, 1985.

ERIC HOBSBAWM 1917–

The son of Leopold Percy Hobsbawm and Nelly Grün, Eric John Ernest Hobsbawm (1917–) was educated in Vienna and Berlin before moving to England in 1932. He continued his education at St Marylebone Grammar School and at King's College, Cambridge, where he completed a BA and a PhD. He has spent the bulk of his academic career at Birkbeck College, London.[1] Hobsbawm has written scores of works on a wide range of political and historical themes, but he is best known for his history of the 'triumph and transformation of capitalism', beginning with the 'dual revolution' (the first industrial revolution in Britain and the French political revolution) and ending with the widespread collapse of communist regimes in the 1980s and 1990s (*The Age of Revolution: Europe 1789–1848*, 1962; *Industry and Empire; an Economic History since 1750*, 1968; *The Age of Capital 1848–1875*, 1975; *The Age of Empire 1875–1914*, 1987; and *Age of Extremes: the Short Twentieth Century 1914–1991*, 1994).

For Hobsbawm, the age of the 'dual revolution' between 1780 and 1848 saw:

> the triumph not of 'industry' as such, but of *capitalist* industry; not of liberty and equality in general but of *middle class* or '*bourgeois*' *liberal* society; not of the 'modern economy' or the 'modern state', but of the economies and states in a particular geographical region of the world (part of Europe and a few patches of North America), whose centre was the neighbouring and rival states of Great Britain and France.
>
> (*The Age of Revolution*, p. 1)

Britain led the charge through the ceiling which existing social structures and science and technology had imposed on production (ibid., p. 28). There, farming was already predominantly for the market, manufacture had spread throughout the countryside and 'private profit and economic development had become accepted as the supreme objects of government policy' (ibid., p. 31). A relatively small number of landlords acquired much of the land and employed tenant farmers to work their holdings. These tenant-farmers produced food for sale in growing urban markets. The increasing number of peasants who could not find work on the land became mobile wage workers for the non-agricultural sector of the economy (ibid., chap. 8). Initially they worked for urban merchants in shops or homes. New technologies and the expansion of both the export and domestic markets, however, soon saw many people labouring under appalling conditions in factories. This industrial revolution, Hobsbawm argues, left the labouring poor and the emerging industrial proletariat with three choices: they could try to join or follow the precepts of the middle classes, accept their lot in life, or rebel. And such was their lot that 'rebellion was not merely possible, but virtually compulsory'. 'Nothing was more inevitable', he suggests, than the rise of labour and socialist movements, and the revolutions in France, Austria, Prussia, Hungary, Bohemia, and parts of Italy in 1848 (ibid., p. 204). These revolutions were to be unsuccessful, however, for workers 'lacked the organisation, the maturity, the leadership, perhaps most of all the historical conjuncture, to provide a political alternative' (*The Age of Capital*, p. 21).

This was instead to be the age of the triumphant liberal 'bourgeoisie' (1848–75), for, during this period, revolutions defused the explosive discontents of the poor and achieved economic, institutional and cultural hegemony (*The Age of Empire*, p. 9). That hegemony, Hobsbawm believes, was secured via both the industrial (British) *and* political (French) revolutions. For him, the French Revolution (1789–99) was made possible in the main by a consensus of general ideas among the bourgeoisie. They were against the hierarchy of noble privilege and the political power of the Roman Catholic church and for the creation of a 'secular state with civil liberties and guarantees for private enterprise, and government by tax-payers and property-owners' (*The Age of Revolution*, p. 59; see also *Echoes of the Marseillaise*, 1990). The 'dual revolution' thus heralded the global triumph of capitalism in an 'age of capital' (1848–70s):

> the triumph of a society which believed that economic growth
> rested on competitive private enterprise. . . . An economy so
> based, and therefore resting naturally on the sound foundations
> of a bourgeoisie composed of those whom energy, merit
> and intelligence had raised to their position and kept there,

would – it was believed – not only create a world of suitably distributed material plenty, but of ever-growing enlightenment, reason and human opportunity, an advance of the sciences and the arts, in brief a world of continuous and accelerating material and moral progress. . . . The institutions of the world . . . would gradually approximate to the international model of a territorially defined 'nation-state' with a constitution guaranteeing property and civil rights, elected representative assemblies and governments responsible to them, and, where suitable, a participation in politics of the common people within such limits as would guarantee the bourgeois social order and avoid the risk of its overthrow.

(*The Age of Capital*, p. 1)

The history of the nineteenth century was thus lopsided in favour of industrial revolution. However, at the onset of the 1870s depression, which marked the dawn of the 'age of empire' (1875–1914), it became clear that the world created by and for the liberal bourgeoisie would not be the permanent template of the modern industrial world (*The Age of Empire*, p. 11). Politically, the end of the liberal era ushered in the awareness that the hierarchical nobility and the bourgeoisie could no longer speak for the 'lower orders' or rely on their support. The 'lower orders' began to speak for themselves in working-class parties and movements that generally had a socialist orientation. This 'age' also saw the rise of the ideas of 'nation' and 'nationalism' (*The Age of Empire*, chap. 6; see also *Nations and Nationalism since 1780*). It was further characterised by a move away from unrestrained competitive private enterprise, British industrial monopoly, small and medium-sized business and government abstention from interference in business practices, and a move towards large corporations, mass production and consumption, considerable government interference, imperialism – a dichotomy between dominant 'advanced' countries and dominated 'developing' countries – and fierce international competition between rival national economies such as Britain, Germany and the United States.

These rivalries boiled over into the First World War, the first of many global catastrophes in the 'age of extremes' (1914–91). The 'short' twentieth century, Hobsbawm believes, can be divided into three parts: the 'age of catastrophe' (1914–late 1940s), the 'golden age' (late 1940s–1973) and 'the landslide' (1973–91). The 'age of catastrophe' is aptly named. In the period between 1914 and the late 1940s the world was shaken by two 'total' wars, rebellions and revolutions which brought to power a system thought to be an alternative to bourgeois and capitalist society, the collapse of colonial empires, and a world economic crisis. Just how a 'golden age' arose out of the ruins of Europe, Hobsbawm suggests, is still to be explained by historians. What is clear is that the economic, social and cultural transformation that it entailed was 'the greatest, most rapid and most fundamental in recorded history' (*Age of Extremes*, p. 8). In the early 1970s, however, the world struggled against mass unemployment, cyclical slumps, the ever-increasing gap between rich and poor and the breakdown of many socialist countries.

In the 'age of extremes', four things loom large. First, there is the restructuring of the ideas and practices of capitalism, which allowed it successfully to meet the challenges of communism and fascism. In line with this view, Hobsbawm portrays the Russian Revolution primarily as a wake-up call to capitalist societies:

> as we now see in retrospect, the strength of the global socialist challenge to capitalism was that of the weakness of its opponent. Without the breakdown of nineteenth-century bourgeois society in the Age of Catastrophe, there would have been no October Revolution and no USSR.
> (*Age of Extremes*, p. 8; see also 'The Present as History', in *On History*, p. 237)

The Russian Revolution, and fascism, forced capitalism to capture a broad social base and to deliver on its economic promises (*Age of Extremes*, chaps 4, 5, 9).

Second, the world ceased to be Eurocentric. The power of European countries waned as their ideas and industries migrated throughout the globe. This transformation is reflected in the expanding scope of the *Age of . . .* series. Whereas *The Age of Revolution* is focused in the main on developments in Britain and France, *Age of Extremes* encompasses developments throughout the world. Third, it saw the rise of transnational activities. Breakthroughs in communication and transport helped to make the world 'more of a single operational unit'. Fourth, it is marked by the disintegration of the 'Enlightenment project': the establishment of a universal system of moral standards (ibid., pp. 13–15; 'Barbarism: a User's Guide', in *On History*, p. 254).

This is the development of the twentieth century most regretted by Hobsbawm. People who no longer have social guides to action, he argues, do 'unspeakable things'. Intellectuals may argue that the Enlightenment project is nothing but the aspiration of a white male elite writ large, but in Hobsbawm's opinion it is 'the only foundation for all the aspirations to build societies fit for *all* human beings to live anywhere on this Earth, and for the assertion and defence of their human rights as persons'. Take away that foundation and we offer people 'the chance of entering an erotic paradise of the all-is-permitted' ('Barbarism: a User's Guide', in *On History*, p. 254). That, Hobsbawm believes, has been amply demonstrated in the many atrocities committed in the twentieth century. Some historians may believe that such things are not their concern. Indeed Hobsbawm confesses that he used to feel that way:

> I used to think that the profession of history, unlike that of, say, nuclear physics, could at least do no harm. Now I know it can. Our studies can turn into bomb factories like the workshops in which the IRA has learned to transform chemical fertiliser into an explosive.
>
> ('Outside and Inside History', in *On History*, p. 5;
> see also 'Identity History is Not Enough',
> in ibid., p. 277)

History can do harm because the past can be used to legitimise actions. It can be the 'fertiliser' for nationalist, ethnic or fundamentalist ideologies. And if there is no suitable past, then one can be invented (see 'Introduction' in *The Invention of Tradition*, pp. 1–14). In response, historians must defend the supremacy of evidence and fulfil their responsibility of criticising the politico–ideological abuse of history. For Hobsbawm this entails being committed to the belief that historians can distinguish between fact and fiction, between statements based on evidence and those which are not (*On History*, pp. viii, 6, 271–2). This is not to say that historians must stand outside their subject matter as objective observers. All historians, Hobsbawm insists, 'are plunged into the assumptions of our times and places' (ibid., p. 276). But to be worthy of the title 'historian', they must subject their assumptions to critical scrutiny. Though Hobsbawm tells us that these are important matters, he does not explore them in much detail.

He does, however, practise what he preaches. In the introduction to *Age of Extremes*, for instance, he tells of his struggle to write historically about events that he experienced personally (see also 'The Present as History', in *On History*, pp. 228–40). Yet he does not shy away from bringing his voice to the fore. As a number of reviewers have noted, Hobsbawm's personal anecdotes make *Age of Extremes* compelling reading.[2] He is also not frightened to tell us about what he values. It is pretty clear, for instance, that he has a great deal of sympathy for the labouring poor and the industrial proletariat. Consider, for instance, this excerpt from the introduction to *The Age of Capital*:

> The author of this book cannot conceal a certain distaste, perhaps a certain contempt, for the age with which it deals, though one mitigated by admiration for its titanic material achievements and by the effort to understand even what he does not like. . . . His sympathies lie with those to whom few listened a century ago.
>
> (p. 5)

Hobsbawm's commitment to those 'to whom few listened' is also evident in the host of books that he has written on forms of social movement and rebellion: *Labour's Turning Point* (1948), *Primitive Rebels* (1959), *Labouring Men* (1964), *Captain Swing* (with G. Rudé, 1969), *Bandits* (1969), *Revolutionaries* (1973), *Worlds of Labour* (1984) and *The Jazz Scene* (originally published under the pseudonym F. Newton, 1959).[3] But he also resists the temptation to romanticise working-class dissent.[4] In his and George Rudé's account of the English Swing Riots of 1830, for instance, we are not sheltered from the knowledge that some workers engaged in a vengeful campaign of poaching, burning and rural terror (*Captain Swing*, p. 11). Nor does he assume that their actions are equivalent to revolutionary politics. In *Primitive Rebels*, for example, he suggests that many of the forms of social movement in the nineteenth and twentieth centuries were reformist rather than revolutionary. They wanted to restore the values and practices of the past (as they actually were or as they 'remembered' them), not create a new society. He writes of social banditry of the 'Robin Hood type', for instance:

> [It] is little more than endemic peasant protest against oppression and poverty: a cry for vengeance on the rich and the oppressors, a vague dream of some curb upon them, a righting of individual wrongs. Its ambitions are modest: a traditional world in which men are justly dealt with, not a new and perfect world. . . . Social banditry has next to no organisation or ideology, and is totally inadaptable to modern social movements.
>
> (*Primitive Rebels*, p. 5)

Hobsbawm is similarly critical of the writer who inspired him to write such histories: Marx. Hobsbawm is not a Marxist zealot. He has never hesitated to move beyond that which he feels is dated and erroneous in Marx and Marxist thought.[5] Hobsbawm has no doubt that Marx's materialist vision of history offers the best guide to transformations of the world since the Middle Ages ('Preface', in *On History*, p. ix). But he also believes that Marxist history should not be isolated from the remainder of historical thinking and research. For him, Marx is a starting point in research, not a point of arrival ('What do Historians Owe to Karl Marx?', in *On History*, pp. 141–56).

Hobsbawm's strong commitments may not be to everyone's liking. But Hobsbawm does not write solely for the converted.[6] On the contrary, he seems to prefer readers who believe that history is worth arguing about.

Notes

1   P. Keuneman, 'Eric Hobsbawm: a Cambridge Profile 1939', in R. Samuel and G. Stedman Jones (eds), *Culture, Ideology and Politics: Essays for Eric Hobsbawm*, London: Routledge & Kegan Paul, 1982, pp. 366–8.
2   See, for instance, R. McKibbin, 'Capitalism out of Control: Review of *Age of Extremes*', *Times Literary Supplement*, 28 October 1994, 4778: 4–6; and T. Judt, 'Downhill All the Way: Review of *Age of Extremes*', *New York Review of Books*, 25 May 1995, 42(9): 20–5.
3   For details of his papers on forms of social movement and rebellion, see K. McClelland, 'Bibliography of the Writings of Eric Hobsbawm', in Samuel and Stedman Jones (eds), *Culture, Ideology and Politics*, pp. 332–63.
4   E. D. Genovese, 'The Politics of Class Struggle in the History of Society: an Appraisal of the Work of Eric Hobsbawm', in P. Thane, G. Crossick and R. Floud (eds), *The Power of the Past: Essays for Eric Hobsbawm*, Cambridge: Cambridge University Press, 1984, pp. 18–19.
5   Ibid., p. 17.
6   Review of *On History*, *The Economist*, 19 July 1997, 344: 10.

Hobsbawm's major works

(ed.) *Labour's Turning Point, 1880–1900: Extracts from Contemporary Sources*, London: Lawrence & Wishart, 1948.
The Jazz Scene, originally publ. under the pseudonym F. Newton in 1959, London: Michael Joseph, 1993.
Primitive Rebels: Studies in Archaic Forms of Social Movement in the Nineteenth and Twentieth Centuries, Manchester: Manchester University Press, 1959.
The Age of Revolution, Europe 1789–1848, London: Weidenfeld & Nicolson, 1962.
Labouring Men: Studies in the History of Labour, London: Weidenfeld & Nicolson, 1964.
Industry and Empire: an Economic History of Britain since 1750, London: Weidenfeld & Nicolson, 1968.
Bandits, London: Weidenfeld & Nicolson, 1969.
(with G. Rudé) *Captain Swing*, Old Woking, Surrey: Lawrence & Wishart, 1969.

Revolutionaries: Contemporary Essays, London: Weidenfeld & Nicolson, 1973.

The Age of Capital, 1848–75, London: Weidenfeld & Nicolson, 1975.

(with T. Ranger) (ed.) *The Invention of Tradition*, Cambridge: Cambridge University Press, 1983.

Worlds of Labour: Further Studies in the History of Labour, London: Weidenfeld & Nicolson, 1984.

The Age of Empire, 1875–1914, London: Weidenfeld & Nicolson, 1987.

Echoes of the Marseillaise: Two Centuries Look Back on the French Revolution, London: Verso, 1990.

Nations and Nationalism since 1780: Programme, Myth, Reality, Cambridge: Cambridge University Press, 1990, revised edition, 1992.

Age of Extremes: the Short Twentieth Century, 1914–1991, London: Michael Joseph, 1994.

On History, London: Weidenfeld & Nicolson, 1997.

(ed.) *The Communist Manifesto*, by K. Marx and F. Engels, London: Verso, 1998.

See also

Marx, Moody, Thompson.

Further resources

Campbell, J., 'Towards the Great Decision: Review of *The Age of Empire*', *Times Literary Supplement*, 12 February 1988, 4428: 153.

Cronin, J., 'Creating a Marxist Historiography: the Contribution of Hobsbawm', *Radical History Review*, 1979, 19: 87–109.

Genovese, E. D., 'The Squandered Century: Review of *Age of Extremes*', *New Republic*, 17 April 1995, 212: 38–43.

Hampson, N., 'All for the Better? Review of *Echoes of the Marseillaise*', *Times Literary Supplement*, 15 June 1990, 4550: 637.

Judt, T.. 'Downhill All the Way: Review of *Age of Extremes*', *New York Review of Books*, 25 May 1995, 42(9): 20–5.

Landes, D., 'The Ubiquitous Bourgeoisie: Review of *The Age of Capital*', *Times Literary Supplement*, 4 June 1976, 3873: 662–4.

McKibbin, R., 'Capitalism out of Control: Review of *Age of Extremes*', *Times Literary Supplement*, 28 October 1994, 4778: 4–6.

Mingay, G. E., 'Review of *Captain Swing*', *English Historical Review*, 1970, 85(337): 810.

Samuel, R. and Stedman Jones, G. (eds), *Culture, Ideology and Politics: Essays for Eric Hobsbawm*, London: Routledge & Kegan Paul, 1982.

Seton-Watson, H., 'Manufactured Mythologies: Review of *The Invention of Tradition*', *Times Literary Supplement*, 18 November 1983, 4207: 1270.

Smith, P., 'No Vulgar Marxist: Review of *On History*', *Times Literary Supplement*, 27 June 1997, 4917: 31.

Thane, P., Crossick, G. and Floud, R. (eds), *The Power of the Past: Essays for Eric Hobsbawm*, Cambridge: Cambridge University Press, 1984.

Thane, P. and Lunbeck, E., 'Interview with Eric Hobsbawm', in H. Abelove, B. Blackmar, P. Dimock and J. Schneer (eds), *Visions of History*, Manchester: Manchester University Press, 1983, pp. 29–46.

Weber, E., 'What Rough Beast?', *Critical Review*, 1996, 10(2): 285–98.
Wrigley, C. (1984) 'Eric Hobsbawm: an Appreciation', *Bulletin of the Society for the Study of Labour History*, 1984, 48(1): 2.

IBN KHALDUN 1332–1406

Few people have heard of Ibn Khaldun. Those who have, however, describe him as 'the greatest historian and philosopher ever produced by Islam and one of the greatest of all time', and his chief work – the *Muqaddimah* – as 'undoubtedly the greatest work of its kind that has ever yet been produced by any mind in any time or place'.[1] Such comments have foundation, as in the *Muqaddimah* we find one of the earliest systematic explorations of the nature of history.

'Abd-ar-Rahman Abu Zayd Muhammad ibn Khaldun was born in Tunis (the current capital of Tunisia) on 1 Ramadan 732 (27 May 1332). His ancestors enjoyed great prominence in Moorish Spain for many centuries, before crossing over to North-west Africa after the fall of Seville to the Christian King Ferdinand III in 1248. Ibn Khaldun's father provided his son with an education based on the *Koran*, *Hadith* (stories of prophets) and Arabic literature. Ibn Khaldun was also taught by Abelli, an important philosopher and commentator on the works of Averroes and Avicenna.

Ibn Khaldun had an eventful career. After seven years of public service in Tunis, he moved to Fez, Morocco, where he became secretary to the Merinid Sultan Abu 'Inan. This position did not last long, however, as he was suspected of liberating a captured prince. He was thrown into prison in February 1357 and only released after Abu 'Inan died in 1358. Ibn Khaldun was reinstated by the Vizier Al-Hassan ibn 'Umar but, fearing for his safety, he moved to Granada in Spain. There he was given a warm welcome and in 1364 he was entrusted to conduct a peace mission to Pedro the Cruel of Castile. Not long hereafter he returned to Africa to become the Hafsid ruler Abu 'Abdallah's prime minister. After further political troubles he and his family took refuge in the fortified village of Qul-at Ibn Salamah in the province of Oran (in Algeria). There Ibn Khaldun began to write his *Kitab al- 'Ibar* or 'History of the World'. He continued to write after he moved to Cairo and was given an academic position and a judgeship, positions from which he was removed and to which reinstated no fewer than five times. Later, Ibn Khaldun left Egypt on an expedition to Damascus, which was under attack by Tamerlane's armies. Ibn Khaldun was able to meet Tamerlane and to record their discussions. He returned to Egypt in 1401 and died on 25 Ramadan 808 (17 March 1406).

Although Ibn Khaldun mentions only the *Kitab al-'Ibar* in his *Ta'rif* or 'Autobiography', his friend Ibn al-Kahib recorded that he also wrote commentaries on al Burisi's *Burdah* (poem in praise of Muhammad) and Ibn al-Kahib's own poem on law, summaries of most of Averroes' writings and Fakhr-ad-Din-ar-Razi's *al-Muhassal*, and treatises on logic and arithmetic. Of these, only the summary of *al-Muhassal* survives.[2]

The *Kitab al-'Ibar* comprises three books: the first treats the nature of history and society, the second the history of the Arabs and the third the history of the Berbers. In the foreword to the first book, the *Muqaddimah* or 'Preface', Ibn Khaldun makes the following claim:

> I chose a remarkable and original method. In the work, I commented on civilisation, on urbanisation, and on the essential characteristics of human social organisation, in a way that explains to the reader how and why things are as they are. . . . As a result, he will wash his hands of any blind trust in tradition.
>
> (I: 11)[3]

Ibn Khaldun is clearly not modest about his achievements. And perhaps deservedly so, for, unlike other contemporary histories, the *Muqaddimah* is not designed to 'move or charm the reader', 'moralise or convince', or to 'serve any administration or government' (I: 78, 79). Other works of history, he claims, are undermined by 'partisanship for opinions and schools', 'reliance upon transmitters', 'unfounded assumptions as to the truth of a thing', and the lavishing of 'great and high-ranking persons with praise and econiums' (I: 9–71). There is also no shortage of fanciful events in the writings of historians who want to produce great literary works. For instance, he comments on the appearance of djinns in many histories:

> the djinn are not known to have specific forms and effigies. They are able to take on various forms. The story of the many heads they have is intended to indicate ugliness and frightfulness. It is not meant to be taken literally.
>
> (I: 73)

Ibn Khaldun was not the first person to question the role of the fantastic in history, but he went further than his predecessors in showing, through appeal to the ideas of economics, geography, demography, military strategy and tactics, why many historical accounts were inadequate. For example, in criticising claims that Moses counted

600,000 in the ranks of the Israelite army, Ibn Khaldun points out, first, that such a small country could not support an army of that size; second, that such a large army could not be easily controlled in battle; and finally, that it was demographically impossible for such an army to have been raised in the first place (I: 16–18).

Ibn Khaldun also believes that historians who merely emulate the achievements of earlier historians are dull and produce superficial work. He writes:

> They [disregard] the changes in conditions and in the customs of nations and races that the passing of time had brought about. Thus, they [present] historical information about dynasties and stories of events from the early period as mere forms without substance, blades without scabbards, as knowledge that must be considered ignorance, because it is not known what of it is extraneous and what is genuine.
>
> (I: 9)

These historians, Ibn Khaldun argues, have forgotten to 'pay attention to historiography's purpose' (I: 63). That purpose, for him, is to get to the 'inner meaning' of historical events. This involves

> speculation and an attempt to get at the truth, subtle explanation of the causes and origins of existing things, and deep knowledge of the how and why of events. History, therefore, is firmly rooted in philosophy. It deserves to be accounted a branch of philosophy.
>
> (I: 6)

In order to get to the truth, historians must look to the social, political, economic, cultural and physical conditions that give shape to 'umran or civilisations (I: 11). When they look at 'umran in this way, history ceases to be a branch of rhetoric and becomes a science that is rooted in philosophy. It is a science, Ibn Khaldun claims, because it fulfils the three preconditions set by earlier Muslim thinkers: it has its own object (mawdu'), human societies, its own problems (masa'il), those arising from historical events, and its own goal (ghaya), to find the 'inner meaning' of events.[4]

Having declared his purpose to write history as both blade and scabbard, Ibn Khaldun embarks upon an exploration of the characteristics of civilisation in general and in the context of the history of the medieval Maghreb (the region of North Africa bordering on the

Mediterranean Sea). He begins with an analysis of the influence of the physical environment upon events. This is followed with a description of the social nature of people, the characteristics of primitive social organisation and its relationship to higher forms of society. In looking to societies, Ibn Khaldun focuses on the nature of leadership and government, how primitive societies develop into more sophisticated ones and how the latter collapse. His ideas on the nature of society and societal change are thrown into relief in his description of the medieval Maghreb. In this he distinguishes between *'umran badawi* (rural, Bedouin or nomadic life) and *'umran hadari* (urban, sedentary life). These concepts, Mahdi tells us, should be understood as stages in a cycle in which civilisations rise and fall.[5] As such, Ibn Khaldun's distinction between the two is very similar to the distinction between 'hard' and 'soft' societies in classical works such as the histories of Herodotus and Livy. For Ibn Khaldun, *'umran badawi* is the first stage in the development of civilisation and the basis of *'umran hadari* (I: 253). Within *'umran badawi*, Ibn Khaldun further distinguishes between camel nomads of the desert, semi-nomadic groups and sedentary farmers. Within *'umran hadari* he distinguishes between those who live near towns and those who live in them. These different groups represent different levels of development (I: 251, 274, 279, 287).

In Ibn Khaldun's estimation, culture and luxury are the highest goals of *'umran hadari*, but they also mark its decline:

> When civilisation reaches that goal, it turns towards corruption and starts being senile, as happens in the natural life of living things.
>
> (II: 296)

Unlike most living things, however, *'umran hadari* does not 'die' from natural causes. Rather, it is destroyed by people with the characteristics of *'umran badawi*. These conquerors lay the foundations for a new state with many features of the old one, and thus move again towards *'umran hadari*. These people, in turn, will become prone to corruption, and thus conquest.

The mainspring of this cycle is *'asabiya*. *'Asabiya* can only exist in the context of *'umran badawi*. The appearance of *'umran hadari* leads to the disappearance of *'asabiya* and thus to the inevitable decline of the state. Virtually everyone who has written on Ibn Khaldun has their own interpretation of *'asabiya*. It has been variously described as 'the vitality of the state', 'the life force of the people', 'patriotism', 'national awareness', 'national feeling', 'public spirit', 'social solidarity', 'group cohesion', 'common will', 'group feeling', 'the basic protoplasm out of which all bodies politic and bodies social are built up', 'nobility', 'aristocratic structure of society', 'solidarity in battle', 'warlike attitude', 'blood ties', 'agnatic solidarity', 'virtù', 'tribal fanaticism' and 'tribal solidarity'.[6] Most of these descriptions are accurate up to a point, but, as Lacoste points out, the existence of such differences indicates that Ibn Khaldun is describing a combination of elements. It is also clear that 'asabiya is not an abstract, ahistorical notion, but is firmly linked to the history of the medieval Maghreb.[7]

'Asabiya is usually expressed in warlike activities:

> Group feeling produces the ability to defend oneself, to protect oneself and to press one's claims. Whoever loses his group feeling is too weak to do any of these things.
>
> (I: 289)

When the group becomes less warlike, it loses its 'asabiya. If 'asabiya is to exist and develop, the group must have what Ibn Khaldun calls riasa, the tacit but real authority of a great family (I: 269). This entails the existence of a chieftain. Chieftains establish their authority over a group partly by means of the profits that they make from trade but mostly from the spoils of war. As less and less of the wealth is shared, the power of the tribal aristocracy increases at the expense of military egalitarianism. In order to maintain at least an appearance of solidarity, the group is constantly drawn into conflicts with others. The excitement of battle fosters a feeling of unity in the face of an illusory common danger. This unity, plus the crumbs of victory, makes group members go on supporting a leader who is in fact their master.

Subsequently, as gains from war, and now taxes, are appropriated by the chieftain, group members become increasingly aware of the inequality that exists. Furthermore, as the chieftain and his entourage settle in town for comfort, they lose their day-to-day contact with the group. Once the group realise this, they refuse to obey the chieftain. The chieftain tries to find new supporters who cannot challenge his power by appealing to group solidarity among clients, mercenaries and slaves. As a result, the chieftain's own group become his enemies. Weakened by internal divisions, the civilisation is prone to conquest by a group with a high level of 'asabiya. In its turn, that group will suffer the same fate (I: 272–273).

Ibn Khaldun's focus on 'asabiya has led a number of commentators to ask whether he was a secular or a religious thinker. For although Ibn Khaldun often quotes from the Koran in the Muqaddimah, Islam views 'asabiya in a pejorative sense. In Islamic thought, it is at-taqwa (piety, conscientiousness) which deserves and acquires power and leadership, not 'asabiya. This apparent contradiction has led some to declare his writings to be blasphemous and others to conclude that on the whole he was a secular thinker.[8]

Four hundred years after the death of Ibn Khaldun a few fragments of his work were brought to light and translated into French by Silvestre de Sacy (1806). Prior to that time, Turkey and Moorish Spain were probably the only non-African countries aware of his ideas. Europeans had to wait another fifty-two years before the first complete edition of the Muqaddimah was published by Etienne Marc Quatremère. Quatremère was fortunate enough to have discovered the last and the most complete version of the Muqaddimah in Ibn Khaldun's hand. While Quatremère's edition was in press, Nasr al-Hurini produced an Egyptian edition of the Muqaddimah (1857). This was followed by the release of the complete text of the Kitab al-'Ibar in 1868. A complete reprint was released in Beirut in 1879 and in Europe a number of articles by Flügel, Reinard, von Kremer, Wüstenfeld and Flint during the period 1852–93 made Ibn Khaldun's ideas more widely known.

The rediscovery and translation of the Muqaddimah in the nineteenth century coincided with the rise of writings on sociology and the scientific nature of history. Many writers were struck by the similarity between Ibn Khaldun's ideas and their own. As a result, far-reaching comparisons were made. For instance, it has been claimed that Ibn Khaldun anticipated Marx's dialectic, Machiavelli's virtù, Montesquieu's ideas on environment, Tarde's views on imitation and Darwin's ideas on evolution.[9] In the twentieth century, a number of books and articles dealing with Ibn Khaldun's contributions to diverse fields appeared. Understanding of his ideas was also stimulated by Franz Rosenthal's English translation of the Muqaddimah (1958). We still have much to learn, however, about this man who 'realised his own gifts and the opportunities of his historical position in a work that ranks as one of man's important triumphs'.[10]

Notes

1 P. K. Hitti, *Récit de l'histoire des Arabes* and A. Toynbee, *A Study of History*, vol. 3; quoted in Y. Lacoste, *Ibn Khaldun: the Birth of History and the Past of the Third World*, trans. D. Macey, London: Verso, 1984, p. 1.

2 H. Simon, *Ibn Khaldun's Science of Human Culture*, trans. F. Baali, Lahore: Muhammad Ashraf, 1978, chap. 4.

3 Citations correspond to volume and page numbers of F. Rosenthal's translation of the *Muqaddimah*.

4 Simon, *Ibn Khaldun's Science of Human Culture*, chap. 1.
5 M. Mahdi, *Ibn Khaldun's Philosophy of History*, London: G. Allen & Unwin, 1957, pp. 193–5.
6 See, for example, A. Azmeh, *Ibn Khaldun: an Essay in Reinterpretation*, London: Routledge, 1990; C. Issaway, *An Arab Philosophy of History*, London: Methuen, 1950; A. Toynbee, *A Study of History*, vol. 3, London: Oxford University Press, 1934; H. Ritter, 'Irrational Solidarity Groups: a Socio-psychological Study in Connection with Ibn Khaldun', in *Oriens*, 1948, 1(1): 15–32; N. Schmidt, *Ibn Khaldun: Historian, Sociologist and Philosopher*, Lahore: Universal Books, 1978; H. Simon, *Ibn Khaldun's Science of Human Culture*; and Lacoste, *Ibn Khaldun*.
7 Lacoste, *Ibn Khaldun*, chap. 6.
8 See S. M. A. Imam, *Some Aspects of Ibn Khaldun's Socio-political Analysis of History: a Critical Appraisal*, Karachi: Khurasan Islamic Research Centre, 1978; and F. Rosenthal, 'Translator's Introduction', *The Muqaddimah*, vol. 1, p. lxxiii.
9 See, for example, Lacoste, *Ibn Khaldun*, part II.
10 F. Rosenthal, 'Translator's Introduction', p. lxxxvii.

Ibn Khaldun's major works

The Muqaddimah, 3 vols, ed. and trans. F. Rosenthal, Princeton, NJ: Princeton University Press, 1958 and 1967.
The Muqaddimah, trans. F. Rosenthal, ed. and abr. N. J. Dawood, Princeton, NJ: Princeton University Press, 1967.

See also

Herodotus, Livy, Machiavelli (MP), Marx, Toynbee.

Further resources

Azmeh, A., *Ibn Khaldun: an Essay in Reinterpretation*, London: Routledge, 1990.
Imam, S. M. A., *Ibn Khaldun: his Life and Work*, Lahore: Muhammad Ashraf, 1944.
Lacoste, Y., *Ibn Khaldun: the Birth of History and the Past of the Third World*, trans. D. Lacey, London: Verso, 1984.
Lawrence, B. L. (ed.), *Ibn Khaldun and Islamic Ideology*, Leiden: E. J. Brill, 1984.
Mahdi, M., *Ibn Khaldun's Philosophy of History: a Study in the Philosophical Foundation of the Science of Culture*, London: G. Allen & Unwin, 1957.
Rosenthal, F., 'Translator's Introduction', in *The Muqaddimah*, vol. 1, Princeton, NJ: Princeton University Press, 1967.
Simon, H., *Ibn Khaldun's Science of Human Culture*, trans. F. Baali, Lahore: SH. Muhammad Ashraf, 1978.

IMMANUEL KANT 1724–1804

At first sight it might seem odd to find Kant in a book dedicated to key thinkers on history. Kant had no desire to be an historian and his philosophy appears singularly ahistorical. Just as Copernicus reversed the way people thought about the relationship of the Earth to the sun, Kant reversed the way people thought about the relationship of the world of experience to the mind. For Kant, the mind is not shaped by the world of experience; rather, the world of experience is shaped by the unchanging forms and categories of the mind which exist a priori and are neither derived from nor testable by sense experience. Since the mental dispositions of individuals can neither develop nor appear, there would seem to be no place for history in Kant's writings. It is reason alone that tells us about the nature of mind. Why, then, is Kant here? There are three principal responses to this question. First, Kant wrote a number of essays on the nature of history between the publication of two of his best-known works, the *Kritik der reinen Vernunft* and the *Kritik der praktischen Vernunft* (trans. *Critique of Pure Reason, Critique of Practical Reason*). Second, though these essays have traditionally been set against his main ideas, recent German and Anglo-American scholarship has contended that Kant's moral interest in history locates it at the heart of his philosophy. Finally, Kant's 'Copernican revolution' changed the way that people thought about historical research.

Immanuel Kant was born and raised in the Prussian university town of Königsberg (now Kaliningrad). In 1740 he entered the university to study theology, then natural science and philosophy. He was trained by followers of Wilhelm von Leibniz and Christian Wolff, but was also greatly influenced by the writings of Isaac Newton, Jean Jacques Rousseau and David Hume. The death of his father forced him to discontinue his studies and he worked as a private tutor between 1746 and 1755. In 1755 he returned to the University of Königsberg and a year later he was granted a degree and a lectureship. By that time he had written on philosophy and astronomy (in *Kant's gesammelte Schriften*, vol. 1). Most of his works at this time were scientific but some contained criticisms of Leibnizian-Wolffian philosophy (ibid.). In 1770 he was made a professor, but until 1781, he published very little. After that time and up to 1790 he produced his most important works. In 1781 he published his most famous work, the *Critique of Pure Reason*. In this he explored the principles which underlie our knowledge of what is the case. In 1785 he published *Grundlegung zur Metaphysik der Sitten* (trans. *Foundations of the Metaphysics of Morals*) and, in 1787, the *Critique of Practical Reason*, both of which aim to describe and demonstrate the legitimacy of the principles which underlie our knowledge of what we ought to do. The 'third critique', the *Kritik der Urteilskraft* (1790) (trans. *Critique of Judgement*), examines the principles which are at the root of our search for purpose in our explanations of natural phenomena and our apprehension of beauty.[1]

Kant's first works on the nature of history appeared in 1784. In that year he published two essays, 'What is Enlightenment?' and 'Idea for a Universal History from a Cosmopolitan Point of View'. The following year he reviewed the first two parts of Herder's *Ideen* for the *Allgemeine Literaturzeitung* of Jena and in 1786 wrote 'Conjectural Beginning of Human History', a work similar to Herder's 'The Most Ancient Document of the Human Race'. In 'The End of All Things' (1794) Kant's attention shifted from the genesis of humanity to the end of the world. A year later he argued that individuals and nations are morally obliged to seek peace ('Perpetual Peace'). Finally, in 1798, he looked to the idea of progress in history in 'An Old Question Raised Again: Is the Human Race Constantly Progressing?'.[2]

According to Kant, there are two types of history (*Geschichte*). *Empirical* history, roughly speaking, is a record of past events written without preconceptions. Empirical historians simply look to past actions and ideas and draw their conclusions from the evidence they have found. In contrast, *rational* historians try to find an intelligible pattern in the apparently chaotic human past. Ostensibly, the rational historian's task seems difficult, because world history appears to be 'woven together from folly, childish vanity, even from childish malice and destructiveness' ('Idea for a Universal History from a Cosmopolitan Point of View', in *Kant: On History*, p. 12). Anyone who looks to the past expecting to see examples of wisdom and virtue will be sorely disappointed.[3] There is some purpose to this folly, however, even though individuals may be unaware of it (ibid.). According to Kant, humans possess a number of potentialities. As nature creates nothing in vain, we must assume that these potentialities develop. Potentialities such as reason, however, may take more than the lifetime of a single individual to develop. We must therefore further assume that nature has some means of helping people to realise these potentialities over a long period of time (ibid., pp. 13–14). Echoing Plato and Hobbes, Kant claims that this means is humanity's 'unsocial sociability' (ibid., pp. 15–16).[4] People seek isolation but need to associate with others in order to survive and thrive.[5] People can thus neither tolerate nor withdraw from others.

In community, individuals seek to impose their wishes upon others, which leads to confrontation and conflict. It is a case of 'can't live with them, can't live without them'. This 'unsocial sociability' also takes place on an international level. Nations try to pursue their own interests but they also depend on other nations for economic well-being. Knowing from its own experience that it wishes to harm the other, each state suspects the other of the same and expects to be suspected in return; in order to forestall being the victim, it is tempted to become the aggressor. This leads to fundamental international instability. Although this resembles the conflict of individuals, on the international level there is no central government and no enforceable law. While there is an obvious negative side to conflict, Kant believes that it drives individuals and societies toward morality (ibid., pp. 15, 18–20; 'Perpetual Peace', in ibid., pp. 106–8; 'Conjectural Beginning of Human History', in ibid., pp. 66–7). Conflict leads states to seek constitutions built not on mutual antagonism but on mutual recognition and respect, and nations to seek a league of nations, lawful regulations and a common authority. This may come about through rebellion or through peaceful means. Progress is thus towards the ideal moral community, where conflict will give way to solidarity. Human beings are blind to this end, but they will be led to it despite their intentions. There is no short-cut to the ideal moral community; humanity must realise its potentialities step by step over a long period of time ('Idea for a Universal History from a Cosmopolitan Point of View', in ibid., p. 13). This means that there is a certain injustice to history, for only later generations will profit from the labour of early generations (ibid., p. 14).

As the above course of events is brought about not by rational activity but by nature, Kant's views on history are generally seen as incompatible with his main philosophical ideas. Recently, however, a number of scholars have begun to question this conclusion. In Anglo-American circles, the most influential work has been Yovel's *Kant and the Philosophy of History* (1980).[6] Though Yovel admits that Kant's historical writings describe more of a natural history than a rational history, he claims that we can find the latter in the account of the 'highest good', as developed in the three 'Critiques' and *Die Religion innerhalb der Grenzen der blossen Vernunft* (1790, trans. *Religion within the Limits of Reason Alone*), and in his remarks on the history of religion and of philosophy. A history of philosophy which merely describes developments would be empirical history, but one which reveals philosophers to be players in a drama of reason which culminates in Kant's critical philosophy is rational history (see 'The History of Pure Reason' in *Critique of Pure Reason*, A852 B880; *Logic*, introduction, pp. 542–3).[7] Similarly, the history of religion is the progressive development of different forms of religion, culminating in the one true moral and rational religion described in *Religion within the Limits of Reason Alone* (pp. 98–122). Thus the development of reason underlies the history of religion and the history of philosophy. As Kant never seriously attempted to write such histories himself, however, they remain simply suggestions.[8] It is only in the writings of Hegel that we see what these histories would be like. Such endeavours, however, do not prove that 'reason rules the historical world'; for that, Yovel argues, we must look to the concept of the 'highest good' as a factor in human conduct.[9]

At the heart of Kant's ideas on human conduct is the categorical imperative. The categorical imperative states that a person should '[a]ct only according to that maxim whereby you can at the same time will that it should become a universal law' (*Foundations of the Metaphysic of Morals*, p. 30). To explain this, Kant offers the example of someone who borrows money, promises to pay it back, but has no intention of doing so. If this were a universal law – that is, if everyone acted in this way – promises would become meaningless. The idea of a 'promise' would no longer make any sense. We thus see that for 'promises' to mean something, we have to keep them. In recognising this imperative we are self-determined, not only because we determine our action freely, but also because we accept that it makes *rational sense* to keep promises. We are autonomous when we accept the categorical imperative because we follow our own law. As soon as we begin to think of ends such as rewards or punishments, which are not determined by reason, then we are no longer masters of ourselves. While Kant believes that the categorical imperative is fundamental to our lives, there is also another imperative: to 'act to promote the highest good in the world'. As Kant writes in the *Critique of Judgement*:

> The moral [categorical] law is the formal rational condition of the employment of our freedom and, as such, of itself alone lays its obligation upon us, independently of any end as its material condition. But it also defines for us a final end, and does so a priori, and makes it obligatory upon us to strive towards its attainment. This end is the highest good in the world.
>
> (II: p. 118)

When an individual disregards their own self-interest and acts in accordance with the categorical imperative, they still want results that contribute to the realisation of morality in the world (*Religion within the Limits of Reason Alone*, VI, p. 4). The highest good satisfies 'our natural need to conceive of some sort of final end for all our actions and abstentions, taken as a whole, an end which can be justified by reason and the absence of which would be a hindrance to moral decision' (ibid.). For Yovel, the highest good operates on two levels: personal and universal. On the personal level, citing the highest good enables us to give an account of how we are subject to moral law, but even so hope for personal happiness. Even though we may not get what we deserve in this life, we hope that God will reward our virtue in the next life. Yet not only do we hope for the highest good, but we also have a duty to promote it. As Yovel writes:

> It follows that, as duty, the highest good incorporates not only my personal final end (my private happiness and virtue), but an ultimate design for the entire moral universe. It is now defined as 'the highest good that reason presents to *all* rational beings as the goal of *all* their moral wishes': a universal human system which will combine the greatest and the most widespread happiness with the strictest morality of all rational beings.[10]

The highest good is our world brought to moral perfection.[11] We are thus obliged as a matter of duty to act in order to make the future as moral as we can. Nature can aid us in this goal by forcing us to seek peaceful political arrangements both in and between states, but this is not enough. For the highest good to be realised, people must overcome their laziness and cowardice and break the hold that nature has over their lives. We can break the hold of nature, Yovel argues, because we have experienced the Enlightenment, the motto of which was 'Have courage to use your own reason' ('What is Enlightenment?', in *Kant: On History*, p. 3).[12] We can now see the meaning of past actions and understand what we ought to do in order to realise the highest good. Henceforth morality is pursued intentionally. Here, Yovel concludes, we can see the emergence of Kant's idea of rational history.

Though Yovel's work has led many scholars to reassess their conclusions about Kant's views on history, it has also met with a number of criticisms. In their reviews, W. A. Galston, W. H. Walsh and T. E. Willey point out four issues that need to be addressed.[13] First, there is some doubt as to whether an ethical system (based on the categorical imperative) that shuns ends can accommodate a 'final end'. Second, it is not clear how, in the transformation of the personal highest good to the universal highest good, hope turns into duty. Third, it has to be asked whether conscious awareness of one's obligation to realise the highest good makes one any more able to perform it. Finally, and most seriously, why should the realisation of the highest good produce rational *history*? If the highest good is realised, Walsh points out, we will more accurately have a 'rational state of affairs'. This is different from rational history because it happens all at once while history must take the form of a development over time. Walsh writes: 'Would not the attaining of the highest good . . . : mark not the institution of rational history, but the point at which the historical process ceases to be of any moral interest?'[14]

While there is still some doubt about the place of history in Kant's philosophy, there is no question that his Copernican revolution in the philosophy of mind brought about a corresponding revolution in the philosophy of history. In *The Idea of History*, R. G. Collingwood clearly describes what this revolution entails:

> Throughout the course of his work the historian is selecting, constructing, and criticising. . . . By explicitly recognising this fact it is possible to effect what, . . . borrowing a Kantian phrase, one might call a Copernican revolution in the theory of history: the discovery that, so far from relying on an authority other than himself, to whose statements his thought must conform, the historian is his own authority and his thought is autonomous, self-authorising, possessed of a criterion to which his so-called authorities must conform and by reference to which they are criticised.[15]

After Kant's death, writers such as Hegel, Ranke, Dilthey, Simmel, Windelband, Troeltsch, Rickert, Weber, Lange, Cassirer and Collingwood explored the authority and autonomy of historians. Their works, in turn, inspired debates on such topics as relativism and historicism, which dominate current scholarship. Kant would be shocked (and perhaps horrified) to learn how much his steady world of 'the starry skies above and the moral world within' has changed the way we think about history.

Notes

1 For a more general account of Kant's ideas, see Kant (MP).
2 These essays are reprinted in *Kant: On History*, (ed.) L. W. Beck, The Library of Liberal Arts, New York: Macmillan, 1963.
3 This is the point of Voltaire's *Candide*, which mocks the Leibnizian confidence that all is for the best in the best of all possible worlds.
4 Plato, *Republic*, book 2. On Hobbes and Kant, see P. J. Kain, 'Hobbes, Revolution, and the Philosophy of History', in C. Walton and J. J. Johnson (eds), *Hobbes's 'Science of Natural Justice'*, Dordrecht: Martinus Nijhoff, 1987, pp. 208–18; id., 'Kant's Political Theory and Philosophy of History', *Clio*, 1989, 18(4): 325–45.

5 As Rousseau pointed out in *Discourse on the Origin of Inequality*, selfishness is only possible in a social setting. J. J. Rousseau, *The First and Second Discourses*, trans. R. D. Masters and J. R. Masters, New York: St Martin's Press, 1964, p. 222.

6 See also S. Anderson-Gold, 'Kant's Ethical Anthropology and the Critical Foundations of the Philosophy of History', *History of Philosophy Quarterly*, 1994, 11(4): 405–19.

7 'A' refers to the 1781 edition, 'B' to the 1787 edition.

8 Walsh points out that we can see similar thinking in Kant's comments on other forms of intellectual history, especially the history of mathematics and of the natural sciences. W. H. Walsh, 'Review of *Kant and the Philosophy of History*', *History and Theory*, 1981, 20(1): 195.

9 Y. Yovel, *Kant and the Philosophy of History*, Princeton, NJ: Princeton University Press, 1980.

10 Ibid., p. 64.

11 Ibid., p. 72.

12 Ibid., p. 269.

13 W. H. Walsh, 'Review of *Kant and the Philosophy of History*', pp. 191–203; T. E. Willey, *Canadian Journal of History*, 1981, 16(1): 145–8; and W. A. Galston, *Philosophical Review*, 1983, 92(2): 288–91.

14 Walsh, 'Review of *Kant and the Philosophy of History*', p. 203.

15 R. G. Collingwood, *The Idea of History*, revised edition, ed. W. J. Van der Dussen, Oxford: Oxford University Press, 1993, p. 236.

Kant's major works

Kant's gesammelte Schriften, 29 vols, Berlin: Georg Reimer, 1900– .

Critique of Pure Reason (1781 and 1787 editions), trans. N. Kemp Smith, London: Macmillan, 1970.

Critique of Practical Reason, trans. L. W. Beck, The Library of Liberal Arts, New York and London: Macmillan, 1956.

Critique of Judgement, trans. J. C. Meredith, Oxford: Oxford University Press, 1952.

Kant: On History, L. W. Beck (ed.), The Library of Liberal Arts, New York and London: Macmillan, 1963.

Foundations of the Metaphysics of Morals, trans. L. W. Beck, Chicago: Chicago University Press, 1950.

Logic, trans. R. S. Hartman and W. Schwarz, The Library of Liberal Arts, New York and London: Macmillan, 1974.

Religion within the Limits of Reason Alone, trans. T. M. Greene and H. H. Hudson, New York: Harper & Row, 1960.

Online versions of many of Kant's works can be found at: http://www.hkbu. edu.hk/~ppp/K1texts.htm

See also

Collingwood, Dilthey, Foucault, Hegel, Hume (MP), Leibniz (MP), Lyotard (CT), Ranke, Rousseau (MP).

Further resources

Arens, K., 'History as Knowledge: Herder, Kant and the Human Sciences', in W. Koepke (ed.), *Johann Gottfried Herder: Academic Disciplines and the Pursuit of Knowledge*, Studies in German Literature, Linguistics and Culture, Columbia, SC: Camden, 1996, pp. 106–19.

Booth, W. J., *Interpreting the World: Kant's Philosophy of History and Politics*, Toronto: University of Toronto Press, 1986.

Cagvill, H., *A Kant Dictionary*, Oxford: Blackwell, 1996.

Collingwood, R. G., *The Idea of History*, revised edition, (ed.) W. J. Van der Dussen, Oxford: Oxford University Press, 1993.

Despland, M., *Kant on History and Religion*, Montreal: McGill-Queen's University Press, 1973.

Fackenheim, E. L., 'Kant's Concept of History', *Kant Studien*, 1957, 48(2): 381–98.

Galston, W. A., *Kant and the Problem of History*, Chicago, IL: Chicago University Press, 1975.

Walsh, W. H., *An Introduction to the Philosophy of History*, London: Hutchinson, 1951.

Yovel, Y., *Kant and the Philosophy of History*, Princeton, NJ: Princeton University Press, 1980.

THOMAS SAMUEL KUHN 1922–96

It is no exaggeration to say that Thomas Samuel Kuhn's *The Structure of Scientific Revolutions* (1962) is a revolutionary work. Not only did it change the way in which people thought about the history and philosophy of science, but it also made 'paradigm', 'paradigm shift' and 'scientific revolution' household terms.

Thomas Samuel Kuhn was born on 18 July 1922 in Cincinnati, Ohio. He was educated at Harvard and was professor of philosophy there, at the University of California at Berkeley, at Princeton and at the Massachusetts Institute of Technology. He died in 1996.

Traditionally, Kuhn asserts, the primary goal of historians of science was 'to clarify and deepen an understanding of *contemporary* scientific methods or concepts by displaying their evolution' ('The History of Science', in *The Essential Tension*, p. 107). This entailed relating the progressive accumulation of breakthroughs and discoveries. Only that which survived in some form in the present was considered relevant. In the mid-1950s, however, a number of flaws in this view of history became apparent. Closer analysis of scientific discoveries, for instance, led historians to ask whether the dates of discoveries and their discoverers can be identified precisely. Some discoveries seem to entail numerous phases and discoverers, none of which can be identified as definitive. Furthermore, the evaluation of past discoveries and discoverers according to present-day standards does not allow us to see how significant they may have been in their own day. Nor does the traditional view recognise the role that non-intellectual factors, especially institutional and socio-economic, play in scientific developments. Most importantly, however, the traditional historian of science seems oblivious to the fact that the concepts, questions and standards that they use to frame the past are themselves subject to historical change (*The Structure of Scientific Revolutions*, pp. 2, 7, chap. 6; 'Introduction', in *The Essential Tension*, p. xi; and 'The History of Science', in *The Essential Tension*, pp. 109–10).

The identification of such flaws, Kuhn claims, led to a 'historiographic revolution'. New historians of science considered historicity and tried to 'display the historical integrity of [a] science in its own time' by '[climbing] inside the heads of the members of the group which practices some particular scientific specialty during some particular period'.[1] In order to do this, historians must identify and master the scientific problems, concepts, values and norms of the group under study.[2] This is no easy task, for it requires them to read texts in an 'hermeneutic' manner. By this Kuhn means making the following assumptions: a text can be interpreted in numerous ways; not all interpretations of a text are of equal value; preference should be given to interpretations with the greatest plausibility and coherence; the best interpretation of an older text may be the one furthest from that of modern readers; and passages that appear erroneous or implausible to modern readers may signal the need for them to seek greater understanding.[3]

If we study the history of science carefully, Kuhn posits in *The Structure of Scientific Revolutions*, we discover minor variants of the following pattern:[4]

preconsensus science $\rightarrow$ normal science$_1$ $\rightarrow$ crisis$_1$ $\rightarrow$ extraordinary science$_1$ $\rightarrow$ revolution$_1$ $\rightarrow$ normal science$_2$ $\rightarrow$ crisis$_2$ . . .

Kuhn's pattern begins with a 'preconsensus' or 'proto-science' phase, which is characterised by competition between schools which address the same subject-matter from different perspectives (*The Structure of Scientific Revolutions*, pp. ix, 4, 12–13, 16, 17, 47–8, 61–2, 96, 163, 178–9).[5] Kuhn cites as examples of this phase the study of optics before Newton, electricity before Franklin, motion before Aristotle, statics before Archimedes, heat before Black, chemistry before Boyle and Boerhaave and historical geography before Hutton.[6] As there is no universal consensus about the subject-matter under study, each school must explain and justify its ideas and activities. The lack of consensus also means, though, that they are relatively free to decide what will count as legitimate ideas and activities. Consequently, Kuhn suggests, significant ideas and problems cannot be unequivocally identified, and those problems selected for analysis offer no guarantee of solution or guidance for the selection of future problems. This is why, for Kuhn, preconsensus research is 'something less than a science' (*The Structure of Scientific Revolutions*, pp. 13–18, 20, 21, 47–8, 61, 76, 163; 'The History of Science' in *The Essential Tension*, p. 118).

Typically, the victory of one of the schools over the others heralds the transition to what Kuhn calls 'normal science' (*The Structure of Scientific Revolutions*, pp. 17–19, 178). Competing schools gradually disappear, though not all of their adherents need switch to the victorious school. Thus the transition to normal science is neither a precisely datable event nor so gradual as to be unidentifiable. Transitions, Kuhn believes, generally take place over decades. Transition periods mean that adherents of different schools will have enough in common to recognise a significant achievement. For Kuhn, normal science is like puzzle solving. The scientist and puzzle solver share in common the recognition of regulations, the expectation of a solution, a lack of openness to fundamental innovation, a lack of interest in testing the regulations and the hope of enhancing their standing in the community.[7] In both normal science and puzzle solving, the legitimacy of ideas and activities is determined by 'rules of play'. That is, the scientist and the puzzle solver are not free to choose just any problem or solution. Many of the regulations that constrain the activities of normal scientists are conveyed implicitly in paradigms.

'Paradigm' is arguably one of the best-known and least-understood concepts in Kuhn's writings. That this is the case is due in no small part to Kuhn's broad usage of the term. Indeed, some critics have noted with glee Masterman's identification of at least twenty-one meanings in *The Structure of Scientific Revolutions* alone.[8] Though the scope of the term has waxed and waned in his writings, Kuhn usually uses 'paradigm' to refer to concrete problem solutions that also provide guides for scientific practice.[9] That is, paradigms are not just accepted as solutions to particular problems; they are also guides to future practice, in that the researcher can use their conceptual systems or 'lexicons' to identify and solve hitherto unexplored problems.[10] How a paradigm guides scientific practice cannot be explained explicitly. In order to illustrate this important point, Kuhn looks to Ludwig Wittgenstein's discussion on concepts in *Philosophical Investigations*.[11] Wittgenstein shows us that attempts to explicate the attributes that all 'games' and only 'games' have in common are unsuccessful. Though many 'games' will share attributes in common, there is no one set of attributes that will cover all of them and them alone. Rather, concepts like 'game' are families made up of networks of resemblances. Thus, when we apply the term 'game' to an activity we have never seen before, we do so because it bears a 'family resemblance' to things we previously learned to call 'games'. Similarly, paradigms cannot be reduced to an explicit set of rules and assumptions. The scientist gains knowledge of them not by studying definitions, but through education and exposure to literature. Much of the scientist's knowledge is thus tacit, in the sense developed by Michael Polanyi: 'Its precise scope and content are, of course, impossible to specify, but it is sound knowledge nonetheless' ('Logic of Discovery or Psychology of Research', in *The Essential Tension*, p. 285).[12]

Normal scientists and puzzle solvers also expect that there will be a solution to a problem that accords with the regulations. Furthermore, they show little interest in seeking innovations that challenge the regulations. This is not to say that the work of normal scientists cannot be innovative. Kuhn's point is that normal scientists do not make 'unexpected' discoveries. Indeed, he claims that normal scientists display a dogmatic tendency to steer away from and set aside problems that call the regulations into question (*The Structure of Scientific Revolutions*, pp. 5–6, 24, 62, 64). Hence Kuhn's description of normal science as an attempt 'to elucidate topographical detail on a map whose main outlines are available in advance' ('The Essential Tension', in *The Essential Tension*, p. 235). The normal scientist, like the puzzle solver, does not consider his activities to be a test of the regulations (*The Structure of Scientific Revolutions*, pp. 80, 144–5; 'The Function of Measurement in Modern Physical Science' and 'Logic of Discovery or Psychology of Research', in *The Essential Tension*, pp. 187, 192, 197, 270–2). Rather, they engage in their chosen activities to prove their ability as experts to their communities (*The Structure of Scientific Revolutions*, p. 36).

Despite his portrayal of the activities of normal scientists as dogmatic and pedestrian, Kuhn still believes that they can lead to 'linear' and 'cumulative' progress in the acquisition of knowledge (*The Structure of Scientific Revolutions*, pp. 52, 53, 96, 139, 163). As normal science steers away from the unexpected, insights gained through research are compatible and combinable with previous insights. Each solved problem thus improves or expands a community's understanding of the subject-matter under study. But, as Kuhn notes in *The Structure of Scientific Revolutions*, the judgement that progress has been made may rest 'simply in the eye of the beholder' (p. 163).

Though normal scientists deal primarily with the anticipated, they sometimes make discoveries that appear to go against their expectations. Kuhn calls these discoveries anomalies. Normal scientists tend, however, to set them aside because little would be gained from investing time and resources to account for them. And indeed many anomalies eventually disappear by themselves. Still, some anomalies resist solution. Kuhn calls these 'serious', 'meaningful', 'troublesome', 'crisis-provoking' or 'significant' anomalies ('The Function of Measurement in Modern Physical Science', in *The Essential Tension*, pp. 204, 205, 209, 211; *The Structure of Scientific Revolutions*, pp. 77, 81, 82, 86, 97, 186). Some anomalies trigger 'scientific revolutions'.[13] Traditionally, the term 'scientific revolution' has been applied to those earth-shattering episodes in which the replacement of one theory or perspective by another led to changes in scientific views, research practices and possibly even popular consciousness. The achievements of Copernicus, Newton, Darwin and Einstein spring to mind. Kuhn, however, extends the concept to cover, first, changes that have far-reaching consequences within a science but have minimal impact outside it, and second, discoveries of new phenomena.

When faced with a significant crisis, scientists may respond by engaging in 'extraordinary science' or 'science in the crisis state' (*The Structure of Scientific Revolutions*, pp. 6, 82, 86, 87, 91, 101, 154). In extraordinary or crisis science, the 'rules of play' which were previously taken for granted are subjected to scrutiny. Extraordinary scientists try to change the regulations in such a way as to preserve as many previous problem solutions as possible and to account for those anomalies that triggered the crisis in the first place. After this 'paradigm shift', a term that has become almost hackneyed in its wide application, 'normal science' is resumed under new rules. Kuhn portrays revolutions as 'destructive-constructive' because they interrupt the accumulation of knowledge in normal science and give rise to a new view of the subject-matter that is *incommensurable* with the previous one (*The Structure of Scientific Revolutions*, p. 66).[14] Kuhn's changing understanding of the concept of 'incommensurability' has been a popular topic of discussion among philosophers and has given rise to an enormous body of literature. In the 1960s and 1970s, Kuhn drew on the work of the philosopher Quine to argue that two views of the world are incommensurable if there is no 'neutral observation language' 'into which at least the empirical consequences of both can be translated without loss or change'. But in the 1980s, mention of a neutral observation language disappears and the idea of 'untranslatability' comes to the fore. In this later literature, two perspectives are considered to be incommensurable if the structure of their 'lexicons' is different. That is, if views are incommensurable it is impossible for us systematically to match the meaning and scope of their concepts. This is not to say, as some critics have concluded, that the incommensurability of successive paradigms means that they are *incomparable* or that the continuity between periods of natural science is undermined. In *The Structure of Scientific Revolutions* Kuhn suggests that at least part of the achievements of normal scientists prove to be permanent, because after a revolution

> much of [the scientist's] language and most of his laboratory instruments are the same as they were before. As a result, postrevolutionary science invariably includes many of the same manipulations, performed with the same instruments and described in the same terms as its revolutionary predecessor.
> (Ibid., p. 130)

Progress is made because problem-solving capacity increases, but this alone does not entitle us to say that scientific progress is a drawing closer to truth. For Kuhn, this is so for two reasons. First, the claim that successive theories draw closer to truth asserts that the later theories are better approximations of the truth than earlier ones. But the study of history, Kuhn contends, shows that this is not the case. For instance, when we consider Aristotelian physics, Newtonian mechanics and Einsteinian relativity, it is not outrageous to say that the first and the third are more closely related than the second and the third. Second, how is it possible to judge whether a theory corresponds to the truth? Are we able to stand aside from our perspectives and contemplate the world as it *really* is? Kuhn thus believes that scientific progress should be seen merely as the instrumental improvement of scientific knowledge. He writes:

> Conceived as a set of instruments for solving technical puzzles in selected areas, science clearly gains in precision and scope with the passage of time. As an instrument, science undoubtedly does progress.[15]

Many researchers, including historians, have embraced Kuhn's ideas with wild enthusiasm. Some have tried to demonstrate that minor variants of his pattern of scientific development may also be found in intellectual history, while others have been content simply to adopt terms such as 'paradigm' and 'incommensurable'. Indeed, as David Fischer has suggested, Kuhn's ideas appear to be 'relevant to all fields' of history.[16] Such enthusiasm, however, may be met with a number of serious concerns. First, to what extent are Kuhn's ideas specific to the natural sciences? For instance, is the history of a social group like that of a scientific community, in which individuals have had 'similar educations' and 'professional initiations', read the same technical literature and have 'drawn many of the same lessons from it'? Second, is a clear account of the central tenets of Kuhn's thesis possible? Interpretations of Kuhn's ideas, as was noted earlier in the case of 'paradigm', are remarkably varied. Are his ideas so broad as to be insubstantive? Third, questions may be raised about the adequacy of Kuhn's thesis as a historiography of science. Why, for instance, should scientific *communities* be taken as the basic units of analysis for the history of science? Are normal scientists as dogmatic as Kuhn suggests? Finally, more general philosophical questions may be raised about Kuhn's ideas. For example, why can't the ways in which a paradigm guides scientific practice be explicated? Furthermore, if Kuhn's view of his subject-matter is, like that of scientists, shaped by assumptions and values, then what status should we accord his thesis? Perhaps it is time that we subjected Kuhn's 'rules of play' themselves to scrutiny.

Notes

1 *Structure of Scientific Revolutions*, p. 3; and 'History of Science', in P. D. Asquith and H. E. Kyburg (eds), *Current Research in Philosophy of Science*, Ann Arbor, MI: Edwards, 1979, p. 122.

2 'Commensurability, Comparability, Communicability', in P. D. Asquith and T. Nickles (eds), *Proceedings of the 1982 Biennial Meeting of the Philosophy of Science Association*, East Lansing, MI: Philosophy of Science Association, 1983, pp. 677–8.

3 P. Hoyningen-Heune, *Reconstructing Scientific Revolutions: Thomas S. Kuhn's Philosophy of Science*, trans. A. T. Levine, Chicago, IL: University of Chicago Press, 1993, pp. 21–2.

4 A variation on A. F. Chalmers, *What is this Thing Called Science? An Assessment of the Nature and Status of Science and its Methods*, Milton Keynes: Open University Press, 1978, p. 86.

5 In the first edition of *The Structure of Scientific Revolutions* Kuhn calls this a 'pre-paradigm' phase, but by 1969 he admits that 'preconsensus science' is also shaped by paradigms. See *The Structure of Scientific Revolutions*, pp. ix, 20, 47, 61, 76, 163, 178–9; 'Second Thoughts on Paradigms', in *The Essential Tension*, p. 295, n.4; and 'Reflections on my Critics', in I. Lakatos and A. Musgrave (eds), *Criticism and the Growth of Knowledge*, Cambridge: Cambridge University Press, 1970, p. 272, n.1.

6 He is, however, hesitant about tagging 'an extended historical episode with a single and somewhat arbitrarily chosen name'. See *The Structure of Scientific Revolutions*, p. 15.

7 On the limits of this analogy see P. Hoyningen-Heune, *Reconstructing Scientific Revolutions*, pp. 171–80.

8 M. Masterman, 'The Nature of a Paradigm', in Lakatos and Musgrave (eds), *Criticism and the Growth of Knowledge*, p. 61.

9 'Second Thoughts on Paradigms', in *The Essential Tension*, p. 307, n.16, 319; 'Reflections on my Critics', in Lakatos and Musgrave (eds), *Criticism and the Growth of Knowledge*, pp. 235, 272; and 'Dubbing and Redubbing: the Vulnerability of Rigid Designation', in C. W. Savage (ed.), *Scientific Theories*, Minnesota Studies in Philosophy of Science, no. 14, Minneapolis, MN: University of Minnesota Press, 1990, pp. 302, 314, 316, n.9.

10 Hoyningen-Heune, *Reconstructing Scientific Revolutions*, p. 160.

11 L. Wittgenstein, *Philosophical Investigations*, trans. G. E. M. Anscombe, Oxford: Basil Blackwell, 1953, pp. 31–6.

12 See *The Structure of Scientific Revolutions*, pp. 44, n.1, 196; M. Polanyi, *Personal Knowledge*, London: Routledge & Kegan Paul, 1973, and M. Polanyi, *Knowing and Being*, London: Routledge & Kegan Paul, 1969.

13 Though Kuhn was convinced that crises are usually the prelude to revolutions, in his later writings he allowed that they might in rare cases be started in other ways. He also conceded that a crisis need not be triggered by anomalies within the field at issue. See Hoyningen-Heune, *Reconstructing Scientific Revolutions*, pp. 232–3; M. Mandelbaum, 'A Note on Thomas S. Kuhn's *The Structure of Scientific Revolutions*', *Monist*, 1977, 60(4): 446–7; and J. W. Watkins, 'Against "Normal Science"', in Lakatos and Musgrave (eds), *Criticism and the Growth of Knowledge*, pp. 30–1.

14 In *The Structure of Scientific Revolutions* Kuhn likens revolutions to Gestalt switches, but in the 1980s he admitted that revolutions are gradual to a much greater degree than the analogy suggests. See, for example, 'Response to Commentators', in S. Allén (ed.), *Possible Worlds in Humanities, Arts, and Sciences*, Berlin: de Gruyter, 1989, p. 49.

15 'Metaphor in Science', in A. Ortony (ed.), *Metaphor and Thought*, Cambridge: Cambridge University Press, 1979, p. 418.

16 D. H. Fischer, *Historian's Fallacies: Toward a Logic of Historical Thought*, London: Routledge & Kegan Paul, 1971.

Kuhn's major works

The Structure of Scientific Revolutions, third edition, Chicago, IL: University of Chicago Press, 1996.

The Essential Tension: Selected Studies in Scientific Tradition and Change, Chicago, IL: University of Chicago Press, 1977.

See also

Collingwood, Hempel, Popper (MP), Quine (MP), Wittgenstein (MP).

Further resources

Agassi, J., 'Towards an Historiography of Science', *History and Theory*, 1963, 2(4): 1–17.

Barnes, B., *T. S. Kuhn and Social Science*, London: Macmillan, 1982.

Gutting, G. (ed.), *Paradigms and Revolutions: Applications and Appraisals of Thomas Kuhn's Philosophy of Science*, Chicago, IL: University of Notre Dame Press, 1980.

Hacking, I. (ed.), *Scientific Revolutions*, Oxford: Oxford University Press, 1981.

Hoyningen-Heune, P., *Reconstructing Scientific Revolutions: Thomas S. Kuhn's Philosophy of Science*, trans. A. T. Levine, Chicago, IL: University of Chicago Press, 1993.

Kragh, H., *An Introduction to the Historiography of Science*, Cambridge: Cambridge University Press, 1987.

Lakatos, I. and Musgrave, A. (eds), *Criticism and the Growth of Knowledge*, London: Cambridge University Press, 1970.

Mandelbaum, M., 'A Note on Thomas S. Kuhn's *The Structure of Scientific Revolutions*', *Monist*, 1977, 60(4): 445–52.

Maudgil, A., 'World Pictures and Paradigms: Wittgenstein and Kuhn', in P. Weingartner and G. Schurz (eds), *Reports of the Thirteenth International Wittgenstein Symposium 1988*, Vienna: Höller-Pichler-Tempsky, 1989, pp. 285–90.

Meiland, J. W. and Krausz, M. (eds), *Relativism, Cognitive and Moral*, Chicago, IL: University of Notre Dame Press, 1982.

Newton-Smith, W. H., *The Rationality of Science*, London: Routledge, 1981.

Rorty, R., *Philosophy and the Mirror of Nature*, Princeton, NJ: Princeton University Press, 1979.

EMMANUEL LE ROY LADURIE 1929–

Emmanuel Le Roy Ladurie, who has been described variously as the 'standard-bearer' of the third generation of *Annales* historians and 'the rock star of medievalists', has played a leading role in the extension of the territory of history. Le Roy Ladurie has shown many historians that much can be gained from considering the insights of social scientists, taking fresh approaches to well-known sources, using quantitative methods and studying 'drops' of the sea of humanity.

Emmanuel Bernard Le Roy Ladurie was born in Les Moutiers-en-Cinglais, France, in 1929. He attended the Collège Saint-Joseph in Caen, the Lycée Henri-IV in Paris, and the Lycée Lakanal in Sceaux, obtained his agrégation in history from the Ecole Normale Supérieure, and his doctorat dès lettres from the Faculty of Letters at the University of Paris. After teaching at the Lycée de Montpellier and the University of Montpellier, he became director of studies at the Ecole Pratique des Hautes Etudes in Paris. Since 1970 he has been professor of geography and the social sciences at the University of Paris and, on the retirement of Ferdinand Braudel, professor of the history of modern civilisation at the Collège de France.

Le Roy Ladurie established his reputation as an innovative historian with the publication of his doctoral thesis, 'Les paysans de Languedoc' (trans. *The Peasants of Languedoc*).[1] In it he draws on quantitative data such as tax, tithe, wage, rent and profit figures, and the insights of François Simiand, David Ricardo, Thomas Malthus, Freud, Weber, Lévi-Strauss, Ernest Labrousse, Michel Foucault and Braudel, to argue that the history of Languedoc from the late fifteenth century to the early eighteenth century is '*l'histoire immobile*'. Put crudely, nothing of consequence altered in that time (on *l'histoire immobile*, see *The Mind and Method of the Historian*, pp. 1–27). In the first part of the work, Le Roy Ladurie argues that, while climate plays an important part in human history, he does not believe that climatic change correlates exactly with economic change (*The Peasants of Languedoc*, p. 18; see also *Times of Feast, Times of Famine: a History of Climate since the Year 1000*).

Nor does the study of French rural history from the late fifteenth century to the early eighteenth century suggest the progressive accumulation of rural property by capitalists. Rather, it reveals phases of growth and decline. In the first phase, what Le Roy Ladurie calls 'the low water mark', economic expansion was triggered by a dramatic growth in population in the wake of the Black Death. The growth in population led to the reclamation of forests and poorer lands for cultivation, subdivision of property and a drop in wages. Those who gained most from this situation were landowners who managed their own properties.

These conditions gave rise to the second phase, 'the advance'. Until 1530, the population continued to grow and landowners enjoyed healthy profits. At that time, however, the 'stubborn inelasticity' of agricultural practices triggered a phase of decline (ibid., p. 290). Cultivators planted more grain, but were unable (whether because of technical conservatism, lack of capital or the absence of innovation) to increase production to match population growth. People struggled to live on less food. Many emigrated or married later. They were aware that times were tough, but were 'preoccupied to the point of self-immolation' with religious issues (ibid., p. 291). Protestants and Catholics struggled over claims to salvation and to church land, tithes and taxes. These struggles, Le Roy Ladurie claims, gave rise both to anti-tax movements and to witchcraft, which promised but could not deliver social inversion (ibid., pp. 191–218). 'The Malthusian curse' had fallen upon Languedoc because population growth negated gains in productivity (ibid., p. 311).

In the third phase – 'maturity' (after 1600) – the birth rate grew level with the death rate. The accumulation of private wealth, however, was slowed both by agricultural conservatism and the dramatic rise of 'parasitic phenomena' such as loans, rents, tithes to the church and taxes to the state.

In phase four, 'the long period of recession', taxes, declining production, unemployment, poverty, poor sanitary conditions, emigration, late marriages and even some birth control arrested both population growth and the subdivision of land. A period of land consolidation, to the advantage of capitalists, set in.

In summary, two centuries of population growth and land subdivision were ultimately reversed, hence 'l'histoire immobile'. This was caused in large part, Le Roy Ladurie concludes, by the inability of society to raise productivity. He writes:

> Some have spoken of a *natural* ceiling on productive resources. But 'nature' in this case is actually culture; it is the customs, the way of life, the mentality of the people; it is a whole formed by technical knowledge and a system of values, by the means employed and the ends pursued.
>
> (Ibid., p. 298)

That is, the people of Languedoc not only lacked progressive technology; they also lacked 'the conscience, the culture, the morals, the politics, the education, the reformist spirit, and the unfettered longing for success' (ibid., p. 302). What Le Roy Ladurie traced was not a cycle in the strict sense, however, for the end of expansion did not bring Languedoc society back to its point of departure. Even if the economy as a whole stagnated, there were pockets of growth. Vine and silk cultivation spread, as did cloth manufacture. These, combined with the spread of elementary education, the weakening of religious fanaticism and 'a general improvement in behaviour' allowed an 'economic "takeoff"' in the eighteenth century (ibid., pp. 302, 307).

In *The Peasants of Languedoc*, Le Roy Ladurie is interested above all in identifying the long-term, slowly developing mental and material patterns ('structures') underlying the more visible and fleeting events and trends ('*conjoncture*') favoured by supporters of *histoire événementielle* (history of events). Here he echoes the approach of Braudel. Unlike Braudel, however, Le Roy Ladurie believes that it would be a pity to extinguish the history of events and individual biography (*The Territory of the Historian*, pp. 111–32). Such reflections, and much of his subsequent research, suggest an attempt to combine both events and 'structures'. This is seen clearly, for instance, in *Le Carnaval de Romans: de la chandeleur au mercredi des cendres* (trans. *Carnival in Romans*), a work that grew out of a five-page description in *The Peasants of Languedoc*. In this book Le Roy Ladurie focuses on the massacre of at least twenty artisans and their leader in the town of Romans during carnival time in 1580. From two descriptions of the massacre, one sympathetic to the murdered artisans and the other hostile, household tax lists, plague lists and the ideas of a wide range of historians and social theorists, Le Roy Ladurie derives the conclusion that the upheaval at Romans reflected the social, political and religious antagonisms of late sixteenth-century French rural society. *Carnival in Romans* shows Le Roy Ladurie's interest in values, attitudes, popular customs, religious beliefs and behaviour.[2]

A similar interest in the everyday life of ordinary people underpins his most important and popular work, *Montaillou, village occitan de 1294 à 1324* (trans. *Montaillou: the Promised Land of Error*). *Montaillou* is based on the register of Jacques Fournier, Bishop of Pamiers in Ariège from 1318 to 1325, concerning the interrogation and punishment of people accused of Catharism. Catharism was one of the more persistent Christian heresies of the Middle Ages and survived up to the fourteenth century in Pyrenean villages such as Montaillou. Cathars believed that while God was the creator of good spirits, the Devil was the creator of the material world. Salvation could thus only be achieved through the liberation of the soul from flesh. Fournier's register was published in 1965 and is well known to historians. Le Roy Ladurie, however, was one of the first scholars to suggest that an Inquisition register such as Fournier's could offer insights into rural life. Le Roy Ladurie took the records of interrogations with twenty-five individuals from Montaillou and rearranged them into a bipartite portrait of village life. In the first part of his account, Le Roy Ladurie looks to the material culture of Montaillou: its houses, agricultural practices, ecclesiastical and secular powers and relationship with other villages. In the second part he looks to the mental world of the villagers: their associations and intrigues, understanding of space, time, ageing, death, sexuality, God, sin, marriage, fate, magic and salvation. His work, Le Roy Ladurie claims:

> is much more than a courageous but fleeting deviation. It is the factual history of ordinary people. It is Pierre [Clergue] and Béatrice [des Planissoles] and their love; it is Pierre Maury and his flock; it is the breath of life restored through a repressive Latin register that is a monument of Occitan literature.
>
> (*Montaillou*, p. 356)

The 'breath of life' that Le Roy Ladurie restored to medieval France won him a widespread public audience and much scholarly acclaim and criticism. Montaillou even became a popular tourist destination. Though scholars applauded Le Roy Ladurie's imaginative and innovative approach to history, they complained about his uncritical reliance upon the Fournier register. For, rather than being a testimony of the peasants about themselves, the register records testimonies translated from Occitan to Latin and elicited by punishment or the threat of punishment. Some critics thus consider the register to be a tainted and fragile foundation for a historical study. Other scholars criticised Le Roy Ladurie's use of certain quotations several times to support widely different ideas; his lack of discussion on how he constructed his account; and his frequent use of clichés, neologisms and Franglais terms such as 'une one-man-town' and 'le wait-and-see'.[3]

These criticisms have also been levelled at some of Le Roy Ladurie's more recent works, particularly *La sorcière de Jasmin* (trans. *Jasmin's Witch*) and *Le siècle des Platter, 1499–1628* (trans. *The Beggar and the Professor: a Sixteenth Century Family Drama*).[4] In the former, Le Roy Ladurie supports Carlo Ginzburg's contention that witchcraft, as understood by medieval peasants, was a far cry from the practices attributed to witches in church and court records.[5] His aim is to piece together the 'total social fact of witchcraft' through the Occitan poem *Françouneto*, published in 1842 by Jacques Boé ('Jasmin') (*Jasmin's Witch*, p. 59). This poem was based on a traditional tale – still known by some inhabitants of Roquefort and Agen at the time Le Roy Ladurie wrote his book – about a young woman accused of witchcraft. Despite Jasmin's literary flourishes, Le Roy Ladurie claims that the poem captures many popular beliefs about witchcraft in the south of France in the seventeenth and eighteenth centuries (ibid., pp. 146–8). The 'witch' Françouneto, like the Mimalé family (ibid., pp. 31–52) and the wife of Ramonet de Lola (ibid., pp. 62–3), violated the principle of limited wealth. That is, others believed that they (knowingly or unknowingly) harmed other people and property in order to increase their own wealth (ibid., pp. 25, 44–61, 74).[6] The mental scope of *The Beggar and the Professor* is much larger. Le Roy Ladurie claims that the memoirs and correspondence of three generations of the Platter family illuminate a host of sixteenth-century values, beliefs and attitudes, particularly those concerning learning, religious reform, taxation, medicine, debt, crime and social agitation.

Carnival in Romans, *Montaillou*, *Jasmin's Witch* and *The Beggar and the Professor* are all examples of what has been called 'microhistory'.[7] Through the study of a family, life, event or locality, the historian hopes to shed light on a society's mental and material 'structures'. Though microhistory has become popular partly because of Le Roy Ladurie's works, questions have been raised about typicality. That is, what do the experiences of the people of Romans, Montaillou, Roquefort and Agen, and the Platters, point to? Are we justified in extrapolating from their experiences to make comments on the experiences of people in France? In Western Europe? In the Middle Ages and the Modern Era? Or are they the experiences of those small groups alone? Critics have also questioned Le Roy Ladurie's understanding of 'structures'. His lack of a clear description of that term, it has been repeatedly argued, leaves one wondering what criteria are used to identify them, why similar structures produce very different effects, why structures change, why they arise, and whether the world of structures does indeed exist.[8]

Though Le Roy Ladurie has given much attention to the experiences of ordinary people, he has also written histories of the royal French state between 1460 and 1774. In *L'Etat royal: de Louis XI à Henri IV, 1460–1610* (trans. *The Royal French State: 1460–1610*), he argues that the early modern state was defined by aristocratic politics, religious conflicts and economic developments. He also claims that it existed largely to assist with foreign expansion into Provence, Burgundy and Italy, and to match the colonial ambitions and resources of Spain. In *Ancien Régime: de Louis XIII à Louis XV, 1610–1774* (trans. *The Ancien Régime*), he focuses on shifts between periods of relative openness and rationality in the conduct of domestic and foreign affairs with those characterised by aggression abroad and authoritarianism at home. Among the former he places the reign of Louis XV which, despite hesitations during the 1750s, was characterised by a progression towards pragmatic liberalism. Among the latter he identifies the age of Richelieu and the last half of the reign of Louis XIV. At the close of these two volumes, Le Roy Ladurie suggests that irreversible progress towards liberalism, religious division, anti-clericalism and the emergence of the ideas of the Enlightenment pointed towards the revolution of 1789.[9]

Le Roy Ladurie has also demonstrated his ability as an essayist, penning articles on a wide range of topics such as the unification of the globe by disease, the use of computers in historical research, patterns of delinquency in nineteenth-century French conscripts and the use of magic in the sixteenth century to induce impotence (*The Territory of the Historian*; *The Mind and Method of the Historian*; *L'historien, le chiffre et le texte*). His other major works include *Love, Death and Money in the Pays d'Oc*, *The French Peasantry: 1450–1660* and reflections on his past allegiance to the French Communist Party (*Paris-Montpellier, PC-PSU, 1945–63*). Le Roy Ladurie's publications have made him a highly influential intellectual in France. He has appeared frequently on state television and in the pages of the newspapers *Le Monde*, *L'Express* and

Le Nouvel Observateur. He is also the director of the Bibliothèque de France. Due in large part to his efforts, the continuing international development of the *Annales* view of history – which began with Bloch and Febvre and continued with Braudel – seems assured.

Notes

1 Part one, much of the statistical appendix and a number of short sections have been removed and Part four is summarised as Part three in the English translation. For reviews of *The Peasants of Languedoc*, see R. Foster, *American Historical Review*, 1967, 72(2): 596–7; R. H. Hilton, *English Historical Review*, 1967, 83(325): 791–5; J. Jacquard, *Economic History Review*, 1967, 20(3): 623; and P. Sonnino, '*Les paysans de Languedoc: vingt-sept ans après*' (English text), *Proceedings of the Annual Meeting of the Western Society for French History*, 1994, 21: 293–300.

2 For reviews of *Carnival in Romans*, see W. Beik, *Journal of Interdisciplinary History*, 1980, 11(2): 307–9; L. Stone, 'In the Alleys of Mentalité', *New York Review of Books*, 8 November 1979, 26(17): 20–4; A. MacFarlane, *Journal of Modern History*, 1980, 52(3): 520–3; and R. J. Knecht, *History*, 1981, 66(217): 297–8.

3 Stone, 'In the Alleys of Mentalité', p. 22; D. Herlihy, *Social History*, 1979, 4(3): 517–20; E. Weber, *Journal of the History of Ideas*, 1979, 40(3): 481–90; and F. X. Hartigan, 'Montaillou', *Proceedings of the Annual Meeting of the Western Society for French History*, 1994, 21: 275–83.

4 On a smaller scale, see Le Roy Ladurie's description of the experiences of the sixteenth-century noble Gilles de Gouberville in 'In Normandy's Woods and Fields', in *The Territory of the Historian*, pp. 133–71. For reviews of *Jasmin's Witch*, see M. Broers, *History*, 1989, 74(241): 317–18, and E. L. Newman, 'Le Roy Ladurie's Magic, Jasmin's Witch', *Proceedings of the Annual Meeting of the Western Society for French History*, 1994, 21: 285–92. For reviews of *The Beggar and the Professor*, see D. J. Sturdy, *English Historical Review*, 1997, 112(447): 738–9; E. Weber, *New York Times Book Review*, 13 April 1997, p. 28; D. A. Bell, *New Republic*, 5 May 1997, 216(18): 39–41; M. S. Kimmel, *Nation*, 21 April 1997, 264(15): 28–30; S. Carroll, *Times Literary Supplement*, 1 December 1995, 4835: 9; L. Jardine, *New Statesman*, 16 May 1997, 126(4334): 47–8; and anon., *The Economist*, 12 July 1997, 344(8025): 76–7.

5 See, for instance, C. Ginzburg, *The Cheese and the Worms: the Cosmos of a Sixteenth Century Miller*, Baltimore, MD: Johns Hopkins University Press, 1980.

6 On the persistence and rearrangement of themes in folk-tales, see also 'Mélusine down on the Farm: Metamorphosis of a Myth', in *The Territory of the Historian*, pp. 203–20.

7 This term was initially used to describe Ginzburg's *The Cheese and the Worms*. See P. Burke, *The French Historical Revolution: the Annales School, 1929–1989*, Cambridge: Polity, 1990, p. 82.

8 D. North, 'Comment', *Journal of Economic History*, 1978, 38(1): 77–80; R. Brenner, 'Agrarian Class Structure and Economic Development in Pre-industrial Europe', *Past and Present*, 1976, 70: 30–74; and Sonnino, '*Les paysans de Languedoc: vingt-sept ans après*'.

9 For reviews of *The Royal French State: 1460–1610*, see A. D. Thomas, *History*, 1995, 80(258): 120–1; D. Parker, *English Historical Review*, 1996, 111(443): 972–3; J. Powis, *Times Literary Supplement*, 14 October 1994, 4776: 11; M. Wolfe, *Sixteenth Century Journal*, 1996, 27(1): 150–2; and J. Bergin, *History Today*, 1995, 45(7): 60–1. For reviews of *The Ancien Régime*, see D. Parker, *Times Literary Supplement*, 13 December 1996, 4889: 9; and N. Henshall, *History Today*, 1997, 47(7): 56–7.

Le Roy Ladurie's major works

Times of Feast, Times of Famine: a History of Climate since the Year 1000, trans. B. Bray, Garden City, NY: Doubleday, 1971.

The Peasants of Languedoc, trans. J. Day, Urbana, IL: University of Illinois Press, 1974.

Montaillou: the Promised Land of Error, trans. B. Bray, New York: Vintage, 1979.

Carnival in Romans, trans. M. Feeny, New York: Braziller, 1979.

The Territory of the Historian, trans. B. and S. Reynolds, Hassocks, Sussex: Harvester, 1979.

The Mind and Method of the Historian, trans. B. and S. Reynolds, Brighton: Harvester, 1981.

Love, Death and Money in the Pays d'Oc, trans. A. Sheridan, New York: Braziller, 1982.

Paris-Montpellier: PC-PSU 1945–1963, Paris: Gallimard, 1982.

Jasmin's Witch, trans. B. Pearce, New York: Braziller, 1987.

The Royal French State, 1460–1610, trans. J. Vale, Oxford: Basil Blackwell, 1994.

The Ancien Régime: a History of France, 1610–1774, trans. M. Greengrass, Oxford: Basil Blackwell, 1996.

The Beggar and the Professor: a Sixteenth Century Family Saga, trans. A. Goldhammer, Chicago, IL: University of Chicago Press, 1997.

L'historien, le chiffre et le texte, Paris: Fayard, 1997.

See also

Bloch, Braudel, Davis, Febvre, Foucault, Lévi-Strauss (CT), Marx.

Further resources

Barzun, J., *Clio and the Doctors: Psycho-history, Quanto-history and History*, Chicago, IL: University of Chicago Press, 1974.

Burke, P., *The French Historical Revolution: the Annales School, 1929–1989*, Cambridge: Polity, 1990.

Cantor, N. F., *Inventing the Middle Ages: the Lives, Works and Ideas of the Great Medievalists in the Twentieth Century*, New York: W. Morrow, 1991.

Carrard, P., 'The New History and the Discourse of the Tentative: Le Roy Ladurie's Quotation Marks', *Clio*, 1985, 15(1): 1–14.

——, *Poetics of the New History: French Historical Discourse from Braudel to Chartier*, Baltimore, MD: Johns Hopkins University Press, 1992.

Hartigan, F. X., 'Montaillou', *Proceedings of the Annual Meeting of the Western Society for French History*, 1994, 21: 275–83.

Himmelfarb, G., *The New History and the Old: Critical Essays and Reappraisals*, Cambridge: Cambridge University Press, 1987.

Newman, E. L., 'Le Roy Ladurie's Magic, Jasmin's Witch', *Proceedings of the Annual Meeting of the Western Society for French History*, 1994, 21: 285–92.

Sonnino, P., 'Les paysans de Languedoc: vingt-sept ans après' [English text], *Proceedings of the Annual Meeting of the Western Society for French History*, 1994, 21: 293–300.

Stone, L., 'In the Alleys of Mentalité', *New York Review of Books*, 8 November 1979, 26(17): 20–3.

Willis, F. R., 'The Contribution of the Annales School to Agrarian History: a Review Essay', *Agricultural History*, 1978, 52(4): 538–48.

LIVY *c.* 64 BC–*c.* AD 12

The Roman historian Titus Livius has long been maligned as a prodigious writer with little historical skill; a 'transparent overlay', careless translator and 'lost babe in the woods' who wandered from source to source without much idea of where his writing was headed. When held up against the standards of historical research in the nineteenth and early twentieth centuries, Livy was found seriously wanting. With the recent questioning of such 'standards', however, a growing number of scholars have called for a reconsideration of Livy's merits as a historian.

Of the 142 books that Livy wrote for his history of Rome, only 35 survive (1–10, 21–45). The rest are known from brief summaries or *periochae*. These were made from the first century on, because the size of the work made it practically unreadable. Though Livy tells us that it was his intention to write a history of Rome *ab urbe condita* ('from the founding of the city') to the murder of Cicero in 43 BC, the work also covers the years 42–49 BC. The elder Pliny explains this extension by saying that 'he had already achieved a sufficient measure of fame and could have stopped writing, were it not that his restless spirit thrived on hard work'.[1] Many of the events covered in the first five books, Livy tells us, such as the fall of Troy and the foundation of Rome by Romulus and Remus, are 'deeds that are obscured by too much antiquity, like things which are barely visible from a long distance' (6.1.2).[2] Later events can be spoken of with more accuracy, but the amount of evidence for such brings its own problems. As Livy writes:

> I see in my mind's eye that, like men who, attracted by the shallow water near the shore, wade out into the sea, I am being carried on, whatever progress I make, into depths more vast and, as it were, into the abyss, and that the task almost waxes

greater which, as I finished each of the earlier portions, seemed to be growing smaller.

(31.1.1)

This statement is supported by the rapid decline in the period of time covered in books 1 to 20 and the near steady treatment of approximately a year per book from there on.

The sheer size of Livy's project is remarkable; he must have written approximately three books per year. This estimated pace of composition has led a number of critics to conclude that Livy must have copied his primary sources – Valerius Antias, C. Licinius Macer, Aelius Tubero, Claudius Quadrigarius and the Greek historian Polybius – in an unthinking fashion. In many instances, he does appear either unwilling or unable to question dubious evidence or to pass judgement on conflicting sources (for example, 1.3.3; 26.49.6; 2.21.3; 38; 39.43.4). For him, the facts 'must be stated as they have been handed down, lest I deny credit to any of my authorities' (8.18.2–3).

On occasion, however, he is critical about his sources. In some passages he praises and criticises earlier historians (such as 3.5.12–15; 26.49.3; 30.19.11–12; 33.10.7–10; 36.38.67; 30.45.5; 33.10.10). In other places he expresses his doubts about the quality of the evidence concerning Rome's early history (for instance, preface 6–8; 3.5.12; 4.23.3; 6.1.1–3; 7.6.1–6) and various battles (like 3.5.12–13; 25.39.11–17; 26.49.1–6; 30.19.11–12; 33.10.7–10; 34.15.9; 36.38.6–7; 38.23.6–9; 45.43.8). Analysis of the books in which he used Polybius extensively also shows that he read ahead before writing, translated with a fair degree of accuracy, recast information to fit in with key events and themes and tried to explain the unfamiliar to his audience (books 31–45).[3] Overall, though, he looked for sources that would allow him to write the most comprehensive account of Roman history possible. Thus, in the first books of the history, Livy willingly suspends disbelief in the interest of providing as detailed an account as possible (preface 6; 5.21.8–9; 7.6.6; 8.18.3; 6.12.2–6; 29.14.9).[4]

Recent scholarship has also shown that Livy did much to structure his work. It is almost universally agreed that the surviving books were composed and published in units of five books (pentads), the length of which was determined by the size of a papyrus roll. The shape of books 1–45 is thus thought to be as shown on p. 204.[5] It is also thought that Livy further structured his work by placing speeches and major events such as battles and peace settlements at the beginning, middle and end of individual books. Intervening events were then made to fit into the remaining gaps. In some instances he had to stretch what

1–15: Early Rome
- 1–15: From Foundation until the sack of Rome by the Gauls
- 6–15: The Samnite Wars and the Conquest of Italy

16–30: The Punic Wars
- 16–20: The First Punic War
- 21–30: The Second Punic War

31–45: The Conquest of the East
- 31–35: The War with Philip V
- 36–40: The War with Antiochus
- 41–45: The War with Perseus

little material he had a long way, while in others he had to abridge material quite considerably (see, for example, books 31–35).[6] As important structural devices such as speeches were generally excluded from the *periochae*, however, opinion is divided as to whether he continued with the arrangement of material according to pentads in books 46 onwards.[7]

We thus have some idea of how Livy wrote his *Ab Urbe Condita*. What remains to be explained is *why*. Why did Livy spend his life writing a 142-book history? Livy's idea of writing a history of Rome down to the present day was not a new one, but the perspective he brought to that task was. Unlike earlier writers such as Q. Fabius Pictor, the elder Cato, L. Calpurnius Piso, C. Licinius Macer and Sallust, Livy was not active in politics. For him, historical events were not to be explained in political terms and used to support the political ideologies of his day. Rather, for him, history has a moral purpose. An account of the virtues and vices that made up the Roman national character at various points, he believed, would edify those who heard or read his work. This purpose is clearly stated in his preface. Each reader, he writes, should pay close attention to

> what life and morals were like; through what men and by what policies, in peace and in war, empire was established and enlarged; then let him note how, with the gradual relaxation of discipline, morals first gave way, as it were, then sank lower and lower, and finally began the downward plunge which has brought us to the present time when we can endure neither our vices nor their cure.
>
> What chiefly makes the study of history wholesome and profitable is this, that you behold the lessons of every kind of experience set forth as on a conspicuous monument; from

these you may choose for yourself and for your own state what to imitate, from these mark for avoidance what is shameful in the conception and shameful in the result.

(Preface 9–10)

Here Livy draws on a popular Roman educational device in which important ideas and exempla to be remembered are arranged in a mental architectural structure.[8] His hope is that the reader will look carefully at the features of his 'conspicuous monument', try to understand its representations and implement that understanding. Study of the past thus offers more than an escape from the woes of the present; it may also lead one to virtuous behaviour.

Although earlier writers such as Sallust also believed that Rome had declined into a state where 'neither our vices nor their cure' could be endured, Livy offers a novel explanation for that decline. Echoing the ideas of Greek writers such as Herodotus, Livy's predecessors argued that current moral woes were due to a destructive preoccupation with wealth and the absence of the fear of an external enemy (*metus hostilis*). For Livy, however, the three main symptoms of moral decline – preoccupation with wealth, partisan rivalry and neglect of the gods – were due to evils inherent in humans and contact with foreign practices and ideas (for example, 37.54.1; 37.54.18–28; 38.17.3–9; 1.6.4).[9] Unlike his predecessors, he also believed that such a decline could be contained and reversed. Livy's optimism is seen clearly in his account of how Roman character was formed. At foundation, he tells us, Romulus quickly established a social and political hierarchy and used religion to secure his rule (1.8.1; 1.8.7; 1.13.6–8; 1.12.7; 1.9.6–10). His authoritarian approach, Livy believes, prepared the populace for the responsibilities of *libertas* or freedom:

For what would have happened if that plebeian population, shepherds and immigrants, refugees from their own peoples, had attained freedom, or at least impunity, under the protection of inviolable sanctuary, and, released from fear of a king, had begun to be stirred up by the tribunes' stormings and, in a city not their own, had begun to sow conflicts with the fathers before the guarantees of wives and children and affection for the soil itself (to which one becomes accustomed by the long passage of time) had joined their minds?

(2.1.4–5)

Livy also expresses his admiration for Numa, who hoped to instil in the populace respect for the gods, Servus Tullius, who introduced constitutional reforms to establish *mores* (conventions thought to be essential to a community) and Camillus, 'Romulus and parent of the fatherland, and second founder of the city' (1.21.1; 1.19.4; 1.46.5; 5.49.7). Livy thus believes that strong leaders can help people to turn away from evil. He probably hoped that strong leaders would also help his contemporaries to escape moral decline.

Despite doubts about Livy's abilities as a historian, scholars have long admired his style. Not only was he familiar with conventional writing styles and vocabularies but he also displayed a keen interest in experimentation. His accounts of military action, for instance, incorporate conventional military vocabulary, 'communiqué style' (terse, report language), invented and reported speeches (*oratio obliqua* and *oratio recta*), neologisms and invented clichés.[10] Miles has also suggested that Livy might have deliberately blurred the stylistic convention used by earlier historians to distinguish between visual and oral evidence. In the ancient world, first-hand observation was the most reliable basis on which to construct an account of events. Oral evidence (from oral tradition or written works read aloud) was thought to be a poor substitute. Accordingly, in works of history, distant events were mentioned briefly and through indirect speech in order to convey the historian's refusal to take responsibility for their truth or reliability. In the opening books of Livy's history, however, there appears to be no consistent rationale behind his use of direct and indirect discourse. While this may be taken as the sign of a poor writer, it is also possible that Livy actively reformulated the convention.[11]

Though Livy had some doubts about the reception of his project (Preface 1–3), the *Ab Urbe Condita* was widely read and quoted during the Roman Empire. It is even reported by Pliny the Younger that a man travelled all the way from Cadiz (Spain) to Rome just to look upon Livy.[12] However, praise was soon eclipsed by complaint. Emperor Gaius Caligula dubbed him 'a verbose and careless historian',[13] and at the collapse of the Western Empire interest in his work was kept alive only by a few dedicated individuals such as Orosius and Cassiodorus. Fridugis of Tours, Lupus of Ferrièrs and Theatbert of Duurstede renewed interest in Livy during the Carolingian period, but his ideas did not gain widespread currency until they were studied and adapted by the Italian Renaissance thinkers Dante, Boccaccio and, most importantly, Machiavelli. Livy's work became a popular quarry for later thinkers such as the nineteenth-century English historian Thomas Babington Macaulay. In the nineteenth and early twentieth centuries a group of German scholars tried to identify what literary sources Livy had used and how. Their suggestion that Livy was a poor translator of

Polybius and that he had little political and military experience encouraged the perception of him as a stylist who stood up poorly against their standards of historical research. More recently, a number of scholars have sought to demonstrate Livy's originality and talent as an historian by looking at the way that he structured his work, adapted his sources, set about writing and depicted Roman national character. For them, Livy was a gifted writer who formulated and reformulated some of the central ideas and historiographical principles of his age.

Notes

1 The Elder Pliny, *Natural History*, trans. H. Rackham, Loeb Classical Library, London: Heinemann, 1958, vol. 1, preface, §16.
2 Citations correspond to the book, chapter and section number of the Loeb edition of the history.
3 T. J. Luce, *Livy: the Composition of his History*, Princeton, NJ: Princeton University Press, 1977, chaps 2–4; J. Briscoe, A *Commentary on Livy, Books 34–37*, Oxford: Oxford University Press, 1981.
4 Luce, *Livy*, p. 146.
5 Based on ibid., p. 6. See also P. A. Stadter, 'The Structure of Livy's History', *Historia*, 1972, 21(2): 287–307.
6 Ibid., chap. 2.
7 See, for example, R. Syme, 'Livy and Augustus', *Historia Philosophia*, 1959, 64(1): 27–87; P. G. Walsh, *Livy: his Historical Aims and Methods*, Cambridge: Cambridge University Press, 1961; R. M. Ogilvie, *A Commentary on Livy Books 1–5*, Oxford: Oxford University Press, 1965; and Luce, *Livy*.
8 C. S. Kraus and A. J. Woodman, *Latin Historians*, Oxford: Oxford University Press, 1997, pp. 55–8.
9 G. B. Miles, *Livy: Reconstructing Early Rome*, Ithaca, NY: Cornell University Press, 1995, pp. 152–4; Luce, *Livy*, p. 282.
10 Kraus and Woodman, *Latin Historians*, pp. 67–8.
11 Miles, *Livy*, chap. 1.
12 Pliny the Younger, *Letters and Panegyricus*, trans. B. Radice, Loeb Classical Library, London, Heinemann, 1975, vol. 1, 2.3.8.
13 Suetonius, *Lives of the Caesars*, trans. J. C. Rolphe, Loeb Classical Library, London: Heinemann, 1920, vol.1, 4.34.2.

Livy's major works

Livy: From the Founding of the City, 14 vols, trans. B. O. Foster, E. T. Sage and A. C. Schlesinger, Loeb Classical Library, Cambridge, MA: Harvard University Press. Online version at: http://www.perseus.tufts.edu/Texts.html

See also

Froissart, Gibbon, Herodotus, Ibn Khaldun, Macaulay, Polybius, Tacitus.

Further resources

Briscoe, J., *A Commentary on Livy, Books 34–37*, Oxford: Oxford University Press, 1981.

Dorey, T. A. (ed.), *Livy*, London: Routledge & Kegan Paul, 1971.

Jaegar, M., *Livy's Written Rome*, Ann Arbor, MI: University of Michigan Press, 1997.

Kraus, C. S. and Woodman, A. J., *Latin Historians*, Oxford: Oxford University Press, 1997.

Luce, T. J., *Livy: the Composition of his History*, Princeton, NJ: Princeton University Press, 1977.

Mellor, R., *The Roman Historians*, London: Routledge, 1999.

Miles, G. B., *Livy: Reconstructing Early Rome*, Ithaca, NY: Cornell University Press, 1995.

Ogilvie, R. M., *A Commentary on Livy, Books 1–5*, Oxford: Oxford University Press, 1965.

Packard, D. W., *A Concordance to Livy*, Cambridge, MA: Harvard University Press, 1968.

Stadter, P. A., 'The Structure of Livy's History', *Historia*, 1972, 21(2): 287–307.

Walsh, P. G., *Livy: his Historical Aims and Methods*, Cambridge: Cambridge University Press, 1961.

——, *Livy*, Oxford: Oxford University Press, 1974.

THOMAS BABINGTON MACAULAY 1800–59

There was a time when the works of Thomas Babington Macaulay could be found on bookshelves throughout the British Empire. Macaulay made historical writing a recognised part of British literature and generated world-wide interest in the revolution of 1688. Today, however, his works are more likely to be found in bargain bins in second-hand bookstores, the victim of his enormous appeal to Victorian thought.

The son of Selina Mills and Zachary Macaulay, Thomas Babington Macaulay was born on 25 October 1800 in Leicestershire. Zachary Macaulay was the editor of the *Christian Observer* and a committed member of the 'Clapham Sect', an Anglican movement that pushed for the abolition of slavery in the British Empire. Zachary inculcated in Thomas the ideas of the sect, while Selina, who had been educated by the religious writer Hannah More, encouraged him to read widely. Thomas 'talked printed words' when he was four, showed an interest in Latin and Greek composition at the age of six and wrote a number of essays and hymns by the age of eight. He attended a day school in Clapham until 1813 and then left home to attend the Reverend Preston's boarding school in Cambridgeshire. A gifted and precocious student, Thomas won a place at Trinity College, Cambridge, before he was eighteen. Though he was awarded a Craven scholarship, a Latin declamation prize and the Chancellor's English verse medal twice, he took a baccalaureate without honours in 1822 for want of mathematical prowess. In 1824 he won a fellowship at Trinity.

While at Cambridge, Macaulay wrote for the short-lived *Knight's Quarterly Magazine*. His contributions to *Knight's* included love poems, book reviews, satirical allegories and historical fiction. His historical writings covered the Huguenot defeat at Moncontour in 1569 and victory at Livry in 1590, the Cavaliers' march on London in 1642 and the Roundheads' victory at Naseby in 1645. Though he was interested in the deeds of individuals, he believed that they should be viewed in context. Historians, he claimed, should describe the past as fully as possible in order to make sense of the actions of individuals. For example, in his review of Mitford's *History of Greece*, he argues that the historian should study

> all that is interesting and important in military and political transactions; but he will not think anything too trivial for the gravity of history, which is not too trivial to promote or diminish the happiness of man. He will portray in vivid colours the domestic society, the manners, the amusements, the conversation of the Greeks. He will not disdain to discuss the state of agriculture, of the mechanical arts, and of the conveniences of life. The progress of painting, of sculpture, and of architecture, will form an important part of his plan. But above all, his attention will be given to the history of that splendid literature from which has sprung all the strength, the wisdom, the freedom, and the glory, of the western world.
>
> (*Works*, 3, p. 302)

Zachary did not approve of some of the material that Thomas had written, and persuaded him to sever his connection with the magazine.

Macaulay managed to make amends with his father by writing an essay on slavery in the West Indies for the *Edinburgh Review*. This became the first of a number of highly successful contributions to that magazine. Between 1825 and 1832 he wrote on the abolition of slavery, the extension of university education to the middle class, the civil rights of Jews, Machiavelli and Samuel Johnson (see *Critical and Historical Essays Contributed to the Edinburgh Review*). Though some are more polemical than others, political issues are debated in all of them. Many readers assume that Macaulay was a Whig: a supporter of the political party that aimed to subordinate the power of the Crown to that of the Parliament and the upper classes.

A close look at these essays, however, suggests that he took a more moderate stance. For Macaulay, the antagonism in all societies between the upper classes and those discontented with them threatened the social order. The discontented could become rebellious and threaten revolution, while the upper classes could suppress rebelliousness without addressing legitimate grievances. In Britain during Macaulay's day, the conflict was between a defensive and repressive governing class and an aggrieved radical movement. Macaulay's remedy for this conflict was to steer a middle course between these two extremes, to support order without despotism and freedom without anarchy.[1] For Macaulay the middle ground meant the promotion of free trade and personal liberty, the greatest good of the greatest number, and the restriction of government and church power. As he wrote in 'Southies Colloquies':

> Our rulers will best promote the improvement of the nation by . . . leaving capital to find its most lucrative course, commodities their fair price, industry and intelligence their natural reward, idleness and folly their natural punishment. . . . Let the Government do this: the People will assuredly do the rest.
>
> (*Works*, 7, p. 502)

These essays also reveal more of his views on history. In 'History', for instance, he argues that history is a 'debatable land':

> It lies on the confines of two distinct territories. It is under the jurisdiction of two hostile powers; and, like other districts similarly situated, it is ill defined, ill cultivated, and ill regulated. Instead of being equally shared between its two rulers, the Reason and the Imagination, it falls alternately under the sole and absolute dominion of each. It is sometimes fiction. It is sometimes theory.
>
> (*Works*, 7, p. 177)

According to Macaulay, while ancient historians such as Herodotus, Thucydides, Tacitus and Livy excel in the art of narration, they are weak in analysis. Modern historians such as Hume, Gibbon and Mitford, on the other hand, are strong in analysis but neglect the art of narration. For Macaulay, history should be a balance of narration and analysis. His aim of counterbalancing the contemporary emphasis on analysis with narration led him to stress the relationship between history and other literary genres. Historians, he claims, should learn from successful writers of fiction how to select and present materials. He also believes that historians have much to learn from painters:

> History has its foreground and its background: and it is principally in the management of its perspective that one artist differs from another. Some events must be represented on a large scale, others diminished; the great majority will be lost in the dimness of the horizon; and a general idea of their joint effort will be given by a few slight touches.
>
> (*Works*, 7, p. 178)

These ideas appear again and again in Macaulay's writings; for example, in his criticism of Courtney for neglecting the 'arts of selection and compression' (*Edinburgh Review*, 68: 114), of Gleig for writing 'three big bad volumes, full of undigested correspondence and undiscerning panegyric' (ibid., 74: 160), and of Orme for being 'minute even to tediousness' (ibid., 70: 296).

In February 1830 Lord Lansdowne invited Macaulay to stand for the vacant parliamentary seat at Calne in Wiltshire, his pocket or 'rotten' borough (a parliamentary seat under the control of one person or family). Macaulay agreed, and took a seat in the House of Commons during a time of great significance in British parliamentary history. The long rule of the Tories (for the established order in church and state) was coming to an end amid calls for parliamentary reform. When the government collapsed, it left the way open for a Whig administration under Lord Grey. Grey introduced a Parliamentary Reform Bill in March 1831. A third version of the Bill passed in mid-1832. Although Macaulay's seat at Calne was marked for abolition, he was an enthusiastic supporter of the Bill. Parliamentary reform, he thought, would preserve the constitution and save Britain from revolution.[2]

In 1832 Macaulay won a seat in the newly enfranchised borough of Leeds, and two years later he was awarded a post on the newly created Supreme Council of India (*Works*, 9, pp. 543–86). Macaulay had no real desire to go to India but he needed the annual salary of £10,000 to secure his family's financial position. From India, Macaulay played a leading role in persuading the governments of Peel and Melbourne that censorship should be lifted from the press, that Englishmen and Indians should be equal before the law and that the penal system should be reformed. He also tipped the balance of the debate over the language in which university education should be conducted in favour of English.

During this time Macaulay also wrote *Lays of Ancient Rome*, although it was not published until 1842. Shortly before its publication, Macaulay described his project to Macvey Napier, then editor of the *Edinburgh Review*:

> You are acquainted, no doubt, with Prizonius's theory about the early Roman History, – a theory which Niebuhr revived, and which Arnold has adopted as fully established. I have myself not the smallest doubt of its truth. It is that the stories of the birth of Romulus and Remus, the fight of the Horatii and Curatii, and all the other romantic tales which fill the first three or four books of Livy, come from the lost ballads of the early Romans. I amused myself in India with trying to restore some of these long perished poems.[3]

In the *Lays*, Macaulay explored the successful defence of Rome against the ousted Tarquins ('Horatius'), the defeat of the Latin army attacking Rome in the same cause ('The Battle of Lake Regillus'), the seizure of a young woman by a magistrate and her murder by her father ('Virginia'), and the foretellings of a seer to Romulus about the power of Rome ('The Prophecy of Capys'). Each of these poems includes a preface in which he describes the legends that inspired it. Twenty-three thousand copies of the *Lays* were sold in the first ten years of its release in Britain alone, and parts survived as texts for reading or recitation in schools until the mid-twentieth century.

Macaulay also continued to write for the *Edinburgh Review*. Three of his articles from the 1830s ('Mirabeau', 1832; 'Bacon', 1837; 'Gladstone', 1839) are on political matters; the remainder are historical ('Hampden', 1831; 'Burleigh', 1832; 'War of Succession in Spain', 1833; 'Horace Walpole', 1833; 'The Earl of Chatham', 1834; 'Mackintosh', 1835; 'Sir William Temple', 1838). Though these essays were usually named after one person, they are more accurately broad sketches of an age. They were well received, though the editor of Mackintosh's *History of the Revolution in England in 1688*, William Wallace, was so enraged by 'Mackintosh' that he challenged Macaulay to a duel. Macaulay managed to avoid the duel but promised to remove his harshest comments from any reprint of the essay.

When Macaulay returned from India in 1838, he proposed to write a history of England that would extend from the seventeenth century to the 1832 Reform Bill. He began writing and collecting materials in early 1839, but a year later he set the project aside to be the Secretary of War in Melbourne's cabinet. The War Office, at a time of peace, did not demand much of Macaulay. *The Times*, building on reports of Macaulay's rapid manner of speech, christened him 'Mr Babbletongue Macaulay' and even Melbourne remarked that he would prefer to sit 'in a room with a chime of bells, ten parrots and Lady Westmorland' than with him.[4] Macaulay lost his seat in 1847, and before he regained it five years later, he tried to complete his *History of England*. Macaulay considered this to be a far more serious work than his essays but he none the less wanted to 'produce something which shall for a few days supersede the last fashionable novel on the tables of young ladies' (*Works*, 9, p. 119).

The *History of England* covers the first 2,000 or so years of British history, from the discovery of its inhabitants by the Phoenicians to the restoration of Charles II, in the first 160 pages. The following 1,000 or so pages are dedicated to forty-two years, of which the reigns of James II and William III take up the bulk of the space. Volume 2 culminates with the 1688 revolution and the crowning of William and Mary. In Macaulay's opinion, 'It is because we had a preserving revolution in the seventeenth century that we have not had a destroying revolution in the nineteenth' (*Works*, 3, p. 288).

Volumes 3 and 4, which were published in 1855, and volume 5, which appeared posthumously in 1861 (edited by Macaulay's sister Hannah), focused primarily on William III. After the publication of volume 4, Macaulay's publisher gave him a cheque for £20,000. The *History* was so widely read that for a time he rivalled Dickens. Macaulay was especially pleased with the popularity of the work among ordinary readers. To some his popularity proved the shallowness of the work and the ease with which an uncritical audience could be swayed.

After suffering a heart attack in 1852, Macaulay had to delay taking up his seat in Edinburgh. He ultimately resigned his seat in January 1856 to concentrate on the *History*. He was made a peer in 1857. He died on 28 December 1859 and was buried in Westminster Abbey at the foot of the statue of Addison.

Muted criticism during Macaulay's lifetime gave way to bitter criticism after his death. He was seen by writers such as Carlyle, Acton, Arnold and Ruskin as transfixed by 1832, an uncritical voice for Whig ideas, naïvely optimistic, pompous, superficial and base. Later scholarship also revealed that he ignored some events (such as the 'Settlement' Act of 1662), was uncritical or sloppy in his treatment of sources and exaggerated (for example, the number of executions and transportations at the 'Bloody Assizes' and treatments of Judge Jeffreys and Marlborough).[5] The result of these criticisms was devastating: very few people are familiar with Macaulay's works today. Those who are, however, realise that they are an excellent indicator of Victorian style and thought.

Notes

1 J. Hamburger, *Macaulay and the Whig Tradition*, Chicago, IL: University of Chicago Press, 1976.
2 M. Cruikshank, *Macaulay*, Boston, MA: Twayne, 1978.
3 Quoted in J. Millgate, *Macaulay*, London: Routledge & Kegan Paul, 1973, pp. 70–1.
4 Quoted in K. Young, *Macaulay*, Harlow: Longman, 1976, p. 15.
5 For a discussion on the reputation of Macaulay in the twentieth century, see G. Himmelfarb, 'Who Now Reads Macaulay?' *The New Criterion*, 1982, 1(4): 41–7.

Macaulay's major works

The Complete Works of Lord Macaulay, 20 vols, ed. Lady Trevelyan, London: G. P. Putnam's Sons, 1898.
Critical and Historical Essays Contributed to the Edinburgh Review, London: Longmans Green, 1843.
The History of England from the Accession of James II, 4 vols, London: Longmans Green, 1848–61.
The Letters of Thomas Babington Macaulay, 6 vols, ed. T. Pinney, Cambridge: Cambridge University Press, 1974–81.

See also

Michelet, Ranke.

Further resources

Clive, J. L., *Macaulay, the Shaping of the Historian*, New York: Knopf, 1973.
Cruikshank, M., *Thomas Babington Macaulay*, Boston, MA: Twayne, 1978.
Firth, C. H., *A Commentary on Macaulay's History of England*, London: F. Cass, 1964.
Gay, P., *Style in History*, New York: McGraw-Hill, 1974.
Geyl, P., *Debates with Historians*, New York: Meridian, 1958.
Hamburger, J., *Macaulay and the Whig Tradition*, Chicago, IL: University of Chicago Press, 1976.
Levine, G., *The Boundaries of Fiction: Carlyle, Macaulay, Newman*, Princeton, NJ: Princeton University Press, 1968.
Millgate, J., *Macaulay*, London: Routledge & Kegan Paul, 1973.
Rosemary, J., *The Art and Science of Victorian History*, Columbus, OH: Ohio State University Press, 1985.
Young, K., *Macaulay*, Harlow: Longman, 1976.

KARL MARX 1818–80

Of late, there has been much discussion on those individuals who played a significant role in the shaping of the twentieth century. Though he lived in the nineteenth century, the German philosopher and revolutionary thinker Karl Marx has featured heavily. This is because his writings have been so influential in economics, politics, sociology and history that it is hard to conceive of what these fields would have been like without him.[1]

Karl Marx was born in Trier, Germany, on 5 May 1818. He commenced studies in law at the University of Bonn in 1835 but was transferred to the University of Berlin a year later at his father's request after being wounded in a duel and arrested for drunkenness. At Berlin he turned from law to philosophy and was heavily influenced by the ideas of Hegel and his interpreters, such as Bruno Bauer and Ludwig Feuerbach. He was awarded a doctorate for his account of the differences between the ideas of Democritus and Epicurus in 1841, but, unable to find a lectureship, he turned to journalism to make a living. Initially he wrote for and edited the *Rheinische Zeitung*, a liberal democratic newspaper, but after this was banned by the Prussian government in 1843 he moved to Paris to write for the *Deutsch–Französische Jahrbücher*. In Paris he explored political, economic, historical and philosophical ideas and struck up a friendship with Friedrich Engels, the son of a wealthy textile manufacturer, who was also interested in the philosophy of Hegel. Marx and Engels penned *Die Heilige Familie* (1845, trans. *The Holy Family, Selected Writings*, pp. 131–55), a critical examination of the philosophy of Bauer, before Marx and his family were forced to leave Paris for Brussels.

Against the wishes of the authorities in Brussels, Marx established an organisation that aimed to keep communists around the world in contact (the Communist Correspondence Committee), and co-authored a number of works with Engels in which they criticised popular French and German philosophical and socialist ideas (see *Die deutsche Ideologie*, 1845, trans. and abr. *The German Ideology, Selected Writings*, pp. 159–91 and *La misère de la philosophie*, 1847, trans. *The Poverty of Philosophy, Collected Works*, vol. 6, pp. 105–212). In 1847 he participated in the second Congress of the League of Communists in London. The League embraced Marx and Engels' ideas with enthusiasm and invited Marx to write about its beliefs and aims. The result was *Das Kommunistische Manifest* (1848, trans. *The Communist Manifesto*), published at a time of political instability in Europe.

Marx's hopes of living in a free, fair society led him and his family to move to Paris, to Germany, back to Paris and then finally to London, where he spent the rest of his life. There he contributed regular articles to the *New York Tribune*, published *Zur Kritik der politischen Ökonomie* (1859, trans. *A Critique of Political Economy, Collected Works*, vol. 16, pp. 465–77), *Das Kapital* (1867, trans. *Capital*), *Der Französische Bürgerkrieg* (1871, trans. and abr. *The Civil War in France, Selected Writings*, pp. 539–58), *Das achtzehnte Brumaire des Louis Bonaparte* (1851, trans. *The Eighteenth Brumaire of Napoleon Bonaparte, Selected Writings*, pp. 300–25), *Kritik des Gothaer Programms* (1891, trans. and abr. *Critique of the Gotha Programme, Selected Writings*, pp. 564–70), participated in political reform movements and squabbled with other socialists and communists. He also worked on volumes 2 and 3 of *Capital*, but these were only guided to publication by Engels after Marx's death in 1880. Since then, a variety of his other manuscripts have been published.

According to Marx, Hegel's writings were the root of his philosophy ('Economic and Philosophic Manuscripts', *Selected Writings*, p. 98). For Hegel, the study of history reveals the progressive manifestation of 'Mind', which takes place along a path that entails struggle. In the *Phenomenology of Spirit*, for instance, Hegel argues that people who are not aware that they are part of Mind see one another as rivals. They struggle, and some enslave others. In the relationship of master and slave, Hegel believes that Mind is 'alienated' from itself because individuals consider others to be foreign and hostile to themselves. This master/slave relationship is not stable, however, because through their work the slave becomes self-conscious and the master becomes dependent on the slave. Eventually the slave is liberated, and people begin to realise that they are unified and free.

After Hegel's death, there was much debate on his idea of 'Mind'. For the 'Young Hegelians' at the University of Berlin, 'Mind' could be viewed as a collective term for all human minds. Seen in this way, Hegel's writings became an account of humanity freeing itself from the illusions that stand in the way of self-understanding, unity and freedom. The goal of history was thus the liberation of humanity. One of the Young Hegelians, Ludwig Feuerbach, thought that orthodox religion was the obstacle that prevented humanity from achieving freedom. God, he argued, was invented by humans as a projection of their own ideals, an invention which led to the alienation of humans from their true nature.

Drawing on the ideas of Hegel and the Young Hegelians, Marx argued that it was neither religion nor ignorance of Mind, but current economic and material conditions that prevented humans from achieving freedom.[2] As such, philosophy and social criticism alone cannot end human alienation ('Theses on Feuerbach', *Selected Writings*, p. 158). It can only be addressed

> [in] the formation of a class with radical chains . . . a sphere of society having a universal character because of its universal suffering . . . a sphere, in short, that is the *complete loss* of humanity and can only redeem itself through the *total redemption of humanity*. This dissolution of society as a particular class is the proletariat.
>
> ('Towards a Critique of Hegel's *Philosophy of Right*: Introduction', *Selected Writings*, pp. 72–3)

Human alienation, Marx claims, requires a practical solution. For him, that solution would be a social revolution led by a class that could enlist a large part of society to join it in opposing the prevailing system. To have its claim accepted, such a class must act in the interests of all of the people. Marx thought that the key to such acceptance was poverty. The propertyless working class, or 'proletariat' as he calls them, have nothing to lose and everything to gain. As he puts it in words that were to become the motto of many a twentieth-century revolutionary: 'The proletarians have nothing to lose but their chains. They have a world to win' (*The Communist Manifesto*, p. 77). Other groups stand to lose private property and social status, and so cannot be relied on to act in a selfless manner.

However, Marx is not simply rephrasing Hegel in economic terms. He has a fundamentally different approach to history:

> In direct contrast to German philosophy, which descends from heaven to earth, here we ascend from earth to heaven. That is to say, we do not set out from what men say, imagine, conceive, nor from men as narrated, thought of, imagined, conceived, in order to arrive at men in the flesh. We set out from real, active men, and on the basis of their real-life process we demonstrate the development of the ideological reflexes and echoes of this life-process. The phantoms formed in the human brain are also, necessarily, sublimates of their material life-process, which is empirically verifiable and bound to material premises. Morality, religion, metaphysics and all the rest of ideology and their corresponding forms of consciousness no longer seem to be independent. They have no history or development. Rather, men who develop their material

production and their material relationships alter their thinking and the products of their thinking along with their real existence. Consciousness does not determine life, but life determines consciousness.

(*The German Ideology, Selected Writings*, p. 164)

Where Hegel starts with philosophy, Marx starts with people's experiences. The material conditions of life determine the nature of human consciousness and society, rather than the other way around. These ideas, making up the 'materialist conception of history', are explored in more detail in the preface to *A Critique of Political Economy*:

In the social production which men carry on they enter into definite relations that are indispensable and independent of their will; these relations of production correspond to a definite stage of development of their material powers of production. The sum total of these relations of production constitutes the economic structure of society – the real foundation, on which rise legal and political superstructures and to which correspond definite forms of social consciousness. The mode of production of material life conditions the general character of the social, political and spiritual processes of life. It is not the consciousness of men that determines their existence, but, on the contrary, their social existence determines their consciousness. At a certain stage of their development the material forces of production in society come into conflict with the existing relations of production or – what is but a legal expression for the same thing – with the property relations within which they had been at work before. From forms of development of the forces of production these relations turn into their fetters. Then comes the epoch of social revolution.

(*Selected Writings*, p. 389)

Here Marx divides society into three parts. First, there are the 'productive forces', which consist of the machinery, raw materials and skills people employ in order to live. The productive forces give rise to the 'relations of production', which are the relations between people and/or people and things. These relations constitute the 'economic structure of society', and it, in turn, gives rise to the 'superstructure' or the political and legal institutions of a society and the ways in which members of that society conceive of themselves and their relations. Thus to understand the institutions, laws, art and morality of a society and the changes that a society undergoes, it is necessary to understand the nature of its productive forces and relations of production.[3]

For Marx the study of history reveals that society has passed through a number of distinct 'modes of production': forms or stages of economic organisation, defined by a characteristic form of relations of production. These are the primitive communal mode, ancient mode, feudalism, and capitalism.[4] In primitive communal societies, property is communal rather than private. Work may be communal or undertaken by particular families, and there is no clear division of labour between urban craft work and agricultural work and specialist and non-specialist tasks. This form of social organisation, Marx claims, was widespread in the early history of Europe (*Capital*, vol. 3, pp. 333–4). Though such a form of social organisation can last indefinitely, Marx believes that migration and warfare may have stimulated the disintegration of primitive communism in Europe. In the place of primitive communism there emerged first in Greece, Rome and some parts of the Middle East the ancient mode of society. In such a society, labour is divided between town and country but the country dominates the city. City occupations such as craft and trading are held in low regard and full citizenship is denied those who engage in such activities. Conquest secures new land and slaves, but most of the spoils are given to the social and military leaders of the society. Growing reliance on slave labour leads to the emergence of a dispossessed urban 'proletarian rabble', a mob who have nothing to offer the state but their *proles* or offspring (*The German Ideology*, *Selected Writings*, p. 162). Though the proletariat were unable to 'lose their chains' in Greece and Rome, they left Rome vulnerable to attacks by Barbarians.

The fall of Rome, Marx claims, stimulated the development of the feudal institution of serfdom. Though slaves and serfs are 'organic accessories of the land', serfs cannot be sold. They can, however, be forced from the land if they cannot pay taxes and rent and feed themselves. Those who fled from the land during the 'feudal stage', Marx tells us, flocked to towns. Urban commerce grew, as did calls for trade regulations. Though casual labourers occasionally attempted revolts, they were ineffective against the organised power of the 'town fathers' ('Critique of Hegel's *Philosophy of Right*'; *German Ideology*; 'Letter to Annenkov', *Selected Writings*, pp. 30, 162–3, 193; *The Communist Manifesto*, pp. 34–5).

In Marx's view, at the end of the Middle Ages there existed the three preconditions for the development of industrial capitalism. First, there were large numbers of labourers who were 'free' in the double sense that 'neither they themselves [formed] part and parcel of the means of production, as in the case of slaves, bondsmen, etc., nor [did] the means of production belong to them, as in the case of peasant proprietors' (*Capital*, vol. 1, p. 714). As commerce developed between town and countryside, serfs were often able to buy exemptions from various manorial duties. This led to a society of independent or semi-independent propertied peasants. In the seventeenth century, however, they were expelled from the land. In the case of England and Scotland, which Marx examines in detail in chapters 27 to 29 in volume 1 of *Capital*, the expulsion of the peasantry from the land was brought about by the need to produce more wool for the newly developed 'manufactures' of Flanders. The advent of the Reformation also hastened the process of dispossession, as confiscated Catholic lands were for the most part 'given away to rapacious royal favourites, or sold at a nominal price to speculating farmers and citizens, who drove out, *en masse*, the hereditary sub-tenants' (ibid., p. 721). By 1750, independent peasants had all but disappeared. Many of those forced off the land had no choice but to beg or engage in criminal activities to stay alive. Governments throughout Europe responded with cruel legislation. This new proletariat had little choice but to work for wages.

Second, there was a considerable mass of merchant capital (private wealth). This had been accumulated through the expansion of domestic and foreign markets. Third, urban craft outgrew the guild system. This development began with the division of production between particular towns. The outcome of such specialisation was 'manufacture', which was established throughout much of Europe by the sixteenth century (ibid., chap. 14). In this system labour is made more efficient both through centralisation – a large number of workers being concentrated in one place – and through an increase in the division of labour. Different specialised workers each carry out a particular operation. The co-operation of a large number of workers tends to save costs both in outlay for workplace, training and tools, and flattens out the differences in efficiency between labourers. The new division of labour also allows the worker to perfect a limited skill to an extent that would have been previously impossible:

> The habit of doing only one thing converts [the worker] into a never failing instrument, while his connection with the whole mechanism compels him to work with the regularity of the parts of a machine.
>
> (Ibid., p. 339)

Machinery, which first made its appearance on a large scale in England during the eighteenth century, brought about considerable changes in both the organisation and nature of industry. Machinery made strength less essential to a variety of jobs. This led to an increase in demand for cheaper female and child labour. Families were not better off, however, as the price of labour dropped in proportion to this change. Machinery also allowed 'capitalists' (the owners of private wealth) to lengthen the working day and to produce more goods in the same amount of time (ibid., chap. 15). The growth of capitalist enterprise forced smaller and weaker competitors out of business. Some of the displaced workers were re-employed in thriving businesses, but usually at lower wages. They, like all other workers, however, had to accept such conditions because they faced the threat of replacement by the 'industrial reserve army' of the unemployed (ibid., chap. 25, §§4, 5). In capitalist society, Marx concludes, workers exist in a state of alienation. They are alienated from their productive activity, having no say in what they do or how they do it; from the product of that activity, having no control over what is made or what happens to it; from other human beings, with competition replacing co-operation; and from nature, being unable to share in what has become private property ('Economic and Philosophic Manuscripts', *Selected Writings*, pp. 77–87).

Capitalism, Marx believes, comes into the world 'dripping from head to foot from every pore, with blood and dirt', and as such, sows the seeds of its own destruction. The constant cycle of boom and bust and the dehumanisation of workers as commodities that it entails feeds in workers the need to become free. Before long, they will realise that to be human, they will have to bring an end to the conditions which make for capitalist society. Capitalists will be forcibly ousted, and after a transitional period in which workers are the ruling class, there will arise a new form of society. In this form of society, called 'communism' by Marx, people will act in accordance with plans devised for the good of all (*The Communist Manifesto*, passim; *Critique of the Gotha Programme, Selected Writings*, pp. 564–70).

Even before Marx's death, the variety of interpretations of his thought led Marx himself to declare that he was sure at least that he wasn't a Marxist. A number of early Marxists were avowedly anti-intellectual, arguing that Marx had called for practical solutions to problems. Others felt that Marx's writings lacked a strong philosophical base, and drew on other thinkers to shore up his ideas. For instance, Karl Kautsky looked to Darwin; Eduard Bernstein and Max Adler to Kant; Plekhanov and Lenin to Feuerbach; Henri de Man to Freud; Georg Lukács, Karl Mannheim, Herbert Marcuse and Jean-Paul Sartre to Hegel; and

Antonio Gramsci and Giovanni Gentile to the Italian neo-Hegelians. The result was an explosion in the varieties of Marxism. This led political thinkers and leaders such as Rosa Luxemburg, Lenin, Trotsky, Stalin, Mao Zedong, Khrushchev and Ernesto Che Guevara to establish and enforce a particular doctrinaire version of Marxism called 'Orthodox Marxism'. Many states in Eastern Europe during the twentieth century were underpinned by Stalin's understanding of Orthodox Marxism. Orthodox Marxism was challenged by 'Western Marxists', whose first generation comprised Lukács, Karl Korsch, Bela Forgarasi and Josef Revai. Their writings influenced the Frankfurt school of critical theory, which included writers like Theodor Adorno.[5] The writings of the Frankfurt school, and those of the French Marxist Louis Althusser, have, in turn, anticipated many developments of postmodern thought. More recently, the collapse of the Soviet Union, the emergence of social and political movements organised around gender, race and nationalism and the growth of environmentalism have led to a far-reaching reassessment of Marxism.[6]

Countless historians and historiographers have also adopted, adapted and criticised Marx's thought. Their debates have ranged across a number of issues, including the role of ethics in historical materialism, the idea that people's actions depend on their being toolmakers and producers, whether Marx imposed his theory of history on a very selective view of the past, whether revolutions are best explained by class conflict, the role of Asia and the developing world in revolutionary activities, and whether the productive forces are the prime determinant of the character of society.[7]

This last issue has been given a great deal of attention by Anglo-American historiographers and philosophers. By far the most influential work on this question is G. A. Cohen's *Karl Marx's Theory of History: a Defence* (1978). Cohen argues that the forces of production alone determine the relations of production and the superstructure of a society. For Cohen the nature of the determination involved is functional: the existence of a particular economic structure is explained by its being optimal, at that time, for the development of the forces of production.[8] There are several places in Marx's writings where he claims that the productive forces alone determine the nature of society. Critics such as Richard Miller, Jon Elster, Melvin Rader and J. Roemer have pointed out, however, that there are some writings in which Marx acknowledges the role of both the relations of production and the superstructure in the shaping of society.[9] As the liveliness of this and other debates on Marx's ideas attests, he will probably continue to loom large in the twenty-first century.

Notes

1 For a more general account of Marx's thought, see Marx (MP).

2 In earlier works such as 'On the Jewish Question', Marx did argue that religion was an obstacle to freedom. See *Selected Writings*, pp. 39–62.

3 For a discussion on the role of consciousness in Marx's theory of historical materialism, see C. W. Mills, 'Determination and Consciousness in Marx', *Canadian Journal of Philosophy*, 1989, 19(3): 421–45; D. A. Duquette, 'The Role of Consciousness in Marx's Theory of History', *Auslegung*, 1981, 8(2): 239–59; and G. H. R. Parkinson, 'Hegel, Marx and the Cunning of Reason', *Philosophy*, 1989, 64(3): 287–302.

4 There are also two modes not in the main sequence: simple commodity production, where independent producers own the means of production; and the Asiatic mode, where communal village producers are exploited by tax-rent.

5 For a more detailed account, see L. Kolakowski, *Main Currents of Marxism*, 3 vols, trans. P. S. Falla, Oxford: Oxford University Press, 1978.

6 See, for example, A. E. Buchanan, *Marx and Justice: the Radical Critique of Liberalism*, Totowa, NJ: Rowman & Littlefield, 1982; Z. R. Eisenstein (ed.) *Capitalist Patriarchy and the Case for Socialist Feminism*, New York: Monthly Review Press, 1979; J. Habermas, *Legitimation Crisis*, trans. T. McCarthy, Boston, MA: Beacon Press, 1975; A. Kuhn and A. Wolpe (eds) *Feminism and Materialism: Women and Modes of Production*, London, Routledge, 1978; J. Le Grand and S. Estrin (eds) *Market Socialism*, Oxford: Oxford University Press, 1989; and M. Reich, *Racial Inequality: a Political Economic Analysis*, Princeton, NJ: Princeton University Press, 1981.

7 See, for example, S. Lukes, *Marxism and Morality*, Oxford: Oxford University Press, 1985; H. Aronovitch, 'Marxian Morality', *Canadian Journal of Philosophy*, 1980, 10(3): 351–76; R. Young, *White Mythologies: Writing History and the West*, London: Routledge, 1990; M. Ferro, *Colonization*, London: Routledge, 1996; B. Mazlish, 'Marx's Historical Understanding of the Proletariat and Class in Nineteenth Century England', *History of European Ideas*, 1990, 12(6): 731–47; R. F. Hamilton, *The Bourgeois Epoch: Marx and Engels on Britain, France and Germany*, Chapel Hill, NC: University of North Carolina Press, 1991; J. Amariglio and B. Norton, 'Marxist Historians and the Question of Class in the French Revolution', *History and Theory*, 1991, 30(1): 37–55; F. Furet, *Marx and the French Revolution*, ed. C. Lucien, trans. D. Kan, Chicago, IL: University of Chicago Press, 1988; and L. Krieger, 'Marx and Engels as Historians', *Journal of the History of Ideas*, 1953, 14(3): 381–403.

8 G. A. Cohen, *Karl Marx's Theory of History: a Defence*, Princeton, NJ: Princeton University Press, 1978, chaps 6 and 8. For a similar view, see W. H. Shaw, *Marx's Theory of History*, Palo Alto, CA: Stanford University Press.

9 M. Rader, *Marx's Interpretation of History*, New York: Oxford University Press, 1979; R. Miller, *Analyzing Marx: Morality, Power and History*, Princeton, NJ: Princeton University Press, 1984; J. Elster, *Making Sense of Marx*, Cambridge: Cambridge University Press, 1985; and J. Roemer (ed.) (1986) *Analytical Marxism*, Cambridge: Cambridge University Press. See also P. Wetherly (ed.) *Marx's Theory of History*, Avebury: Brookfield, 1992; D. A. Duquette, 'A Critique of the Technological Interpretation of Historical Materialism', *Philosophy of the Social Sciences*, 22(2): 157–86; P. Warren, 'Explaining

Historical Development: a Marxian Critique of Cohen's Historical Materialism', *Clio*, 1991, 20: 253–70; and C. W. Mills, 'Is it Immaterial that there's a "Material" in "Historical Materialism"?' *Inquiry*, 32: 323–42.

Marx's major works

Collected Works, 16 vols, London: Lawrence & Wishart, 1975–81.
Capital: a Critique of Political Economy, trans. S. Moore and E. Aveling, ed. F. Engels, 3 vols, New York: International Publishers, 1967.
(with F. Engels) *The Communist Manifesto*, trans. S. Moore, ed. E. Hobsbawm, London: Verso, 1998.
Selected Writings, ed. D. McLellan, Oxford: Oxford University Press, 1977.
A wide selection of Marx's writings can also be found online at: http://csf. colorado.edu/psn/marx/

See also

Diop, Fukuyama, Hegel, Hobsbawm, Lenin (IRT), Marx (MP and ME), Nietzsche (MP), Rowbotham, Sartre (MP), Thompson (CT).

Further resources

Berlin, I., *Karl Marx: his Life and Environment*, Oxford: Oxford University Press, 1978.
Best, S., *The Politics of Historical Vision: Marx, Foucault, Habermas*, New York: Guilford, 1995.
Cohen, G. A., *Karl Marx's Theory of History: a Defence*, Princeton, NJ: Princeton University Press, 1978.
Cohen, M., Nagel, T. and Scanlon, T. (eds) *Marx, Justice, and History*, Princeton, NJ: Princeton University Press, 1980.
Hobsbawm, E., 'Marx and History', *New Left Review*, 1984, 143: 39–50.
Kolakowski, L., *Main Currents of Marxism*, trans. P. S. Falla, 3 vols, Oxford: Oxford University Press, 1978.
McLellan, D., *Karl Marx: his Life and Thought*, New York: Harper & Row, 1973.
——, *Marxism after Marx: an Introduction*, Boston, MA: Houghton Mifflin, 1979.
Rader, M., *Marx's Interpretation of History*, Oxford: Oxford University Press, 1979.
Shaw, W. H., *Marx's Theory of History*, Palo Alto, CA: Stanford University Press, 1978.
Tagliacozzo, G. (ed.) *Vico and Marx: Affinities and Contrasts*, Princeton, NJ: Atlantic Highlands Humanities Press, 1983.
Wetherly, P. (ed.) *Marx's Theory of History*, Avebury: Brookfield, 1992.

JULES MICHELET 1798–1874

Michelet was the first person to apply the word 'Renaissance' to a period of history, and to write the first modern work on witchcraft. He also brought the Neapolitan philosopher Giambattista Vico to the mainstream of Western thought. Most of all, however, he dedicated his life to the promotion of liberty and unity in his beloved France. Believing that these ends could be achieved through the study of history, Michelet devoted his energies to writing the monumental *Histoire de France* (1833–69, 17 vols, trans. *History of France*), *Histoire de la Révolution française* (1847–53, 7 vols, trans. *History of the French Revolution*) and *Histoire du dix-neuvième siècle* (1872–74, 3 vols). Michelet's conception of France and its history influenced generations of his countrymen and he was recognised as the official historian of France during the Third Republic (1871–1940). Though today he is often dismissed as the writer of biased histories, many French historians still claim him as their chief source of inspiration.

Jules Michelet was born in Paris on 21 August 1798 to Jean-Furcy Michelet, a printer, and Angélique-Constance Millet. Michelet helped his father with the running of his print-shop from a very early age, and kept it going with the help of his Uncle Narcisse after his father was imprisoned for debt in 1808. He did not start school until 1809, and, though he initially struggled with his studies at the Mélot Latin School (1809–12) and Collège Charlemagne (1812–17), he soon became the most distinguished student in his class. In 1811, mounting debts led to the seizure of the family's possessions and not long thereafter the print-shop was closed under the conditions of Napoleon Bonaparte's decree that the number of printing presses be reduced. Jean-Furcy found a new job at the sanatorium of Dr Duchemin, and after Angélique-Constance died (1815) he and Michelet moved onto the premises. In 1817 Michelet passed the baccalauréat with high honours and was offered a teaching position at the Briand Institute. In 1819 he was awarded the doctorat dès lettres for essays on the moral philosophy of Plutarch and John Locke's idea of infinity. He continued to teach at the Briand Institute until he passed the agrégation in 1821, the first year the examination was taken. He served as a substitute teacher at the Collège Charlemagne for a year and was then appointed to teach history at the Collège Sainte-Barbe. At that time, history had only recently been added to the curriculum and was viewed with great suspicion by the government. In order to minimise the chance of social unrest, the study of history was restricted to younger students and was not to include the 1789 Revolution. Michelet wanted to teach older students, and so requested a transfer to the newly reconstituted Ecole Normale Supérieure.

In the early 1820s, Michelet's reading ranged widely over ancient and modern history, philosophy, literature and science. He proposed to study many areas of history, including customs, law, language, religion, politics, industry, science and philosophy, as well as their relations to one another. His goal of a total synthetic history mirrored in part the ideas of writers such as Cousin, Comte, Saint-Simon, Fourier and Hegel but his writings also showed the influence of Giambattista Vico, whom he later called 'his only master'.[1] Michelet translated parts of Vico's *New Science*, *Autobiography*, *Roman Wisdom from the Ancient Days* (see *Oeuvres choisies de Vico*, *Oeuvres complètes*, vol. 1, pp. 279–605). Though he was not the most accurate of translators, his simplified and shortened versions of Vico's works proved an immediate success and were the standard route to Vico's ideas for more than 100 years. Michelet was very sympathetic to Vico's idea that history is the record of humanity's self-creation. We can understand history, both Vico and Michelet believe, because people made it.

In 1827, Michelet was invited to teach philosophy and history at the Ecole Normale. While he thought that philosophy could help people to understand the ideas and actions of individuals, only history could account for the ideas and actions of groups of people in different times and places. In *Introduction à l'histoire universelle* (1831, *Oeuvres complètes*, vol. 2, pp. 217–313), for instance, he claims that the study of world history – from India, through Persia, Greece and Rome, to contemporary France – reveals humanity's movement from enslavement to liberty; the sacred to the profane; and the dominance of the female to the dominance of the male. France, Michelet believes, has a crucial role to play in the next phase of the world's story: the unification of humanity (ibid., p. 258).

Believing that France held the key to the future, Michelet sought to learn every detail of its past. The products of his efforts – the *History of France*, *History of the French Revolution* and *Histoire du dix-neuvième siècle* – took forty-one years to complete. Michelet was not the first person to undertake such a monumental project. Augustin and Amédée Thierry, Prosper de Barante and François Guizot had published *Lettres sur l'histoire de France*, *Histoire de la conquête de l'Angleterre*, *Histoire des Gaulois*, *Histoire des ducs de Burgogne*, and *Essais sur l'histoire de France* and Henri Martin and J. C. L. Sismonde de Sismondi were working on *Histoire de France* and *Histoire des Français*. Michelet was well acquainted with these works and mentioned them in the preface to the *History of France*. He praised them for their creative and innovative works, but claimed that he was the first to embrace 'history in the living unity'. Rather than focusing on one aspect of French history, he claimed that his *History of France* was no less than the 'resurrection of the fullness of life'.[2]

That is a fair claim. In books 1–6, for instance, we see the fusion of anthropology, geography and history. The early history of France, he claims, reveals the victory of people over racial and geographical determination. In the 'Picture of France' (*History of France*, pp. 110–42), he writes:

> The true starting point of our history is a political division of France, founded on its natural and physical division. At first, history is altogether geography. It is impossible to describe the feudal or *provincial* period . . . without first tracing the peculiarities of the provinces. Nor is it sufficient to define the geographical form of these different countries. They are to be thoroughly illustrated by their fruits alone – I mean by the men and the events of their history.
>
> (Ibid., p. 110)

Rivers, mountains and valleys separated groups of people and made them virtual prisoners of specific geographical areas. Gradually, however, they came together. Though Paris was the only unified area in the eleventh century, during the Middle Ages feudal and provincial diversities began to be superseded by political and social centralisation. The two institutions around which France had attempted to unite during the Middle Ages were the church and the monarchy. These two shaped much of the character of modern France. They, in turn, were shaped by notable figures such as Joan of Arc. Michelet adores Joan of Arc. In his view, her character and the ideals of a united, harmonised France were one.[3] His view of Joan is thus dramatically different from the portrayal of her as a 'foul accursed minister of hell' in Shakespeare.[4]

In the 1840s Michelet's attention turned from history to contemporary social and political problems. His attacks on the Jesuits and the wider church for brainwashing the French people (*Des Jésuites*, 1843; *Du prêtre, de la femme et de la famille*, 1845, *Oeuvres complètes*, vol. 4) broadened to a general attack on the intellectual and political establishment. In *Le peuple* (1846, trans. *The People*), for instance, Michelet called on the people of France to destroy the barriers separating town from country, educated from non-educated, artisan from non-artisan and poor from rich and to realise the revolutionary ideals of fraternity and social justice. Michelet also spread his ideas through lectures at the Collège de France (1838–52). His lectures attracted enormous crowds and government surveillance. The Guizot government and King Louis-Philippe were unhappy with the attention that Michelet gave to the 1789 Revolution, and on 6 January 1848 he was suspended from teaching duties. The Revolution of 22–24 February 1848 led to his reinstatement but he was again suspended for refusing to swear allegiance to Napoleon III (Louis-Napoleon Bonaparte).

While Michelet was suspended he wrote the work for which he is best known: *The History of the French Revolution*. In this work Michelet continued his story of the unification of the French people, culminating in the Fête de la Fédération of 1790. Contemporaries such as Louis-Adolphe Thiers and Auguste Mignet saw the Revolution as an affair led by bourgeois legislators; Thomas Carlyle, as the substitution of one form of anarchy for another; Philippe Buchez, as a socialist and working-class uprising; Edgar Quinet, as the realisation of primitive Christian principles; Alphonse de Lamartine, as an event given much shape by individuals; and Jean Blanc, as a transformation in ideas and politics. Michelet, however, considered it to be the birth of a new, world-wide religion of humanity.

Michelet's story of France redeeming humanity has a deeply religious character.[5] For example, in the preface he writes:

> I am endeavouring to describe today that epoch of unanimity, that holy period, when a whole nation, free from all distinction, as yet a comparative stranger to the opposition of classes, marched as one beneath the flag of brotherly love. Nobody can behold that marvellous unanimity, in which the self-same heart beats together in the breasts of twenty millions of men, without returning thanks to God. These are the sacred days of the world.
>
> (*History of the French Revolution*, vol. 1, p. 13)

Michelet not only makes free use of biblical language and imagery but he also suggests analogies to Gospel stories. The eve of the Revolution, for instance, is likened to the nativity of Jesus:

> Behold our new kings, put out, kept out of doors, like unruly scholars. Behold them wandering about in the rain, among the people, on Paris avenue. . . . The deputy Guillotin . . . [made a motion] to repair to Old Versailles, and take up their quarters in the Tennis-court (Jeu-de-Paume), a miserable, ugly, poor and unfurnished building, but the better on that account. The Assembly was also poor, and represented the people, on that day, so much the better. They remained standing all day long, having scarcely a wooden bench. It was like the manger of the new religion, – its stable of Bethlehem!
>
> (Ibid., pp. 120–1)

The Revolution is the 'heir and adversary' of Christianity because, whereas both seek justice, only the former offers it to all (ibid., p. 22). To support this view, Michelet revisits the Middle Ages. Instead of a France slowly progressing towards harmony and unity, Michelet now sees the church plotting against humanity, manipulating the minds of people and attacking those who held other beliefs (ibid., pp. 31–7). Fortunately, however, a sense of justice survived in the minds of intellectuals like Montesquieu, Voltaire and Rousseau. The conjunction of these men's ideas, Michelet argues, helped to bring about the 1789 Revolution.

Events from the convocation of the Estates-General in 1789 until the Fête de la Fédération in 1790 make up a 'new gospel' (ibid., p. 246). The National Assembly enshrined in its 'credo of the new age' – the Declaration of Rights – the principles of a new human morality based upon rights, duty, law and justice. In the Fête de la Fédération Michelet sees the transcendence of personal and regional differences and the selfless unity of all people. He writes:

> Where, then, are the old distinctions of provinces and races of men? Where those powerful and geographical contrasts? All have disappeared: geography itself is annihilated. There are no longer mountains, rivers or barriers between men. . . . All at once, and without even perceiving it, they have forgotten the things for which they would have sacrificed their lives the day before, their provincial sentiment, local tradition, and legends. Time and space, those material conditions to which life is subject, are no more. A strange *vita nuova*, one eminently spiritual . . . is now beginning for France. It knew neither time nor space.
>
> (Ibid., 1: 444)

It seems, as Hegel suggested, that the realisation of liberty brings history to an end.

The *History of the Revolution* has all the vitality and melodrama of a great drama. Michelet fills his pages with colourful and larger-than-life representations of individuals, groups and the 'people'. He seems to be totally engrossed by developments. As Kippur has noted, statements such as 'I hope to kill Mirabeau tomorrow' were common in his journal and letters during the composition of this work.[6] His description of the 'Terror' – the period between 3 September 1793 and 27 July 1794 ('Thermidor') when harsh measures were taken against suspected enemies of the Revolution – is especially vivid. In Michelet's opinion, the Terror was the result of unconditional love. The Revolution, he believes, was made possible by the love of everything, including the monarchy, the church and 'even England' (ibid., p. 22). In so loving, the people of France were prone to attack by seekers of power both from within and without. The problem was that not all people embraced the ideals of fraternity and social justice. That problem remained in the France of Michelet's day. He writes:

> Fraternity! Fraternity! It is not enough to re-echo the word to attract the world to our cause, as was the case at first. It must acknowledge in us a fraternal heart. It must be won over by the fraternity of love, and not by the guillotine.
>
> (Ibid., p. 8)

From 1854 to his death in 1874, Michelet devoted himself to the regeneration of social justice and fraternity. This aim even pervades his works on natural history: *L'oiseau* (1856), *L'insecte* (1857), *La mer* (1861) and *La montagne* (1868) (*Oeuvres complètes*, vols 17 and 19).[7] Drawing on the ideas of Jean-Baptiste Lamark, Goethe and Geoffrey Saint-Hilaire, he writes of a 'metamorphosis' from minerals 'seeking' animality, through the emergence of morality in female mammals and artistic creativity in birds to the human quest for reason, unity and liberation.

While Michelet was alive, many people felt that he spoke for France. After his death, however, the popularity of his works waned dramatically. His *History of the French Revolution* became a standard source but later studies revealed numerous factual errors. Many people also cringed at his vivid language and colourful writing style. In the twentieth century, Michelet's reputation was to some extent rehabilitated by *Annales* historians such as Febvre, Bloch, Braudel, Le Goff and Le Roy Ladurie.[8] They acknowledged their debt to Michelet for helping them to see the importance of describing the past in its totality, recognising the relationship between geography and history, drawing on a wide range of sources and looking for the details of life among ordinary people.

Notes

1 Preface of 1869 to *Histoire de France*, in E. K. Kaplan, *Michelet's Poetic Vision: a Romantic Philosopher of Nature, Man and Woman*, Amherst, MA: University of Massachusetts, 1977, p. 148.
2 *Histoire de France*, vol. 1, p. 60; quoted in S. A. Kippur, *Jules Michelet: a Study of Mind and Sensibility*, Albany, NY: State University of New York Press, 1981, p. 3.

3 See *Joan of Arc*, trans. A. Guérard, Ann Arbor, MI: University of Michigan Press, 1957.
4 W. Shakespeare, *Henry VI, Part One*, ed. A. Cairncross, London: Methuen, 5.5.93–4.
5 L. Gossman, *Between History and Literature*, Cambridge, MA: Harvard University Press, 1990, pp. 201–27; and Kippur, *Jules Michelet*, pp. 150–9.
6 Kippur, *Jules Michelet*, p. 161.
7 Kaplan, *Michelet's Poetic Vision*, chap. 1.
8 T. Burrows, 'Their Patron Saint and Eponymous Hero: Jules Michelet and the *Annales* School', *Clio*, 1982, 12(1): 67–81.

Michelet's major works

Oeuvres complètes, 22 vols, ed. P. Villaneix, Paris: Flammarion, 1977–87.
History of France, 2 vols, trans. G. H. Smith, New York: D. Appleton, 1869.
History of the French Revolution, trans. C. Cocks, ed. G. Wright, Chicago, IL: University of Chicago Press, 1967.
The People, trans. J. P. McKay, Urbana, IL: University of Illinois Press, 1973.

See also

Barthes (CT), Bloch, Braudel, Febvre, Hegel, Le Roy Ladurie, Vico.

Further resources

Burrows, T., 'Their Patron Saint and Eponymous Hero: Jules Michelet and the *Annales* School', *Clio*, 1982, 12(1): 67–81.
Crossley, C., *French Historians and Romanticism: Thierry, Guizot, the Saint-Simonians, Quinet, Michelet*, London: Routledge, 1993.
Gossman, L., *Between History and Literature*, Cambridge, MA: Harvard University Press, 1990.
Haac, O. A., *Jules Michelet*, Boston, MA: Twayne, 1982.
Kaplan, E. K., *Michelet's Poetic Vision: a Romantic Philosophy of Nature, Man, Woman*, Amherst, MA: University of Massachusetts Press, 1977.
Kippur, S. A., *Jules Michelet, a Study of Mind and Sensibility*, Albany, NY: State University of New York Press, 1981.
'Michelet Issue', *Clio*, 1977, 6(2).
Mitzman, A., *Michelet, Historian: Rebirth and Romanticism in Nineteenth Century France*, New Haven, CT: Yale University Press, 1990.
Orr, L., *Jules Michelet: Nature, History and Language*, Ithaca, NY: Cornell University Press, 1976.
White, H., *Metahistory*, Baltimore, MD: Johns Hopkins University Press, 1973.
Wilson, E., *To the Finland Station: a Study in the Writing and Acting of History*, Harmondsworth: Penguin, 1991.

THEODORE WILLIAM MOODY 1907–84

Interpretation of the history of Ireland – a history scarred by waves of colonisation, religious strife, political instability and cultural conflict – presents a formidable challenge to the historian. In the 1930s, Theodore William Moody accepted that challenge and resolved to initiate a 'scientific' historiographical revolution that would give historians the power to dissolve the popular myths that kept the different communities of Ireland divided.

Moody was born in Belfast on 26 November 1907. Though his parents earned little from iron turning and dressmaking, they sent Moody to the best day school available, the Belfast Academical Institution (1920–26). At first his strongest subjects were Latin and science, but in preparing for a scholarship to the Queen's University, a teacher called Archie Douglas turned his attention to history. At Queen's, Moody's love for history was nurtured by James Eadie Todd, and he resolved to pursue graduate study. He enrolled at the Institute of Historical Research in London, and between 1930 and 1932 undertook research on the Londonderry plantation (English settlement) in Ulster in the seventeenth century. Out of this research came a doctoral thesis (1934), a number of articles, and a book, *The Londonderry Plantation, 1609–41: the City of London and the Plantation of Ulster*. To historians writing after the destruction of the Irish Public Record Office in 1922, the amount of evidence that Moody assembled must have seemed remarkable. This was because, to a large extent, historians had traditionally relied on state papers. Moody, however, based his account on the private records of a number of London companies and the Irish Society. Though the English response to *The Londonderry Plantation* was lukewarm, Irish reviewers recognised what an original and important work it was. In *The Londonderry Plantation*, they saw the innovative synthesis of private records, a consideration of Irish history in the context of British history and objective scholarship. Moody's book was to remain unrivalled until the 1970s.[1]

In London, Moody met his wife, Margaret Robertson. He also had many discussions with R. Dudley Edwards on Irish history.[2] Moody and Edwards agreed that a revolution in the aims, method and style of Irish historical scholarship was badly needed, and they resolved to introduce reforms when they got back to Ireland. In 1932 Moody returned to Queen's as an assistant to Todd, and in 1935 he assumed responsibility for the teaching of Irish history. Though there were a number of Irish history lecturers throughout the island, they tended to work in isolation from one another. Moody felt strongly that both established and emerging scholars needed a forum to present their work. With the help of Todd, and Samuel Simms, a doctor and book collector, Moody established the Ulster Society for Irish Historical Studies in February 1936. Later that year, Edwards established the Irish Historical Society in Dublin. From the very beginning these two societies endeavoured to work together. In 1938 they created the Irish Committee of Historical Studies so that Ireland could be represented on the Comité International des Sciences Historiques, and established *Irish Historical Studies*, the first journal of its kind in Ireland. Moody and Edwards saw *Irish Historical Studies* as having two aims: to encourage new research and revisions of accepted views on particular topics, and to make school teachers and the public aware of advances in scholarship ('Preface', *Irish Historical Studies*, 1938, 1(1): 1–3). Like other historians at that time, they believed that historical research should be conducted in a 'scientific' manner by critical and objective analysis of evidence. Both the Committee and the journal quickly earned international recognition for their promotion of high standards of scholarship.

In June 1939 Moody accepted a fellowship at Trinity College, Dublin, and in 1943 he became head of the school of history. Although Trinity College had few students (there were only fifteen or so history students per year) and had weak links with the community, Moody had high hopes. He aimed to

> teach history in various fields, including the history of Ireland to undergraduates; to encourage and direct research on Irish history, especially by young history graduates; to set new standards of objectivity and technical excellence in the conduct of the research and in the presentation of its results; to promote and assist the publication of articles and books based on such work and thus to bring a new historiography to bear on the teaching of Irish history and on public thinking about the Irish past; to encourage cooperation among historians and communications between the historians and the concerned public; and to contribute directly to the new historiography.
>
> ('Notes on my Career as an Historian', pp. 4–5)[3]

Under his leadership, enrolments rose steeply and Trinity began to acquire a reputation as a major centre of research in both medieval and modern Irish history. Moody revised and expanded the undergraduate course a number of times and established a graduate seminar. He also helped many new scholars to publish their work. Though he had already created a forum for new research in *Irish Historical Studies*, he also managed, with the help of Edwards (now professor of modern history at University College, Dublin) and David Quinn (who was to become professor of history at Liverpool University), to persuade the publisher Faber & Faber to launch a new monograph series called 'Studies in Irish History'. The first publication in the series was R. B. McDowell's *Irish Public Opinion, 1750–1800* (1948), and a second series published by Routledge & Kegan Paul began in 1960 with R. S. Lyons' *The Fate of Parnell, 1890–91*.

Moody's aim of making the public aware of advances in historical scholarship also absorbed a great deal of his energy. In 1954 he organised a series of twelve radio lectures on Ulster since 1800, which were broadcast on Northern Ireland Radio. The series proved to be very popular, and the lectures were released as a paperback (*Ulster since 1800: a Political and Economic Survey*, 1954). A second series was commissioned by Northern Ireland Radio; twenty-two lectures were broadcast during 1957; and again released in paperback (*Ulster Since 1800, Second Series: a Social Survey*, 1957). In both series, the lecturers addressed many issues that are still salient. Moody also promoted Irish history through radio in the Republic of Ireland. In 1953 he established the 'Thomas Davis Lectures', a regular series of half-hour talks named after a leading member of the Young Ireland movement in the nineteenth century who had hoped to unite the different groups in Ireland.[4] The success of the series rapidly exceeded all expectations and a number of the lectures were published.

Moody was quick to see the possibilities for communication through television and took a leading role in the creation of the twenty-one-part Radio Telefís Èireann series 'The Course of Irish History'. The aim of the series, Moody and F. X. Martin noted, was 'to present a survey of Irish history that would be both popular and authoritative, concise but comprehensive, highly selective while at the same time balanced and fair minded, critical but constructive and sympathetic' (*The Course of Irish History*, preface). Though the lecture format of the series is rather dated, the accompanying book is still in print.[5] The clarity and balanced perspective of *The Course of Irish History* has made it a popular course book for school and university students both in Ireland and abroad.

Between 1943 and 1984 Moody was also a member of the Irish Manuscripts Commission, the advisory committee for cultural relations (1949–63), the government commission on higher education ('1960–62), the Comhairle Radio Èireann (the Irish Broadcasting Council, 1953–60) and its successor, the Irish Broadcasting Authority (1960–72). This last appointment ended abruptly in 1972 when the entire body was dismissed by the government for allegedly breaching a directive not to broadcast 'any matter that could be calculated to promote the aims or activities of any organisation which engages in, promotes, encourages or advocates the attaining of any particular objective by violent means'. Moody agreed broadly with the governmental directive, but felt that the dissemination of information was paramount. In an interview with *The Irish Times*, he argued that:

> Much of our problem springs from a refusal to face unpalatable facts, an addiction to make believe, a tendency to prefer myths to truth. But a new realism, a new questioning of case-hardened assumptions has emerged, and this has been greatly, perhaps decisively, encouraged and stimulated by the development of broadcasting. If the measure of freedom that the RTE [Radio Telefís Èireann] has had is now to be drastically reduced, one of the first casualties will be truth, and the process of awakening the public mind to the realities of the Irish predicament may be disastrously halted. We need more, not less, communication in Ireland.
>
> (27 November 1972)[6]

Despite these obligations, Moody still managed to undertake research. During his time at Trinity, his interest in nineteenth-century history grew. This change in focus was partly inspired by the fact that he had been entrusted with the papers of Michael Davitt, the founder of the Irish Land League and a leading figure in nationalist and labour movements. Moody published a number of papers on Davitt and completed a biography in 1981 (*Davitt and the Irish Revolution, 1846–82*). In his research on Davitt, Moody hoped to rewrite or revise Irish political history in a more objective manner.

He believed, however, that Irish history in general needed to be revised, and used his presidential address to the Irish Historical Society in 1962 to call for a 'New History of Ireland' ('Towards a New History of Ireland', *Irish Historical Studies*, 1969, 16(63): 243). Moody envisaged a twelve-to-fourteen-volume work that would embrace every imaginable aspect of Irish history. This, he suggested, would require the close collaboration of a multitude of scholars and financial support from the state. Though some historians doubted that such a large project could be completed, 'Moody's history' was formally adopted by the Irish Historical Society in October 1963. By that time, Moody's original plan had been modified. *The New History of Ireland* was to be written in two stages. Stage 1 was to be produced as quickly as possible, and would consist of a general history of Ireland in two volumes of text and one volume of reference material. Stage 2, which would resemble the original plan that Moody had advanced, would be released over a longer time-span. Later, Moody and the other editors, F. X. Martin and F. J. Byrne, settled on a ten-volume format, seven volumes of which would contain 'primary narrative' and 'complementary structure' (specialised chapters on such topics as music, art, literature and law) and three of which would contain reference material.[7] The first volume of *The New History* (vol. 3), dealing with the history of modern Ireland (1543–1691), was published in 1976. Though dogged by delays, only one volume of 'primary narrative', concerning events post-1921, remains to be published. A number of ancillary volumes of a literary, bibliographic and statistical nature have also been published.[8] Although the reception of *The New History* in Ireland and abroad has generally been favourable, a number of reviewers have noted that lengthy delays between composition and publication have made many of the contributions out of date.[9] For instance, most of the essays for volume 4 (*Eighteenth-century Ireland, 1691–1800*) were completed in 1973, revised in 1981–82 and published in 1986.

While working on *The New History*, Moody continued his research on Davitt and revisited the history of Ulster. Most notable among his publications during this period is *The Ulster Question, 1603–1973* (1974). Though this is in the main an historical survey, it also conveys Moody's views on Northern politics after the outbreak of the 'troubles' in late 1968. Moody was greatly saddened by the 'troubles', but was none the less hopeful that the government elected to take office on 1 January 1974 would restore peace and promote social justice (*The Ulster Question*, p. vii). Unfortunately, by the time an advance copy had been produced, the power-sharing agreement introduced by the Sunningdale Agreement was already shattered.

The continuing violence, Moody believed, was fuelled in part by popular myths. In his valedictory speech, 'Irish History and Irish Mythology' (1977),[10] he argued that it was the duty of historians to dissolve such myths ('received views' which combine 'fact and fiction'). Though Moody felt that myths concerning the origin of the Anglican-Irish church, the role of Catholicism in the struggle against Elizabeth I's conquest of Ireland, Irish nationalism, the racial and religious nature of 'true' Irishmen, the uprising of the native Irish in Ulster in 1641, Orangeism, the famine (1845–50) and the land war (1879–82) urgently needed demolition, he singled out for special attention the myth that the struggle against England is central to Irish history. This myth was by far the most dangerous, he asserted, because it was used by the Provisional IRA as the primary justification for its activities.

That Ireland was the prisoner of myth was not a new idea. Shaw's critical analysis of the 1916 Rising and Conor Cruise O'Brien's study of Northern Ireland had generated some debate, but historians had generally remained silent on contemporary matters.[11] Moody's speech ended this silence. Several well-known historians such as Ronan Fanning, Michael Laffan, F. S. L. Lyons, John A. Murphy and Tom Dunne echoed Moody's claim that historians were obliged to question and explode the myths that gripped contemporary Ireland.[12] Steven Ellis, too, applied Moody's idea to his research on late medieval and early modern Ireland. In 'Nationalist Historiography and the English and Gaelic Worlds', published in *Irish Historical Studies*, he claimed that previous Irish historians had failed to appreciate the significance of the similarities between the medieval lordship in Ireland and English governance in Wales and the north of England because they had been blinded by Irish nationalism.[13] Though Ellis's paper gained the support of a number of historians, others, such as Brendan Bradshaw, saw it as an example of a malaise that had infected Irish historical writing ever since Moody and Edwards had declared their intent to bring about a historiographical revolution.

For Bradshaw, Moody and Edwards were at best politically and intellectually naïve. Under the pretence of objectivity, their work had simply served to de-sensitise modern historical writing to the suffering and injustices of Ireland's past.[14] Furthermore, they had encouraged scepticism towards the history of Irish nationalism. Thus they had not only masked over the injustices suffered by past generations, but also denigrated the achievements of those who had successfully challenged English rule. Bradshaw's article expressed with great clarity the growing dissatisfaction among some historians with Moody's ideas. Bradshaw's thesis seemed to accord with Desmond Fennell's (a political and cultural commentator with nationalist sympathies) complaint that historians revised history simply to meet the 'needs of the establishment'.[15] The majority of practising historians, however, failed or refused to see that such a problem existed; and insisted to the contrary that their critics' case was not merely politically motivated, but rested more seriously on a fundamental misunderstanding of what the practice of scholarly history involved.

That Moody and Edwards hoped to bring about a revolution simply to denigrate the claims of Irish nationalists is not true. Such a view neglects the parallels with historiographical debates elsewhere. Along with many other historians and social scientists such as Charles Beard, Carl Becker and the 'new historians' in the United States and H. Butterfield, J. H. Clapham, R. H. Tawney and A. F. Pollard in

England, Moody and Edwards tried to formulate the principles of history in response to the threat posed by historicism. They acknowledged the relativity of events but maintained that it was still possible to offer statements about the past which were both internally coherent and externally defensible. In pursuit of the latter, they looked to science, which was seen to provide methods which could combat personal bias and render historical interpretations subject to external assessment and evaluation. Furthermore, Moody and Edwards's ideas on the revision of Irish history are similar to those central to debates concerning slavery and African American history in the United States, the nature of the Third Reich and the 'final solution' in Germany, the significance of the French Revolution, and the role of women in history.[16] Historians in these fields, like Moody and Edwards, recognise how much power visions of the past can hold over the present.

Notes

1 R. Gillespie, 'T. W. Moody, *The London Plantation, 1609–41* (1939)', *Irish Historical Studies*, 1994, 29(113): 109–13.

2 See R. W. D. Edwards, 'T. W. Moody and the Origins of Irish Historical Studies: a Biographical Memoir', *Irish Historical Studies*, 1991, 26(101): 1–2.

3 Quoted by F. S. L. Lyons, 'T. W. M', in F. S. L. Lyons and R. A. J. Hawkins (eds), *Ireland under the Union: Varieties of Tension: Essays in Honour of T. W. Moody*, Oxford: Oxford University Press, 1980, p. 11.

4 F. X. Martin, 'The Thomas Davis Lectures, 1953–67', *Irish Historical Studies*, 1967, 15(59): 276–302. For Moody on Davis, see *Thomas Davis, 1814–45: a Centenary Address Delivered in Trinity College, Dublin, on 12 June 1945 at a Public Meeting of the College*, Dublin, Trinity College, 1945; and 'Thomas Davis and the Irish Nation', in *Hermathena*, 1966, 103: 5–31.

5 The first edition of *The Course of Irish History* was published in 1966. A chapter was added to the revised 1984 edition, and another to the revised 1995 edition, in order to bring events up to date.

6 Quoted by Lyons, 'T. W. M.', in *Ireland under the Union*, pp. 20–1.

7 T. Moody, 'A New History of Ireland', *Irish Historical Studies*, 1969, 16(63): 241–57; T. Moody, 'A New History of Ireland', *Ireland Today: Bulletin of the Department of Foreign Affairs*, 15 December 1976, 898: 6–8.

8 See, for example, P. W. A. Asplin (ed.) *Medieval Ireland, c.1170–1496: a Bibliography of Secondary Works*, Dublin: Royal Irish Academy, 1971; W. E. Vaughan and A. J. Fitzpatrick (eds) *Irish Historical Statistics: Population 1821–1971*, Dublin: Royal Irish Academy, 1978; B. M. Walker (ed.) *Parliamentary Election Results in Ireland, 1801–1922*, Dublin: Royal Irish Academy, 1978; *Expugnatio Hibernica: the Conquest of Ireland, by Giraldus Cambrensis*, H. B. Scott and F. X. Martin (eds), Dublin: Royal Irish Academy, 1978.

9 See, for example, E. Larkin, 'Review of a New History of Ireland, vol. 4, Eighteenth-century Ireland, 1691–1800', *Journal of European Economic History*, 1991, 20(1): 217–18; and C. A. Empay and M. Elliott, 'Review of the New History of Ireland', *Irish Historical Studies*, 1977, 25(100): 423–31.

10 'Irish History and Irish Mythology', *Hermathena*, 1978, 124: 7–23. Reprinted in C. Brady (ed.), *Interpreting Irish History: the Debate on Historical Revisionism 1938–1994*, Dublin: Irish Academic Press, 1994, pp. 71–86.

11 F. Shaw, 'The Canon of Irish History: a Challenge', *Studies*, 1972, 61(1): 113–57; C. C. O'Brien, *States of Ireland*, New York: Pantheon, 1972.

12 See Brady (ed.), *Interpreting Irish History*, pp. 87–104; *The Crane Bag*, 1984, 8(1); *Irish Review*, 1986 and 1988, 1 and 4; R. Fanning, '"The Great Enchantment": Uses and Abuses of Modern Irish History', in J. Dooge (ed.), *Ireland and the Contemporary World: Essays in Honour of Garret Fitzgerald*, Dublin: Gill & Macmillan, 1986, pp. 131–46.

13 S. Ellis, 'Nationalist Historiography and the English and Gaelic Worlds', *Irish Historical Studies*, 1986, 25(100): 1–18; reprinted in Brady (ed.), *Interpreting Irish History*, pp. 161–80.

14 B. Bradshaw, 'Nationalism and Historical Scholarship in Modern Ireland', *Irish Historical Studies*, 1989, 26(104): 329–51. Ellis responded in 'Historiographical Debate: Representations of the Past in Ireland: Whose Past and Whose Present?', *Irish Historical Studies*, 1990, 27(108): 289–308.

15 D. Fennell, *Beyond Nationalism*, Dublin: Ward River Press, 1985; *The Revision of Irish Nationalism*, Dublin: Ward River Press, 1989; *Heresy*, Belfast, 1993; quote from 'Against Revisionism', *Irish Review*, 1988, 4(1): 22, reprinted in Brady (ed.), *Interpreting Irish History*, pp. 183–90. On the concept of 'revisionism', see R. Fanning, 'The Meaning of Revisionism', *Irish Review*, 1988, 4(1): 15–19; and R. Foster, 'We are All Revisionists Now', *Irish Review*, 1986, 1(1): 1–5.

16 See P. Novick, *That Noble Dream: the 'Objectivity' Question and the American Historical Profession*, Cambridge: Cambridge University Press, 1988, pp. 469–629; C. Maier, *The Unmasterable Past: History, the Holocaust and German National Identity*, Cambridge, MA: Harvard University Press, 1988; and B. A. Carroll (ed.), *Liberating Women's History*, Urbana, IL: University of Illinois Press, 1976.

Moody's major works

The Londonderry Plantation, 1609–41: the City of London and the Plantation in Ulster, Belfast: William Mullan & Son, 1939.

Thomas Davis, 1814–45, Dublin: Hodges, Figgis, 1945.

(ed. with J. C. Beckett) *Ulster since 1800: a Political and Economic Survey*, London: British Broadcasting Corporation, 1954, revised edition, 1957.

(ed. with J. C. Beckett) *Ulster since 1800, second series: a Social Survey*, London: British Broadcasting Corporation, 1957, revised edition, 1958.

(ed. with F. X. Martin) *The Course of Irish History*, Cork: Mercier Press, 1967, revised editions, 1984 and 1994.

(ed.) *The Fenian Movement*, Cork: Mercier Press, 1968.

'A New History of Ireland', *Irish Historical Studies*, 1969, 16(63): 241–57.

(ed.) *Irish Historiography, 1936–70*, Dublin: Irish Committee of Historical Sciences, 1971.

The Ulster Question, 1603–1973, Dublin: Mercier Press, 1974.

(ed., with F. X. Martin and F. J. Byrne) *A New History of Ireland*, 10 vols, vol. 1, *Prehistoric and Early Ireland*; vol. 2, *Medieval Ireland, 1169–1534*; vol. 3, *Early Modern Ireland, 1534–1691*; vol. 4, *Eighteenth-century Ireland, 1691–1800*;

vol. 5, *Ireland under the Union, I, 1801–1870*; vol. 6, *Ireland under the Union, II, 1870–1921*; vol. 8, *A Chronology of Irish History to 1976*; vol. 9, *Maps, Genealogies, Lists*, Oxford: Oxford University Press, 1976– .
'The First Forty Years', *Irish Historical Studies*, 1977, 20(80): 377–83.
'Irish History and Irish Mythology', *Hermathena*, 1978, 124: 7–23.
Davitt and the Irish Revolution, 1846–82, Oxford: Oxford University Press, 1981.

See also

Diop, Hobsbawm, Woodson.

Further resources

Bartlett, T., 'Review of a New History of Ireland', *Past and Present*, 1987, 116: 206–19.
Boyce, D. G. and O'Day, A. (eds) *The Making of Modern Irish History: Revisionism and the Revisionist Controversy*, London: Routledge, 1996.
Bradshaw, B., 'Nationalism and Historical Scholarship in Modern Ireland', *Irish Historical Studies*, 1989, 25(104): 329–51.
Brady, C. (ed.) *Interpreting Irish History: the Debate on Historical Revisionism 1938–1994*, Dublin: Irish Academic Press, 1994.
Curtis, L. P., 'The Greening of Irish History', *Eire–Ireland*, 1994, 29(2): 7–28.
Edwards, R. W. D., 'T. W. Moody and the Origins of Irish Historical Studies: a Biographical Memoir', *Irish Historical Studies*, 1988, 26(101): 1–2.
Gillespie, R., 'T. W. Moody, *The Londonderry Plantation, 1609–41* (1939)', *Irish Historical Studies*, 1994, 29(113): 109–13.
Heasom, A., '"Revisionism" and its Critics: Recent Writing in Irish History', *Durham University Journal*, 1992, 84(2): 305–9.
Kearney, H., 'The Irish and their History', *History Workshop Journal*, 1991, 31: 149–55.
Lee, J. (ed.) *Irish Historiography, 1970–1979*, Cork: Cork University Press, 1981.
Lyons, F. S. L. and Hawkins, R. A. J. (eds) *Ireland under the Union: Varieties of Tension: Essays in Honour of T. W. Moody*, Oxford: Oxford University Press, 1980.
Martin, F. X., 'Theodore William Moody', *Hermathena*, 1984, 136: 5–7.
Mulvey, H. F., 'Theodore William Moody (1907–1984): an Appreciation', *Irish Historical Studies*, 1984, 24(94): 121–30.

MICHAEL OAKESHOTT 1901–90

'Modality', as Oakeshott explains on the cover of *Experience and its Modes*, is

> human experience recognised as a variety of independent, self consistent worlds of discourse, each the invention of human intelligence, but each also to be understood as abstract and an arrest in human experience.

While this brief description captures much of Oakeshott's view of our world, it can also be used to describe *our* understanding of Oakeshott. For most of his readers, Oakeshott is a conservative political thinker. To view him as such, however, is an 'arrest', the contemplation of his work from a very limited standpoint, because it ignores not only his liberal belief in the importance of the individual, of self-reliance, of property rights, of governmental power and of the rule of law, but also his many ideas on the nature of science, practical thought, poetry, religion, morality and history.

Michael Joseph Oakeshott was born on 11 December 1901 in Chelsford in Kent. He attended St George's, a Quaker-sponsored coeducational school, from 1912 to 1920 and then Gonville and Caius College, Cambridge, from 1920 to 1926. He continued his studies in Tübingen and Marburg, and returned to Gonville and Caius in 1929 as a lecturer in history. During this time Oakeshott published his first major philosophical work, *Experience and its Modes* (1933), and *The Social and Political Doctrines of Europe* (1939, second edition 1941), a critical collection of texts illustrating the doctrines of representative democracy, Catholicism, communism, fascism and National Socialism. He served in the British Army in England, France and Germany from 1942 to 1945. Upon his return to Cambridge, he edited Hobbes's *Leviathan* (1946) and established *The Cambridge Journal* (1947). Oakeshott wrote many articles and reviews for *The Cambridge Journal*, and some were reprinted in his most famous work, *Rationalism in Politics and other Essays* (1962).

Common to a number of these essays is an attack on 'rationalists': people who think that they can apply intellectual blueprints to the world of politics, solve concrete problems by the light of abstract generalisations and introduce into politics the methods of the *Polytechnicien* or engineer. Oakeshott was passed over for a chair in political science in Cambridge, and took up a fellowship at the newly established Nuffield College, Oxford (1950–51). He may have been passed over for the chair, it has been suggested, partly because of the enthusiasm for horse racing he made public in *A New Guide to the Derby: How to Pick the Winner* (with G. T. Griffith, 1947).[1]

In 1951 he was awarded the chair of political science at the London School of Economics and Political Science, and he held that post until his retirement in 1967. After he retired, Oakeshott published *On Human Conduct* (1975), an exposition on the ideal of civil association implicit in modern European history; *Hobbes on Civil Association* (1975), a collection of most of his essays on Hobbes; *On History and other Essays* (1983), a collection of papers on the nature of historical knowledge, political authority, civil association and the modern relevance of the Biblical story of the tower of Babel; the first paperback edition of *Experience and its Modes* (1983); and *The Voice of Liberal Learning: Michael Oakeshott on Education* (1989), an account of teaching and learning that aims to realise civil association. Since his death on 19 December 1990, a revised and expanded version of *Rationalism in Politics* (1991), two collections of essays (*Religion, Politics and the Moral Life*, 1993; *Morality and Politics in Modern Europe: the Harvard Lectures*, 1993) on the history of political thought since the sixteenth century, religion, theology, rationalism and civil association and a recently discovered manuscript on rationalism (*The Politics of Faith and the Politics of Scepticism*, 1996) have been published.

For Oakeshott, as for earlier 'idealists' such as Kant, Hegel, T. H. Green and F. H. Bradley, the human mind creates the world it understands. That is, reality is of our own making, and nature and body have no existence apart from us. The only reality is consciousness and experience. Furthermore, all of human experience is interrelated; no thing or person is separate, unique or isolated. It is a unity,

> in which every element is indispensable, in which no one is more important than any other and none is immune from change and rearrangement. The unity of a world of ideas lies in its coherence not in its conformity to or agreement with any one fixed idea. It is neither 'in' nor 'outside' its constituents, but is the character of its constituents in so far as they are satisfactory in experience.
>
> (*Experience and its Modes*, pp. 32–3)

The unity of experience is not arrived at by abstracting from a collection of particulars a common element or factor, but rather by seeing that all of our experiences are linked. We are capable of realising what Oakeshott calls a 'coherent' world of experience through philosophy, but are prone to 'arrest'. This 'arrest' or 'mode of experience' is a view of the whole of experience from a very limited standpoint. Whereas Hegel and Collingwood posit a linked hierarchy of modes of experience, Oakeshott, following Bradley, argues that the modes of experience are categorically distinct and that none is primary (*On History*, p. 2).[2] In order to free ourselves from arrest, we must expose and question the assumptions that give them shape. It is philosophy, Oakeshott contends, that reveals to us how inadequate our assumptions are. In philosophy we 'never look *away* from a given world to another world, but always *at* a given world to discover the unity it implies' (*Experience and its Modes*, pp. 29–31). Although theoretically the number of potential arrests is unlimited, Oakeshott explored four in depth: historical, scientific, practical and poetic thought.

According to Oakeshott, 'history' as it is commonly viewed incorporates two distinct ideas. First, it can refer to the 'notional grand total' of all that humanity has experienced or 'a passage of somehow related occurrences distinguished in this grand total by being specified in terms of a place and a time and a substantive identity' (*On History*, p. 1). Here, 'history' refers to 'what actually happened there and then' and is made by the participants in historical occurrences irrespective of whether we know anything about them. Second, 'history' may refer to an historian's inquiry into or attempt to understand historical occurrences. Historians, Oakeshott contends, are the *creators* rather than the *discoverers* of the past which they describe. They aim not to revive a dead past, for that would be a piece of 'obscene necromancy' ('The Act of being an Historian', *Rationalism in Politics and other Essays*, 1991, p. 181), but to transform historical evidence or 'survivals' into an account in which they understand 'men and events more profoundly than when they were understood when they lived and happened' ('Mr Carr's First Volume', *Cambridge Journal*, 1950–51, 4: 350; see also *On History*, pp. 52–8). History is thus an activity which accounts for the nature and existence of historical survivals and the historian contributes to a coherent account of the *present* world. This does not mean, however, that historians are free to write what they please, because their work must accommodate historical evidence. The 'truth' of their accounts will depend not on their correspondence with the past as 'it really was' but on their coherence and comprehensiveness. Coherence, Oakeshott writes, 'is the sole criterion [of truth]: it requires neither modification nor supplement, and is operative always and everywhere' (*Experience and its Modes*, p. 37), because 'there is no external means by which truth can be established' (ibid., p. 34).

Thus for the historian, the past 'is a certain way of reading the present'. In 'The Activity of being an Historian' (*Rationalism in Politics*, pp. 151–83), Oakeshott identifies four attitudes that can be taken towards the past: contemplative, scientific, practical and historical. The first of these, the 'contemplative' attitude, is seen in the works of historical novelists, poets or artists. For them, the past is a 'storehouse of mere images' which 'provoke neither approval nor disapproval, and to which the categories "real" and "fictitious" are alike inapplicable' (ibid., pp. 164, 158). This attitude is not historical, Oakeshott claims, because it would be irrelevant to ask how accurate Shakespeare's portrayal of Henry V was. Second, there is the 'scientific' attitude, in which we try to regard events independently of their relation to us and our interests (ibid., p. 163). The 'scientist' seeks to relate events through the ideas of 'cause' and 'effect', and this entails regarding the past as exemplifying general laws (ibid., p. 159). This is also not an historical attitude, Oakeshott points out, because the subject-matter of history does not fall under generalisations. Historians do utilise general terms such as 'revolution', 'Christian' and 'war', but these terms are merely 'conveniences' (*Experience and its Modes*, pp. 119, 148). That is because there may be so little in common between any two of them that a generalisation will not be applicable. This, Oakeshott notes, accords with Huizinga's observation that terms such as 'Carolingian', 'Christian' and 'feudal' are not to be used as 'foundations upon which large structures may be built' ('The Activity of being an Historian', p. 177; see also *On History*, chap. 3, and *Morality and Politics in Modern Europe*, pp. 3–15). Historical events are not so unique that they cannot be articulated, but they are individual in a sense that would rule out covering descriptions of different historical events.

Third, there is the practical attitude, about which Oakeshott has much to say. Those who adopt this attitude to the past are concerned about the relationship between past and present:

> Wherever the past is merely that which preceded the present, that from which the present has grown, wherever the significance of the past lies in the fact that it has been influential in deciding the present and future fortunes of man, wherever the present is sought in the past, and wherever the past is regarded as merely a refuge from the present – the past involved is a practical and not an historical past.
>
> (*Experience and its Modes*, p. 103)

This practical attitude – seen, for instance, in searching for the origins of events and value judgements, and pointing to future events – infects much of historical scholarship. For example, statements such as 'He died too soon', 'It would have been better if the French Revolution had never taken place', 'the evolution of parliament', 'The loss of markets for British goods on the Continent was the most serious consequence of the Napoleonic Wars', and 'The next day the Liberator addressed a large meeting in Dublin' contain contemporary values and rest on causal connections that historical evidence cannot support ('The Activity of being an Historian', p. 163). Thus, as Smith has noted, for Oakeshott there is a close relationship between the practical attitude to the past and 'ideology' (any sort of premeditated political concept or moral abstraction).[3] Not only are notions such as 'Marxism', 'Liberalism' and 'democracy' ideological, but so too are 'freedom', 'equality' and 'happiness'. An attitude to the past is also practical if the inquirer brings any moral concerns to their study. As Oakeshott writes in 'The Activity of being an Historian':

> The categories of 'right' and 'wrong', 'good' and 'bad', 'justice' and 'injustice' etc. relate to the organisation and understanding of the world in respect of its relationship to ourselves.
>
> (Ibid., p. 159; see also pp. 179, 181)

Practical historians merely pick out 'emblematic actions and utterances' from the vast storehouse that is the 'living past': 'occurrences, artefacts and utterances, transformed into fables, relics rather than survivals, icons not informative pictures' (*On History*, pp. 39–40).

In contrast, those who adopt an 'historical' attitude are interested in the past for its own sake ('The Activity of being an Historian', p. 170). They must give no thought to utility, moral or value judgements, descriptions of events as accidents or interventions, or what caused or influenced what:

> The world has neither love nor respect for what is dead, wishing only to recall it to life again. It deals with the past as with a man, expecting it to talk sense and have something to say apposite to its plebeian 'causes' and engagements. But for the 'historian', for whom the past is dead and irreproachable, the past is feminine. He loves it as a mistress of whom he never tires and whom he never expects to talk sense.
>
> (Ibid., pp. 181–2)

This is, for Oakeshott, the way in which the study of history should be approached. As with the philosophy in Nietzsche's *Beyond Good and Evil*, the historian pursuing the truth is like an earnest, clumsy man trying to win over a woman. The historian as necrophiliac, as Himmelfarb points out, is one of the most bizarre suggestions of modern historiography.[4] It is an inquiry in which historical survivals are used to build up a coherent account of a past that has not survived. In a 'coherent' account, everything in the past is related to everything else in an 'internal and intrinsic' manner (*Experience and its Modes*, p. 141); but how specific items are to be thought of as related is never fully explained. As Dray argues, in lieu of detailed descriptions, we are supplied with analogies.[5] For instance, in *On History*, Oakeshott portrays the historian as the builder of a 'dry wall', a wall in which the stones (historical occurrences) are fitted so well together that no mortar is needed, and as the composer of a tune,

> What an historian has are shapes of his own manufacture, more like ambiguous echoes which wind in and out, touch and modify one another; and what he composes is something more like a tune (which may be carried away by the wind) than a neatly fitted together, solid structure.
>
> (*On History*, p. 117)

Oakeshott's view of an 'historical' attitude to the past is so narrow as to exclude most of what we would call historical scholarship. Indeed, by his own admission, most of his own work is overtly practical. For instance, in *On Human Conduct* he looks for the origins of the moral relationships that ground the civil constitution of modern European states, and in his 'Introduction to *Leviathan*' (in *Rationalism in Politics*) he claims that Hobbes is a brilliant contributor to the political myths of our civilisation. It seems that the historical attitude to the past is a goal to which we must aspire.

But, even if we were to aim for an 'historical' attitude to the past, we should remember that in the world of *Experience and its Modes*, history is still an 'arrest'; it is still an 'abstraction', 'backwater' and 'mistake' that 'stands in the way of a finally coherent world of ideas' (*Experience and its Modes*, pp. 148–9).[6] In one of his later essays, however, Oakeshott suggests that we should foster a 'conversation in which all universes of discourses meet' ('The Voice of Poetry in the Conversation of Mankind', in *Rationalism in Politics*, p. 491). These voices are not 'divergences from some ideal' as the modes of experience were from the ideal of absolute coherence; 'they diverge only from one another' (ibid., p. 497). His view that 'there is only one kind of experience' seems to be abandoned in favour of one in which 'there is no symposiarch or arbiter' because the voices are too different to be judged in comparison with one another.[7] This seems to be very different from his earlier view, and the relationship between the two is still the subject of debate.

When *Experience and its Modes* was first published in 1933 it was given a very cold reception. This was largely because Oakeshott, like Collingwood, was one of the few British philosophers who did not abandon idealism in favour of the newly emerging 'analytic' approach to philosophy espoused by Russell and Moore in Cambridge. The book would, however, go on to become a classic of British idealism, and Oakeshott's ideas are now in vogue with conservative and radical thinkers alike. For example, Alan Beattie draws on Oakeshott to defend the study of history in schools for its own sake against those 'who would use it as a vehicle of moral propaganda or who pursue the false gods of relevance by turning it into current affairs', while Keith Jenkins uses Rorty's interpretation of Oakeshott to argue for a 'non-foundationalist' view of philosophy and history.[8] Such attempts to appropriate Oakeshott for a particular tradition, however, are tenuous. Beattie argues that we must protect history education from peril, but makes no mention of it being an 'arrest' that is to be surpassed in favour of a coherent view of experience. Rorty and Jenkins argue for surpassing foundationalism and blurring the boundaries between disciplines, but ignore Oakeshott's claims that the 'voices' in the conversation of mankind are distinct and should not be muddled and that philosophy, at least in *Experience and its Modes*, supersedes and judges the other modes of experience.

Notes

1   M. Cranston, 'In Memoriam: Michael Oakeshott 1901–1990', *Political Theory*, 1991, 19(3): 323.
2   D. Boucher, 'The Creation of the Past: British Idealism and Michael Oakeshott's Philosophy of History', *History and Theory*, 1984, 23(1): 197.
3   T. W. Smith, 'Michael Oakeshott on History, Practice and Political Theory', *History of Political Thought*, 1996, 17(4): 605.
4   G. Himmelfarb, 'Supposing History is a Woman – What Then?', *American Scholar*, 1984, 53(4): 494–505.
5   W. H. Dray, *On History and Philosophers of History*, London: E. J. Brill, 1989, p. 219.
6   History can also stand as a barrier to religious experience. See 'Religion and the World', and 'The Importance of the Historical Element in Christianity', in *Religion, Politics and the Moral Life*, pp. 27–38, 63–73.
7   T. Modood, 'Oakeshott's Conceptions of Philosophy', *History of Political Thought*, 1980, 1(2): 315–22.
8   A. Beattie, *History in Peril: May Parents Preserve it*, London: Centre for Policy Studies, 1987, p. 35; K. Jenkins, *On 'What is History?' From Carr to Elton to Rorty and White*, London: Routledge, 1995.

Oakeshott's major works

Experience and its Modes, Cambridge: Cambridge University Press, 1933, pbk edition 1986.
The Social and Political Doctrines of Contemporary Europe, Cambridge: Cambridge University Press, 1939.
Rationalism in Politics and other Essays, London: Macmillan, 1962, expanded edition, ed. T. Fuller, Indianapolis, IN: Liberty Press, 1991.
On Human Conduct, Oxford: Oxford University Press, 1975.
On History and other Essays, Oxford: Basil Blackwell, 1983.

Morality and Politics in Modern Europe: the Harvard Lectures, ed. S. R. Letwin, New Haven, CT: Yale University Press, 1993.

Religion, Politics and the Moral Life, ed. T. Fuller, New Haven, CT: Yale University Press, 1993.

See also

Bradley (MP), Collingwood, Croce, Hegel, Kant.

Further resources

Boucher, D., 'The Creation of the Past: British Idealism and Michael Oakeshott's Philosophy of History', *History and Theory*, 1984, 23(1): 193–214.

——, 'Human Conduct, History and Social Science in the Works of R. G. Collingwood and Michael Oakeshott', *New Literary History*, 1993, 24(3): 697–717.

Collingwood, R. G., *The Idea of History*, revised edition, ed. W. J. Van der Dussen, Oxford: Oxford University Press, 1993.

Franco, P., *The Political Philosophy of Michael Oakeshott*, New Haven, CT: Yale University Press, 1990.

Grant, R., *Oakeshott*, London: Claridge Press, 1990.

Himmelfarb, G., 'Supposing History is a Woman – What Then?', *American Scholar*, 1984, 53(4): 494–505.

King, P. 'Michael Oakeshott and Historical Particularism', *Politics* [Australia], 1981, 16(1): 85–102.

King, P. and Parekh, B. C., *Politics and Experience: Essays Presented to Professor Michael Oakeshott on the Occasion of his Retirement*, London: Cambridge University Press, 1969.

Sanderson, J. B., 'Professor Oakeshott on History', *Journal of Philosophy*, 1966, 44(2): 210–23.

Smith, T. W., 'Michael Oakeshott on History, Practice and Political Theory', *History of Political Thought*, 1996, 17(4): 591–614.

Walsh, W. H., *An Introduction to the Philosophy of History*, London: Hutchinson, 1951.

POLYBIUS *c.* 200–*c.* 118 BC

> Can anyone be so indifferent or idle as not to care to know by what means, and under what kind of Policy, almost the whole inhabited world was conquered and brought under the domination of the single city of Rome, and that too within a period of not quite fifty three years?

So begins Polybius in his *Histories*, a work which has been judged both as the finest history of the ancient world and as so dull that it is unreadable.[1]

Most of what we know about the life of Polybius derives from his own *Histories*. Born into one of the leading families of the Arcadian city of Megalopolis, Polybius was from very early on groomed for a political career. His education was fairly practical, including lessons in riding and hunting, and though he had much confidence in his own literary skill, his knowledge of literature and philosophy was rather perfunctory (for example, 29.8; 31.14.3; 36.1.4–5).[2] As an adolescent he was present at debates within the Achaean faction led by Philopoemen and his father Lycortas (22.19), and in 182 BC he was selected to carry the ashes of Philopoemen to burial.[3] He later wrote an account of Philopoemen's life in three books, which are now lost (10.21.6). In 181/180 he was chosen by the Achaeans for membership on an embassy to Egypt and he also served on a commission establishing the frontier between Megalopolis and Messene (24.6.5).

Polybius was made a cavalry commander for the Achaean League in 170/169, a time of war between Rome and Perseus of Macedon. The Achaean League supported the Romans in war but also sought to maintain its independence. After the Roman victory at Pydna in 168, a purge took place through the Greek cities whose loyalty to Rome was open to any doubt. Polybius was one of 1,000 Achaean citizens denounced by the pro-Roman Callicrates of Leontium and was detained in Italy without trial for sixteen years. Polybius thought this a totally unjust catastrophe (3.13.9–11). In Rome, Polybius befriended Scipio Aemilianus, the commander of Roman troops at Pydna. Through Scipio, he was able to learn about Roman politics and military procedures. It is likely that he also travelled with Scipio to Spain and Africa, and across the Alps. Shortly after his political detention had ended (150), Polybius joined Scipio at the fall of Carthage (146) and undertook a voyage of exploration in the Atlantic.

In the meantime, war broke out between Rome and Achaea (146). Rome won the war quickly, and Polybius resolved to secure a favourable settlement for his countrymen. His efforts were recognised throughout Achaea and some statues were even raised in his honour (39.3.11). Of his later career little is known. He travelled to Alexandria (34.14.6) and Sardes (21.38.7) and kept up contact with his Roman friends. A reference in the *Histories* to the measuring of the Via Domitia in southern Gaul (3.39.8) suggests that he lived until 118 BC. According to Pseudo-Lucian, Polybius died at the age of eighty-two after falling from his horse.[4]

From his arrival in Italy in 167 to his death Polybius worked on documenting the rise of Rome as a world power. Of the forty books that he wrote, only books 1–5 are intact. Much of book 6 has survived, but the material from book 7 onwards is fragmentary, taking the form either of extracts or quotations in the works of later writers such as Diodorus of Sicily, Dio Cassius, Plutarch and Livy, or extracts prepared under the direction of the tenth-century Byzantine emperor Constantine Porphyrogenitius in order to illustrate such themes as 'on being deceived', 'virtues and vices' and 'on generalship'.

Polybius' original plan was to outline the history of the fifty-two years (220–168) during which Rome made itself master of the known world. In line with this, in books 1 and 2 he sets the scene by detailing Roman history during the time of the first Punic War (264–241). In this war, Rome and Carthage fought to establish control over the islands of Sicily and Corsica. It ended with Carthage ceding Sicily and the Lipari islands to Rome and agreeing to pay an indemnity. In the years directly after the war, Rome wrested Corsica and Sardinia from the Carthaginians and forced them to pay an even greater indemnity. In book 3, Polybius offers a modified plan, proposing to describe how the Romans maintained their supremacy and captured Carthage in 146.

In books 3–29 he focuses on events from 241 to 168, especially the second Punic War of 218–201. Under the leadership of Hamilcar Barca, his son Hannibal and son-in-law Hasdrubal, Carthage acquired a new base in Spain whence they could renew war with Rome. After capturing Saguntum (Sagunto) on the east coast of the Iberian peninsula, Hannibal led his army through Spain and Gaul and across the Alps into Italy. Having established a hold over northern Italy (218–217), he marched on to Capua. He annihilated a huge Roman army at Cannae (216) but was only able to hold Capua until 211. Hasdrubal followed Hannibal's route across the Alps, but his advance into Italy was checked by Gaius Nero and the southern Roman army on the banks of the Metauros River. Hannibal maintained his position in southern Italy until 203, when he was ordered to return to Africa. Meanwhile, in Spain, Publius Scipio won a decisive battle at Ilipa in 206 and forced the Carthaginians out. Scipio sailed for Africa and went into battle against the massed Carthaginian army at Zama in 204. The Carthaginians were defeated, and were forced to pay an indemnity and to surrender their navy and gains in Spain and the Mediterranean islands.

Books 30–39 cover the period 168–146 and focus in particular on events in Greece, the Mediterranean islands, Asia Minor and Carthage. Though the first two Punic Wars effectively deprived Carthage of its political power, its commercial enterprises expanded and thus excited the envy of Rome's mercantile community. When the Carthaginians resisted Masinissa's aggressions by force of arms, they broke their treaty with Rome. A Roman army was dispatched to Africa, and though the

Carthaginians tried to negotiate, they were goaded into revolt. Carthage resisted the Roman siege for two years before it was captured by Scipio Aemilianus and razed, and its citizens were sold into slavery.

Though the *Histories* focus primarily on the struggle between Carthage and Rome, Polybius also details developments in places such as Macedonia, Syria, Gaul and Asia Minor. Prior to his efforts, he tells us:

> the world's history had been, so to speak, a series of disconnected transactions, as widely separated in their origins and results as in their localities. But from this time forth History becomes a connected whole; the affairs of Italy and Libya are involved with those of Asia and Greece, and the tendency of all is to unity.
>
> (1.3.3–4; see also 1.4.1–2)

In addition, four of the forty books stand outside the narrative of the events of 220–146. Book 40, now lost, is thought to have contained a summary of the contents of the *Histories* book by book (see 39.8.3). Book 34, following the precedent of earlier Greek historians such as Herodotus, is a geographical description of the area covered in the main narrative.[5]

The topics of books 6 and 12 are more unusual. In the first of these, Polybius describes the constitution, army procedures and early history of Rome. Such things, he believes, are fundamental in the explanation of how Rome managed to conquer the world in fifty-three years. According to Polybius, there are six constitutional forms: three of them are good (primitive monarchy, aristocracy and democracy), and three of them are corrupted (tyranny, oligarchy and mob-rule). Each good form degenerates into a corrupted form and then develops into a successive good form in a perpetual cycle that he calls '*anacyclôsis*'.[6] *cyclical!* Thus primitive monarchy (control by one individual) gives way to tyranny, which gives way to aristocracy, and so on. As the cycle is regular, Polybius tells us that once a person can identify the stage that a community is at, then they can predict what the future will bring. Rome, Polybius claims, managed temporarily to arrest this cycle through the 'mixture' or balance of the three good constitutional forms (6.10, 11.18). 'Monarchy' corresponds to the two consuls, 'aristocracy' to the senate and 'democracy' to popular assemblies. These three groups work with one another and prevent one of them from becoming dominant. The success of Rome, he argues, can also be attributed to its army procedures. Polybius' detailed description of those procedures –

from the movement of camps to recruitment – leaves the reader in no doubt that Rome was a well-oiled machine.[7]

Polybius would also like his readers to think that his *Histories* are well organised. This hope is conveyed most clearly in book 12. In that book, Polybius uses Timaeus of Tauromenium's works on Africa, Sicily and Italy as a point of departure for a description of his own views of history. There are, he claims, three ways of gathering material: with one's eyes, by actually witnessing events; with one's ears, by interviewing witnesses; and also with one's ears, by reading written accounts aloud (12.27.1–4). The last approach, that used by Timaeus, is the least accurate. Witnessing is best, Polybius argues, but historians must also have the proper experience in order to understand what they see. For Polybius, the best experience is to have taken part in similar events (12.28a; see also 20.12; 7.25.4; 27.28). For example, one of the reasons Polybius gives for choosing 220 as a starting point for his *Histories* is that he witnessed many of the events detailed (4.2.2). He could not have seen all the events that happened, however, and this is where his ears came in. If historians are unable to witness an event, then they can build up an account of what happened by critically interviewing witnesses. Written sources may also be consulted, but historians must compare their facts to get at the heart of what really happened (12.28.3, 4, 7; 12.25.1–14; 27.5). The historian can also explore the places in which events happened. For example, Polybius tells us that he retraced Hannibal's route over the Alps 'in order to learn the truth and see with [his] own eyes' (3.48.57–59).

Like Thucydides, Polybius believes that getting to the heart of the past entails revealing the links in the chains of causation which lead to events such as wars (3.6.3).[8] Unlike Thucydides, however, he distinguishes between three elements in a causal analysis, not two: a beginning (*archai*), a pretext (*prophaseis*) and a cause (*aitiai*). For example, in the case of a war, *archai* are the first actions of the war itself, *aitiai* are those states of mind which lead individuals to seek war, and the pretext alleged for going to war is the *prophaseis*.[9]

Polybius uses this scheme to dissect such conflicts as the second Punic War. This war, he tells us, has three causes: Hamilcar's resentment at being defeated in the first Punic War, Rome's unjust annexation of Sardinia and demand for heavy reparations, and the success of the Carthaginians in Spain. It had two beginnings: Hannibal's capture of Saguntum and his crossing of the Ebro River (the northern boundary of Carthaginian control in Spain). Finally, it had a single pretext: Hannibal's claim that he was avenging the execution of some of Saguntum's citizens by the Romans. On such a pretext, Polybius concludes, Carthage was to blame for the war. If they had cited Sardinia and heavy reparations as a pretext, however, then Rome would have been to blame (3.15, 30).

Historians, Polybius also argues, should have no interest in the sensational or the fantastic. The historian's aim, he writes:

> should not be to amaze his readers by a series of thrilling anecdotes; nor should he aim at producing speeches which *might* have been delivered, nor study dramatic propriety in details like the writer of a tragedy: but his function is above all to record with fidelity what was actually said or done, however commonplace it may be. For the purposes of drama and of history are not the same, but widely opposed to each other. In the former the object is to strike and delight by words as true to nature as possible; in the latter to instruct and convince by genuine words and deeds; in the former the effect is meant to be temporary, in the latter permanent. In the former, again, the power of carrying an audience is the chief excellence, because the object is to create illusion; but in the latter the thing of primary importance is truth, because the object is to benefit the learner.
>
> (2.56; see also 2.13–16; 3.20, 48; 7.1–2;
> 14.36; 15.1–36; 16.20)

Many historians, particularly those who write monographs, are driven to 'magnify small matters, to touch up and to elaborate brief statements and to transform incidents of no importance into momentous events and actions' (29.12.3; see also 7.7). Though such pronouncements smack of self-righteousness, Polybius did put his ideas into practice. He had extensive military and political experience, he travelled widely throughout the Mediterranean region and consulted a wide range of Roman and Greek sources in a critical manner (for example, 29.14.3; 10.9.3; 30.4.10–11; 3.26.1).[10] Furthermore, he very rarely succumbed to sensational description. This is why he has acquired the reputation of being rather dull.

Style must take a back seat to more important considerations. Through the study of history, Polybius claims, we can prepare ourselves to face moral problems and the vicissitudes of fortune (*tyche*). He writes:

> There are two roads to reformation for mankind – one through misfortunes of their own, the other through those of others: the former is the most unmistakable, the latter less painful.

. . . It is this which forces us to consider that the knowledge gained from the study of true history is the best of all educations for practical life. For it is history, and history alone, which, without involving us in actual danger, will mature our judgement and prepare us to take right views, whatever may be the crisis or the posture of affairs.

(1.35)

The *Histories* is not unlike those voluminous training manuals which are characteristic of our own times. Polybius' target audience are practising and aspiring statesmen. In his work, they will find detailed descriptions of practical skills (such as fire-signalling, 10.43–47), tactical ideas (as how to find allies and supporters, 3.12), and the principles that underpin successful states (book 6). Thus his conclusion that '[i]f you take away from history its capability to give practical instruction, what is left is utterly unexceptional and has nothing to teach us' (12.25g).

Given Polybius' didacticism and long-windedness, it is not surprising that the *Histories* has long been unpopular. He was not included among the Greek authors whom Byzantine scholars brought to the West, and his work remained virtually unknown in Europe until the mid-fifteenth century. Polybius' ideas were rediscovered in Florence in around 1418–19, when Leonardo Bruni drew on the *Histories* to write a history of the first Punic War and subsequent Illyrian and Gallic wars. Not long after, Pope Nicholas V chose Polybius as one of a number of Greek writers to be translated into Latin. Niccolò Perotti was entrusted with the task, and his translation (1414) became the vehicle through which Polybius was known up to the sixteenth century. In the sixteenth century, Machiavelli and his contemporaries began to recognise the value of Polybius' political ideas.[11] After Machiavelli, translations of the military chapters of book 6 multiplied. Meanwhile French (1545–46), Italian (1546), English (1568) and German (1574) translations were produced. Between 1789 and 1795, Johannes Schweighaeuser published a monumental translation in ten volumes. This was the basis for a number of subsequent editions, including that by Buttner-Wobst (1866–1904). This in turn gave rise to English translations by Shuckburgh (1889) and Paton (1922–27).

Today, Polybius' *Histories* has a small but devoted band of followers. They realise that within its sea of pages there are islands of narrative that are more accurate *and* exciting than works by more 'sensational' historians. Open the *Histories* at Hannibal's crossing of the Alps (3.33.5), for instance, and see for yourself.

Notes

1 Dionysius of Halicarnassus, *De compositione verborum*; quoted in K. Sacks, 'Polybius on the writing of history', *Classical Studies*, 1981, 24, special issue, p. 30.
2 Citations correspond to the book, chapter and section number of the Shuckburgh translation of the *Histories*.
3 Plutarch, *Lives*, trans. B. Perrin, Loeb Classical Library, London: Heinemann, vol. 10, Philopoemen, 21.5.
4 On the details of Polybius' life, see A. M. Eckstein, 'Notes on the Birth and Death of Polybius', *American Journal of Philology*, 1992, 113(3): 387–406.
5 Several later geographical passages were also inserted in earlier books. See, for example, 1.41.7–42.6; 2.14.3–17.12; 3.36–39, 47.2–4, 57–59; 4.39–42; 5.21.3–22.4, 44.3–11; 10.10–11; and 27.4–11, 48. For a discussion on whether Polybius' later interest in geography was at the expense of his interest in history, see F. W. Walbank, *Polybius*, Berkeley, CA: University of California Press, 1990, p. 117.
6 For a more detailed description of what this cycle entails, see T. J. Luce, *The Roman Historians*, London: Routledge, 1997, pp. 136–7.
7 Ibid., p. 137.
8 Thucydides, *History of the Peloponnesian War*, trans. C. F. Smith, Loeb Classical Library, London: Heinemann, 1919, vol. 1, 1.23.6.
9 D. W. Baranowski, 'Polybius on the Causes of the Third Punic War', *Classical Philology*, 1995, 90(1): 16–32; and A. M. Eckstein, 'Hannibal at New Carthage: Polybius 3.15 and the Power of Irrationality', *Classical Philology*, 1989, 84(1): 1–15.
10 For a discussion on Polybius' supposed bias towards Rome, see A. M. Eckstein, 'Polybius, Demetrius of Pharos, and the Origins of the Second Illyrian War', *Classical Philology*, 1994, 89(1): 46–59; D. W. Baranowski, 'Polybius on the Causes of the Third Punic War'; and A. Momigliano, *Alien Wisdom: the Limits of Hellenization*, Cambridge: Cambridge University Press, 1975, pp. 22–48.
11 A. Momigliano, *Essays in Ancient and Modern Historiography*, Oxford: Basil Blackwell, 1977, p. 88.

Polybius' major works

The Histories of Polybius, 2 vols, trans. E. S. Shuckburgh, intro. F. W. Walbank, Bloomington, IN: Indiana University Press, 1962.
Polybius: the Histories, 6 vols, trans. W. R. Paton, Loeb Classical Library, London: Heinemann, 1922–27.
Polybius: the Rise of the Roman Empire, trans. and abr. I. Scott-Kilvert, Harmondsworth: Penguin, 1979.

See also

Herodotus, Livy, Machiavelli (MP), Thucydides.

Further sources

Bagnall, N., *The Punic Wars*, London: Hutchinson, 1990.

Eckstein, A. M., *Moral Vision in the Histories of Polybius*, Berkeley, CA: University of California Press, 1995.

Momigliano, A., *Essays in Ancient and Modern Historiography*, Oxford: Basil Blackwell, 1977.

Sacks, K., *Polybius on the Writing of History*, Classical Studies, 1981, vol. 24, special issue.

von Fritz, K., *The Theory of Mixed Constitutions: a Critical Analysis of Polybius's Political Ideas*, New York: Columbia University Press, 1954.

Walbank, F. W., *A Historical Commentary on Polybius*, 3 vols, Oxford: Oxford University Press, 1957.

——, *Polybius*, Berkeley, CA: University of California Press, revised edition, 1990.

LEOPOLD VON RANKE 1795–1886

> Ranke is the representative of the age which instituted the modern study of history. He taught it to be critical, to be colourless, and to be new. We meet him at every step, and he has done more for us than any other man.[1]

Thus wrote Lord Acton of Leopold von Ranke, a nineteenth-century German historian of the modern world. These days, calling someone 'colourless' is equivalent to the kiss of death. Colourless means boring, and boring means unreadable. In Acton's day, however, 'colourlessness' – hiding one's views and sticking to the facts – was something to which one aspired. Ranke, as Acton suggests, did teach history to be new and critical: he encouraged historians to preserve, organise and critically examine evidence; and many also believed that he showed them how to be colourless. Whether Ranke was himself colourless, however, is questionable.

Leopold Ranke was born in Wiehe, Germany, in 1795. Ranke's early education at home and at the renowned Gymnasium of Schulpforta fostered in him Lutheran pietism and a love of classical languages. After graduating in 1814 he enrolled at the University of Leipzig. There he studied theology and classics, concentrating particularly on philology and the translation of texts. During his years at Leipzig Ranke also showed an interest in the ideas of J. G. Fichte, Friedrich Schlegel, Goethe, Friedrich Schelling, Kant, Thucydides, Livy, Dionysius of Halicarnassus and Barthold Georg Niebuhr. As he later recalled, however, he did not read many works of modern history because in them he 'saw only an immense number of facts, whose arid incomprehensibility scared [him]'.[2] In 1817, he was appointed teacher of classics at Friedrichs Gymnasium in the Prussian town of Frankfurt an der Oder. While there (1817–25), Ranke began to take more of an interest in modern history. This was prompted by the combination of his quest to seek the signature of God in humanity and his ambition to make an impression on the new field of professional historical studies.[3]

Out of his interest in modern history arose his first book, *Geschichte der romanischen und germanischen Völker von 1494 bis 1514* (1824, trans. *History of the Latin and Teutonic Nations, 1494 to 1514*). In the introduction, Ranke tries to demonstrate the unity of the six nations formed in the Carolingian Empire (the Latin nations of France, Italy and Spain and the Teutonic nations of Germany, England and Scandinavia) through the three medieval 'respirations' of the great migration (*Völkerwanderung*), the Crusades and colonisation.[4] In these developments, he claims, 'one can almost perceive the unity of a single, closed event' which produces a shared history that 'binds nations in a closer unity' (*History of the Latin and Teutonic Nations*, preface). In the main text, however, Ranke explores developments in each of the six nations separately until they become embroiled in a struggle in Italy in the fifteenth and sixteenth centuries.

The *History of the Latin and Teutonic Nations* is known chiefly for the statement that

> History has had assigned to it the office of judging the past and of instructing the account for the benefit of future ages. To show high offices the present work does not presume; it seeks only to show what actually happened [*wie es eigentlich gewesen*].
> (*History of the Latin and Teutonic Nations*, p. vii)

The meaning of Ranke's aim to study the past '*wie es eigentlich gewesen*' has been subject to much debate among historians. A number of writers have translated the phrase as 'what actually happened' and take it to be an endorsement of 'colourless' history. Historians, they claim, should stick to the facts. There should be no evidence of their views and commitments in their writings. It is only when they remove all trace of themselves that they can revive the past 'as it really was'. More recent commentators such as Iggers, however, have argued that such a translation is not accurate because it does not reveal Ranke's 'idealistic' conception of history. Iggers prefers to translate the phrase as '[History] merely wants to show how, essentially, things happened.'[5] That is, historians must try to offer a factual representation of the past devoid of their views, but they must also go beyond the facts and seek the general tendencies or leading ideas which gave an individual or institution its character. Historians, Ranke claims, try to unveil the 'holy hieroglyph' that is God's presence in the world. So history is more than just facts; the historian has a 'joy in the particular' but also an 'eye for the universal'.[6] In the appendix of *History of the Latin and Teutonic Nations*, Ranke also argues that it is impossible to write sound history without recourse to primary evidence (evidence contemporary with an event).

Upon publication of the *History*, Ranke was appointed to a professorship at the University of Berlin. The University of Berlin was founded in 1810 largely on the prompting of Wilhelm von Humboldt, a philosopher who was then head of education in the Prussian Ministry of the Interior. Hegel held the chair of philosophy, Friedrich Schleiermacher taught theology, and Friedrich Savigny law. In the humanities, opinion was sharply divided between those who agreed with Hegel that history was the story of universal freedom and those who stressed with Savigny the individuality and variety of experiences in history. Ranke sided with Savigny, and objected to Hegel's positing of a view of history above and independent of concrete historical facts and events. He believed that universal and divine ideas were dependent upon people's concrete experiences for their realisation. In the library at Berlin Ranke discovered forty-seven volumes of reports by Venetian ambassadors in the sixteenth and seventeenth centuries, which formed the basis of a number of his future works. Primary materials were very important to Ranke. As he later wrote:

> I see the time approaching when we shall base modern history, no longer on the reports even of contemporary historians, except insofar as they were in possession of personal and immediate knowledge of facts; and still less on work yet more remote from the source; but rather on the narratives of eyewitnesses, and on genuine and original documents.
>
> (*History of the Reformation in Germany*, I: x)

A generous grant from the Prussian government also allowed Ranke to consult archives in Vienna, Venice, Florence and Rome.

Not long after his return to Berlin in 1831, the Prussian Foreign Minister, Count Bernstorff, asked Ranke to edit a new journal: the *Historisch-Politische Zeitschrift*. This journal, it was hoped, would counter the liberal political ideas that arose in Germany after the French and Belgian revolutions of 1830. Ranke was unable to enlist many writers or readers, and he had to write a number of the articles that appeared in its short run of four issues (1833–36). In some of these we get a clearer impression of his 'idealism'. In 'Dialogue on Politics' (1836) and 'The Great Powers' (1833), for instance, he argues that each state is shaped by a particular spiritual and moral idea which derives from God. Individuals, Ranke tells us, should work to realise the idea that lies at the heart of their state. Thus in his opinion French revolutionary ideas and activities should not be encouraged in Germany. Rather, each state should 'organise all its internal resources for the purpose of self-preservation'.[7] This means, above all, protecting the state from outside ideas. In these writings, Ranke stands particularly close to the ideas of Hegel. Both claimed that the state was the manifestation of an idea and that it was not subject to external moral principles. The problems of such a view are now evident: if states cannot be judged from the outside, then they may resort to extreme measures, even violence, to 'protect' themselves from other states. In the twentieth century, a number of writers criticised Ranke and his followers for leaving Germany susceptible to totalitarianism.[8]

While working on the *Historisch-Politische Zeitschrift*, Ranke wrote *Die römischen Päpiste, ihre kirche und ihr Staat im sechzehnten und siebzehnten Jahrhundert* (1834–36, trans. *History of the Popes, their Church and State*). Though as a Protestant he was barred from consulting papal archives, he managed to describe the rise of Rome and the church in the first half of the sixteenth century on the basis of private manuscripts that he had seen in Venice and Rome. While some Protestants thought that the work was too impartial and the Papacy condemned it as hostile, Ranke was widely praised for his description of the Catholic church as an historical phenomenon and the interplay of religious and secular issues in the Counter Reformation (a term he coined), and vivid portraits of Popes Paul IV, Pius V and Ignatius Loyola.

He next turned his attention to a complementary subject, writing *Deutsche Geschichte im Zeitalter der Reformation* (1845–47, trans. *History of the Reformation in Germany*). Ranke drew on ninety-six volumes of reports by the Frankfurt ambassadors to the German Imperial Diet during the Reformation to develop his account of how political intrigues and conflicts determined the outcome of religious reform in Germany. The work was the first scholarly treatment of that period and soon became a national classic.

After he was appointed to the position of Royal Historiographer by King Friedrich Wilhelm IV of Prussia in 1841, Ranke penned a history of Prussia (*Neun Bücher preussischer Geschichte*, 1849, trans. *Memoirs of the House of Brandenburg and History of Prussia, during the Seventeenth and Eighteenth Centuries*, 1949, later expanded to twelve volumes) covering the history of the Hohenzollern monarchy from the late Middle Ages through to the age of Frederick the Great. Ranke's conservative depiction of Prussia as an exemplary provincial territorial state rather than as a key participant in German unity was criticised by many writers.[9] Between 1852 and 1868 he aimed to portray 'those epochs which have had the most effectual influence on the development of mankind' and through which particular nations acquired a 'world historical character'.[10] Ranke expanded his views on epochs in a series of lectures that he gave to Maximilian Joseph of Bavaria (later King Maximilian Joseph). In these lectures, Ranke argues that each era is unique and must be studied on its own terms, rather than through present ways of thinking or as a stepping-stone to a subsequent era. Unlike writers such as Herder and Hegel, Ranke does not believe that there is a general directing will that guides the development of the human race from one point to another or a progression of the spirit which drives humanity towards a defined goal. All eras are equal to God, and they must be so to the historian. The historian can divine 'leading ideas' within individual eras, but history does not evidence general progress or development.

Ranke retired from the University of Berlin in 1871 and devoted his energies to collecting and editing his complete works. He also continued his research on German history, publishing and editing works on such topics as Albrecht Wallenstein, the revolutionary wars of 1791–92, Prussian statesman Hardenberg and the correspondence of Wilhelm IV with Christian Bunsen. His reputation continued to grow and he was awarded many honours. He was granted a hereditary nobility (thus adding 'von' to his surname) in 1865, made a Privy Councillor in 1882 and an honorary citizen of Berlin in 1885. In 1884 the newly formed American Historical Association made him its first honorary member.[11] Despite failing eyesight he began work in 1880 on what he claimed would be a universal history of mankind. With the help of assistants, he published a volume a year of his 'universal history', tracing events from the ancient Egyptian and Hebrew civilisations down to the death of Otto in the twelfth century (six volumes), before his death on 23 May 1886. His student, Alfred Dove, used Ranke's lecture notes and those of his students to bring the account up to 1453, at which point his publications on modern history commenced. Though this work ideally should have included everything in human life from its very beginnings, Ranke excluded prehistory and 'primitive' people (just about everyone outside Europe) because of a lack of evidence (see *Universal History*).

Ranke's critical method became the model of historical research in the nineteenth century in Germany and the wider world. Despite the interest in his ideas, however, he was little understood. British and

American historians seized on his comments that historians must study 'the past as it actually was', stick to 'the strict presentation of facts' and 'extinguish' themselves, and revered him as the exemplar of a 'scientifically' trained historian.[12] By the turn of the century, however, reverence turned to scathing criticism. Many historians in the United States, France and Germany called for a turn away from Rankean fact-orientated political and religious history and towards a broader vision of history. Increasingly, Fitzsimons notes, he was 'blamed for what he wrote, the misuse of what he wrote and for what he did not write at all'.[13] In the latter part of the twentieth century, 'Rankean' became shorthand for outdated, naïve, dry-as-dust histories. Recent scholarship, stimulated in part by the publication of a number of previously unpublished manuscripts, has shown how unfair that view is. Ranke, scholars now claim, was a colourful historian because he sought facts *as well as* ideas.

Notes

1 Lord Acton, 'Inaugural Lecture on the Study of History', quoted in G Himmelfarb (ed.) *Essays on Freedom and Power*, Cambridge, MA: Harvard University Press, 1948, p. 20.

2 'Autobiographical Dictation, November 1885', *The Secret of World History: Selected Writings on the Art and Science of History*, ed. R. Wines, New York: Fordham University Press, 1981, p. 36.

3 Ibid., pp. 36–8; L. Kreiger, *Ranke: the Meaning of History*, Chicago, IL: University of Chicago Press, 1977, p. 97.

4 In two letters to his brother Heinrich (28 November 1822 and 25 August 1827), Ranke uses the word 'breath' to suggest divine presence in the world. Quoted in L. Kreiger, *Ranke*, p. 27.

5 G. G. Iggers, 'Introduction', in G. G. Iggers and K. von Moltke (eds) *The Theory and Practice of History*, Indianapolis, IN: Bobbs-Merrill, 1973, pp. xli–xlii.

6 Letter to Heinrich Ranke, 1820, 'The Pitfalls of a Philosophy of History' (lecture on universal history from the 1840s), 'History and Philosophy' (manuscript from the 1830s), *The Secret World of History*, pp. 103, 241; Iggers and von Moltke (eds) *The Theory and Practice of History*, pp. 31, 47–50.

7 'Dialogue on Politics', in Iggers and von Moltke (eds) *The Theory and Practice of History*, p. 118.

8 For a level-headed discussion on post-war criticisms of Ranke, see P. Geyl, 'Ranke in the Light of the Catastrophe', in *Debates with Historians*, New York: Meridian, 1958, pp. 9–29.

9 G. P. Gooch, *History and Historians in the Nineteenth Century*, New York: Longmans, 1935, p. 235.

10 *The Secret World of History*, p. 15.

11 H. B. Adams, 'Leopold von Ranke', *American Historical Association Papers*, 1888, vol. III, pp. 101–20.

12 G. G. Iggers, 'The Image of Ranke in American and German Historical

Thought', *History and Theory*, 1962, 2(1): 17–40; D. Ross, 'On the Misunderstanding of Ranke and the Origins of the Historical Profession in America', in G. G. Iggers and J. M. Powell, *Leopold von Ranke and the Shaping of the Historical Discipline*, Syracuse, NY: Syracuse University Press, 1990, pp. 154–69; G. G. Iggers, 'The Crisis of the Rankean Paradigm in the Nineteenth Century', in ibid., pp. 170–9; D. S. Goldstein, 'History at Oxford and Cambridge', in ibid., pp. 141–53; S. Bann, 'The Historian as Taxidermist: Ranke, Barante, Waterton', in *Comparative Criticism*, 1981, 3(1): 21–49; P. Novick, *That Noble Dream: the 'Objectivity' Question and the American Historical Profession*, Cambridge: Cambridge University Press, 1988.
13 M. A. Fitzsimons, 'Ranke: History as Worship', *Review of Politics*, 1980, 42(3): 553.

Ranke's major works

Sammtliche Werke, 54 vols, Leipzig: Dunker & Humboldt, 1867–90.

History of the Latin and Teutonic Nations, 1494–1514, trans. G. R. Dennis, London: G. Bell, 1915.

The Ottoman and Spanish Monarchies in the Sixteenth and Seventeenth Centuries, trans. W. K. Kelly, London: Whittaker, 1843.

History of the Popes, their Church and State, trans. E. Foster, London: Whittaker, 1845.

History of the Reformation in Germany, trans. S. Austin, ed. R. A. Johnson, New York: E. P. Dutton, 1966.

Memoirs of the House of Brandenburg and History of Prussia during the Seventeenth and Eighteenth Centuries, trans. Sir A. and Lady Duff Gordon, New York: Haskell House, 1969.

Civil Wars and Monarchy in France in the Sixteenth and Seventeenth Centuries: a History of France, trans. M. A. Garvey, New York: Harper & Brothers, 1973.

History of England principally in the Seventeenth Century, trans. G. W. Kitchin and C. W. Boase, Oxford: Oxford University Press, 1875.

Universal History: I. The Oldest Historical Group of Nations and the Greeks, trans. G. W. Prothero, London, 1884.

The Theory and Practice of History, trans. and ed. G. G. Iggers and K. von Moltke, Indianapolis, IN: Bobbs-Merrill, 1973.

The Secret World of History: Selected Writings on the Art and Science of History, trans. and ed. J. Wines, New York: Fordham University Press, 1981.

See also

Dilthey, Hegel, Turner.

Further resources

Gay, P., *Style in History*, New York: McGraw-Hill, 1974.

Geyl, P., *Debates with Historians*, New York: Meridian, 1958.

Gilbert, F., *History: Politics or Culture? Reflections on Ranke and Burckhardt*, Princeton, NJ: Princeton University Press, 1990.

Gooch, G. P., *History and Historians in the Nineteenth Century*, New York: Longmans, 1935.

Iggers, G. G. and Powell, J. M. (eds) *Leopold von Ranke and the Shaping of the Historical Discipline*, Syracuse, NY: Syracuse University Press, 1990.

Kreiger, L., *Ranke: the Meaning of History*, Chicago, IL: University of Chicago Press, 1977.

Novick, P., *That Noble Dream: the 'Objectivity' Question and the American Historical Profession*, Cambridge: Cambridge University Press, 1988.

von Laue, T. H., *Leopold von Ranke, the Formative Years*, Princeton, NJ: Princeton University Press, 1950.

White, H., *Metahistory*, Baltimore, MD: Johns Hopkins University Press, 1973.

PAUL RICOEUR 1913–

We are forgetful beings. Assumptions give shape to our ideas and actions. Sometimes they are transparent to us; we know that they are open to question and redescription. But more often than not, we forget that they are assumptions and take them to be self-evident truths. This seems sensible, for it would not be practically possible to subject all of our ideas and actions to continual scrutiny. In our forgetfulness, though, we can lose sight of what we are and what we might be. Overcoming that forgetfulness can be difficult, for the things under our noses, so to speak, are often the hardest to see. Many remedies for such forgetfulness have been advanced over time, but the one offered by the French philosopher and historian Paul Ricoeur – entailing the interpretation of texts – offers rich possibilities for those interested in history.

Orphaned at a young age, Jean Paul Gustave Ricoeur (born in 1913 in Valence, France) was raised by his paternal grandparents and his aunt in Rennes. Ricoeur was an outstanding student at the University of Rennes and planned to pursue graduate studies in classical languages. One of his instructors, Roland Dalbiez, however, encouraged him to study philosophy, and in 1933 Ricoeur took a position as a teacher of that subject at a lycée in Brittany. In 1934 he enrolled at the Sorbonne to study for the agrégation, and in the following year he was placed second. While at the Sorbonne, Ricoeur met the philosopher Gabriel Marcel, whose ideas would be an influence on his work. He also married Simone Lejas, a childhood friend. Before the war, he taught philosophy at lycées in Colmar (near Alsace) and Lorient (on the south-west coast of Brittany) and undertook obligatory military service. At the outbreak of hostilities, Ricoeur was called to active service with the 47th Infantry. In 1940 he was captured at Dormans, a small village in the Marne Valley. He was kept in various prison camps for almost five years. While a prisoner, Ricoeur read, wrote and taught philosophy. He outlined drafts of what were to become his doctoral theses: *Voluntaire et l'involuntaire* (1950, trans. *Freedom and Nature: the Voluntary and the Involuntary*) and a translation and commentary on Edmund Husserl's *Ideen I* (1950). After his liberation, he set down and published many of the ideas that he had formulated as a prisoner (see *Philosophie*, 1932; *Karl Jaspers et la philosophie de l'existence* (with Mikel Dufrenne), 1947; and *Gabriel Marcel et Karl Jaspers: philosophie du mystère et philosophie du paradoxe*, 1948).

In 1948 he was invited to teach the history of philosophy at the University of Strasbourg and eight years later he succeeded Raymond Bayer in the chair of general philosophy at the Sorbonne. When not teaching classes on the history of philosophy and the philosophy of language, he devoted his energies to writing. This was a productive time: he published *Histoire et vérité* (1955, trans. *History and Truth*), *Finitude et culpabilité I: L'homme faillible* (1960, trans. *Fallible Man*), *Finitude et culpabilité II: La symbolique du mal* (1960, trans. *The Symbolism of Evil*) and *Essai sur Freud* (1965, trans. *Freud and Philosophy: an Essay on Interpretation*). In 1967 Ricoeur decided to leave the Sorbonne for a new campus of the University of Paris being built in the western suburb of Nanterre (now the University of Paris X-Nanterre). Although he managed to published a collection of articles called *Le conflit des interprétations: essais d'herméneutique* (1969, trans. *The Conflict of Interpretations: Essays in Hermeneutics*), disruptive and even violent political demonstrations on the campus made work difficult. In 1969 he requested a three-year leave from the French university system. During that break, he taught at the University of Louvain and the University of Chicago, and published *The Religious Symbolism of Atheism* (1969, with Alasdair MacIntyre), *La métaphore vive* (1975, trans. *The Rule of Metaphor: Multi-disciplinary Studies of the Creation of Meaning in Language*) and *The Contribution of French Historiography to the Theory of History* (1980). He returned to France, and since his retirement from the University of Paris (1980) and the University of Chicago (1991) he has published a number of books and articles, including *Temps et récit* (1983–85, 3 vols, trans. *Time and Narrative*) and *Soi-même comme un autre* (1990, trans. *Oneself as Other*).

At the centre of Ricoeur's writings is 'hermeneutics'. Prior to the nineteenth century, the concern of hermeneutics was taken to be the interpretation of particular texts, such as the Bible. After that time, however, the recognition that all ideas and actions are shaped by particular historical contexts led writers like Schleiermacher and Dilthey to question whether an immediate and undistorted understanding of them is possible. They assumed rather that misunderstanding happens as a matter of course and that understanding can only be achieved through interpretation. For Schleiermacher and Dilthey, interpretation entails recovering and reflecting on the experiences of others. Ricoeur is also interested in exploring the conditions that make understanding possible. This is an *epistemological* pursuit, because it entails questions about how we come to know things. In addition, however, he draws on the ideas of thinkers like Kant, Fichte and Heidegger to show that, because in a certain significant way humanity *is* language, in laying out the principles of linguistic meaning we learn something about ourselves. This is an *ontological* pursuit, because it entails questions about what we *are* and what it means to *be*. Ricoeur's writings on hermeneutics are thus shaped by the epistemological and ontological hope that through interpretation we can learn about what we are and how we know about our world (*The Symbolism of Evil*, pp. 351, 355).

During the period between *The Symbolism of Evil* (1960) and *Freud and Philosophy* (1965), Ricoeur portrays hermeneutics as the task of deciphering double-meaning expressions (*Freud and Philosophy*, pp. 8–9). Linguistic expressions, he suggests, may be divided between concepts or single-meaning expressions and symbols or double-meaning expressions. Concepts have a 'primary, literal, manifest meaning'; for instance, if I say, 'That carpet is stained,' it is clear what I mean. Symbolic expressions, however, convey a meaning which is suggestive and figurative rather than literal; for instance, in saying, 'That man is stained,' I may not mean that he has been discoloured by a foreign substance. On the contrary, I may be suggesting that his 'soul' is unclean (*The Symbolism of Evil*, p. 15). Ricoeur's point is that in symbolic expression the literal meaning suggests a second, symbolic meaning on the basis of a resemblance. Both the carpet and the man are tainted, but in different ways. Symbols, Ricoeur believes, have a 'mixed texture' that invites both the 'hermeneutics of suspicion' and the 'hermeneutics of belief'. He writes:

> Hermeneutics seems to me to be animated by [a] double motivation: willingness to suspect, willingness to listen; vow of rigour, vow of obedience. In our time we have not finished doing away with *idols* and we have barely begun to listen to *symbols*. It may be that this situation, in its apparent distress, is instructive: it may be that extreme iconoclasm belongs to the restoration of meaning.
>
> (*Freud and Philosophy*, p. 27)

Symbolic language shows us that we cannot take words at face value. It suggests different ways of looking at the world. When we look at symbolic expressions, we must be careful that we do not impose our own views of the world. When someone says, 'We have fallen,' for instance, they may not mean, as we might, that we have physically taken a tumble or that we have fallen from favour with God. An expression may also have a meaning of which the person using it is unaware. Thus we must 'do away with idols' and be suspicious of our own and others' readings of expressions.[1]

Three 'masters', Ricoeur believes, dominate the school of suspicion: Marx, Nietzsche and Freud (*Freud and Philosophy*, p. 32). These three claimed that people were unaware of the meaning of religion. Marx thought that the function of religion was to provide a 'flight from the reality of inhuman working conditions' and to make 'the misery of life more endurable', Nietzsche considered it to be the refuge of the weak, and Freud thought that it was a wish for a father-God. Thus they believed that it is possible to reveal or unmask an understanding that more faithfully correlates with reality. So when we approach an expression, we ought to query whether what it appears to say corresponds with its true message. Furthermore, we need to be suspicious about ourselves and ask whether we are imposing our own meaning on the studied expressions. But we also need to 'listen' to the meanings we lay bare because they can tell us much about our assumptions about the world and ourselves. Expressions can also help us to think about ourselves and the world in new ways.[2]

In works after *Freud and Philosophy*, Ricoeur's understanding of hermeneutics broadens considerably.[3] He looks beyond the analysis of *symbols* to the interpretation of *texts*. The term 'text', Ricoeur believes, can be applied to anything that can be interpreted, including dreams, ideologies, narratives and human actions.[4] Thus the social sciences and history are hermeneutical disciplines. Texts, as distinct from speech acts, endure and give rise to what Ricoeur calls the 'autonomy of the text'. A text, because it can outlive its author, escapes their intention. That is, it may be used in a way never intended by the writer, as when, for example, a poem is appropriated by a rock group. It also outlasts and escapes its original audience and its original context.

In seeking understanding, the reader tries to reveal the meaning that the author hoped their texts would convey. In talking of the author's meaning or intention, Ricoeur is not calling for re-enactment. Rather, he wants the reader to understand that the text is the product of an implied author. As he writes in *Time and Narrative*:

> Rhetoric can escape the objection of falling back into the 'intentional fallacy' and, more generally, of being no more than

a psychology of the author inasmuch as what it emphasises is not the alleged creation process of the work but the techniques by means of which a work is made communicable. These techniques can be discerned in the work itself. The result is that the only type of author whose authority is in question here is not the real author, the object of biography, but the implied author.

(Vol. 3, p. 160)

The implied author is and is not the author. That is, the existence of the text implies the existence of an author, but does not allow us to make statements with any precision about their desires, moods or hopes. This *distanciation* makes the traditional hermeneutic aim of recapturing the author's ideas and desires difficult, but it also opens up the possibility of the reader being able to make the text 'their own'. Like the philosopher Gadamer, Ricoeur believes that the reader engages in a conversation with the text and tries to make sense of what it says in the light of their experiences. You and I, for instance, may 'converse' with a piece of historical evidence in very different ways. Unlike Gadamer, however, he also believes that the meaning of a text is not entirely dependent on the reader. The text is not the reader's, for it possesses an expressive structure that the reader did not create. This structure does not fully determine the meaning of the text, but it is an indispensable part of that meaning. It is therefore possible for the reader to misinterpret a text.

Reader and text, Ricoeur claims, meet in a 'hermeneutical arc'. At one end of the arc are the features of the text independent of the reader and at the other end are the reader's life experiences (*Hermeneutics and the Human Sciences*, p. 164). In the middle there is discourse. In looking at a piece of historical evidence, for instance, I might learn something of the 'forgotten assumptions' that shaped an historical agent's ideas and actions. But I may also become aware of my own forgetfulness and see that other ways of looking at myself and the world are possible. I 'talk' of my own experiences but I also 'listen' to the experiences of others. Interpretation can thus help us to understand our world better, and to contemplate new directions for that world. It is because interpretation can help the reader to contemplate actual and possible norms that Ricoeur portrays hermeneutics as an ethical enterprise (*Oneself as Another*, p. 115).

Symbols, metaphors and narratives, Ricoeur argues, offer rich possibilities for self-understanding and the exploration of new worlds (see *The Rule of Metaphor*). Narratives, Ricoeur believes, are especially promising because they reveal the temporal nature of human life. They show us that we draw together past, present and future: our experiences are shaped by our hopes and previous experiences and in turn shape future experiences and hopes. They also show us that we can take responsibility for our own assumptions. Historical narratives can help us become aware of our responsibilities, Ricoeur claims, because they show us other worlds and are always provisional (*Time and Narrative*, 1, p. 155). They are provisional because they can be undermined when new ideas and facts are brought to light or when better explanations of existing evidence are produced. If, he believes, we see that the ideas and hopes that underpin historical accounts may be subject to scrutiny, then we may come to understand that our own ideas and hopes are also open to question.

According to Ricoeur, not only history, but all texts, whether they be works of literature, dances, plays or games, can show us the actual and the possible. While this seems a plausible view of our world, it is not without its problems. First, Ricoeur's broad vision of hermeneutics leads us to wonder whether it has boundaries at all, and if so, where those boundaries lie. Are *all* human actions 'texts'? If so, should we try to interpret all actions? If this is not possible, on what grounds can we argue that some actions are better interpreted than others? Second, Ricoeur's presentation of interpretation as a conversation between the text and the reader leads one to ask what kind of conversation it will be. Will both participants contribute equally, or will there be cases where the domination of one participant is appropriate? If so, what conditions would we consider 'appropriate'? Finally, Ricoeur's discussion on the study of history is dominated by his hope that it will lead to self-understanding and the contemplation of new possibilities. Is it possible to talk of studying history for other reasons, reasons outside ourselves? Such questions do not fatally undermine Ricoeur's view of hermeneutics, but signal, rather, the beginning of what promises to be a fruitful conversation.

Notes

1 A. Thisleton, *New Horizons in Hermeneutics*, Grand Rapids, MI: Zondervan, 1992, p. 26.
2 *Freud and Philosophy*, pp. 27–34; discussed in D. Stewart, 'The Hermeneutics of Suspicion', *Journal of Literature and Theology*, 1989, 3(2): 296–307. See also G. D. Robinson, 'Paul Ricoeur and the Hermeneutics of Suspicion: a Brief Overview and Critique', *Premise*, 1995, 2(8); online at http://capo.org/premise/
3 'From Existentialism to the Philosophy of Language', in C. Reagan and D.

Stewart (eds) *The Philosophy of Paul Ricoeur: an Anthology of his Work*, Boston, MA: Beacon Press, 1978, pp. 88–91.

4 See *Time and Narrative; Lectures on Ideology and Utopia*, ed. G. H. Taylor, New York: Columbia University Press, 1986; and 'The Model of the Text: Meaningful Action Considered as Text', *Social Research*, 1971, 38(3): 529–62.

Ricoeur's major works

History and Truth, trans. C. Kelbey and others, Evanston, IL: Northwestern University Press, 1965.

The Symbolism of Evil, trans. E. Buchanan, New York: Harper & Row, 1967.

Freud and Philosophy: an Essay on Interpretation, trans. D. Savage, New Haven, CT: Yale University Press, 1970.

The Conflict of Interpretations: Essays in Hermeneutics, trans. D. Ihde, Evanston, IL: Northwestern University Press, 1974.

The Philosophy of Paul Ricoeur: an Anthology of his Work, eds C. Reagan and D. Stewart, Boston, MA: Beacon Press, 1978.

The Rule of Metaphor: Multi-disciplinary Studies of the Creation of Meaning in Language, trans. R. Czerny with K. McLaughlin and J. Costello, Toronto: University of Toronto Press, 1978.

Hermeneutics and the Human Sciences, ed. and trans. J. Thompson, Cambridge: Cambridge University Press, 1981.

Time and Narrative, 3 vols, trans. K. McLaughlin, D. Pellauer and K. Blamey, Chicago, IL: University of Chicago Press, 1984–88.

From Text to Action: Essays in Hermeneutics II, trans. K. Blamey and J. Thompson, Evanston, IL: Northwestern University Press, 1986.

Lectures on Ideology and Utopia, ed. G. H. Taylor, New York: Columbia University Press, 1986.

Oneself as Other, trans. K. Blamey, Chicago, IL: University of Chicago Press, 1992.

See also

Dilthey, Freud (CT), Heidegger, Nietzsche (MP and CT), Sartre (MP), White.

Further resources

Carr, D., 'Review Essay: *Temps et récit*, volume one', *History and Theory*, 1984, 23(3): 357–70.

Carr, D., Ricoeur, P., Taylor, C. and White, H., 'Round Table on *Temps et récit*, volume one', *University of Ottowa Quarterly*, 1985, 55(4): 287–322.

Clark, S. H., *Paul Ricoeur*, London: Routledge, 1990.

Gehart, M., 'Imagination and History in Ricoeur's Interpretation Theory', *Philosophy Today*, 1979, 23(1): 51–68.

Ihde, D., *Hermeneutic Phenomenology: the Philosophy of Paul Ricoeur*, Evanston, IL: Northwestern University Press, 1971.

Kellner, H., 'Narrativity in History: Post-structuralism and Since', *History and Theory*, 1987, 26(4): 1–29.

Kemp, P. and Ramussen, D. (1989) *The Narrative Path: the Later Works of Paul Ricoeur*, Cambridge, MA: MIT Press, 1989.

Klemm, D. E. (1983) *The Hermeneutical Theory of Paul Ricoeur: a Constructive Analysis*, Lewisburg, WV: Associated University Press, 1983.

Pucci, E., 'History and the Question of Identity: Kant, Arendt, Ricoeur', *Philosophy and Social Criticism*, 1995, 21(5–6): 125–36.

Reagan, C. (ed.) *Studies in the Philosophy of Paul Ricoeur*, Athens, OH: Ohio University Press, 1979.

——, *Paul Ricoeur: his Life and Work*, Chicago, IL: University of Chicago Press, 1996.

Robinson, G. D., 'Raul Ricoeur and the Hermeneutics of Suspicion: a Brief Overview and Critique', *Premise*, 1995, 2(8); online at: http://capo.org/premise/

White, H., *The Content of the Form: Narrative Discourse and Historical Representation*, Baltimore, MD: Johns Hopkins University Press, 1987.

Wood, D., *On Paul Ricoeur: Narrative and Interpretation*, London: Routledge, 1991.

SHEILA ROWBOTHAM 1943–

Until comparatively recently, the idea of dedicating an entry to a women's historian in a book such as this would probably have been met with surprise or even scorn. Women's activities and perspectives were of little interest to historians because it was felt either that they had contributed little to events or that their experiences were adequately covered by the description of men's experiences. By the end of the 1960s, however, the many silences of history were thrown into sharp relief. While some historians drew attention to the lives of men previously ignored, others such as Sheila Rowbotham declared their intention to write a new form of history that would tell of the experiences of both men and women.

The daughter of an office clerk and an engineering salesman, Sheila Rowbotham first became interested in the study of history at secondary school. Kings and queens, wars and explorations 'left her cold', she later recalled, but Olga Wilkinson, a teacher at the Methodist college she attended, showed her that history 'belonged to the present, not to history textbooks' ('Search and Subject, Threading Circumstance', in *Dreams and Dilemmas*, pp. 166–7).[1] The history syllabus that she encountered at St Hilda's College, Oxford, however, did little to develop her growing fascination with the lives of ordinary people and the relationship between the past and the present. Its mixture of Bede, Macaulay, de Tocqueville and Gibbon and Roman, Anglo-Saxon and nineteenth-century European history left her bewildered and determined to seek other views of the past. Through friends in the socialist movement and the Committee for Nuclear Disarmament, Rowbotham was led to the ideas of Karl Marx (ibid., pp. 168–9).[2] Marx gave voice to her own suspicions that the economic and material conditions of modern capitalist society forced workers to sell their labour power as a commodity in order to survive. In doing so, they had to relinquish control over what they made and to compete with other workers in order to avoid unemployment and starvation. Some Marxist historians presumed that the oppression of the working class in modern capitalist society was determined solely by economic factors. Others, such as Dorothy and Edward Thompson, however, believed that it was possible for workers to become aware of their status in society and unite to bring about change.

Marx's view of history, as interpreted by Edward and Dorothy Thompson, focuses on the experiences and perspectives of ordinary men and women. But it also offers, Rowbotham claims, a means of understanding how women have, on occasion, become aware of oppression on the grounds of gender. In capitalist society, the dominant class not only controls economic and material conditions, but also language, morality, law and religion. Thus the struggle of the oppressed is both material and ideological. But the nature and extent of the oppression of women, Rowbotham shows us, is only hinted at in Marx's writings. In *Capital*, for instance, Marx focuses on societies in which people's labour power is sold as a commodity. In doing so, Rowbotham argues, Marx neglects the double role that women played outside the wage economy. Not only are women the biological producers, educators and nurturers of the next generation of workers, but also their work as housekeepers is necessary for the support of current wage earners ('Search and Subject, Threading Circumstance', in *Dreams and Dilemmas*, p. 185). Consequently, Marxist historians have neglected sexuality, maternity, unwaged work and the personal and social relations within families. For her, a more meaningful history will not only take account of the roles that men and women have played in revolutions, political organisations, trade unions and radical movements and how they have responded to change. It will also take account of the different material, personal and social relationships:

> in different historical periods between procreation, the production of new life which will make existence possible in the future, housework, the labour in the home which enables workers to go out and continue to labour in the wages system in capitalism, child rearing, making the survival of the future makers of new life possible, and women's work outside the home for wages.
>
> ('Search and Subject, Threading Circumstance', in
> *Dreams and Dilemmas*, p. 188)[3]

Such a view of history underpins Rowbotham's most well-known publications, *Women, Resistance and Revolution: a History of Women and Revolution in the Modern World* (1972) and *Hidden from History: Rediscovering Women in History from the Seventeenth Century to the Present* (1974). In these, Rowbotham looks to the experiences of women in Britain, France, the Soviet Union, China, Cuba, Vietnam and Algeria, and charts their resistance to oppression in popular radical, socialist, Utopian, trade-union, suffrage and feminist movements from the seventeenth century to the present day.[4] What emerges from these histories is the message that liberal agitation and discourse failed to produce any real prospect for the emancipation of all women, or to make women aware of their identity. Rather, it is only through socialist revolutionary movements that women's liberation has really been taken seriously (*Women, Resistance and Revolution*, p. 205).

Unfortunately, however, while men accept the participation of women in overthrowing existing social conditions, they 'tend to see the future society as one in which women are put back firmly in their place' (ibid.). Rowbotham demonstrates this point clearly in an examination of the changes brought about by the Russian Revolution of 1917. Despite superstition, poverty, illiteracy and the popular view of women as the property of their fathers or husbands, the women's department (*Zhenotdel*) set up by the Bolsheviks managed to introduce socialised health care, laundries and restaurants. These were all introduced in order to free women for work in the wage economy. Abortion, divorce and contraception were legalised and marriage became a civil, not a religious, ceremony. Such far-reaching changes, however, were short lived. By the late 1920s what gains women had made were reversed by Stalin in the name of economic progress. By the 1930s, women were expected not only to work, but also to shoulder the burden of house-keeping and child-care. History demonstrates, Rowbotham concludes, that what is needed is a 'revolution within a revolution' or, in the case of the developing world, liberation from the 'colony within the colony': the overturning of both capitalist conditions and the understanding of liberation as the power to control other things. This requires a radical transformation of the 'cultural conditioning of men and women, upbringing of children, shape of the places we live in, legal structure of society, sexuality, and the very nature of work' (ibid., pp. 245, 249).

The reception of these works by academics was decidedly mixed. Whereas some praised Rowbotham's efforts to challenge contemporary views of the nature and scope of history, others were troubled by her almost exclusive reliance upon secondary sources, her socialist agenda and her attempts to spin a history out of what amounted to no more than 'a few moon rocks dotted in a rather inexpert manner through the years'.[5] For countless women, however, *Women, Resistance and Revolution* and *Hidden from History* introduced them to a tradition of resistance in which their own efforts to bring about change could be grounded, and suggested ways of organising to change sex, race and class relations. They quickly became standard texts in women's studies courses both in Britain and abroad and are still recognised by feminist scholars today as landmark works.

In response to critical reviews of her work, Rowbotham penned *Woman's Consciousness, Man's World* (1973). In this she draws on her own experience of childhood and evidence of women's economic and social oppression under capitalism to make her modification of the vocabulary of Marxism more explicit. She also suggests that the origin of women's subordination within the family can be found in pre-capitalist societies. She writes, for instance, that, 'in the relation of husband and wife there is an exchange of services which resembles the bond between *man* and *man* in feudalism' (p. 63; see also pp. 64–5, and 'When Adam Delved, and Eve Span . . . ', in *Dreams and Dilemmas*, pp. 199–207).[6] This excerpt might be taken as supporting the claim that women should struggle against capitalism *and* against patriarchy. But in 'The Trouble with Patriarchy', Rowbotham cautions that it is difficult to struggle against 'patriarchy' if you haven't got a clear idea of what it is:

> The term has been used in a great variety of ways. 'Patriarchy' has been discussed as an ideology which arose out of men's power to exchange women between kinship groups; as a symbolic male principle; and as the power of the father (its literal meaning). It has been used to express men's control over women's sexuality and fertility; and describe the institutional structure of male domination. Recently the phrase 'capitalist patriarchy' has suggested a form peculiar to capitalism.
>
> (*Dreams and Dilemmas*, pp. 208–9)[7]

Furthermore, those who support the struggle against patriarchy, she argues, often deny men a role in the liberation of women.[8] For Rowbotham, both men and women will achieve liberation in the struggle against capitalism:

> Just as the abolition of class power would release people outside the working class and thus requires their support and involvement, so the movement against hierarchy which is carried in feminism goes beyond the liberation of a sex. It contains the

possibility of equal relations not only between women and men but also between men and men, and women and women, and even between adults and children.

(Ibid., p. 214)

As this extract shows, Rowbotham is interested in liberation for all, not just for women.

In *Women, Resistance and Revolution, Hidden from History* and *Woman's Consciousness, Man's World*, Rowbotham draws upon a wide range of sources, including songs, novels, governmental and organisational records, pamphlets, other historical works and her own experiences. She also values the oral testimonies of women, as can be seen clearly in *Dutiful Daughters* (edited with Jean McCrindle in 1977). Rowbotham and McCrindle look into the lives of fourteen working-class and lower-middle-class women of various ages. Though not intended to be representative of women's experiences, *Dutiful Daughters* offers the reader a fascinating account of how individual women view themselves and what significance they give to personal and public events. These testimonies, Rowbotham is careful to stress, are not histories. They are fragments: glimpses of individual lives frozen in writing. History only emerges when such fragments are combined with other sources in an account that helps us to understand not only where we have been, but also where we might go in future (ibid., pp. 1–9).

Rowbotham's commitment to this view of history is also seen in her political activism. In *Beyond the Fragments*, for instance, Rowbotham, Lynne Segal and Hilary Wainwright call for the fragmentary groups of the Left to come together to create a movement that will foster socialist consciousness and grassroots activism among working people. In this, as with works such as *The Friends of Alice Wheeldon* (1986), *The Past is Before Us* (1989), *Women in Movement: Feminism and Social Action* (1992), *Dignity and Daily Bread* (1993), *Homeworkers Worldwide* (1993) and *Women Encounter Technology* (1995); her contributions to the periodicals *Red Rag, Spare Rib, Black Dwarf, Islington Gutter Press, Jobs for Change, History Workshop, Radical America, Radical History Review;* and her work for the Greater London Council (1982–86), technical and further education colleges, secondary schools and universities, Rowbotham tells us that grassroots movements in the developed and developing world can bring about change.

As is clear from her writings, her audience are ordinary men and women. Not surprisingly then, she rejects much of the current literature of gender studies, Marxist theory and historiography. For her, the importation of French structuralist and post-structuralist perspectives have not only made academic writing inaccessible to the public, but have also discouraged academics from taking an interest in the developing world and in the life and work of people with different heritages from their own. Historians must never lose sight of the goal of social transformation that, to be realised, requires the unity of men and women, past and present.

Thanks to writers like Rowbotham, historians now listen to many more 'voices'. Few people have appreciated, however, her commitment to ordinary women *and* men; she does not speak only of and for women. Rowbotham reminds us that it is one thing to listen to 'voices' and another to bring them together.

Notes

1   'Search and Subject, Threading Circumstance' first appeared in the American edition of *Hidden from History*, New York: Pantheon, 1974.
2   See also D. Copelman, 'Interview with Sheila Rowbotham', in H. Abelove, B. Blackmar, P. Dimock and J. Schneer (eds) *Visions of History*, Manchester: Manchester University Press, pp. 50–2.
3   See also *Women's Liberation and the New Politics*, Nottingham: Bertrand Russell Peace Foundation, 1971.
4   On Rowbotham's view of the suffragettes, see B. Caine, *English Feminism 1780–1980*, Oxford: Oxford University Press, 1997, pp. 260–1.
5   For reviews of *Women, Resistance and Revolution*, see M. Foot, *Books and Bookmen*, August 1973, 18: 106–7; F. Howe, *American Scholar*, 1973, 42(3): 682, 4; anon., *The Economist*, 3 March 1973, 246: 93–4; anon., *Times Literary Supplement*, 23 March 1973, 3707: 321. For reviews of *Hidden from History*, see anon., *Times Literary Supplement*, 30 November 1973, 3743, 1473; E. Long, *New York Times Book Review*, 16 March 1975, pp. 12, 14; and P. S. Prescott, *Newsweek*, 20 January 1975, 85: 74.
6   'When Adam Delved, and Eve Span . . . ' originally appeared in *New Society*, 4 January 1979.
7   'The Trouble with Patriarchy' originally appeared in the *New Statesman*, 21–28 December 1979, pp. 970–1.
8   See S. Alexander and B. Taylor, 'In Defence of "Patriarchy"', *New Statesman*, 1 February 1980, p. 161.

Rowbotham's major works

Women, Resistance and Revolution: a History of Women and Revolution in the Modern World, London: Allen Lane, 1972.
Woman's Consciousness, Man's World, Harmondsworth: Penguin, 1973.
Hidden from History: Rediscovering Women in History from the Seventeenth Century to the Present, New York: Vintage Books, 1976 (English edition 1973).
(ed. with J. McCrindle) *Dutiful Daughters*, London: Allen Lane, 1977.
Dreams and Dilemmas: Collected Writings, London: Virago, 1983.

A Century of Women: the History of Women in Britain and the United States, London: Viking, 1997.

See also

Davis, Hobsbawm, Marx, Scott, Thompson.

Further resources

Alexander, S. and Taylor, B., 'In Defence of "Patriarchy"', *New Statesman*, 1 February 1980.

Caine, B., *English Feminism 1780–1980*, Oxford: Oxford University Press, 1997.

Copelman, D., 'Interview with Sheila Rowbotham', in H. Abelove, B. Blackmar, P. Dimock and J. Schneer (eds) *Visions of History*, Manchester: Manchester University Press, 1981, pp. 49–69.

Degler, C. N., *Is there a History of Women?* Oxford: Oxford University Press, 1975.

Kaye, H. J. (1984) *The British Marxist Historians*, Cambridge: Polity, 1984.

Radical History Review, 1995, 63: 141–65.

Seccombe, W., 'Sheila Rowbotham on Labour and the Greater London Council', *Canadian Dimension*, 1987, 21(2): 32–7.

Swindells, J., 'Hanging up on Mum or Questions of Everyday Life in the Writing of History', *Gender and History*, 1990, 2(1): 68–78.

Zissner, J. P., *History and Feminism: a Glass Half Full*, New York: Twayne, 1993.

JOAN WALLACH SCOTT 1941–

Joan Wallach Scott (née Joan Wallach), historian of gender and feminist theorist, was born in Brooklyn on 18 December 1941. After gaining a bachelor of arts at Brandeis University in 1962, she completed a masters and then a doctoral degree at the University of Wisconsin. After working at the University of Illinois at Chicago, Northwestern University and the University of North Carolina at Chapel Hill, she was appointed the Nancy Duke Lewis University Professor and a professor of history at Brown University. At Brown, she was also the founding director of the Pembroke Center for Teaching Research on Women. It was at the Pembroke Center, Scott later claimed, that she learned 'to think about theory and gender' (*Gender and the Politics of History*, p. ix).[1] Since 1985 she has been a professor of social science at the Institute for Advanced Study in Princeton.[2] As a child, the sacking of her father – Samuel Wallach – for refusing to co-operate with investigations into communist activities impressed upon her the need to close the gap between what academic freedom is and what it ought to be.[3] Since 1993 she has served on the American Association of University Professors

academic freedom committee (committee A). She has published more
than forty articles and thirteen books on history, feminism and higher
education, most notably *The Glassworkers of Carmaux* (1974); *Women,
Work, and Family* (with L. Tilly, 1978); *Gender and the Politics of History*
(1988, revised edition 1999); *Only Paradoxes to Offer: French Feminists and
the Rights of Man* (1996); and *Feminism and History* (editor, 1996).

Scott's work is characterised by a determination to unmask the
fixation of Western historians upon the idea of a centre. Many historians
seek Truth and the realisation of the ideal form of historical research.
The problem with such centres or ideals, for Scott, is that they are
built upon a foundation of exclusion. Any views of 'Truth' or 'History'
that do not conform to those of the dominant group (in the case of
historical research, white, middle-class, educated men) are marginalised
or pushed to the outside. Furthermore, despite the fact that any ideal
or centre 'rests on – contains – repressed or negated material and so is
unstable, not unified', those privileged by ideals or centres have tried
to fix them by suggesting that they are 'natural' or the only ones possible
('Introduction', in *Gender and the Politics of History*, p. 7). It is Scott's aim
to make us aware that prevailing views of the subject-matter and
methods of historical research are built upon a foundation of privilege
and exclusion and that they are open to change. This way of looking at
historiography, labelled 'deconstruction' by the French post-structuralist
Jacques Derrida,

> undermines the historian's ability to claim neutral mastery
> or to present any particular story as if it were complete,
> universal, and objectively determined. Instead, if one grants
> that meanings are constructed through exclusions, one must
> acknowledge and take responsibility for the exclusions involved
> in one's own project.
>
> (Ibid.)

However, it also challenges the view that conflicts and disagreements
about the content, uses and meanings of historical knowledge are
unhealthy and thus ought to be avoided at all costs ('History in Crisis?
The Others' Side of the Story', *American Historical Review*, 1989, 94(3):
680–92).[4]

Scott's interest in contesting the privilege of white, middle-class,
educated men can be found in all her historical writings. Early in her
career, E. P. Thompson's work *The Making of the English Working Class*
(1963) provided her with a model for writing 'socially relevant history'
('Women in *The Making of the English Working Class*', in *Gender and the*

Politics of History, p. 69). Through his study of the tradition of worker radicalism in England between 1790 and 1830, Thompson challenged the popular assumption that working people were not historical agents because they were incapable of formulating and acting on revolutionary ideas. For instance, with Eric Hobsbawm, Scott explored the remarkable reputation of nineteenth-century shoemakers as political radicals in three senses: as agents of militant action in movements of social protest; as associates with movements of the political Left; and as ideologists of the common people.[5] Like Thompson, she also subjected to question assumptions about how working-class unrest was triggered. In her study of the glassworkers of Carmaux in south-western France, for instance, she shows us that working-class unrest may be attributed not – as was assumed by public officials and historians alike – to economic and geographical dislocation, but to the stability afforded through land ownership and the identification of one's fortunes with a particular institution or location (*The Glassworkers of Carmaux*, 1974).[6] With Louise Tilly she has also shown that industrialisation did not – as many people assume – guarantee the transformation of women's work or liberation from subjugation (*Women, Work, and Family*, 1978).[7]

Though Scott owed much to Thompson, she became aware that *The Making of the English Working Class* was of limited usefulness for those trying to draw attention to the experiences of another group on the periphery of history: women. As she was later to argue, Thompson's work is primarily a story about men, and class is constructed as a masculine identity, even when not all the actors are male:

> the organisation of the story and the master codes that structure the narrative are gendered in such a way as to confirm rather than challenge the masculine representation of class. Despite their presence, women are marginal in the book; they serve to underline and point up the overwhelming association of class with the politics of male workers.
>
> ('Women in *The Making of the English Working Class*',
> in *Gender and the Politics of History*, p. 72)

Thus, while he focuses much attention on the privileging of middle-class and elite experiences over those of the working class, the domination of men over women is left unquestioned (see also Scott's critical analysis of Gareth Stedman Jones's *Languages of Class*, 'Language and Working Class History', in *Gender and the Politics of History*, pp. 56–67). But women's history too, Scott claims, leaves the designation of male as centre and female as periphery largely unscathed.

In Scott's view, the two major forms of women's history – social history and 'her-story' – are seriously flawed. In the 1960s and 1970s, social historians tried to shift attention in history away from the deeds of elite statesmen towards the experiences of ordinary people. Alongside studies of peasants, workers and racial and ethnic minorities emerged those of women. As social historians typically write within the Marxist tradition, however, they assume that women are no different from other groups mobilising resources, being modernised or exploited, contending for power, or being excluded from a polity. Thus questions about the distinctiveness of women and the centrality of the social relations between the sexes tend to be displaced or subsumed by questions about the role of economic forces in determining actions ('Women's History', in *Gender and the Politics of History*, p. 22). 'Her-storians', on the other hand, who focus exclusively on female agency, have tended to conflate the valuation of women's experiences and the positive assessment of everything that women did, and to isolate women as a special and separate topic of history. Social history thus fosters total integration; 'her-story', ghettoisation. Neither of these ways of writing women's history, Scott believes, encourages *all* historians to take the experiences of women and the relations between the sexes seriously. Neither leads to a new form of history – as distinct from a new history of women – because they do not foster a critical re-examination of the premises and standards of existing historical work. The concept of 'gender', however, offers a way out of this dead end.[8]

Traditionally, relations between the sexes have been considered to be 'natural', that is, determined strictly by anatomy. Many scholars thus thought it pointless to explain how and why relations between the sexes came to involve male domination and female subordination and how this state of affairs could be changed. In the twentieth century, however, scholars began to argue that the connection between biology and relations between the sexes could be cut. Drawing on anthropological evidence and the experiences of transsexuals and persons whose biological sex was open to dispute, writers like Oakley and Chodorow showed that sexual identity was primarily a social and cultural construction. Differences between the sexes were found to exist throughout the world, but those differences varied from culture to culture. For example, 'femininity' might be identified with self-sufficiency in one culture and dependency in another.[9] To escape the biological determinism assumed in concepts like 'sex' and 'relations between the sexes', feminists began to use 'gender' to refer to the social organisation of the relationship between the sexes. Gender was also preferred because it was thought that its relational nature would lead to a critical examination of many economic, social and political institutions. That is, because men and women are defined in terms of one another, the study of how they relate may lead to critical awareness of the subordination of women.

Echoing these developments, Scott sees much promise in the historical study of the relation between the sexes. In the essay 'Gender: a Useful Category of Historical Analysis', though, she insists that the three major theoretical approaches to gender are limited. Patriarchy theory and psychoanalysis rest on the shaky premise that there is a fixed difference between men and women, and Marxist feminism subsumes gender relations to economic forces. In Scott's view, gender relations are open to historical change ('Gender: a Useful Category of Historical Analysis', in *Gender and the Politics of History*, pp. 33–41). Moreover, drawing on the ideas of Michel Foucault, she claims that gender 'is a primary field within which or by means of which power is articulated', because gender metaphors are used to construct and endorse a great variety of unequal social relations that have no logical connection to sexual difference. She writes:

> concepts of gender structure perception and the concrete and symbolic organisation of all social life. To the extent that these [concepts] establish distributions of power (differential control over or access to material and symbolic resources), gender becomes implicated in the conception and construction of power itself.
>
> (Ibid., p. 45)

Scott's point is that society's conceptions of gender give shape to a host of institutional structures such as the family, the labour market, class, spirituality, education, the polity and historical research (ibid., pp. 44–5). Indeed, the designation of male as centre and female as periphery is largely seen as ubiquitous. Given the centrality of gender in social organisation, it thus follows for Scott that all historians should attend critically to gender relations in history and in the methods of historical research. When they do so, she claims, it will be possible to lay bare inequalities and to show that they are contestable ('Introduction', in *Gender and the Politics of History*, pp. 3, 6, 11).

In parts 2 and 3 of *Gender and the Politics of History* and in *Only Paradoxes to Offer: French Feminists and the Rights of Man*, Scott shows us how concepts of gender permeate social institutions, past and present. In 'Language and Working Class History' and 'Women in *The Making of the English Working Class*', for instance, she argues that in response to the rise of industrial capitalism, male workers formed a specifically male form of agitation and community to protect their social and political status. In doing so, they (knowingly and sometimes unknowingly) pushed women to the margins of work and society (*Gender and the Politics of History*, pp. 53–90). Furthermore, she claims that many of the concepts of gender adopted by male workers may also be found in the writings of social theorists and in the polity. In *Only Paradoxes to Offer*, for example, Scott traces how the French feminists Olympe de Gouges, Jeanne Deroin, Hubertine Auclert, Madeleine Pelletier and Louise Weiss responded to the contradictory legacy of the French Revolution: a universal, abstract, rights-bearing individual as the unit of national sovereignty, embodied as a man. The idea of an abstract individual made it possible for women to claim the political rights of active citizens, but its embodiment as male suggested either that rights themselves, or at least how and where they were exercised, depended on the physical characteristics of male bodies. This paradox, Scott argues, led feminists to demand either the affirmation of equality (sameness) or difference. Elsewhere, Scott questions the view that equality and difference are dichotomous, and suggests that equality may entail indifference to differences. In her estimation, then, it is possible to be both different and equal (see 'The Sears Case', in *Gender and the Politics of History*, pp. 167–77; see also '"L'ouvrière! Mot impie, sordide . . . ": Women Workers in the Discourse of French Political Economy, 1840–1860', in *Gender and the Politics of History*, pp. 139–63). Scott has also argued that historians in the United States labour under the shadow of 'a single prototypical figure represented in the historical subject: white, Western man' ('American Women Historians: 1884–1984', in *Gender and the Politics of History*, pp. 178–98). Thus the discipline of history also offers women a paradoxical legacy.

Scott's critique of women's history – and history in general – is astute and her vision of gender history is original and promising. Reactions to her writings, however, have been mixed. For example, while *Gender and the Politics of History* attracted numerous positive reviews and the American Historical Association's Joan Kelly Memorial Prize, it also led to claims that her focus on the language of gender in society had come at the expense of the experiences of ordinary people, that she had been unfair in her dismissal of social history and that she had 'accepted Derridian and literary deconstructionism too uncritically'.[10] Though in the minority, these criticisms are not without foundation. Her eagerness to appropriate the vocabulary of post-structuralists like Derrida and Foucault means that she does not always question their assumptions. For instance, is it true that 'there is no social reality outside to or prior to language'? ('Language and Working Class History', in *Gender and the Politics of History*, p. 56). Is it possible to distinguish between the objects of literary and historical study? Are centres and ideals necessarily unstable and incomplete? Is the theory of power that Scott draws upon gendered? And does radical history require radical epistemology?[11]

Notes

1 At the time of writing, the revised edition of *Gender and the Politics of History* had not been published. Page numbers thus correspond to the 1988 edition.

2 On Scott's appointment to the Institute for Advanced Study, see K. Hinds, 'Joan Wallach Scott: Breaking New Ground', *Change*, 1985, 17(4): 48–53.

3 J. W. Scott, 'Academic Freedom as an Ethical Practice', in L. Menand (ed.) *The Future of Academic Freedom*, Chicago, IL: University of Chicago Press, 1996, pp. 163–80; see also E. Abelson, D. Abraham and M. Murphy, 'Interview with Joan Scott', *Radical History Review*, 1989, 45: 41–59.

4 See also 'Forum: Raymond Martin, Joan W. Scott and Cushing Strout on *Telling the Truth about History*', *History and Theory*, 1995, 34(4): 329–34; 'The Rhetoric of Crisis in Higher Education', in M. Bérubé and C. Nelson (eds) *Higher Education under Fire: Politics, Economics and the Crisis of the Humanities*, New York: Routledge, 1995, pp. 293–304; and 'Border Patrol: a Crisis in History? On Gérard Noiriel's *Sur la crise de l'histoire*', *French Historical Studies*, 1998, 21(3): 383–97.

5 E. Hobsbawm and J. W. Scott, 'Political Shoemakers', *Past and Present*, 1980, 89: 86–114.

6 See also J. W. Scott, 'The Glassworkers of Carmaux', in S. Thernstrom and R. Sennett (eds) *Nineteenth Century Cities: Essays in the New Urban History*, Yale Studies of the City 1, New Haven, CT: Yale University Press, 1969, pp. 3–48.

7 See also 'Women's Work and the Family in Nineteenth Century Europe' (with L. Tilly), in *Comparative Studies in Society and History*, 1975, 17(1): 36–64; L. Tilly, J. W. Scott and M. Cohen, 'Women's Work and European Fertility Patterns', *Journal of Interdisciplinary History*, 1976, 6(3): 447–76; and J. W. Scott, 'The Mechanization of Women's Work', *Scientific American*, September 1982: 167–87.

8 Scott also suggests that the feminist 'equality versus difference' debate is another privilege-protecting dead end. See 'The Sears Case', in *Gender and the Politics of History*, pp. 167–77.

9 A. Oakley, *Sex, Gender and Society*, New York: Harper Colophon Books, 1972; and N. Chodorow, 'Being and Doing: a Cross-cultural Examination of the Socialization of Males and Females', in V. Gornick and B. Moran (eds) *Women in Sexist Society*, New York: Basic Books, 1971, pp. 259–91.

10 For reviews of *Gender and the Politics of History*, see M. J. Boxer, *Journal of Social History*, 1989, 22(4): 788–90; C. Koonz, *Women's Review of Books*, 1989, 6(1): 19–20; W. H. Sewell, *History and Theory*, 1990, 29(1): 71–82; L. Tilly, 'Gender, Women's History and Social History', *Pasato et Presente*, 1989, 20–1: 14–25; and E. Weber, *New Republic*, 1988, 199(3848): 43–6.

11 See, for example, N. Hartsock, *Money, Sex and Power: Toward a Feminist Historical Materialism*, New York: Longman, 1983.

Scott's major works

The Glassworkers of Carmaux: French Craftsmen and Political Action in a Nineteenth Century City, Cambridge, MA: Harvard University Press, 1974.

(with L. Tilly), *Women, Work, and Family*, New York: Holt, Rinehart & Winston, 1978.

(with E. Hobsbawm), 'Political Shoemakers', *Past and Present*, 1980, 89: 86–114.

Gender and the Politics of History, New York: Columbia University Press, 1988, revised edition 1999.

'History in Crisis? The Others' Side of the Story', *American Historical Review*, 1989, 94(3): 680–92.

'Women's History', in P. Burke (ed.) *New Perspectives on Historical Writing*, London: Polity, 1991, pp. 43–66.

'Forum: Raymond Martin, Joan W. Scott and Cushing Strout on *Telling the Truth about History*', *History and Theory*, 1995, 34(4): 329–34.

'After History?', *Common Knowledge*, 1996, 5(3): 9–26.

(ed.) *Feminism and History*, Oxford Readings in Feminism, Oxford: Oxford University Press, 1996.

Only Paradoxes to Offer: French Feminists and the Rights of Man, Cambridge, MA: Harvard University Press, 1996.

'Border Patrol: a Crisis in History? On Gérard Noiriel's *Sur la crise de l'histoire*', *French Historical Studies*, 1998, 21(3): 383–97.

See also

Davis, Derrida (CT), Foucault, Hobsbawm, Rowbotham, Thompson.

Further resources

Abelson, E., Abraham, D. and Murphy, M., 'Interview with Joan Scott', *Radical History Review*, 1989, 45: 41–59.

Downs, L. L. 'If "Woman" is Just an Empty Category, then Why am I Afraid to Walk Alone at Night?' and 'Reply to Joan Scott', in *Comparative Studies in Society and History*, 1993, 35(2): 414–51.

Fontana, B., 'Review: *Only Paradoxes to Offer*', *Times Literary Supplement*, 28 February 1997, 4900: 31.

Goodman, D., 'More than Paradoxes to Offer: Feminist History as Critical Practice', *History and Theory*, 1997, 36(3): 392–405.

Kent, C., 'Victorian Social History: Post-Thompson, Post-Foucault, Postmodern', *Victorian Studies*, 1996, 40(1): 97–133.

Koonz, C., 'Review: *Gender and the Politics of History*', *Women's Review of Books*, 1989, 6(1): 19–20.

Scott, J. W., Palmer, B. D., Stansell, C. and Rabinbach, A., 'Class, Sex, and Language in Nineteenth-century Britain', *International Labor and Working Class History*, 1987, 31: 1–36.

Sewell, W. H., 'Review: *Gender and the Politics of History*', *History and Theory*, 1990, 29(1): 71–82.

Tilly, L., 'Gender, Women's History and Social History', *Pasato et Presente*, 1989, 20–1: 14–25.

Varikas, E., 'Gender, Experience and Subjectivity: the Tilly–Scott Disagreement', *New Left Review*, 1995, 211: 89–101.
Zissner, J. P., *History and Feminism: a Glass Half Full*, New York: Twayne, 1993.

OSWALD SPENGLER 1880–1936

Ever since the publication of Spengler's *Der Untergang des Abendlandes* (trans. *The Decline of the West*) in 1918, historians have been perplexed as to what they should do about it. Though they have almost universally condemned it as too speculative, full of errors and even fantastic, people the world over stubbornly refuse to take heed of their verdict. For them, it seems, Spengler's story of the disintegration of Western civilisation offers confirmation of their belief in 'the darkness of this time'.[1]

Oswald Spengler was born in Blankenburg, north Germany on 29 May 1880. He studied classics, mathematics and science at the universities of Munich, Berlin and Halle, and earned his doctorate and teaching certificate in 1904 for two dissertations – one on the pre-Socratic philosopher Heraclitus and the other on sight in 'the higher ranks of the animal kingdom' (*Heraklit eine Studie* and *Der metaphysische Grundgedanke der Heraklitschen Philosophie*). He taught for a short time at Saarbrücken and Düsseldorf before taking up a position at a Gymnasium in Hamburg (1908). As the Gymnasium was new and only had a small teaching staff, Spengler taught German, history, mathematics and science. When his mother died in 1910 she left him enough money to support himself. He taught for another year and then resolved to give writing a try. Finding that the climate in Hamburg aggravated the severe headaches from which he suffered, he moved to Munich. In Munich he tinkered with poetry, drama and short stories, but the events that were unfolding in Europe led him to politics and history. He later wrote:

> At that time the World War appeared to me both as imminent and also as the inevitable outward manifestation of the historical crisis, and my endeavour was to comprehend it from an examination of the spirit of the preceding centuries – not years.
> (*The Decline of the West*, vol. 1, p. 46)

Spengler began work on a book that was to be called 'Conservative and Liberal', but the scope of the work widened as his inquiry progressed. By the outbreak of the war the organisation of what was now called *Der Untergang des Abendlandes* had taken its final form. In this work, Spengler offered a comparative study of the birth, growth, decline and death of eight cultures: Babylonian, Indian, Chinese, Egyptian, Mayan-Aztec (Mexican), Classical (Greco-Roman), Magian (Arabian, Syrian, Jewish, Byzantine and Islamic)˙and the ominously named 'Faustian' (Western Europe).

With the outbreak of the First World War, the foreign sources of his mother's legacy were cut off. Spengler was twice rejected by the Army on health grounds and was left in a state of poverty. Despite this, he managed to finish the first volume of *The Decline of the West* by the end of the war. He had difficulty finding a publisher, but eventually it was accepted by a firm in Vienna. By the time volume 2 was published in 1922, however, no fewer than 100,000 copies of the first volume had been sold. Spurred on by the public success of the book, Spengler resolved to take an active part in politics. He had little faith in the Weimar Republic. Democracy, he believed, would soon give way to an age of dictatorships and Caesarism. He therefore felt it his duty to search for and support someone who would lead Germany out of its woes. Such ideas made Spengler attractive to the fledgling Nazi Party, and he was approached repeatedly by Georg Strasser to become a propagandist. Spengler rejected this offer, however, because he was repulsed by the fanatical anti-Semitism and racism of Hitler and his followers (*Politische Schriften*, p. x).[2] In his view, Germany needed a strong but benevolent dictator (see *Preussentum und Sozialismus*, 1919). He thought that General von Seeckt, the head of a small army permitted by the terms of the Treaty of Versailles, was just the person to assume that role, but Seeckt refused to have anything to do with such a plan.

With the stabilisation of the German economy in 1925 and the subsequent period of prosperity, Spengler's popularity waned. Sales of *The Decline of the West* had earned him a great deal of money, though, and he used it to give lectures throughout Germany and in Italy, Spain, Lithuania, Latvia and Finland. He turned back to history and wrote *Früzheit der Weltgeschichte* (1925) and *Der Mensch und die Technik* (1931, trans. *Man and Technics*). In this work, Spengler employs the symbols of lava, crystal and amoeba to illustrate the character of the successive prehistorical cultures (100,000–20,000 BC, 20,000–8000 BC and 8000–3000 BC). In the first of these periods, humans spread across the earth like lava from a volcano. In the 'crystal age' they began to see that they were different from other animals. In the 'age of amoeba' people became aware of themselves as individuals, and different languages and tribes emerged. They were, like amoebas, mobile and expansive. Out of these ages arose three cultures: Atlantis (centred on Spain, Morocco and north Sahara), Kasch (centred on the Persian Gulf, Oman, Baluchistan and Hyderabad) and Turan (stretching from Scandinavia to Korea).[3] Strangely enough, his ideas on people being like lava and amoebas never caught on with prehistorians. In *Man and Technics*, Spengler argued that the gift of Western industrial techniques to less developed countries (most of the countries outside Western Europe) would lead those peoples to mount a world revolution.

Shortly before his death Spengler returned to politics. In *Die Jahre der Entscheidung* (*The Hour of Decision*, 1933), for instance, he foretold the coming of a war that would do Germany harm. This book was already in wide circulation before the Nazis realised that it contained veiled repudiations of Hitler and his followers. Further circulation of the book was prohibited and newspapers were forbidden to mention Spengler's name. He died on 8 May 1936.

Historians, Spengler argues in the introduction to *The Decline of the West*, commonly see history 'as a sort of tape-worm industriously adding on to itself one epoch after another' (vol. 1, p. 21). For them, history is linear and culminates in modern Western civilisation. Europe is thus the centre of history, and all other cultures are made to follow orbits about it. Such a view, Spengler claims, is meaningless and egocentric. He writes:

> I see, in the place of that empty figment of *one* linear history which can only be kept up by shutting one's eyes to the overwhelming multitude of the facts, the drama of a *number* of mighty cultures, each springing with primitive strength from the soil of a mother-region to which it remains firmly bound throughout its whole life-cycle, each stamping its material, its mankind, in *its own* image; each having *its own* idea, *its own* passions, *its own* life, will and feeling, *its own* death. . . . I see world-history as a picture of endless formations and transformations, of the marvellous waxing and waning of organic forms.
>
> (Ibid.)

History is without centre: it is the story of a potentially unlimited number of cultures that 'grow with the same superb aimlessness as the flowers of the field' (ibid.). 'Grow' is an apt word, for Spengler, like Herder, believes that cultures develop in ways analogous to the life-cycle of plants or animals. He also often portrays such ageing in terms of the succession of the four seasons. Cultures have their spring when life is rural, agricultural and feudal; their summer when towns emerge, an aristocracy of manners develops and named artists succeed their anonymous predecessors; their autumn when cities and commerce spread, monarchies are centralised and religion and tradition are challenged; and their winter when scepticism, materialism, imperialism, constant conflict and the 'megalopolis' (world cities, with large populations of workers) arise. For instance, the Classical and Faustian cultures had their 'spring' with the Homeric period and the Middle Ages respectively; 'summer' in the rise of the Greek city-state, and the Renaissance; 'autumn' with the Peloponnesian War, and the eighteenth century; and 'winter' with the Sophists and Socrates and Plato, and the nineteenth century. Historians, Spengler argues, must aim to produce a 'physiognomic' comparative 'morphology' of cultures: an account of cultures as organisms that are born, grow, decline and die.

Such a method of study, Spengler believes, will allow historians to make predictions about the future of particular cultures. Indeed, Spengler presents his work as the first serious attempt to predetermine the 'duration, rhythm, meaning and product of the *still unaccomplished* stages of our Western history' (ibid., vol. 1, p. 112). He even insists that cultures have a life-cycle of approximately 1,000 years and plots out with a fair degree of exactitude the 'lives' of four cultures (Faustian, Classical, Chinese and Egyptian) in three tables appended to volume 1. In other places, however, he claims that the actual life-span of cultures may vary considerably. Some cultures may linger in a state of suspension for considerably longer than 1,000 years, as he thinks the examples of India and China show. A culture may also perish after a relatively short time because of external assault, as in the case of Mayan-Aztec culture, or be stunted by 'pseudomorphosis'. Pseudomorphosis refers to those cases in which an older alien culture dominates a young culture to such an extent that the normal development of the latter is arrested (ibid., vol. 1, p. 183). Spengler thought that pseudomorphosis was evident in Russia, because he believed that the import of Marxism had halted its growth. He is also careful to note that the 'destiny' of a culture depends a great deal 'on the character and capacities of individual players' (ibid., vol. 1, pp. 38, 145; vol. 2, p. 446). Spengler's varying statements make it hard to judge where he stands on the issue of determinism.

Cultures, Spengler also believes, are shaped by distinctive 'prime symbols' or key ideas. The symbols that shape cultures are so different from one another that intercultural understanding is open to few people (ibid., vol. 1, pp. 4, 174). Spengler is evidently one of the few. For the Magians (AD 0 to 1000), for instance, the world is like a cavern in which light battles against the darkness. This view of the world, Spengler claims, is seen in the 'magic' of algebra, the Ptolemaic view of the universe and the architecture of the basilica and mosque. Western

European culture (AD 900–) is 'Faustian' because of the limitless ambition of its people. The spires of its cathedrals soar heavenwards, its paintings offer a depth of perspective previously unseen, its ships conquer the seas, and its weapons bring levels of destruction hitherto unknown.

Reading *The Decline of the West*, you cannot help but wonder why it was so popular. The answer has to do with timing. *The Decline of the West* gave voice to the public suspicion that the collapse of Germany between 1918 and 1923 was a symptom of a wider malaise. In the twentieth century, people lost faith in the idea of historical progress. Rather, they saw the many conflicts of their time as evidence of decline. Spengler confirmed their vision of the world.

Very few German scholars found anything to commend in *The Decline of the West*. Even those who professed support for Spengler did so with qualification. Manfred Schroeter, for instance, was impressed by Spengler's 'demoniacal strength' but thought his constructions crude and violent, and though Eduard Meyer thought that there was much to Spengler's judgement of the present as a time of decline, he refused to accept that all actions are expressions of a prime symbol and that cultural interaction is next to impossible.[4] Outside Germany, the reception was scarcely better. Benedetto Croce dismissed the *Decline* as a mere repetition of what Vico had said in *The New Science* two centuries earlier, André Fauconnet accused him of being a German chauvinist, R. G. Collingwood questioned his account of 'prime symbols' and his grasp of ancient history, and J. T. Shotwell denied that democracy would lead to further decline. The list of charges built up. Historians argued that he selected and even invented historical details to fit his scheme, that he could not support the claim that cultures are radically different from one another and that it was absurd to argue that intercultural understanding is open to few in a book written for the general public.[5]

The public, however, disregarded such verdicts. The *Decline* was translated into numerous languages and, though sales waned in the 1920s, there have been a number of revivals of interest. In the 1940s works by new cyclical historians such as Arnold Toynbee, Pitrim A. Sorokin and Alfred L. Kroeber invited comparison.[6] Though these 'new Spenglerians' were really 'anti-Spenglerians', they recognised that Spengler had shattered the prevalent linear model of history and opened a discourse on the 'lives' of world cultures. Spengler's ideas were also adopted and adapted by poets such as T. S. Eliot, Ezra Pound, Yeats and W. H. Auden, novelists like F. Scott Fitzgerald and philosophers such as Ludwig Wittgenstein.[7] In the 1960s and 1970s, fears of overpopulation and the rapid expansion of communism into Asia led many to turn back to Spengler. In *Twilight of the Evening Lands*, for instance, James Fennelly saw much to suggest that the West was in a state of decline. Similarly, pessimistic works can also be found from the 1980s and 1990s.[8] In the 1990s Spengler's ideas also began to appear in a number of neo-fascist and racist web sites.[9] Given Spengler's views on Nazism, this is ironic. The continuing popularity of *The Decline of the West* is not due to what Spengler says about the past, but to what he says about the present. As Hughes concludes:

> It formulates more comprehensively than any other single book the modern malaise that so many feel and so few can express. It has become the classic summary of the now familiar pessimism of the twentieth century West with regard to its own historical future.[10]

Notes

1 L. Wittgenstein, *Philosophical Remarks*, ed. R. Rhees, trans. R. Hargreaves and R. White, New York: Barnes & Noble, preface.

2 Quoted in H. S. Hughes, *Oswald Spengler, a Critical Estimate*, New York: Scribner, 1952, p. 127.

3 J. Farrenkopf, 'The Transformation of Spengler's Philosophy of World History', *Journal of the History of Ideas*, 1991, 52(3): 463–85.

4 M. Schroeter, *Der Streit um Spengler: Kritik seiner Kritiker*, Munich: C. H. Beck, 1922; id., *Die Metaphysik des Untergangs*, Munich: Leibniz-Verlag, 1949; id., *Spengler-Studien*, Munich: C. H. Beck, 1965; E. Meyer, *Spenglers Untergang de Abendlandes*, Berlin: 1925. For a description of these, see Hughes, *Oswald Spengler*, p. 93.

5 See, for instance, H. Barth, *Truth and Ideology*, Berkeley, CA: University of California Press, 1976; D. A. Messer, *Oswald Spengler als Philosoph*, Stuttgart: Drud von Streder, 1927; E. Heller, *The Disinherited Mind*, New York: Harcourt Brace Jovanovich, 1975, pp. 179–96; M. Braun, 'Bury, Spengler and the New Spenglerians', *History Today*, 1952, 7(8): 525–9; and W. Lewis, *Time and Western Man*, revised edition, ed. P. Edwards, Santa Rosa, CA: Black Sparrow Press, 1993.

6 A. Toynbee, *A Study of History*, 12 vols, London: Oxford University Press, 1935–61; P. A. Sorokin, *Social and Cultural Dynamics*, New York: American Book Company, 1937–41; and A. L. Kroeber, *Configurations of Culture Growth*, Berkeley, CA: University of California Press, 1944.

7 On the influence of Spengler on twentieth-century poetry, see N. Frye, 'The Decline of the West by Oswald Spengler', *Daedalus*, 1972, 103(1): 1–13. On Fitzgerald and Spengler, see J. S. Whitley, 'A Touch of Disaster: Fitzgerald, Spengler and the Decline of the West', in A. R. Lee (ed.) *Scott Fitzgerald: the Promises of Life*, London: St Martin's Press, 1990, pp. 157–80; and J. Kirkby, 'Spengler and Apocalyptic Typology in F. Scott Fitzgerald's *Tender is the Night*', *Southern Review: Literary and Interdisciplinary Essays*, 1979, 12(3): 246–61. And on Spengler and Wittgenstein, see J. Bouveresse, '"The Darkness of this Time":

Wittgenstein and the Modern World', in G. A. Phillips (ed.) *Wittgenstein Centenary Essays*, Cambridge: Cambridge University Press, 1991, pp. 11–39; and W. M. DeAngelis, 'Wittgenstein and Spengler', *Dialogue* [Canada], 1994, 33(1): 41–61.

8 See J. F. Fennelly, *Twilight of the Evening Lands: Oswald Spengler a Half Century Later*, New York: Brookdale Press, 1972; T. Sunic, 'History and Decadence: Spengler's Cultural Pessimism Today', *Clio*, 1989, 19(1): 51–62; and K. P. Fischer, *History and Prophecy: Oswald Spengler and the Decline of the West*, New York: Peter Lang, 1989.

9 On Spengler and the web, see, for example, the article by R. Eatwell of the *Manchester Guardian Weekly*, 24 September 1995. See also R. C. Thurlow, 'Destiny and Doom: Spengler, Hitler and "British" Fascism', *Patterns of Prejudice*, 1981, 15(4): 17–33.

10 Hughes, *Oswald Spengler*, p. 165.

Spengler's major works

Heraklit eine Studie, Halle: Kaemmerer, 1904.

Der metaphysische Grundgedanke der Heraklitschen Philosophie, Halle: Kaemmerer, 1904.

The Decline of the West, trans. C. F. Atkinson, 2 vols, New York: Alfred A. Knopf, 1926–8.

Preussentum und Sozialismus, Munich: C. H. Beck, 1926.

Man and Technics; a Contribution to a Philosophy of Life, trans. C. F. Atkinson, New York: Alfred A. Knopf, 1932.

Politische Schriften, Munich: C. H. Beck, 1933.

The Hour of Decision, trans. C. F. Atkinson, New York: Alfred A. Knopf, 1934.

See also

Ibn Khaldun, Polybius, Toynbee, Vico, Wittgenstein (MP).

Further resources

Collingwood, R. G., 'Oswald Spengler and the Theory of Historical Cycles', *Antiquity*, 1927, 1: 311–25, 435–46.

Costello, P., *World Historians and their Goals: Twentieth Century Answers to Modernism*, DeKalb, IL: Northern Illinois University Press, 1993.

Farrenkopf, J., 'Hegel, Spengler and the Enigma of World History: Progress or Decline?' *Clio*, 1990, 19(4): 331–44.

——, 'The Transformation of Spengler's Philosophy of World History', *Journal of the History of Ideas*, 1991, 52(3): 463–85.

Fennelly, J. F., *Twilight of the Evening Lands: Oswald Spengler a Half Century Later*, New York: Brookdale Press, 1972.

Fischer, K. P., *History and Prophecy: Oswald Spengler and the Decline of the West*, New York: Peter Lang, 1989.

Frye, N., 'The Decline of the West by Oswald Spengler', *Daedalus*, 1972, 103(1): 1–13.

Hughes, H. S., *Oswald Spengler, a Critical Estimate*, New York: Scribner & Sons, 1952.

McNeill, W. H., 'The Changing Shape of World History', *History and Theory*, 1995, 34(2): 8–26.

Sunic, T., 'History and Decadence: Spengler's Cultural Pessimism Today', *Clio*, 1989, 19(1): 51–62.

Toynbee, A., *A Study of History*, 12 vols, London: Oxford University Press, 1934–61.

SSU-MA CH'IEN *c. 145–c.* 90 BC

Nearly all that we know of the life of the 'grand historian of China', Ssu-ma Ch'ien (also spelt Sima Qian and Se-ma Ts'ien), derives from two sources: the 'Postface' to his *Shih chi* (also spelt *Shi ji*, trans. *Records of the Grand Historian*) and a letter that he wrote to Jen Shao-ch'ing.[1] Ssu-ma Ch'ien was the son of Ssu-ma T'an, the grand historian/astrologer at the court of the Han Emperor Wu from 140 to 110 BC.[2] The duties of this office included selecting lucky days for the performance of important affairs, travelling with the ruler at times of important sacrifices and keeping a record of daily events. At the age of ten, Ssu-ma Ch'ien could 'read the old writings' and by twenty he had travelled extensively ('Shih chi 130', in *Ssu-ma Ch'ien, Grand Historian of China*, p. 48). He entered court service, and after his father died succeeded him in the post of grand historian/ astrologer. He started to write the *Shih chi* but before he completed it 'disaster' overtook him and he was made to 'submit to the worst of all punishments'.[3] In coming to the aid of a defeated general, Li Ling, Ssu-ma Ch'ien offended Emperor Wu. The Emperor sentenced him to death, and then reduced the penalty to castration. Ordinarily, those who could not afford to commute the sentence with a large cash payment committed suicide. Ssu-ma Ch'ien, however, submitted to the punishment in order to complete the *Shih chi*.

Underpinning Ssu-ma Ch'ien's decision to complete the *Shih chi* is a respect for and identification with Confucius.[4] It was, Ssu-ma Ch'ien tells us, his father's dying wish that he complete the historical record that he had begun. The act of writing the *Shih chi* was thus bound up with respect for the Confucian virtue of filial devotion. But his father also suggested that in completing the *Shih chi* Ssu-ma Ch'ien would continue the work of Confucius, in gathering and reviving Chinese traditions and *li* or moral principles (ibid., pp. 49–50). One of the products of Confucius's efforts was thought to be the *Spring and Autumn Annals*. Ostensibly, the *Annals* is a terse chronicle of the reigns of twelve dukes of the state of Lu from 722 to 484 BC. To scholars of its three commentary traditions – *Tso*, *Kung-yang* and *Ku-liang* – however, Confucius's order of presentation and choice of material and even words suggest judgements upon the events of the past. For them, the *Annals* is a guide to moral conduct. Ssu-ma Ch'ien views the *Annals* in a similar fashion:

> It distinguishes what is suspicious and doubtful, clarifies right and wrong, and settles points which are uncertain. It calls good good and bad bad, honours the worthy, and condemns the unworthy. It preserves states which are lost and restores the perishing family. It brings to light what was neglected and restores what was abandoned.
>
> (Ibid., p. 51)

Ssu-ma Ch'ien's *Shih chi* is written with the same purpose in mind. This aim is apparent throughout the work, but emerges particularly clearly in chapter 61. There he asks:

> Some people say: 'It is Heaven's way, without distinction of persons, to keep the good perpetually supplied.' Can we say then that Po I and Shu Ch'i were good men or not? They clung to righteousness and were pure in their deeds . . . and yet they starved to death. . . . Robber Chih day after day killed innocent men, making mincemeat of their flesh. . . . But in the end he lived to a great old age. For what virtue did he deserve this? . . . I find myself in much perplexity. Is this so-called 'Way of Heaven' right or wrong?
>
> (In *Ssu-ma Ch'ien, Grand Historian of China*, pp. 188–9)

In response he cites a number of aphorisms of Confucius, including: 'The sage arises and all creation becomes clear.' Ssu-ma Ch'ien's point is that, although the wicked may sometimes prosper and the good suffer, wise historians will eventually restore the reputation of the good and show the wicked for what they are.[5] Such a belief clearly motivates comments like this:

> Su Ch'in and his two brothers all achieved fame among the feudal lords as itinerant strategists. Their policies laid great stress upon stratagems and shifts of power. But because Su Ch'in died a traitor's death, the world has united in scoffing at him and has been loath to study his policies. . . . Su Ch'in arose from the humblest beginnings to lead the Six States in

the Vertical Alliance, and this is evidence that he possessed an intelligence surpassing the ordinary person. For this reason I have set forth this account of his deeds, arranging them in proper chronological order, so that he may not forever suffer from an evil reputation and be known for nothing else.[6]

Pointing to the good and the bad could get a writer in trouble. One way to avoid such trouble was to follow the tradition of oblique criticism attributed to Confucius in the *Spring and Autumn Annals*. At the end of chapter 110, Ssu-ma shows that he is aware of that tradition:

> When Confucius wrote the *Spring and Autumn Annals*, he was very open in treating the reigns of Yin and Huan, the early dukes of Lu; but when he came to the later period of Dukes Ding and Ai, his writing was much more covert. Because in the latter case he was writing about his own times, he did not express his judgements frankly, but used subtle and guarded language.
>
> (*Records of the Grand Historian*, 110:II:162)[7]

It is unlikely, as Watson suggests, that Ssu-ma Ch'ien intended every word of his writings to convey moral judgements. There are places, however, where one gets the impression that he is being critical about his times.[8] For example, Ssu-ma Ch'ien's comments on Confucius's use of oblique criticism are located in a chapter on the Hsiung Nu barbarians and may signal his disagreement with Emperor Wu's policies towards them (see also 10:I:310).[9]

He also follows Confucius's directive in the *Analects* to '[h]ear much, but leave to one side that which is doubtful, and speak with due caution concerning the remainder'.[10] He sets boundaries beyond which he cannot obtain reliable information. For example, he tells us that '[t]he ages before the Ch'in dynasty are too far away and the material on them too scanty to permit a detailed account of them here' (ibid., 49:I:324; see also 17:I:423; 18:I:429; 30:II:83; 127:II:431; 129:II:433). He also expresses his doubts about information that appears unbelievable. In chapter 86, for instance, he dismisses as 'ridiculous' the claim that Prince Tan was able to make the heavens rain grain and horses sprout horns.[11] The reliability of information, he believes, can be established by comparison with the six Confucian classics (*Book of Odes*, *Book of History*, *Book of Rites*, *Book of Music*, *Book of Changes* and *Spring and Autumn Annals*). When faced with details not mentioned in the Classics,

Ssu-ma Ch'ien suggests comparison with other documents. In the *Shih chi*, Ssu-ma Ch'ien refers to more than 75 documents, inscriptions and memorials. He also recommends personal observation. Ssu-ma Ch'ien seems to have taken advantage of his office to question individuals in the capital (ibid., 7:I:47–8; 95:I:206; 97:I:231; 104:I:493). He was well travelled, and often mentions information gathered during his journeys:

> When I had occasion to pass through Feng and Pei I questioned the elderly people who were about the place, visited the old home of Xiao He, Cao Can, Fan Kuai, and Xiahou Ying, and learned much about their early days. How different it was from the stories one hears!
>
> (Ibid., 95:I:205; see also 84:I:451–2; 29:II:60)

Ssu-ma Ch'ien questioned the oldest informants available because he thought that they would supply him with the most accurate information. He also examined sites and relics: he tells us he was awe-stricken at the sight of Confucius's carriage, clothes and sacrificial vessels.[12]

Ssu-ma Ch'ien is indebted to Confucian thought in a number of ways. But four important features of the *Shih chi* stand out as original. First, unlike earlier histories, which tended to focus on a particular region or dynasty, the *Shih chi* is a history of the known world. Its 130 chapters cover the history of China and a number of lands on its borders from the time of the legendary Yellow Emperor (2697?–2599? BC) to Ssu-ma Ch'ien's own times. Second, Ssu-ma Ch'ien draws on a more varied collection of source materials than his predecessors. As outlined above, he looked to people, objects and sites, as well as documents, as sources of information. Third, the *Shih chi* looks beyond the boundaries of the court. Finally, in the *Shih chi* Ssu-ma Ch'ien departs from the tradition of chronological arrangement. It is instead organised into five sections: basic annals (*pen-chi*, 12 chapters), chronological tables (*piao*, 10 chapters), treatises (*shu*, 8 chapters), hereditary houses (*shih-chia*, 30 chapters) and biographies (*lieh-chuan*, 70 chapters) ('Shih chi 130' in *Ssu-ma Ch'ien, Grand Historian of China*, pp. 56–7). The basic annals detail the history of dynastic houses and individual emperors. Next come the chronological tables, which present events in graph form. These are followed by treatises on topics such as hydraulic engineering, astronomy, economics, the calendar, rites, music and religious affairs. Following the treatises are the hereditary houses, which detail the history of prominent hereditary office-holding families. The final section, the biographies, is dedicated to the lives of individuals, foreign peoples and peoples of similar disposition, social status or profession (such as the families of empresses, philosophers, frustrated poets, assassins, harsh officials, jesters, diviners and tycoons).[13] Within each of these sections, the chapters are arranged chronologically.

It is through this structure that Ssu-ma Ch'ien conveys his moral judgements. As Watson comments:

> The various large sections and one-hundred-and-thirty chapters of the *Shih chi* represent no merely arbitrary divisions of Ch'ien's material. Each one is a significant formal unit whose contents have been selected and disposed with care and intention.[14]

What he includes and where tell us a great deal about him. In the final chapter, Ssu-ma Ch'ien tells us that the arrangement of his sections is hierarchical; the subjects of the biographies, for instance, wield less power than the subjects of the basic annals. Where Ssu-ma Ch'ien places particular individuals conveys his judgement on how powerful or important they were. For example, Hsian Yü and Empress Lü were the real rulers of China during the reigns of I of Ch'u and Hui of the Han. Ssu-ma Ch'ien includes the former in the place of the latter in the basic annals. Similarly, in granting Ch'en she and Confucius places in the hereditary houses, he sets them apart from the subjects of the biographies section in which they ought to have been included. Ssu-ma Ch'ien is also able to make his judgements known through the distribution of material, as his five-part arrangement allows him to describe the same individual or event in several different chapters. As a number of commentators have noted, he does not always tell the story in the same way. In addition, he mentions details about individuals not found in chapters dedicated to their biography. This can be a form of oblique criticism, as is seen in the case of the rivals Emperor Kao-tsu and Hsiang Yü. In their own chapters in the basic annals, they are presented in a favourable light. Their bad points are revealed in their rivals' chapter.[15] Differences also result when Ssu-ma Ch'ien tries to avoid repeating phrases and words and when he copies earlier histories verbatim.

Finally, Ssu-ma Ch'ien also reveals his personal reactions and moral judgements in the comment sections which can be found at the end of most chapters. For instance, he frequently comments on the consequences of pursuing or failing to pursue Chinese values such as determination, humility, generosity, filial respect and concern for the common people (see, for example, 10:I:310; 53:I:98; 57:I:380; and 84:I:451–2). In addition, we learn something of his view of the nature of historical research. The above discussion on his use of sources, for example, is based in the main on the sections in which 'the grand historian/astrologer speaks'.[16]

Ssu-ma Ch'ien's *Shih chi* has been enormously influential in China, Japan and Korea. Although its form has seldom been replicated, it was the model for many single and multiple dynasty histories. However, his belief that history is a moral endeavour may not be to the modern reader's taste. Nor is the *Shih chi* easy to read. Its length and structure make it hard to find all the relevant information on individuals and events. But one of the things that makes it hard to read – its lack of a unified narrative voice – may in fact make it more appealing. As Hardy has pointed out, Ssu-ma Ch'ien may have much to offer historians such as Davis in this book who are interested in fragmented and multiple voice narratives.[17] It is thus a pity that so little of the *Shih chi* is available in English. Less than half of the work, covering in the main the Han Dynasty, has been translated into English and its five-part structure has not been preserved. Until what remains of the whole work is translated and its structure is restored, we will have a sadly limited understanding of how richly the 'grand historian/astrologer speaks'.[18]

Notes

1 A translation of Ssu-ma Ch'ien's letter may be found on p. xiii of Watson's *Records of the Grand Historian*, and on p. 101 of C. Birch (ed.) *Anthology of Chinese Literature*, New York: Grove Press, vol. 1, 1965.

2 There is some dispute over the translation of the office of *t'ai shih ling*. Watson translated this as 'grand historian', but Dubs and Hardy believe that 'grand astrologer' is more accurate. As the office seemed to entail activities that could be described using both terms, I will opt for 'historian/astrologer'. On this debate, see H. H. Dubs, 'History and Historians under the Han', *Journal of Asian Studies*, 1961, 20(2): 213–15, and G. R. Hardy, 'Objectivity and Interpretation in the "Shih chi"', PhD thesis, Yale University, 1988, pp. 1–2.

3 Ssu-ma Ch'ien's letter to Jen Shao-ch'ing, in Birch (ed.) *Anthology of Chinese Literature*, p. 101.

4 S. W. Durrant, 'Self as the Intersection of Traditions: the Autobiographical Writings of Ssu-ma Ch'ien', *Journal of the American Oriental Society*, 1986, 106(1): 37.

5 Hardy, 'Objectivity and Interpretation in the "Shih chi"', pp. 47–63.

6 Chap. 69, as quoted in ibid., p. 156.

7 Citations refer to the chapter, volume and page number of Watson's translation.

8 B. Watson, *Ssu-ma Ch'ien, Grand Historian of China*, New York: Columbia University Press, 1958, pp. 93–4; id., 'Introduction', *Records of the Grand Historian*, p. xviii.

9 Watson, *Ssu-ma Ch'ien*, pp. 94–5; Hardy, 'Objectivity and Interpretation in the "Shih chi"', p. 80.

10 *The Analects of Confucius*, trans. A. Waley, London: Allen & Unwin, 1989, 15.25. See also 2.18 and *Shih chi*, chap. 13, quoted in Watson, *Ssu-ma Ch'ien, Grand Historian of China*, p. 86.
11 Quoted in Hardy, 'Objectivity and Interpretation in the "Shih chi"', p. 136.
12 Ibid., p. 127.
13 G. R. Hardy's translation. See 'Can an Ancient Chinese Historian Contribute to Modern Western Theory?' *History and Theory*, 1994, 33(1): 20–38.
14 Watson, *Ssu-ma Ch'ien*, p. 95.
15 Ibid., p. 98; Hardy, 'Objectivity and Interpretation in the "Shih chi"', p. 96.
16 On the voice of Ssu-ma Ch'ien in the form of the *Shih chi*, see Watson, *Ssu-ma Ch'ien*, pp. 101–34; Hardy, 'Objectivity and Interpretation in the "Shih chi"', pp. 84–112; and J. R. Allen III, 'An Introductory Study of Narrative Structure in the *Shi ji*', *Chinese Literature: Essays, Articles, Reviews*, 1981, 3(1): 31–66.
17 Hardy, 'Can an Ancient Chinese Historian Contribute to Modern Western Theory?' p. 38.
18 One chapter is missing and several others appear to be incomplete. See Watson, *Records of the Grand Historian*, vol. 1, p. xv.

Ssu-ma Ch'ien's major works

Records of the Grand Historian, 2 vols, trans. B. Watson, New York: Columbia University Press, 1961, revised edition 1993.
The Grand Scribe's Records, ed. and trans. W. H. Nienhauser, Jnr, T.-F. Chang and others, Bloomington, IN: Indiana University Press, 2 vols, 1944– .
'Shi chi 130: the Postface of the Grand Historian', in B. Watson, *Ssu-ma Ch'ien, Grand Historian of China*, New York: Columbia University Press, 1958, pp. 42–69.
Les mémoires historiques de Se-ma Ts'ien, 6 vols, trans. E. Chavannes, Paris: E. Leroux, 1895–1905 and 1969 (vol. 6).

See also

Davis, Froissart.

Further resources

Allen, J. R., 'An Introductory Study of Narrative Structure in the *Shi ji*', *Chinese Literature: Essays, Articles and Reviews*, 1981, 3(1): 31–66.
—— 'Records of the Historian', in B. S. Miller (ed.) *Masterworks of Asian Literature in Comparative Perspective: A Guide for Teaching*, Armonk, NY: Sharpe, 1994, pp. 259–71.
Beasley, W. G. and Pulleyblank, E. G. (eds) *Historians of China and Japan*, London: Oxford University Press, 1961.
Dubs, H. H., 'History and Historians under the Han', *Journal of Asian Studies*, 1961, 20(2): 213–18.
Durrant, S. W., 'Self as the Intersection of Tradition: the Autobiographical Writings of Ssu-ma Ch'ien', *Journal of the American Oriental Society*, 1986, 106(1): 33–40.

Gardner, C. S., *Chinese Traditional Historiography*, Cambridge, MA: Harvard University Press, 1970.

Hardy, G. R., 'Objectivity and Interpretation in the "Shih chi"', PhD thesis, Yale University, 1988.

—— 'Can an Ancient Chinese Historian Contribute to Modern Western Theory?' *History and Theory*, 1994, 33(1): 20–38.

Kroll, J. L., 'Ssu-ma Ch'ien's Literary Theory and Literary Practice', *Altorientalische Forshungen*, 1976, 4: 313–25.

Li, W. Y., 'The Idea of Authority in the *Shih chi* (*Records of the Historian*)', *Harvard Journal of Asiatic Studies*, 1994, 54(2): 345–405.

Moloughney, B., 'From Biographical History to Historical Biography: a Transformation in Chinese Historical Writing', *East Asian History*, 1992, 4: 1–30.

Watson, B. (1958) *Ssu-ma Ch'ien, Grand Historian of China*, New York: Columbia University Press, 1958.

TACITUS *c.* 56–*c.* 117

Historians tell us about the good, the bad and the ugly of the past. One historian who concentrated on the ugly was Tacitus, whose *Histories* and *Annals* of Rome from AD 14–96 capture in vivid terms 'a period rich in disasters, terrible with battles, torn by civil struggles, horrible even in peace' (*Histories*, 1.2).[1]

Few details of Cornelius Tacitus' life are known. As Roman law and convention specified with fair precision the ages and stages of advancement for those who wanted a senatorial career, and because we know some of the dates at which Tacitus held various offices, it can be inferred that he was born around AD 56. He was born either in Cisalpine Gaul (northern Italy) or in southern Gaul (Provence) and moved to Rome to complete his education. In his *Histories* (1.1.3) he tells us that his status as a member of the senatorial order began under Vespasian (69–79), increased under Titus (79–81), and was advanced considerably under Domitian (81–96). Tacitus would have begun his public career in a minor civil post, followed at about the age of twenty by a short period of military service as a tribune. In 77 he married the daughter of Gnaeus Julius Agricola, who was to be governor of Britain. Around 81 he was elected to the quaestorship (which brought membership of the Senate) and in 88 he attained a praetorship and became a member of the college of the *quindecimviri sacris faciundis*, a body of priests who had charge of the oracular Sibylline books (*Annals*, 11.11.1). For four years after his praetorship, during which Domitian undertook a savage purge of the Senate, Tacitus was away from Rome on unspecified assignments. When he returned to Rome he attained the office of suffect consul. During that time he delivered the funeral oration for Verginius Rufus, a soldier who could have claimed power after Nero's death but who preferred to leave the choice of ruler to the Senate.[2] Along with Pliny the Younger, he also took part in the prosecution of Marius Priscus (the proconsul of Africa) on charges of cruelty and maladministration. According to Pliny, 'Cornelius Tacitus made an eloquent speech . . . with all the majesty which characterises his style of oratory.'[3] Around 112 he was appointed to the prestigious proconsulship of Asia. He died probably around 117.

Before he wrote the works for which he is best known – the *Histories* and the *Annals* – Tacitus composed three short essays: *Agricola*, *Germania* and *Dialogus*. The first of these is an account of the life of his father-in-law, Gnaeus Julius Agricola. It begins with an introduction (chapters 1–3), and details of Agricola's birth, early life and training and political career up to the governorship of Britain occupy chapters 4 to 9. Chapters 30 to 34 survey the history of Rome's campaigns and the administrative achievements of Agricola. Chapters 39 to 43 tell of Agricola's recall to Rome, and 44 to 46 detail the last years of his life. *Agricola* is an intriguing work. Though it focuses on the life of Agricola, large segments are also devoted to historical and ethnographical matters; for example, chapters 10 to 12 focus on the history, ethnography and geography of Britain. In these chapters, Tacitus seems to follow the precedent established by Greek historians such as Herodotus of describing the area covered in the main narrative. Thus it appears that *Agricola* is a blend of history and biography.[4]

Agricola also offers us a glimpse of why Tacitus wrote. As in his later works, Tacitus conveys his views of what senators should and should not do. His portrayal of the contemporary Roman political system is highly critical. This is paradoxical, as Martin has pointed out, because Tacitus advanced unhindered through all the stages of a senatorial career.[5] Some commentators have wondered whether he felt guilty about his good fortune during Domitian's rule. It is more likely, however, that he was able to be critical because at the time he wrote a more liberal era had begun under Trajan (98–117). Senators can be openly critical about the emperor, Tacitus tells us. Such openness, though, may lead to their exile or death. He still thinks it possible, however, for senators to discharge their duties and to avoid becoming instruments of the emperor's despotism. To do so, they must serve the state with modesty. This is the course that Gnaeus Julius Agricola tried to follow:

> Despite Domitian's proclivity to an anger that was the more inexorable as it was more concealed, he was appeased by

the restraint and wisdom of Agricola, who did not by a defiant and futile parade of liberty court a renown that must result in his death. Let those who like to admire what is forbidden realise that even under bad emperors great men can exist, if backed by a keen determination, can achieve a renown such as many have attained only by perilous courses that have brought an ostentatious death without any advantage to the state.

(*Agricola*, 42)

Tacitus hoped that his readers would adopt Agricola's approach. He also singles out individuals who acted with self-restraint in his later writings (for example, *Annals*, 4.20; 6.27; 12.12; 14.47).

A number of commentators believe that Tacitus wrote his second work, *Germania*, in order to contrast the virtues of the barbaric Germans with the vices of contemporary Rome.[6] Unlike the Romans, for instance, the Germans do not allow individuals to possess absolute power (*Germania*, chap. 11). Recently this has been argued against on the grounds that the failings of the Germans are emphasised as much as their virtues, and that, where moral comment occurs, it does not involve a criticism of the Roman way of life.[7] For instance, he notes that the Germans were often drunk and were addicted to gambling (chaps 23 and 24). In addition, the second half of the work – devoted to a description of the various German tribes – has little to do with virtues and vices. Some commentators believe that Tacitus wrote *Germania* in order to demonstrate that Germany was Rome's most powerful enemy. For example, in his account of the defeat of the Bructeri at the hands of the Germans he comments:

More than 60,000 fell, not by Roman arms but, what is far grander, before our delighted eyes. I pray that, if not love for us, at least mutual hatred may persist among them, since fortune can give us no greater gift than discord among our foes, as the destinies of empire urge us ever onward.

(Ibid., chap. 33)

This political message, however, seems to occupy only a small part of the work. It is likely that in *Germania*, as in *Agricola*, we see a combination of motives. Tacitus wrote it because he was interested in the German peoples, disappointed with the practices of his contemporaries and fearful of invasion.

Tacitus' third work is *Dialogus de oratoribus*, and its subject is a fictional debate on the decline of oratory. This work is comprised of three sets of speeches: first, Marcus Aper and Maternus argue about the merits of oratory and poetry (chaps 5–13); second, Aper and Maternus argue, respectively, the merits of contemporary oratory and those of 'ancient' oratory (such as Cicero and his contemporaries) (chaps 14–27); and finally, Messalla and Maternus offer their explanations of the decline in oratory. To Messalla the decline is simply the result of falling moral and educational standards. Maternus disagrees and argues that great oratory is the product of social and political instability. With power concentrated in the hands of the emperor, there is no place for contentious oratory. In these last speeches we see that the *Dialogus* is thus not only a work of literary analysis but also an attempt to examine the impact of political change.

Tacitus' fascination with political change is brought to the fore in his two later works, the *Histories* and the *Annals*. When complete, these works comprised thirty books and covered the period from the death of Augustus (AD 14) to the death of Domitian (96). The *Histories* is the earlier of the two, though its fourteen books cover the later period (69–96). Of these only books 1–4 have survived complete, while book 5 breaks off at chapter 26 (August 70).

In introducing his *Histories* Tacitus draws a clear distinction between the eloquent and outspoken historians of the Roman Republic and those of the Empire, who, he claims, were ignorant of politics and either sycophantic or openly hostile to the imperial regime. 'Those who profess inviolable fidelity to truth', he writes, 'must write of no man with affection or hatred' (1.1). This does not mean that Tacitus refrains from moral judgement; simply that he is on guard against partiality and dislike when writing of individuals he did not know personally. With this aim in mind, Tacitus offers a year-by-year account of a period torn by conflict (1.2).

For more than 100 years the Julio-Claudians ruled the Roman world in dynastic succession. Though there were times of tension between the Senate and the emperor, the state was stable. After the suicide of Nero, however, it became clear that only the leaders of the various armies were able to enforce their wishes when there was no clear-cut choice for the throne. People also realised that the emperor could be proclaimed outside Rome (1.4), which led to a bitter struggle for power among military leaders in the years 69–70.

The first four books of the *Histories* are devoted to those two years. In book 1, Tacitus provides a brief account of the reign of Galba, the adoption of Piso Licinianus as his successor, and the revolution that placed Salvius Otho in power and that cost Galba and Piso their lives (1.5–49). Here Tacitus stresses, first, that in passing over Otho as heir for the throne, Galba prompted Otho to seek retribution with the help of the Praetorian Guard, and second, that the Roman people acted purely out of self-interest. This is followed by an account of the uprising of the legions in Germany, where Vitellius was proclaimed emperor, the advance of these troops towards Italy and Otho's preparations to meet them (1.50–90). In the opening of book 2 Tacitus directs our attention to another contender for power: Vespasian. He then turns back to Italy and to the struggle between the forces of Otho and Vitellius, which ends with Otho's defeat at the battle of Bedriacum and his suicide (2.11–50). The rest of book 2 covers the reign of Vitellius, which was quickly threatened by the proclamation in Egypt and Syria of Vespasian as emperor (2.51–101). Tacitus clearly dislikes Vitellius: he is portrayed as an indolent, self-indulgent man who is easily manipulated by his lieutenants (1.62). Book 3 focuses on the struggles between the adherents of Vespasian and Vitellius. The latter is defeated and meets a miserable end at the hands of a mob. In what remains of book 5, we learn of the revolt of Claudius Civilis in Gaul and Germany and the Jewish war conducted by Vespasian and his son Titus.

politics

After Tacitus wrote the *Histories*, he looked backward, not forward. He sought the causes of current political problems in the early years of the Empire. The result, the *Annals*, covered the period from the death of Augustus (AD 14) to the death of Nero (68). The death of Augustus and the reign of Tiberius occupy six books, all of which survive except much of book 5; Gaius Caligula and Claudius were dealt with in a further six books, of which only the last book and a half of Claudius' reign survive (AD 47–57); for Nero's reign, three-and-a-half books have survived (books 13–16), taking the narrative from his accession in 54 to mid-66.

In both the *Histories* and the *Annals*, Tacitus concentrates much of his attention on the actions and intentions of individuals. Though he hoped to write of the emperors 'without anger and partiality' he often had to rely on authorities, some of which he considered to be biased. Sometimes he names these authorities, but more often he talks in general terms of 'writers', 'we have received the following account', 'there is agreement', 'it is disputed whether', 'following the majority of writers' and 'it is believed/rumoured/said' (for example, *Histories*, 3.38; *Annals*, 1.13, 3.71, 4.57, 13.20). In line with the opinion of earlier writers, Tacitus believed that if an individual's character seemed to change, the only explanation was that in the earlier stages of their life their real character had not yet been revealed. This view of character underpins Tacitus' account of Tiberius. Tacitus believed that Tiberius sought to conceal his true character from those about him. He thus considers it his duty to let his readers know what Tiberius was really like. For example, he writes:

> the diction of Tiberius, by habit or by nature, was always indirect or obscure, even when he had no wish to conceal his thought; and now, in the effort to bury every trace of his sentiments, it became even more intricate, uncertain, and equivocal than ever.
>
> (*Annals*, 1.11)

Tacitus thus warns his readers that an individual's ideas and actions can be deceptive. Others are more obviously dangerous. Nero, for instance, was given to self-indulgence and self-display. In Tacitus' opinion, Nero behaved in a disgraceful manner:

> It was an old desire of his to drive a chariot and team of four, and an equally repulsive ambition to sing to the lyre in the stage manner. . . . He could no longer be checked, when Seneca and Burrus decided to concede one of his points rather than allow him to carry both; and an enclosure was made in the Vatican valley, where he could manoeuvre his horses without the spectacle being public. Before long, the Roman people received an invitation in form, and began to hymn his praises, as is the way of the crowd, hungry for amusements, and delighted if the sovereign draws in the same direction.
>
> (Ibid., 14.14)

Although there are some passages in the *Histories* and the *Annals* that 'ensure that merit shall not lack its record', in many more places it is clear that he wants to 'hold before the vicious word and deed the terrors of posterity and infamy' (ibid., 3.65). While an emperor may be able to burn books when he is alive, he has no control over what is written after his death. Emperors cannot escape, Tacitus tells us, the harsh light of history.

Many commentators agree that Tacitus' works have a rich literary quality. He shows us in striking detail an empire set on a course of self-destruction. To some writers he is 'the authentic voice of ancient Rome' and 'the greatest painter of antiquity'. Every page of his writings shows his extensive rhetorical training, but it emerges with most clarity in his use of speeches to shape and direct the narrative. Tacitus uses direct (*oratio recta*) and invented (*oratio obliqua*) speeches to delineate character, summarise the thoughts of groups of people, convey popular rumour, justify his assertions and highlight political and moral positions. This quality of his writings has made them attractive both to playwrights such as Ben Johnson and Jean Racine and to writers such as Robert Graves. With the adaptation of Graves's writings into the BBC television series I *Claudius* (1976), Tacitus even became a household name for a time. What scholars disagree about is whether Tacitus' writings are too carefully crafted and too judgemental to be works of *history*. To writers like Turtellian, for instance, he is 'a first class chatterbox when it comes to lies'.[8] Tacitus would be puzzled, I believe, at scholars' attempts to demarcate history from fiction and morality.

Notes

1 Citations correspond to book and chapter numbers of the Loeb Classical Library edition.
2 Pliny the Younger, *Letters and Panegyricus*, trans. B. Radice, Loeb Classical Library, London: Heinemann, 1969, vol. 1, 2.1.6.
3 Ibid., vol. 1, 2.11.17–18.
4 On *Agricola*, see F. R. D. Goodyear, *Tacitus*, Oxford: Oxford University Press, 1970, chap. 1.
5 R. Martin, *Tacitus*, Berkeley, CA: University of California Press, 1981, p. 38.
6 For a critical discussion on this view see ibid., pp. 39–49.
7 Ibid., pp. 49–58.
8 Tertullian, *Apologeticus*, trans. G. H. Rendall, Loeb Classical Library, London, Heinemann, 16.3.

Tacitus' major works

Tacitus: Agricola, Germania, Dialogus, Histories, Annals, 5 vols, trans. C. H. Moore, J. Jackson, H. Hutton, R. M. Ogilvie, E. H. Warmington, W. Peterson and M. Winterbottom, Loeb Classical Library, London: Heinemann, 1967–70.
The Histories, trans. K. Wellesley, Harmondsworth: Penguin, 1964.

See also

Froissart, Gibbon, Herodotus, Livy, Polybius, Thucydides, Vico.

Further resources

Benario, H. W., *An Introduction to Tacitus*, Athens, GA: University of Georgia Press, 1975.
Dorey, T. A. (ed.) *Tacitus*, London: Routledge & Kegan Paul, 1969.
Goodyear, F. R. D., *Tacitus*, Oxford: Oxford University Press, 1970.
I Claudius [video recording], The BBC and London Films, 1976, distributed by Network Video Distribution, 1993.
Luce, T. J. and Woodman, A. J., *Tacitus and the Tacitean Tradition*, Princeton, NJ: Princeton University Press, 1993.

Martin, R., *Tacitus*, Berkeley, CA: University of California Press, 1981.

Mellor, R., *Tacitus*, London: Routledge, 1993.

——, *The Roman Historians*, London: Routledge, 1999.

Sinclair, P., *Tacitus the Sententious Historian: a Sociology of Rhetoric in Annals 1–6*, University Park, PA: Pennsylvania State University Press, 1995.

Syme, R., *Tacitus*, 2 vols, Oxford: Oxford University Press, revised edition, 1990.

A. J. P. TAYLOR 1906–90

Alan John Percivale Taylor was, like many of the individuals he wrote about, a troublemaker. He was, Segal suggests, 'a dedicated individualist, a scholar devoted to fostering the angularities and oddities in his personality in society at large, and to resisting the dulling effect of any kind of orthodoxy or respectability on his cherished orneriness'.[1] By being difficult, he hoped to show his readers the instability and inhumanity of the twentieth-century world order.

Taylor's fondness for nonconformity was fostered by his family. His parents valued radical-liberal ideas and insisted that Taylor be educated at Quaker schools. At Bootham, a well-known school in York, Taylor developed a considerable interest in church archaeology, and in 1924 he went to Oriel College, Oxford, to study for a degree in modern history. He was awarded a first class degree, and after a short stint as a legal clerk in London, he spent two years in Vienna studying political and diplomatic records from the Habsburg monarchy. With the help of his supervisor, Alfred Francis Pribram, Taylor secured a teaching position at the University of Manchester. There, Sir Lewis Namier encouraged him to continue archival research and to write what was to be the first of his many works on diplomatic and Central European history: *The Italian Problem in European Diplomacy, 1847–1849* (1934). In 1938 he was appointed lecturer at Magdalen College, Oxford. He continued his exploration of European diplomacy in numerous articles, radio and television broadcasts and books such as *Germany's First Bid for Colonies, 1884–1885* (1938), *The Habsburg Monarchy* (1941), *Course of German History* (1946), *Struggle for Mastery in Europe, 1848–1918* (1954), *Bismarck* (1955) and *The Origins of the Second World War* (1961). The last of these created such a storm when it was published that Taylor was passed over for chairs of history at Oxford and the London School of Economics and was denied an extension of his lectureship; he left Oxford in 1964. Until his death in 1990, he lectured at University College, London, the Polytechnic College of North London (now the University of North London) and the Institute of Historical Research, contributed to radio and television discussions and continued to write for scholars and the public alike.

Taylor's historical writing bears the impression of his commitment to subject to scrutiny the assumptions that shaped societies in the second half of the twentieth century. This is seen most clearly in his discussion of the origins of the Second World War. After the First World War, historians devoted considerable attention to the study of why the war began. It was thought that if the reasons for the war could be uncovered, future conflicts might be avoided. Relatively few historians, however, devoted attention to the origins of the Second World War. This was because, Taylor claims in *The Origins of the Second World War*, most historians accepted the 'Nuremberg Thesis' without question. According to that thesis, the war was desired, planned and initiated by Adolf Hitler. Putting the blame on Hitler, Taylor tells us, was politically and morally convenient for many people. It allowed the German people to say that they had been the innocent victims of the Nazi regime, drew attention away from the policies and actions of other leaders prior to the war and made the Germans acceptable Cold War partners to both the Soviet Union and the United States. Taylor wants to tell a different story. His is a story 'without heroes, and perhaps even without villains' (*Origins of the Second World War*, p. 17). For Taylor, '[t]he war of 1939, far from being premeditated, was a mistake, the result on both sides of diplomatic blunders' (ibid., p. 21).

Central to Taylor's counter-thesis is a revised view of Adolf Hitler. Hitler, Taylor concedes, 'was an extraordinary man', but believes that 'his policy is capable of rational explanation; and it is on these that history is built' (ibid., p. 216). The cornerstone of Taylor's explanation is that Hitler did not cause the war because he did not *intend* it. Like many leaders, he rarely made distant plans. He did have some general aims, such as wanting to free Germany from the burden of the Versailles settlement and to make it 'the greatest power in Europe from [its] natural weight' (ibid., p. 68). He was also happy to exploit situations in order to realise those aims. As Taylor reminds us, however, that is not the same as saying that he wanted to bring about a war in Europe. This was not the accepted view of Hitler. Historians such as Alan Bullock, Hugh Trevor-Roper and Elizabeth Wiskemann looked to documents such as *Mein Kampf*, *Table Talk* and the Hossbach memorandum, and concluded that Hitler planned to launch a war that would end with his being master of the world.[2] For Taylor, Hitler's pronouncements in *Mein Kampf* and *Table Talk* amount to no more than dreams. Charlie Chaplin, he claims, had grasped that idea 'when he showed the Great Dictator transforming the world into a toy balloon and kicking it to the ceiling with the point of his toe' (ibid., p. 69).[3] Nor does Taylor believe that the Hossbach memorandum demonstrates Hitler's intent. The memorandum was a record of statements Hitler made on 5 November 1937 in a meeting with war minister Blomberg, foreign minister Neurath, army chief Fritsch, navy chief Raeder, and air force chief Goering. In this memo, Taylor tells us, Hitler spoke of three main ideas. First, he talked of *Lebensraum* ('living space'), but '[h]e did not specify where this was to be found'. Second, he noted that Germany had to contend with 'two hate inspired antagonists, Britain and France' and that it could only deal with its problems 'by means of force' even though 'this was never without attendant risk'. Third, he suggested that action could be taken against Czechoslovakia if France was distracted by civil war, and against both Czechoslovakia and Austria if France and Italy went to war. In Taylor's estimation, none of the se cases suggested that Hitler wanted a European war and none materialised. Thus, Taylor writes:

> The memorandum tells us, what we knew already, that Hitler (like every other German statesman) intended Germany to become the dominant Power in Europe. It also tells us that he speculated how this might happen. His speculations were mistaken. They bear hardly any relation to the actual outbreak of the war in 1939. A racing tipster who only reached Hitler's level of accuracy would not do well for his clients.
>
> (*Origins of the Second World War*, pp. 131–4)

This excerpt introduces a second argument against the conclusion that Hitler 'caused' the war: that his aims were only to be expected of a leader in his position. For Taylor, Hitler's aims and methods were 'normal' because European leaders had in the past defended their interests by threatening force. Furthermore, the Versailles settlement had denied Germany its 'natural weight' in Europe. Hitler simply followed a foreign policy like 'that of his predecessors, of the professional diplomats at the foreign ministry, and indeed of virtually all Germans' (ibid., p. 68). What Taylor finds strange is the hope on the part of the other European leaders that by appeasing Hitler they could hold down Germany indefinitely. Indeed, as Taylor sees it, Hitler had little choice but to respond to the initiatives and blunders of others. For example, Taylor believes that Hitler was all but compelled by the Austrian Chancellor Von Schuschnigg, that he did not create the German national movement in Czechoslovakia, and that he was forced by the intransigence of Joseph Beck, the Polish foreign minister, to take action over Danzig (ibid., chaps 7, 8 and 11). In each of these cases he did not have preconceived plans; he seized what he was offered.

Furthermore, the message of many of Taylor's earlier articles and books is that Germany set out on a collision course with Europe long before Hitler took power. For Taylor, German plans for mastery were given shape by Habsburg rule. The Habsburg monarchy (also called the house of Austria) was one of the principal sovereign dynasties of Europe from the fifteenth to the twentieth century. In Taylor's view they cared little for their subjects and were happy to play cultural, political and ethnic groups off against one another in order to preserve power. For instance, they encouraged the Germans, Magyars, Poles and Italians to think of themselves as enlightened 'master' peoples and the peoples of Eastern Europe as 'submerged'. In the late nineteenth century, the various peoples ruled by the Habsburgs became increasingly dissatisfied and sought solace in nationalist movements. One such movement was that for the revival of 'great Germany': Charlemagne's Holy Roman Empire of the German Nation. Charlemagne held mastery over Central and Eastern Europe in the ninth century (see *The Habsburg Monarchy, 1815–1918*). From the mid-nineteenth century onwards the Habsburgs also modelled *realpolitik*, the rule of force and self-interest. This emerged, Taylor argues, out of the conflict between those who wanted a 'Concert of Europe' in which Europe was to be dominated by a set number of dynastic powers, and those who wanted to maintain an approximate balance of power in Europe. Nations which had sought peace and balance in Europe tried instead to realise their own interests through brute force (see *The Italian Problem in European Diplomacy, 1847–1849* and *The Struggle for Mastery in Europe, 1848–1918*). It was during this time that a 'small Germany' emerged. German leaders from Bismarck on adopted *realpolitik* and fostered the belief that the state could become 'great' through force. When ordinary German people became politically conscious and were given the vote, Germany set out on a course that ended with Hitler's Third Reich (see *Bismarck, Germany's First Bid for Colonies* and *The Course of German History*).

Taylor's writings on Germany are, as Hett has noted, a thinly veiled 'admonitory fable' on the cause and prevention of war.[4] Even after the death of Hitler the rule of force and self-interest that gave rise to his power lived on, as could be seen by all in the Cold War between the United States and the Soviet Union. Such an international order, Taylor believed, was both unstable and unresponsive to the needs of many people. It also allowed governments and individuals to avoid taking responsibility for their actions (see *The Struggle for Mastery in Europe, 1848–1918*).

Although reviews of Taylor's earlier writings were mixed, the initial response to *The Origins of the Second World War* was overwhelmingly negative. Critics covered wide ground in their reviews. Some pointed out that Taylor was wrong to concentrate solely on diplomatic documents because they alone don't explain the outbreak of the war. Others such as Lambert, Deutscher, Reynolds, Spencer, Segal and Sontag argued that Taylor's account of Hitler was built on misstatements, misuse of evidence and the omission of relevant evidence. Trevor-Roper and Hudson acknowledged that, while Hitler did not have precise plans to start a war in Europe, documents such as the Hossbach memorandum, *Mein Kampf* and *Table Talk* showed that he had *flexible plans*. Even if he did not intend to bring about a general European war, he well knew that his actions would probably lead to war. Furthermore, Trevor-Roper thought it perverse to conclude that Hitler had been *forced* to act. Taylor's suggestion that blame be laid on those who allowed Hitler to do what he did implies that Hitler was unable to make his own decisions.[5] This, as Dray later pointed out, seems to go against Taylor's aim to treat Hitler as a 'normal' statesman. What was clearly at issue in this debate over causes was, first, what counts as an intention to bring something about, and second, what counts as 'normal' behaviour.[6] Some critics even took issue with Taylor's pointed writing style; for instance, his description of the Munich settlement as 'a triumph for all that was best and most enlightened in British life' was much criticised (*Origins*, p. 189). Even his qualification in the revised edition of *The Origins of the Second World War* that he 'ought perhaps to have added "(goak [joke] here)" in the manner of Artemus Ward' raised few laughs (ibid., second edition, 1984, p. 7).[7] Few readers found it amusing because they felt that blame for the war had been shifted from Hitler to Chamberlain and Daladier. One review, for instance, was accompanied by a drawing in which Hitler can be seen offering his blessing to Taylor.[8]

It might be tempting to conclude after reading such reviews that Taylor was an irresponsible contrarian. Taylor's many writings show that he often went against the grain. He did so, however, to show us that many of the ideas that dominate the political world are open to question and that we have a responsibility to change them for the better. In *Englishmen and Others*, for instance, he writes:

> [t]he historian does well to lead a dedicated life; yet however dedicated, he remains primarily a citizen. To turn from political responsibility to dedication therefore is to open the door to tyranny and measureless barbarism.

Notes

1 E. E. Segal, 'Taylor and History', *Review of Politics*, October 1964, 26: 533.

2 See A. Bullock, *Hitler: a Study in Tyranny*, New York: Harper & Row, 1952; H. R. Trevor-Roper, 'Introduction' in *Hitler's Table Talk*, trans. N. Cameron and R. H. Stevens, London, Weidenfeld & Nicolson, 1953; id., *The Last Days of Hitler*, New York: Macmillan, 1947; E. Wiskemann, *Undeclared War*, London: Constable, 1939; and id., *Prologue to War*, New York: Oxford University Press, 1940.

3 On Chaplin's *The Great Dictator*, see G. D. McDonald, M. Conway and M. Ricci (eds) *The Films of Charlie Chaplin*, Secaucus, NJ: Citadel, 1973, pp. 204–10; and the cover of E. Hobsbawm, *Age of Extremes: the Short Twentieth Century, 1914–1991*, London: Michael Joseph, 1994.

4 B. C. Hett, '"Goak Here": A. J. P. Taylor and the Origins of the Second World War', *Canadian Journal of History*, 1996, 31(2): 257–80.

5 For reviews, see W. R. Louis (ed.) *The Origins of the Second World War: A. J. P. Taylor and his Critics*, New York: Wiley & Sons, 1972.

6 W. H. Dray, 'Concepts of Causation in A. J. P. Taylor's Account of the Origins of the Second World War', *History and Theory*, 1978, 17(2): 149–75.

7 Artemus Ward was a comedian who wrote 'goak here' on his scripts – a misspelling of 'joke' – so that no one would miss the punchline. See Hett, '"Goak Here"', p. 257.

8 See the drawing by T. Allen that accompanies W. H. Hale's 'A Memorandum', *Horizon*, 1962, 4(4): 28–9. Reprinted in Louis (ed.) *The Origins of the Second World War*.

Taylor's major works

The Italian Problem in European Diplomacy, 1847–1849, Manchester: Manchester University Press, 1934.

Germany's First Bid for Colonies, 1884–1885, London: Macmillan, 1938.

The Habsburg Monarchy, 1815–1918, London: Macmillan, 1941, revised edition 1948.

The Course of German History, London: Hamish Hamilton, 1945.

The Struggle for Mastery in Europe, 1848–1918, Oxford: Oxford University Press, 1954.

Bismarck: the Man and the Statesman, London: Hamish Hamilton, 1955.

The Troublemakers, London: Hamish Hamilton, 1957.

The Origins of the Second World War, London: Hamish Hamilton, 1961, revised edition 1984.

English History, 1914–1945, Oxford: Oxford University Press, 1965.

Beaverbrook, London: Hamish Hamilton, 1972.

A Personal History, London: Hamish Hamilton, 1983.

An Old Man's Diary, London: Hamish Hamilton, 1984.

See also

Carr.

Further resources

Bosworth, R. J. B., *Explaining Auschwitz and Hiroshima: History Writing and the Second World War, 1945–1990*, London: Routledge, 1993.

Boyer, J. W., 'A. J. P. Taylor and the Art of Modern History', *Journal of Modern History*, 1977, 49(1): 40–72.

Cole, R., *A. J. P. Taylor: the Traitor within the Gates*, London: Macmillan, 1993.

Dray, W. H., 'Concepts of Causation in A. J. P. Taylor's Account of the Origins of the Second World War', *History and Theory*, 1978, 17(1): 149–72.

Great Dictator [video recording], directed by Charlie Chaplin, Universal Pictures, 1940, distributed by Foxvideo FFC.

Hauser, O., 'A. J. P. Taylor', *Journal of Modern History*, 1977, 49(1): 34–9.

Hett, B. C., '"Goak Here": A. J. P. Taylor and the Origins of the Second World War', *Canadian Journal of History*, 1996, 31(2): 257–80.

Louis, W. R. (ed.) *The Origins of the Second World War: A. J. P. Taylor and his Critics*, New York: Wiley & Sons, 1972.

Martel, G. (ed.) *The Origins of the Second World War Reconsidered*, London: Allen & Unwin, 1986.

Mehta, V., *Fly and the Fly Bottle: Encounters with British Intellectuals*, London: Weidenfeld & Nicolson, 1962.

Sisman, A., *A. J. P. Taylor: a Biography*, London: Sinclair-Stevenson, 1994.

Sked, A. and Cook, C. (eds) *Crisis and Controversy: Essays in Honour of A. J. P. Taylor*, London: Macmillan, 1976.

Smallwood, J., 'A Historical Debate of the 1960s: World War II Historiography – the Origins of the Second World War, A. J. P. Taylor, and his Critics', *Australian Journal of Politics and History*, 1980, 26(3): 403–10.

Wrigley, C. (ed.) *A. J. P. Taylor: a Complete Bibliography and Guide to his Historical and Other Writings*, Brighton: Harvester, 1982.

——, *Warfare, Diplomacy and Politics: Essays in Honour of A. J. P. Taylor*, London: Hamish Hamilton, 1986.

E. P. THOMPSON 1924–93

For E. P. Thompson, history is not simply the property of academic historians. Through his studies of the activities of ordinary people in eighteenth- and nineteenth-century England, Thompson hoped to encourage scholars and the public alike to think about and take action on issues of class, poverty and oppression.

Edward Palmer Thompson was born in Oxford in 1924.[1] His parents, Edward John Thompson and Theodosia Jessup Thompson, fostered in him the belief that governments were 'mendacious and imperialist' and that 'one's stance ought to be hostile to government'.[2] Thompson's move towards socialism, though, appears to have been due largely to his older brother Frank's idealism and his death at the hands of Bulgarian fascists in 1939. Thompson and his mother wrote of Frank's views and commitments in *There is a Spirit in Europe: a Memoir of Frank Thompson*

(1947). After commencing studies in history at Cambridge, Thompson followed Frank into the Communist Party and was elected President of the University's Socialist Club (1942). Not long after that he enlisted in the British Army, and served as a tank commander in North Africa, Italy and Austria (1942–45). After the war ended, Thompson returned to Cambridge and completed his degree (1946). He later recalled that he learned much from the writings of Christopher Hill, Christopher Cauldwell and Karl Marx. At Cambridge Thompson also met Dorothy Towers, a member of the Communist League who shared his interest in working-class history. They set up home together in 1945 and were married in 1948. In 1947 Thompson led the British Youth Brigade in an international effort to construct a 150-mile railway line from Samac to Sarajevo. Working on that project, Thompson suggested in *The Railway: an Adventure in Construction* (1948), had taught him the valuable lesson that certain endeavours can help people to 'conceptualise in terms of "our" rather than "my" or "their"'.

When he returned to England, Thompson found work as an adult education lecturer in literature and history at the University of Leeds. He was lucky to get such a position, as many universities denied employment to communists at that time. Initially he had no plans to become an historian but in the course of teaching literature he was 'seized' by the ideas of the nineteenth-century poet and socialist William Morris.[3] Out of this interest grew *William Morris: Romantic to Revolutionary* (1955). In this work, Thompson portrays Morris as a revolutionary Marxist who used art and craft to convey his views. That Thompson wrote the book when he was a member of the British Communist Party is not hard to see. He is quick to use Morris to support the ideals of the Party, as is seen in the following passage:

> Twenty years ago even among Socialists and Communists, many must have regarded Morris's picture of 'A Factory as It Might Be' as an unpractical poet's dream: to-day visitors return from the Soviet Union with stories of the poet's dream already fulfilled. Yesterday, in the Soviet Union, the Communists were struggling against every difficulty to build up their industry to the level of the leading capitalist powers: to-day they have before them Stalin's blue-print of the advance to communism.
>
> (*William Morris*, p. 844)

Those few who reviewed *William Morris* were quick to spot Thompson's bias. An anonymous reviewer in the *Times Literary Supplement*, for instance, declared that the work was too biased by Marxism, too shrill, too long and too ill-tempered.[4] Much later, after he had broken with communism, Thompson revised his study of Morris, tightening up the argument and eliminating its celebration of Stalinism (*William Morris*, revised edition, 1977). This revised edition elicited praise from reviewers: they thought that it was an important account of the transformation of British romanticism, Morris's moral critique of industrial capitalism and the early years of British socialism.[5]

Even when he worked on the first edition of *William Morris*, Thompson harboured doubts about Stalinism. While Morris encouraged workers to take control of and delight in their work, Stalinism appeared to 'lack humanity'. These doubts were brought to the surface in 1956. In that year, Khrushchev's revelations concerning Stalin's reign of terror and the brutal suppression of the Hungarian uprising led many people around the world to dissociate themselves from communism. Thompson was shocked by the events of 1956, but believed that the moral authority of the British Communist Party could be renewed if its leadership acknowledged the crisis and acted upon it. Angered by the lack of response from the Party, Thompson and John Saville launched a journal called the *New Reasoner*, which they hoped to be a forum for discussion on moral rights, human injustice and socialism. Their efforts earned them expulsion from the Party and they joined others of the ten thousand who also left to create the 'new Left'.

On leaving the Party, Thompson argued that Stalinism stood condemned because

> the subordination of the moral and imaginative faculties to political and administrative authority is wrong: the elimination of moral criteria from political judgement is wrong: the fear of independent thought, the deliberate encouragement of anti-intellectual trends amongst the people is wrong: the mechanical personification of unconscious class forces, the belittling of the conscious process of intellectual and spiritual conflict, all this is wrong.[6]

What was needed, he believed, was a 'socialist humanism', a morally conscious version of Marxism that liberated man from 'slavery to things, to the pursuit of profit or servitude to "economic necessity"'. As he wrote in an article for the *New Reasoner*:

> The Stalinist is fixated by Pavlov's dogs: if a bell was rung, they salivated. If an economic crisis comes, the people will

salivate good 'Marxist-Leninist' belief. But Roundhead, Leveller, and Cavalier, Chartist and Anti-Corn Law Leaguer, were not dogs; they did not salivate their creeds in response to economic stimuli; they loved and hated, argued, thought, and made moral choices. Economic changes impel changes in social relationships, in relations between real men and women; and these are apprehended, felt, reveal themselves in feelings of injustice, frustration, aspirations for social changes; all is fought out in the human consciousness, including the moral consciousness. If this were not so, men would be – not dogs – but ants, adjusting their society to upheavals in the terrain. But men make their own history: they are part agents, part victims; it is precisely the element of agency which distinguishes them from the beasts, which is the human part of man, and which it is the business of our consciousness to increase.[7]

In 1959 the *New Reasoner* merged with *Universities* and *Left Review* to form *New Left Review*. Thompson wrote a number of short papers and reviews for the journal, but with the appointment of Perry Anderson as chief editor, he was dismissed from the editorial board.[8] In 'Outside the Whale', Thompson expressed his anger at the assumption among *New Left Review* contributors that the political efforts of the middle and working classes were weak and that they were in need of a group of Marxist intellectuals such as themselves to stimulate sound and lasting political action. This view, Thompson argued, was not only arrogant but erroneous. The working and middle classes were familiar with the ideas of Marx and they had shown in the past that they were capable of bringing about radical social change.[9]

Such apparent ignorance of English history stimulated Thompson to write the book that would make his name familiar to people around the world: *The Making of the English Working Class* (1963). In this work, Thompson tells the story of how, between the years 1790 and 1830, English working people came to feel united among themselves and against their employers. In Part 1, he reviews three traditions inherited by the working class at the beginning of the Industrial Revolution: dissent, particularly as modified by Methodism; 'mob' rule and popular justice; and the 'Englishman's birthright', including various legal guarantees and rights of free conscience and expression. In Part 2 he offers an account of the decline in working conditions and the growing political, social and religious repression stimulated by the Industrial Revolution. In the final part he traces the responses of working people to these changes. As Thompson sees it, working people developed class-consciousness. His chief point is that class is not a thing, theoretical construct, structure or category; it is an historical phenomenon that arises out of human relationships:

> class happens when some men, as a result of common experiences (inherited or shared), feel and articulate the identity of their interests as between themselves, and as against other men whose interests are different from (and usually opposed to) theirs.
>
> (*The Making of the English Working Class*, p. 9)

Class therefore 'owes as much to agency as to conditioning'. Working people drew on English traditions to make themselves into a class. It was not a case of 'steam power and the cotton mill = new working class' (ibid., p. 191).

The Making of the English Working Class was quickly recognised as a work of great significance. Thompson's sympathetic engagement with his subject, the depth of his research, his writing style and his explicit statement of his ideological stance and methodological approach were praised enthusiastically by some reviewers. Others, however, were not only troubled by Thompson's treatment of particular aspects, such as Luddism and Methodism, and his suggestion that a homogeneous working-class consciousness had been 'made' by the early nineteenth century, but also about the validity of a work so clearly written in the light of a firm political commitment.[10] Complaints aside, *The Making of the English Working Class* is still regarded as an indispensable text for those interested in late eighteenth- and early nineteenth-century British history and as a stimulus for labour historians, feminist historians, cultural theorists, anthropologists and sociologists.

In 1965 Thompson was made director of the Centre for the Study of Social History at the newly established University of Warwick. Thompson put a lot of energy into helping his students to see that writing history was 'vital to the health of society' but he also delved further into eighteenth-century England. Out of this research came his next major publication, *Whigs and Hunters: the Origin of the Black Act* (1975). In this book, Thompson looks at the Black Act of 1723, named for groups of armed men (sometimes with faces blackened) who raided the Windsor Forests and some forest districts of Hampshire, which created fifty new capital offences concerned with threats to property. In Thompson's opinion, while the 'Blacks' protested the loss of traditional forest rights, the established classes used the Black Act as an excuse to advance their own interests. Thompson suggests that people sometimes came to know themselves as a class. His point is that struggle precedes class: 'classes do not exist as separate entities, look around, find an enemy class, and then start to struggle'.[11] This idea also underpins his papers on social dissent and price control (the 'moral economy'), the resistance of the labouring poor to the 'severe restructuring of work habits', *charivari* or 'rough music', the disintegration of a 'paternal' model of marketing (marketing in a way that middlemen, dealers and speculators do not exploit the public) and anonymous threatening letters. Thompson thus affirmed his aim to explore class relationships in the light of moral choice, agency and values.[12]

Though Thompson gained some supporters for his 'socialist humanism', he believed that the popularity of Louis Althusser's 'theoretical anti-humanism' made the intellectual climate in Britain hostile to his ideas. For Althusser and his followers, the 'science of history' is concerned not with the conscious actions of individuals, but with the mode of production (form of economic organisation) that exists in a displaced form in the social 'structures' of a society. In *The Poverty of Theory and Other Essays*, Thompson declared 'unrelenting intellectual war' (p. 384) against the Althusserians for constructing an 'orrey' (elaborate mechanism illustrating a series of interconnections or relationships) that legitimised the inhumanity, amorality and irrationalism of Stalinism. He was repulsed not only by Althusser's denial of human agency, but also by his dismissal of ethical protest as mere ideology (a relative, closed system of belief of which most of us are unaware in everyday lived experience). Such a dismissal for Thompson amounts to 'a straightforward ideological police action. It constructs a theory which ensures not only that radical questions about Stalinism, Communist forms, and "Marxism" itself are not asked, but that they cannot be asked' (*The Poverty of Theory*, p. 374). Marxism, Thompson believes, must be capable of self-criticism, self-examination and moral discourse (ibid., p. 148). *The Poverty of Theory* generated an avalanche of criticism. Though critics acknowledged that Thompson had drawn attention to some important questions, they also took issue with his polemical style of argument, the connection he made between Althusserianism and Stalinism and his claim that the former had a firm grip on the Anglo-American world.[13]

The popularity of Althusserianism, Thompson claimed, was itself a symptom of the common assumption that the confrontation of the Soviet and American power blocs was implacable (ibid., p. 266). Attacking Althusserianism was thus not enough. Up to his death in 1993 Thompson tried to generate interest in social and political issues such as the proliferation of nuclear weapons, Soviet and American imperialism, attempts to undermine democratic rights, the monitoring of those engaged in Left struggles and environmental degradation (see *The May Day Manifesto*, 1968; *Warwick University Limited*, 1977; *Zero Option*, 1982; *Protest and Survive*, 1980; *Star Wars*, 1985; *Prospects for a Habitable Planet*, 1987). In these, as in all Thompson's works, we see his belief that history can prompt political action, a belief which Thompson himself lived by.

Notes

1. For an account of Thompson's social and political thought, see Thompson (IRT).
2. M. Merrill, 'Interview with E. P. Thompson', 1976, in H. Abelove *et al.* (eds) *Visions of History*, p. 11.
3. M. Merrill, 'Interview with E. P. Thompson', p. 13.
4. Anon., 'Morris and Marxism', *Times Literary Supplement*, 15 July 1955, p. 391.
5. See, for example, E. Penning-Rowsell, 'The Remodelling of Morris', *Times Literary Supplement*, 11 August 1978, pp. 913–14; and P. Stansky, 'The Protean Victorian', *New York Times Book Review*, 15 May 1977, pp. 7, 48.
6. E. P. Thompson, 'Through the Smoke of Budapest', *New Reasoner*, 1965, 3.
7. E. P. Thompson, 'Socialist Humanism: an Epistle to the Philistines', *New Reasoner*, 1, 1957: 122.
8. See 'At the Point of Decay', 'Revolution' and 'Outside the Whale', in E. P. Thompson (ed.) *Out of Apathy*, London: Verso, 1990.
9. Thompson, 'Outside the Whale'.
10. For favourable reviews, see (for example) E. Hobsbawm, 'Organised Orphans', *New Statesman*, November 1963, 66: 787–8; and C. Hill, 'Worker's Progress', *Times Literary Supplement*, 12 December 1963, pp. 1021–3. For less favourable reviews, see (for example) J. D. Chambers, 'Making of the English Working Class', *History*, 1 June 1966, pp. 183–9; G. Best 'The Making of the English Working Class', *Historical Journal*, 1965, 8(2): 271–81; R. Currie and M. Hartwell, 'The Making of the English Working Class?', in M. Hartwell (ed.) *The Industrial Revolution and Economic Growth*, London, 1971, pp. 361–76; R. A. Church and S. D. Chapman, 'Gravener Henson and the Making of the English Working Class', in E. L. Jones and G. E. Mingay (eds) *Land, Labour and Population in the Industrial Revolution*, London: Macmillan, 1967, pp. 131–61; S. Thernstrom, 'A Major Work in Radical History', *Dissent*, 1965, 12: 90–2; J. Gross, 'Hard Times', *New York Review of Books*, 16 April 1964, pp. 8–10; H. Ausubel, 'The Common Man as Hero', *New York Times Review of Books*, 26 April 1964, p. 44; and G. Himmelfarb, 'A Tract of Secret History', *New Republic*, 11 April 1964, pp. 24–6. Thompson's reply to his critics can be found in the 'Postscript' to the revised (1968) edition of *The Making of the English Working Class*.
11. 'Eighteenth-century English Society: Class Struggle without Class?', *Social History*, 1978, 3(2): 149.
12. 'The Moral Economy of the English Crowd in the Eighteenth Century', 'Time, Work-discipline and Industrial Capitalism', and 'Rough Music: le charivari anglais', all reprinted in *Customs in Common*, London: Merlin Press,

1991; and 'The Crime of Anonymity', in E. P. Thompson (ed.) *Albion's Fatal Tree: Crime and Society in Eighteenth Century England*, London: Allen Lane, 1975.

13 See, for example, P. Anderson, *Arguments within English Marxism*, London: Verso, 1980, pp. 16–58.

Thompson's major works

William Morris: Romantic to Revolutionary, London: Lawrence & Wishart, 1955, revised edition, New York: Pantheon, 1977.

The Making of the English Working Class, London: Victor Gollancz, 1963; second edition, with a new postscript, Harmondsworth: Penguin, 1968; third edition, with a new preface, 1980.

Whigs and Hunters: the Origins of the Black Act, London: Allen Lane, 1975; reprinted with a new postscript, Harmondsworth: Penguin, 1977.

(ed.) *Albion's Fatal Tree: Crime and Society in Eighteenth Century England*, London: Allen Lane, 1975.

The Poverty of Theory and Other Essays, London: Merlin Press, 1978.

Customs in Common, London: Merlin Press, 1991.

See also

Althusser (CT), Davis, Hobsbawm, Marx, Rowbotham, Scott.

Further resources

Anderson, P., *Arguments within English Marxism*, London: Verso, 1980.

History Workshop Journal, 1995, 39: 71–135.

Johnson, R., 'Edward Thompson, Eugene Genovese, and Socialist-humanist History', *History Workshop Journal*, 1978, 6: 7–9.

Kaye, H. J., *The British Marxist Historians*, Cambridge: Polity Press, 1984.

Kaye, H. J. and McClelland, K. (eds) *E. P. Thompson: Critical Perspectives,* Philadelphia, PA: Temple University Press, 1990.

Merrill, M., 'Interview with E. P. Thompson', in H. Abelove *et al.* (eds) *Visions of History*, Manchester: Manchester University Press, 1976, pp. 5–25.

New Left Review, 1993, 201: 3–25.

Palmer, B. D., *The Making of E. P. Thompson: Marxism, Humanism, and History*, Toronto: New Hogtown Press, 1981.

——, *E. P. Thompson: Objections and Oppositions*, New York: Verso, 1994.

Radical History Review, 1994, 58: 152–64.

THUCYDIDES *c.* 460–*c.* 400 BC

Though we know of earlier historians, many writers consider Thucydides to be the father of history. This is because, in their opinion, his *History of the Peloponnesian War* is the earliest example of serious historical research. For them, Thucydides displays the same rigour and respect for truth and evidence as modern-day historians, and is worlds apart from earlier, more literary historians like Herodotus. With the greater appreciation of the relationship between style and history in recent times, however, scholars have begun to look at Thucydides anew as a literary craftsman.

Most of what we know of the life of Thucydides derives from his *History*. He was born probably around 460 BC. Though he was an Athenian citizen, his father's name (Olorus) suggests that he was of Thracian descent. Thucydides had property in Thrace, including gold mines opposite the island of Thasos, and was, he tells us, a man of influence there (4.105.1). Around the time he started work on his *History* he caught the plague that swept through Athens (2.48). Later, in 424, he was made a *strategos*, one of ten annually elected generals. He was given command of the Athenian fleet in the Thraceward region, based at Thasos. He failed to prevent the capture of the valuable city of Amphipolis by the Spartan general Brasidas, who launched a surprise attack in mid-winter (4.106). Thucydides was recalled to Athens, tried and sentenced to exile. While in exile, Thucydides tells us that he had the opportunity to consider events from a Peloponnesian perspective (5.26.5). His exile ended with the fall of Athens and the peace in 404 (5.26). He returned to Athens, and died sometime before 400 BC.

The *History* is divided into eight books: books 1–4 deal with the first ten years of the Peloponnesian War, or Archidamian War, between Athens and Sparta and the peace of Nicias (431–21). The conflict-ridden years between 421 and 413 are dealt with in the remainder of the work; books 6 and 7 describe the Athenian attempts to subjugate Sicily (415–413); and book 8 looks to Sparta's occupation of the fort of Decelea in Athenian territory (also known as the Decelean or Ionian War, 413). Thucydides maintains that these various conflicts comprise a single Peloponnesian war because he did not believe that the agreement of Nicias led to true and lasting peace. Scholars disagree about the order in which the work was composed.

Thucydides had no doubts about the significance of his subject-matter. As he writes in the preface:

> [Thucydides] began the task at the very outset of the war, in the belief that it would be great and noteworthy above all the wars that had gone before, inferring this from the fact that both powers were then at their best in preparedness for war in every way, and seeing the rest of the Hellenic race taking sides with one state or the other, some at once, others planning to

do so. For this was the greatest movement that had ever stirred the Hellenes, extending also to some of the Barbarians, one might say even to a very large part of mankind.

(1.1.1–2)

This point is further developed in the 'Archaeology', an analysis of the forces that underpin the conflicts under study.[1] In Thucydides' opinion, the deepest or 'truest' cause of the Peloponnesian War was Athenian expansionism (1.23.6). Athens and Sparta, Thucydides shows us, were very different from one another. Athens was in the main a naval power. It was an Athens-led navy that allowed Ionia to escape Persian control (see Herodotus, *Histories*). In order to keep its navy crews happy, Athens paid them all wages and made them members of the general assembly of male citizens. Athens was thus democratic in nature. Sparta, on the other hand, was an efficiently run, military state. Sparta was able to support its army of hoplites (heavy armed artillery) by means of compulsory military service and levies on landowners. All activities were designed to keep the male population combat ready. Sparta was the head of a league of Peloponnesus states that included Corinth. As Athens sought to expand its influence, it came into conflict with Corinth over Corcyra (Corfu) and Potidaea (1.24–65). These clashes, Thucydides tells us, initiated the Peloponnesian War.

Following Herodotus, Thucydides aimed to detail recent events. Unlike Herodotus, however, he claims to have followed higher standards of research and accuracy:

from the evidence that has been given, any one would not err who should hold the view that the state of affairs in antiquity was pretty nearly such as I have described it, not giving greater credence to the accounts, on the one hand, which the poets have put into song, adorning and amplifying their theme, and, on the other, which the chroniclers have composed with a view rather of pleasing the ear than of telling the truth, since their stories cannot be tested and most of them have from lapse of time won their way into the region of the fabulous so as to be incredible.

(1.21.1)

This approach, Thucydides argues, may make his work 'less pleasing to the ear' but more likely to endure in the long run (1.22.4).

Thucydides presents the details of his *History* with great confidence. Only in book 8 do we see him, like Herodotus, inviting his readers to analyse alternative explanations (for instance, 8.56.3; 87.2–6). On the whole, however, we are left in no doubt as to what actually happened. From book 1 we gain an impression of the lengths to which Thucydides went to eliminate doubt:

> as to the facts of the occurrences of the war, I have thought it my duty to give them, not as ascertained from any chance informant nor as seemed to me probable, but only after investigating with the greatest possible accuracy each detail, in the case both of the events in which I myself participated and of those regarding which I got my information from others.
>
> (1.22.2)

Much of the *History* is built upon unnamed oral sources and written sources such as Herodotus, Antiochus of Syracuse, Hecataeus of Miletus, Hellanicus and Homer. Numerous scholars have also suggested that he was deeply influenced by tragic drama, epic poetry, Sophist philosophy and Hippocratic views of medicine.[2] As Vico reminds us, however, it is quite possible for two groups to have arrived at similar ideas independently. He also uses inscriptions and evidence supplied by oracles to fill out or shore up his accounts of events. Furthermore, he draws upon material evidence to fill in gaps in accounts of the distant past; for example, he uses archaeological evidence to show that the building of the city walls in Athens in 478 was rushed (1.93.2). However, he rejects the idea supported by Herodotus that the buildings of Athens were an accurate index of its wealth and greatness:

> Suppose that the city of Sparta were to become deserted, and that only the temples and foundations of buildings remained, I think that future generations would, as time passed, find it very difficult to believe that the place had really been as powerful as it was represented to be. . . . If, on the other hand, the same thing were to happen to Athens, one would conjecture from what meets the eye that the city had been twice as powerful as in fact it is.
>
> (1.10.2–3)

Evidence which survives from that period suggests that Thucydides was indeed diligent in his research. Unlike earlier writers, he drew almost exclusively on political and military material and refrained from digressing from the main narrative. Although this results in a very detailed account of the war, we gain only a faint impression of what else was going on in the Mediterranean world.

Thucydides' focus, Luce has suggested, 'was one of fierce, laser-like concentration on a single topic, the war'.[3] This 'laser-like' focus has made him popular among historians. With Thucydides they see the emergence of research methods that are still in use. In the twentieth century, however, historians and the public alike began to appreciate that there is more to Thucydides than methodological rigour. Thucydides was also a great literary craftsman. While his 'voice' can be detected in his selection and arrangement of material, it can be heard with most clarity in his treatment of speeches. In book 1, he tells us about his approach to speeches:

> As for the speeches each side made either in preparing to go to war or during it, it has been difficult for me to remember accurately what was said in regard to those I heard myself and those reported to me from other sources. I have given the speeches as I thought each person or group said what was required on different occasions, keeping as close as possible to the overall sense of what was actually said.
>
> (1.22)

This seems a remarkable admission from a writer who shied away from the merely probable. Could it be that the 'father of history' made things up? Thucydides was not the only ancient historian who composed invented speeches (*oratio obliqua*). What sets him apart from earlier writers is that he tells us *how* he wrote them. When it was impossible to ascertain what was actually said, he tried to keep 'as close as possible to the overall sense'. A close look at a number of his 'invented' speeches, however, shows that he did more than that. In numerous places, Thucydides uses speeches to explain the motives and ambitions of individuals and states but also to draw out important themes. The English philosopher Thomas Hobbes, for instance, believed that Thucydides used invented speeches to convey his doubts about democracy.[4] More recent writers, such as Finlay, however, have pointed out that Thucydides stressed the importance of democracy when writing of Athens' strengths.[5]

In his account of particular events such as the *stasis* (civil strife) that shook Corcyra in 427 BC, we also see his technique of 'history by synecdoche'; that is, experiences at Corcyra are representative of the whole war.[6] At Corcyra, people abandoned social and moral conventions and acted out of self-interest; officials were detained and executed; fathers killed their sons; bodies were left unburied; men were murdered in and near temples; and promises and oaths were broken (3.81). Even the meaning of words changed:

> The ordinary acceptation of words in their relation to things was changed as men saw fit. Reckless audacity came to be regarded as courageous loyalty to party, prudent hesitation as specious cowardice, moderation as a cloak for unmanly weakness, and to be clever in everything was to do naught in anything. . . . In a word, both he that got ahead of another who intended to do something evil and he that prompted to evil one who had never thought of it were alike commended.
>
> (3.82.4–6)

The breakdown in social and moral conventions, he shows us, had widespread implications.

Thucydides' treatment of events at Corcyra also shows his concern to make the reader aware of the suffering involved in the Peloponnesian War. It was important to document the war, he tells us in book 1, because '[n]ever had so many human beings been exiled, or so much human blood been shed' (1.23.2). Knowledge of these events, Thucydides suggests through Hermocrates' speech at Gela, should make us 'more inclined to approach each other with forethought' (4.62.4). It is clear from such excerpts that Thucydides does not want us simply to admire his methodological rigour or literary skill. He also invites us to explore and remember what happens when people no longer have social and moral guides to action. It is this feature of Thucydides' writings that guarantee they will be a 'possession for all time' (1.22.4).

Notes

1 On the similarity between Thucydides' and Foucault's views of 'archaeology', see W. R. Connor, *Thucydides*, Princeton, NJ: Princeton University Press, 1984.
2 See, for example, F. M. Cornford, *Thucydides Mythistoricus*, London: Routledge & Kegan Paul, 1965, p. x; C. Cochrane, *Thucydides and the Science of History*, Oxford: Oxford University Press, 1929, p. 26; C. Macleod, *Collected Essays*, Oxford: Oxford University Press, 1983, p. 157; and A. J. Holladay and J. C. F. Poole, 'Thucydides and the Plague of Athens', *Classical Quarterly*, 1979, 29: 299–300.
3 T. J. Luce, *The Greek Historians*, London: Routledge, 1997, p. 69.
4 See, for instance, L. M. Johnson, *Thucydides, Hobbes and the Intelligence of Reason*, DeKalb, IL: Northern Illinois University Press, 1993.
5 J. H. Finley, *Thucydides*, Cambridge, MA: Harvard University Press, 1942.
6 Luce, *The Greek Historians*, p. 79.

Thucydides' major works

Thucydides: History of the Peloponnesian War, 4 vols, trans. C. F. Smith, Loeb Classical Library, London: Heinemann, 1969.

The Peloponnesian War, trans. R. Warner, Penguin Classics, Harmondsworth: Penguin, revised edition 1972.

Various translations of the *History of the Peloponnesian War* can be found online at: http://www.perseus.tufts.edu/Texts.html

See also

Herodotus, Hobbes (MP), Hobsbawm, Polybius, Tacitus.

Further resources

Adcock, F. E., *Thucydides and his History*, Cambridge: Cambridge University Press, 1963.

Cochrane, C., *Thucydides and the Science of History*, Oxford: Oxford University Press, 1929.

Connor, W. R., *Thucydides*, Princeton, NJ: Princeton University Press, 1984.

Cornford, F. M., *Thucydides Mythistoricus*, London: Routledge & Kegan Paul, 1965.

Finley, J. H., *Thucydides*, Cambridge, MA: Harvard University Press, 1942.

Fornara, C. W., *The Nature of History in Ancient Greece and Rome*, Berkeley, CA: University of California Press, 1983.

Gomme, A. W., Andrewes, A. and Dover, K. J., *An Historical Commentary on Thucydides*, 5 vols, Oxford: Oxford University Press, 1945–81.

Hornblower, S., *Thucydides*, London: Duckworth, 1987.

——, *The History of the Peloponnesian War: an Historical Commentary*, Oxford: Oxford University Press, 1991.

Luce, T. J., *The Greek Historians*, London: Routledge, 1997.

Orwin, C., *The Humanity of Thucydides*, Princeton, NJ: Princeton University Press, 1994.

Rawlings, H. R., *The Structure of Thucydides' History*, Princeton, NJ: Princeton University Press, 1981.

ARNOLD J. TOYNBEE 1889–1975

The sheer mass and scope of Toynbee's writings is enough to make even the most hardy of readers blanch. He wrote big: he penned countless works on religion, ancient and modern history, contemporary events and the nature of history. But he also thought big: one gets the impression that he tried to draw all places and times together in one web.

Born on 14 April 1889 in London, Arnold Joseph Toynbee was the son of Henry Valpy Toynbee, a tea importer turned charity worker, and Sarah Edith Marshall, an unofficial graduate in history from the

University of Cambridge. As a young child, Toynbee was taught by his mother and a governess. He then went to Wootton Court in Kent and Winchester College. Toynbee excelled in his studies, and won a classics scholarship to Balliol College, Oxford. While he enjoyed classics, Toynbee nursed the ambition 'to be a great gigantic historian – not for fame but because there is lots of work in the world to be done, and I am greedy for as big a share of it as I can get'.[1] After completing his degree in 1912, he explored historical sites in Greece and Italy. Though Toynbee enjoyed his travels, he had to cut his trip short in order to seek treatment for dysentery. After his release from hospital he started work as a tutor in ancient history at Balliol. Though he entertained hopes of being able to help his students 'know a different life and civilisation from ours', none of them was able to match his expectations. He devoted his energies instead to what would be his lifelong occupation: writing. He started writing a book on the history of Greece from prehistoric times to the Byzantine era, but before it was completed he became distracted by contemporary events such as the Balkan Wars of 1912 and 1913.[2]

While many of Toynbee's friends were called up at the outbreak of the First World War and subsequently lost their lives, he was rejected from the army on the grounds of ill health. Whether from guilt or gratitude at being spared his life, Toynbee resolved to work towards a just and lasting peace by informing the public about the past and the politics of the war.[3] In *Nationality and the War*, for instance, he hoped to lay bare the ideas and events that lay behind the assassination of Archduke Franz Ferdinand at Sarajevo and to show that a generous settlement with a defeated Germany might lead Europeans away from nationalism and towards co-operation.[4] In 1915 he accepted a position with a newly established governmental propaganda unit in London. There he worked with Lord Bryce to draw international attention to the massacre of Armenians by the Turks. Toynbee took great pains to find reliable evidence, but was later troubled by the one-sidedness of his and Bryce's reports (*Armenian Atrocities: the Murder of a Nation*, 1916; *The Treatment of Armenians in the Ottoman Empire, 1915–16*, 1916; and *The Murderous Tyranny of the Turks*, 1917).[5] Bryce and Toynbee were later asked to investigate reports of German atrocities on other fronts (*The Destruction of Poland: a Study in German Efficiency*, 1916; *The Belgian Deportations*, 1917; and *The German Terror in France*, 1917).[6]

In May 1917 Toynbee was reassigned to the Political Intelligence Department, which aimed to shape British foreign policy during the last stages of the war and at the Versailles peace conference.[7] Toynbee attended the Versailles conference as an adviser on the Ottoman Empire and the Muslims of Central Asia. After he returned to England he was offered the Koraes Chair in Byzantine and Modern Greek Literature and History at the University of London. He was forced to resign that position in 1924, however, because the chair's Greek benefactors were offended by the pro-Turkish tone of his newspaper reports on the war between Greece and Turkey in Anatolia (1921–22).[8] Not long after, he was employed by the British (later Royal) Institute for International Affairs to write a book-length survey of events since the Versailles settlement. The result, *Survey of International Affairs, 1920–1923* (1925), was to be the first of a long line of surveys produced until his retirement in 1953.[9]

Every year, Toynbee managed to turn boxes of information (mostly from newspapers) into reports on contemporary events across the globe. He wrote with confidence about even the most obscure places and drew many connections across space and time. In his spare time, he gave lectures and penned articles.[10] He also began collecting materials for what would become his best-known work: *A Study of History* (12 vols, 1934–61).

Contemporary historical scholarship, Toynbee believed, was deficient because historians were Eurocentric, imitated scientists and undertook research on minute and trivial topics (*Civilisation on Trial and Other Essays*, 1948, p. 85; *A Study of History*, vol. 9, p. 205). What they failed to see, he argued, was that 'the universe becomes intelligible to the extent of our ability to apprehend it as a whole' (*Civilisation on Trial*, p. 11). In that spirit, Toynbee set out to study the 'history of all known civilisations, surviving and extinct' (ibid., p. 143). Within the mass of historical details, he claimed, a pattern could be discerned.

According to Toynbee, civilisations tend to pass through four phases: an age of growth; a time of troubles; a universal state; and interregnum or disintegration. The key to a civilisation's 'age of growth' is what Toynbee calls 'challenge and response'. Put simply, if a 'primitive society' is to develop into a 'civilisation', it must be challenged. It is like 'a climber who has not reached the ledge above him where he may hope to find rest . . . for unless he continues to climb on upward until he reaches the next ledge, he is doomed to fall to his death' (*A Study of History*, vol. 3, p. 373).[11] Challenges at this phase, Toynbee suggests, are posed by external factors such as climate and terrain. Each successful response strengthens the civilisation. If the challenges are extreme, however, the society slumps into a state of stagnation. Such a state, Toynbee claims, may be detected in groups such as the Inuit who live in extreme climates.

The breakdown of a civilisation in a 'time of troubles', on the other hand, is due to internal problems such as excessive concern for the past or the future; nationalism; the imitation of a response that worked for another civilisation (mimesis); the idolisation of a person, technique or institution; smugness about past achievements; and a general loss of creativity. This is why Toynbee suggests that the demise of a civilisation is a matter of suicide. In this phase, wars erupt and a universal state is established by a 'dominant minority'. Peace results, as does short-term prosperity, but prospects for the civilisation are bleak. The establishment of a universal state is merely a holding action and always 'proves to . . . [be] the last phase of a society before its extinction' (ibid., vol. 7, p. 54). Although Toynbee is not as confident as Oswald Spengler that Western civilisation is in decline, he believes that it presents a number of 'suicidal tendencies': the idolisation of technology; the proliferation of nuclear weapons; frequent conflict; nationalism; extreme consumerism; greed; poor treatment of the developing world; and self-centredness (see *A Study of History*, abr., 1972, preface and chap. 1).

In the seven years between the composition of volumes 6 and 7, however, he came to see that '[t]he symbol which a stricken twentieth century sees glimmering through the darkness ahead is not a skull-and-crossbones: it is a question mark' (*A Study of History*, vol. 9, p. 436). This change of view was a consequence of the modification of his ideas on the role of religion in the development of civilisations. He writes:

> In our inquiry into the relation between churches and civilisations up to this point, we have tacitly worked on the assumption that in the interplay between societies of these two species the civilisations had been the protagonists and the role of the churches, whether usefully subsidiary or obnoxiously corrosive, had, on either interpretation, been secondary and subordinate. Now that our operations on these lines have proved fruitless, let us try the effect of reversing our point of view. Let us open our minds to the possibility that the churches might be the protagonists and that vice versa the histories of civilisations might have been envisaged and interpreted in terms, not of their own destinies, but of their effect on the history of religion.
>
> (Ibid., vol. 7, p. 420)

'Universal Churches', he claims, succeed primitive societies and civilisations. In this kind of society, characterised by compassion and selflessness, individuals achieve communion with 'absolute spiritual reality', or what he had previously called God. In light of this new view of history as spiritual progress, Toynbee alters his view of civilisations.

They are now an 'endeavour to create a state of society in which the whole of mankind will be able to live together in harmony, as members of an all-inclusive family' (*A Study of History*, vol. 12, pp. 307–8; see also vol. 4, pp. 420–3; vol. 6, pp. 325–6; vol. 7, pp. 425–6).

Toynbee also modifies and expands his description of how civilisations deteriorate. He argues that the breakdown of civilisations is a three-stage process and that it involves three groups of people: the dominant minority, the internal proletariat and the external proletariat. By proletariat, Toynbee means 'any social element or group which in some way is "in" but not "of" any given society at any given stage of such society's history' (ibid., vol. 7, p. 1, n. 41). The 'dominant minority', Toynbee claims, are those individuals who gain power in the 'age of growth' because of their successful responses to challenges. In the 'time of troubles' they try to maintain their power. This attempt at dominance leads some individuals to withdraw from society and become the 'internal proletariat'. At the same time, groups outside the civilisation ('the external proletariat') start to threaten the 'dominant minority'. Eventually the 'internal proletariat' return to persuade the uncreative majority to follow them along a path that they have opened up (ibid., vol. 5, p. 29).[12] In the majority of cases, Toynbee claims, religion is the contribution that the internal proletariat brings on return (ibid., vol. 9, p. 3; vol. 12, p. 609; see also *An Historian's Approach to Religion*, 1956, chap. 17).[13]

The reception of *A Study of History*, like the content of the work, changed a great deal over time. Volumes 1–3, and to a lesser extent 4–6, were well received by British academics.[14] After the publication of volume 7, however, his popularity among academics began to wane. This was matched, though, by a growth in the popularity of his works with the public, particularly in the USA. Toynbee's warnings about the suicidal tendencies of the West and his calls for the USA to take action in international affairs rang a chord with the masses. Extracts and essays appeared in numerous magazines and newspapers, and Toynbee was heralded as a prophet. His ideas were also popular among science-fiction writers such as Isaac Asimov (*Foundation Trilogy*, 1951–53), Charles Harness (*The Paradox Man*, 1953), Frank Herbert (*Dune*, 1965) and Ray Bradbury (*Toynbee's Convector*, 1988). Even when his ideas lost some of their appeal in the USA, his reputation grew in other parts of the world such as Japan.

Many scholars believe that Toynbee's pronouncements rest on shaky, or even false, evidence. Others believe that his concepts of 'civilisation', 'challenge and response' and so on are so vague that they can be applied to almost any situation. Yet others consider him to be a prophet, not an historian.[15] Still, many probably feel the same sense of fascination with Toynbee's ideas as Pieter Geyl, one of his most persistent critics:

> One follows [Toynbee] with the excitement with which one follows an incredibly supple and audacious tight-rope walker. One feels inclined to exclaim: '*C'est magnifique, mais ce n'est pas l'histoire.*'[16]

Notes

1 Letter, AJT to R. S. Darbishire, 21 May 1911, Toynbee Papers, Bodleian Library, Oxford; quoted in W. H. McNeill, *Arnold J. Toynbee: a Life*, New York: Oxford University Press, 1989, p. 31.

2 See, for example, *Greek Policy since 1882*, London: Oxford University Press, 1914; and 'The Slav Peoples', *Political Quarterly*, December 1914, 4: 33–68.

3 McNeill, *Arnold J. Toynbee*, chap. 3.

4 *Nationality and the War*, London: Dent, 1915, p. 29.

5 *Armenian Atrocities: the Murder of a Nation*, London: Hodder & Stoughton, 1915; *The Treatment of Armenians in the Ottoman Empire, 1915–16*, London: HMSO, 1916; and *The Murderous Tyranny of the Turks*, London: Hodder & Stoughton, 1917.

6 *The Destruction of Poland: a Study in German Efficiency*, London: T. Fisher Unwin, 1916; *The Belgian Deportations*, London: T. Fisher Unwin, 1917; and *The German Terror in France*, London: Hodder & Stoughton, 1917.

7 G. Martel, 'Toynbee, McNeill and the Myth of History', *International History Review* [Canada], 1990, 12(2): 338.

8 R. Beaton, 'Koraes, Toynbee and the Modern Greek Heritage', *Byzantine and Modern Greek Studies*, 1992, 15(1): 1–18; M. Savvas, 'Arnold Toynbee and the Koraes Chair Controversy', *Journal of the Hellenic Diaspora*, 1991, 17(2): 115–23; and R. Clogg, *Politics and the Academy: Arnold Toynbee and the Koraes Chair*, London: Frank Cass, 1986.

9 See S. F. Morton, *A Bibliography of Arnold J. Toynbee*, New York: Oxford University Press, 1980, pp. 39–52.

10 F. Morton's bibliography lists more than 800 articles alone.

11 See the cover from *Time*, 23 March 1947.

12 See also 'The Desert Hermits', *Horizon*, 1970, 12(2): 22–7.

13 C. T. McIntire and M. Perry (eds) *Toynbee: Reappraisals*, Toronto: University of Toronto Press, 1989, introduction.

14 See, for example, L. Woolf, *New Statesman and Nation*, 1934, 8(182): 213; and J. L. Hammond, *Manchester Guardian*, 26 June 1934.

15 See, for example, P. Geyl, P. A. Sorokin and A. J. Toynbee, *The Pattern of the Past: Can We Determine It?* Boston, MA: Beacon Press, 1949; C. T. McIntire and M. Perry (eds) *Toynbee: Reappraisals*; M. Samuel, *The Professor and the Fossil: Some Observations on Arnold J. Toynbee's A Study of History*, New York: Knopf, 1956; M. F. A. Montagu (ed.) *Toynbee and History: Critical Essays and Reviews*, Boston, MA: Peter Sargent, 1956; D. Jerrold, *The Lie About the West: a Response to Professor Toynbee's Challenge*, New York: Sheed & Ward, 1953; C. Frankel, *The Case for Modern Man*, Boston, MA: Beacon Press, 1959; K. Popper, *The*

Open Society and its Enemies, Princeton, NJ: Princeton University Press, 1950; C. Brewin, 'Research in a Global Context: a Discussion of Toynbee's Legacy', *Review of International Affairs*, 1992, 18(2): 115–30; M. Mandelbaum, 'A Note on "Universality" in History', *Revis Univ Madrid*, 1957, 12, pp. 51–7; W. H. Walsh, 'Toynbee Reconsidered', *Philosophy*, 1963, 38(143): 71–8; W. H. Dray, 'Toynbee's Search for Historical Laws', *History and Theory*, 1960, 1(1): 32–54; V. Purcell, *Toynbee in Elysium; a Fantasy in One Act, by Myra Buttle*, New York: Sagamore Press, 1959; and H. R. Trevor-Roper, 'Arnold Toynbee's Millennium', *Encounter*, 1957, 8(45): 14–28.

16 Geyl, Sorokin and Toynbee, *The Pattern of the Past: Can We Determine It?* p. 43.

Toynbee's major works

A Study of History, 12 vols, London: Oxford University Press, 1934–61.
A Study of History, rev. and abr. A. J. Toynbee and J. Caplan, London: Oxford University Press, 1972.
Survey of International Affairs, 22 vols, London: Oxford University Press, 1925–53.
Civilisation on Trial and Other Essays, New York: Oxford University Press, 1948.
The World and the West, London: Oxford University Press, 1953.
An Historian's Approach to Religion, London: Oxford University Press, 1956.
Hannibal's Legacy: the Hannibalic War's Effects on Roman Life, London: Oxford University Press, 1966.
Some Problems of Greek History, London: Oxford University Press, 1969.
Mankind and Mother Earth: a Narrative History of the World, London: Oxford University Press, 1976.

See also

Bergson (MP), Geyl, Hegel, Ibn Khaldun, Marx, Polybius, Spengler, Vico.

Further resources

Geyl, P., *Debates with Historians*, New York: Meridian Books, 1958.
Geyl, P., Sorokin, P. A. and Toynbee, A. J., *The Pattern of the Past: Can We Determine It?* Boston, MA: Beacon Press, 1949.
McIntire, C. T. and Perry, M., *Toynbee: Reappraisals*, Toronto: University of Toronto Press, 1989.
McNeill, W. H., *Arnold J. Toynbee: a Life*, New York: Oxford University Press, 1989.
Montagu, M. F. A. (ed.) *Toynbee and History: Critical Essays and Reviews*, Boston, MA: Porter Sargent, 1956.
Morton, S. F., *A Bibliography of Arnold J. Toynbee*, Oxford: Oxford University Press, 1980.
Perry, M., *Arnold Toynbee and the Crisis of the West*, Washington, DC: University Press of America, 1982.
——, *Arnold Toynbee and the Western Tradition*, New York: Lang, 1996.
Stromberg, R. N., *Arnold J. Toynbee: Historian for an Age in Crisis*, Carbondale, IL: Southern Illinois University Press, 1972.

Thompson, K. W., *Toynbee's Philosophy of World History and Politics*, Baton Rouge, LA: Louisiana State University Press, 1985.

Winetrout, K., *Arnold Toynbee: the Ecumenical Vision*, Boston, MA: Twayne, 1975.

FREDERICK JACKSON TURNER 1861–1932

Frederick Jackson Turner is best known for the view that

> American history has been in a large degree the history of the colonisation of the Great West. The existence of an area of free land, its continuous recession, and the advance of American settlement westward, explain American development.
>
> ('The Significance of the Frontier in American History',
> in *Rereading Frederick Jackson Turner*, p. 31)

Yet he also challenged historians of his day to consider the significance of regional differences in American history; to draw upon a wide range of evidence and research methods; to recognise that events have multiple causes; and to look at the past in the light of the present. These ideas became the hallmark of the 'new history' of James Harvey Robinson, Carl Becker and Carl Beard, and persist today.

Turner was born in 1861 in Portage, Wisconsin. His mother was a teacher; his father was a journalist, printer, minor politician and amateur historian. Turner commenced studies at the University of Wisconsin in 1880. There he was taught by William F. Allen, a medievalist who encouraged his students to use any tool available to uncover the many causes of events and to trace the evolution of societies. Turner's master's thesis, 'The Character and Influence of the Fur Trade in Wisconsin' (1888), which he later expanded into a doctoral thesis at Johns Hopkins University, 'The Character and Influence of the Indian Trade in Wisconsin' (1890), was much influenced by Allen's ideas. Instructors at Johns Hopkins such as Albion Small, Woodrow Wilson and Richard Ely also encouraged Turner to explore the history of the American West.

In 1889 Turner returned to the University of Wisconsin to teach American history. Not long afterwards he published 'The Significance of History' (1891), a paper in which he outlined his views on how and why history ought to be studied. For Turner, good citizenship requires the study of history. This is because history can help us to understand contemporary American events:

> Every economic change, every political change, every military conscription, every socialistic agitation in Europe, has sent us

groups of colonists who have passed out onto our prairies to form new self-governing communities, or who have entered the life of our great cities. These men have come to us historical products, they have brought to us not merely so much bone and sinew, not merely so much money, not merely so much manual skill, they have brought with them deeply inrooted customs and skills. They are important factors in the political and economic life of the nation. Our destiny is interwoven with theirs.

('The Significance of History', in
Rereading Frederick Jackson Turner, p. 27)

As the study of history is entwined with the study of contemporary events, every age 'writes the history of the past anew with reference to the conditions uppermost in its own time'. History is thus 'ever *becoming, never completed*' (ibid., p. 18). In his age, Turner argues, historians cannot afford to be ignorant of European affairs. Nor, if they are to gain a thorough understanding of American society, can they confine themselves to the study of political and economic developments. In order to gain a complete view of society, they must study all the facets of past societies. That requires drawing on a wide range of evidence and research methods.

A year later Turner argued that historians had neglected 'the fundamental, dominating fact in United States history', the expansion of population from east to west. He wrote:

In a sense, American history up to our own day has been colonial history, the colonisation of the Great West. The ever retreating frontier of free land is the key to American development.

('Problems in American History', in
Frontier and Section, p. 29)

Western expansion, he believed, was the key to American identity. Studying it would help to show 'how European life entered the continent, and how America modified that life and reacted on Europe' (ibid., p. 30). Turner sent copies of this article to many historians. One of them, Herbert Adams, recommended that Turner prepare a paper for the 1893 meeting of the American Historical Association at the World's Columbian Exposition in Chicago.

Although more people saw 'Buffalo Bill' Cody's 'Wild West' show than heard Turner speak on 'The Significance of the Frontier in

American History', the latter was eventually to gain such wide influence that it was hailed as the single most important contribution to the writing of American history.[1] In this paper, Turner developed the idea that the frontier – the 'meeting point between savagery and civilisation' – was the key to American history and identity ('The Significance of the Frontier in American History', in *Rereading Frederick Jackson Turner*, p. 32). According to Turner, as settlers moved westward to exploit free land and resources, they found that their customs and habits were inappropriate. This prompted a 'return to primitive conditions': the wilderness overpowered settlers, stripping away their habits and customs, and throwing them into a state of near savagery. Then followed a number of phases of development:

> It begins with the Indian and the hunter; it goes on to tell of the disintegration of savagery by the entrance of the trader, the pathfinder of civilisation; we read the annals of the pastoral stage in ranch life; the exploitation of the soil by the raising of unrotated crops of corn and wheat in sparsely settled farming communities; the intensive culture of the denser farm settlement; and finally the manufacturing organisation with city and factory system.
>
> (Ibid., p. 38)

This pattern of development, Turner claims, epitomises the record of the social evolution of humanity. The result was a new society which differed markedly from those of Europe and the East Coast of America. Western expansion was thus a 'gate of escape from the bondage of the past' (ibid., p. 59). Class distinctions were weakened, social and political equality were demanded and a new spirit of individualism and nationalism emerged as people were 'Americanised in the crucible of the frontier' (ibid., p. 47). To the frontier, Turner thus concludes,

> the American intellect owes its striking characteristics. That coarseness and strength combined with acuteness and inquisitiveness; that practical, inventive turn of mind, quick to find expedients; that masterful grasp of material things, lacking in the artistic but powerful to effect great ends; that restless, nervous energy; that dominant individualism, working for good and for evil, and withal that buoyancy and exuberance which comes with freedom.
>
> (Ibid., p. 59)

With the settlement of all the free land in his times, Turner claimed, the first period in American history had closed. He was uncertain what the next period would be like.

At the time the essay appeared in print, Turner's ideas attracted little attention. Edward Everett Hale called it a 'curious and interesting paper' and Theodore Roosevelt wrote that Turner had 'struck some first class ideas and . . . put into definite shape a good deal of thought which has been floating around rather loosely'.[2] Gradually, however, Turner hammered home his point to historians through a small but steady stream of papers. He also expanded his field of research to embrace the whole trans-Mississippi West and worked hard to take his ideas to a wider audience. For instance, 'The Problem of the West', which appeared in the *Atlantic Monthly* (1896), attracted many favourable reviews, and he built on this success with 'Dominant Forces in Western Life' (*Atlantic Monthly*, 1897), 'The Middle West' (*International Monthly*, 1901) and 'Contributions of the West to American Democracy' (*Atlantic Monthly*, 1903). Scarcely a decade after its appearance, Turner's 'frontier thesis' was common knowledge in historical circles and it 'emerged as an incantation repeated in thousands of classrooms and textbooks'.[3] Turner's thesis, as Roosevelt realised, tapped into existing narratives of frontier mythology and it became a rationale for popular American culture – the culture of cowboys and Indians, 'Little House on the Prairie', Disneyland's 'Frontier Land' and even 'Star Trek'.[4] His ideas were even applied to Australian, African and Russian history.[5]

Turner taught at the University of Wisconsin until 1910 and at Harvard until 1924. He served as president of the American Historical Association from 1909 to 1910 and on the editorial board of the *American Historical Review* from 1910 to 1915. He published more papers on the frontier, but his talk of the concept was increasingly abstract and he chose to focus on pioneer values and ideals. In 'Pioneer Ideals and the State University' (1910), for instance, he suggested that people could engage with, reflect on and change pioneer ideals through scientific research (*Rereading Frederick Jackson Turner*, pp. 101–18). Furthermore, in 'Sections and Nation' (1922), he argued that, although the United States was composed of a number of different cultural 'sections', they were all underpinned by a common inheritance, set of institutions, law, language and spirit. America could even teach Europe something about peaceful coexistence. As he writes:

> We are members of one body, though it is a varied body. It is inconceivable that we should follow the evil path of Europe and place our reliance upon triumphant force. We shall not become

cynical, and convinced that sections, like European nations, must dominate their neighbours and strike first and hardest. However profound the economic changes, we shall not give up our American ideals and hopes for man, which had their origin in our own pioneering experience, in favour of any mechanical solution offered by doctrinaires educated in Old World grievances. . . . We shall continue to present to our sister continent of Europe the underlying ideas of America as a better way of solving difficulties. We shall point to the *Pax Americana*, and seek the path of peace on earth to men of good will.

('Sections and Nation', in
Rereading Frederick Jackson Turner, p. 200)

Though his ideas on sections gained popular acceptance, they did not make as much of a splash as the 'frontier thesis'. Turner also wrote *The Rise of the New West* (the fourteenth volume of A. B. Hart's *The American Nation: a History*) and collected some of his essays together in the volume *The Frontier in American History* (1920), but was still working on *The United States, 1830–1850: the Nation and its Sections* when he died in 1932. It was edited by Merrill H. Crissey, Max Farrand and Avery Craven and released in 1935. A further collection of essays entitled *The Significance of Sections in American History* was released shortly after his death, and Turner was posthumously awarded the Pulitzer Prize for this work.

After Turner's death, critics complained most loudly about the haziness of Turner's language – in particular of his usage of the word 'frontier' – and that he did nothing to remedy the ubiquity of the 'f-word' in American culture.[6] Turner was guilty as charged; he had, for instance, used the word 'frontier' to refer to 'the edge of settled territory', 'the hither edge of free land', 'the line of settlement', 'the West', 'a form of society' and 'a process'. Scholars also took issue with the gaps in the 'frontier thesis'. Charles Beard argued that the frontier could not explain slavery, the growth of the city or industrialisation. Benjamin Wright and Richard White added that frontier culture had been shaped by the East Coast and the Federal Government respectively. George Wilson Pierson complained that Turner had standardised what was a varied pioneer experience.[7] Turner was also accused of playing down European heritage and of giving Indians, women, Hispanics, African-Americans and Asians short shrift.[8] His was a middle-class, white, male account of America's past. Writers like Carlton Hayes even claimed that Turner's thesis was dangerous because it fostered an indifference to international affairs. For many scholars, Turner was simply a myth-maker.[9] A number of writers have come to Turner's defence, but it is now recognised that his ideas cannot be adopted without some pretty far-reaching modifications.[10]

Turner sketched out a framework that has inspired and troubled countless historians of the United States. Scholars have praised him, denounced him and tried to ignore him, but when they talk of the American past, his ideas invariably crop up. That they continue to draw on and adapt his ideas, Turner would probably argue, demonstrates that 'each age writes the history of the past anew'.

Notes

1 R. White, 'Frederick Jackson Turner and Buffalo Bill', in J. R. Grossman (ed.) *The Frontier in American Culture: an Exhibition at the Newberry Library, Chicago, August 6, 1994–January 7, 1995*, Chicago, IL: Newberry Library, 1994, p. 1.

2 R. A. Billington, *The Genesis of the Frontier Thesis: a Study in Historical Creativity*, San Marino, CA: Huntington Library, 1971, p. 13.

3 White, 'Frederick Jackson Turner and Buffalo Bill', p. 12.

4 On Turner, Disneyland and 'Star Trek', see P. L. Limerick, 'The Adventures of the Frontier in the Twentieth Century', in J. R. Grossman (ed.) *The Frontier in American Culture*, pp. 67–102; and W. B. Tyrell, 'Star Trek as Myth and Television as Mythmaker', *Journal of Popular Culture*, 1977, 10: 711–19.

5 See, for example, R. Lawson, 'Towards Demythologising the Australian Legend – Turner's Frontier Thesis and the Australian Experience', in *Journal of Social History*, 1980, 13(4): 577–87; G. Deveneau, 'Frontier in Recent African History', in *International Journal of African Historical Studies*, 1978, 11(1): 63–85; and J. L. Wieczynski, *The Russian Frontier: the Impact of Borderlands upon the Course of Early Russian History*, Charlottesville, VA: University of Virginia Press, 1976.

6 See, for example, G. W. Pierson, 'The Frontier and Frontiersmen of Turner's Essay', in *Pennsylvania Magazine of History and Biography*, 1940, 64: 449–78; and R. Hofstadter, 'Turner and the Frontier Myth', *American Scholar*, 1949, 18: 433–43. On frontier as the 'f-word', see P. L. Limerick, 'The Adventures of the Frontier in the Twentieth Century', in Grossman, *The Frontier in American Culture*, p. 72.

7 For a summary of these criticisms, see H. R. Lamar, 'Frederick Jackson Turner', in M. Cunliffe and R. W. Winks (eds) *Pastmasters: Some Essays on American Historians*, New York: Harper & Row, 1969, pp. 74–109. See also R. White, *'It's Your Misfortune and None of My Own': A History of the American West*, Norman, OK: University of Oklahoma Press, 1991.

8 See the papers by various authors in 'Centennial Symposium on the Significance of Frederick Jackson Turner', in *Journal of the Early Republic*, 1993, 13: 133–249; S. C. Schulte, 'American Indian Historiography and the Myth of the Origins of the Plains Wars', in *Nebraska History*, 1980, 61: 437–46; W. G. Robbins, 'The Conquest of the American West: History as Eulogy', in *Indian Historian*, 1977, 10: 7–13; G. Riley, 'Images of the Frontierswoman: Iowa as a Case Study', in *Western Historical Quarterly*, 1977,

8: 189–202; L. Graaf, 'Recognition, Racism and Reflections on the Writing of Western Black History', in *Pacific Historical Review*, 1975, 44: 22–51; D. C. Smith, 'The Logging Frontier', in *Journal of Frontier History*, 1974, 18: 96–106; and W. R. Jacobs, 'The Indian and the Frontier in American History – a Need for Revision', in *Western Historical Quarterly*, 1973, 4: 43–56.

9 L. M. Hacker, 'Sections – or Classes?', reprinted in G. R. Taylor (ed.) *The Turner Thesis: Concerning the Role of the Frontier in American History*, revised edition, Boston, MA: D. C. Heath, 1956; C. J. H. Hayes, 'The American Frontier – Frontier of What?' in *American Historical Review*, 1946, 51(1): 199–216; R. Hofstadter, 'Turner and the Frontier Myth'; and D. Noble, *Historians against History: the Frontier Thesis and the National Covenant in American Historical Writing since 1830*, Minneapolis, MN: University of Minnesota Press, 1965, pp. 37–55.

10 For examples of re-interpretations of the frontier thesis, see, for example, J. Forbes, 'Frontiers in American History and the Role of the Frontier Historian', in *Ethnology*, 1968, 15: 205, 207; and H. Lamar and L. Thompson (eds) *The Frontier in History: North America and Southern Africa Compared*, New Haven, CT: Yale University Press, 1981.

Turner's major works

Rise of the New West, 1819–1829, vol. 14 of *The American Nation: a History*, ed. A. B. Hart, New York: Harper & Brothers, 1906.

The Frontier in American History, New York: Henry Holt, 1920. Online at: http://xroads.virginia.edu/~HYPER/TURNER/

The Significance of Sections in American History, ed. A. Craven and M. Farrand, New York: Henry Holt, 1932.

The United States, 1830–1850: the Nation and its Sections, ed. M. H. Crissey, M. Farrand and A. Craven, New York: Henry Holt, 1935.

Frontier and Section, ed. R. A. Billington, Englewood Cliffs, NJ: Prentice-Hall, 1961.

Rereading Frederick Jackson Turner, ed. J. M. Faragher, New York: Henry Holt, 1994.

See also

Mill (MP), Ranke, Wilson (IRT), Woodson.

Further resources

Billington, R. A., *The Genesis of the Frontier Thesis: a Study in Historical Creativity*, San Marino, CA: Huntington Library, 1971.

——, *Frederick Jackson Turner: Historian, Scholar, Teacher*, New York: Oxford University Press, 1973.

Carpenter, R. H., *The Eloquence of Frederick Jackson Turner*, San Marino, CA: Huntington Library, 1983.

'Centennial Symposium on the Significance of Frederick Jackson Turner', *Journal of the Early Republic*, 1993, 13(2): 133–249.

Grossman, J. R. (ed.) *The Frontier in American Culture: an Exhibition at the Newberry*

Library, August 26, 1994–January 7, 1995, Chicago, IL: Chicago Library, 1994.

Jacobs, W. R., *The Historical World of Frederick Jackson Turner, with Selections from his Correspondence*, New Haven, CT: Yale University Press, 1968.

Marion, W. E., *Frederick Jackson Turner: a Reference Guide*, Boston, MA: G. K. Hall, 1985.

Nash, G. D., *Creating the West: Historical Interpretations, 1890–1990*, Albuquerque, NM: University of New Mexico Press, 1991.

'New Perspectives on the West', by the American Public Broadcasting Service (PBS), online at: http://www/pbs.org/weta/thewest/

GIAMBATTISTA VICO 1668–1744

It has long been fashionable to view Vico as a neglected genius whose idiosyncratic and esoteric offerings hold the key to much of Western thought. While this view of Vico as a 'difficult' writer has made him appealing to a small number of academics, it has also served to make sure that he remains neglected. This is a great pity, for Vico's views on the nature of historical knowledge and the relationship between the study of history and self-knowledge speak strongly to our times.

The son of a Neapolitan bookseller, Giambattista Vico taught himself Latin, law and philosophy between short spells at a number of schools. At the age of nineteen he left Naples for Salerno to become tutor to the nephews of the jurist Monsignor Rocca. At Salerno Vico delved into the writings of a wide range of thinkers, including Plato, Galileo, Tacitus, Descartes and Francis Bacon, and completed a doctorate in law. On his return he won the competition for a chair of rhetoric at the University of Naples. Vico took up this position in 1699, though he continued to give private lessons and accept literary commissions as he was poorly paid (see *The Autobiography of Giambattista Vico*, pp. 118–36).

At the University of Naples, Vico argued in six orations given between 1699 and 1707 that wisdom and prudence could only be attained through the study of both the arts and the sciences. He stressed that in order to reach the truth and self-knowledge, we must study all the branches of knowledge, past and present (see *On Humanistic Education*). In his orations for 1709 and 1710 he further developed this view of education. In the first of these, *De nostri temporis studiorum ratione* (trans. *On the Study Methods of our Time*), Vico argues that mathematical and scientific knowledge is not certain in the way that writers like Descartes suggest. According to Descartes, certainty is rooted in the criteria of clarity and distinctness. For Vico, on the other hand, scientific and mathematical knowledge is only certain because the symbols and concepts used are the products of the human mind (ibid., pp. 21–4). Here we see the emergence of what was to become the cornerstone of his philosophy: that we can best understand things that have been made by people. Furthermore, Vico claims that the dominance of mathematics and science had led to the neglect of the wide-ranging education he recommended. If students were educated in all forms of knowledge, Vico tells us, then 'they would not feel the impulse to step rashly into discussions while they are still in process of learning; nor would they, with pedestrian slavishness, refuse to accept any viewpoint unless it has been sanctioned by a teacher' (ibid., p. 19).

Vico's 'constructivist' view of knowledge is even clearer in his oration from 1710: *De antiquissima Italorum sapientia ex linguae latinae originibus eruenda* (trans. *On the Most Ancient Wisdom of the Italians Unearthed from the Origins of the Latin Language*). God knows the world, Vico argues, because he made it.[1] Similarly, we – who are made in God's image – can know the world that we have made. So, for instance, I can know this book with more certainty than I can know a rock. This does not mean that the natural world cannot be known at all; it simply means that the knowledge scientists attain by 'imitating God' in experiments is only *perfectly* intelligible to God (ibid., p. 94). Vico sums up this idea in the phrase '*verum et factum convertuntur*' or 'the true is convertible with the made' (ibid., p. 45).

In 1717 a chair of law became vacant at the University of Naples, and Vico hoped to show his qualification for this position through the publication of a multi-part work on Grotius' *The Law of War and Peace* (1717). To that end he wrote *De universi iuris uno principio et fine uno* and *De constantia iurisprudentis* (in *Opere di G. B. Vico*, vol. 2). In these studies, Vico argued that, while the principles underlying the laws of particular nations are subject to change, they correspond to a pattern of growth and decay common to all nations except the Jews. This pattern, Vico believes, is the work of 'Providence'. Exactly what Vico means by 'Providence' is unclear and continues to puzzle commentators. Vico failed to win the chair. In his next work, *Principi di Scienza Nuova di Giambattista Vico d'intorno alla Commune Natura delle Nazioni in Questa Terza Impressione* (trans. *The New Science of Giambattista Vico*), he tried to spell out the pattern of growth and decay in detail. Vico published the first edition of *The New Science* in 1725. In 1728, he was urged to publish an edition in Venice, at that time one of the most important book-printing centres in Europe. He agreed, and enlarged the manuscript with many annotations and additions. He ran into difficulties with the printer, however, and had to reduce the size of the work. This second edition of *The New Science* was released in Naples in 1730. Vico continued to revise the work. The notes that he made formed the basis of a third edition, which he was seeing through publication at the time of his death in 1744 (on the development of *The New Science*, see *The Autobiography of Giambattista Vico*, p. 210).

Many periods of history, Vico argues in *The New Science*, can be described in three ways: the 'age of poetry', the 'age of heroes' and the 'age of humans'. In the human race, he writes,

> first appear the huge and the grotesque, like the cyclopes; then the proud and the magnanimous, like Achilles; then the valorous and just, like Aristides and Scipio Africanus; nearer to us, imposing figures with great semblances of virtue accompanied with great vices, who among the vulgar win a name for true glory, like Alexander and Caesar; still later, the melancholy and reflective, like Tiberius; finally the dissolute and shameless madmen, like Caligula, Nero, and Domitian.
>
> (*The New Science*, §243)[2]

In the 'age of poetry', people are brutish and irrational, but they possess strong imaginative powers. Through myths, which they take to be literal truths, they try to explain their world. Myths underpin their language, their institutions, laws and ideals. People in this age also fear and believe in an all-powerful God. Those who claim to be able to communicate with God are thus accorded a privileged position. In the 'age of heroes', these privileged individuals begin to lose their power. People begin to doubt that they are able to communicate with God. Their clashes highlight the need for a political system based on humanity and justice. This type of system is realised in the 'age of humans'. In the 'age of heroes' and the 'age of humans', people pass from mythic, non-rational consciousness to rational consciousness. These are not superior ages, however, for the loss of imaginative ability leads to doubts about God, and thus, Vico suggests, moral corruption. If this disbelief cannot be arrested or reversed, a society may slump into a 'barbarism of reflection': the stage at which thought has exhausted its creative power.[3] In the 'barbarism of reflection', people seek to recapture belief through mythic consciousness. In the abstract, world history is underpinned by a cyclical pattern (ibid., §114). In reality, however, factors such as climate, disease, conflict and landscape produce variations in the pattern.

Through the study of history, Vico contends, we can gain insight into the ideas that shape our own times. Self-knowledge is important, he believes, because it can help us to avoid a collapse into barbarism. In line with his earlier writings, Vico contends that the study of the past is made possible because 'the true is convertible with the made'. It is 'beyond question', he writes, that 'the world of civil society has certainly been made by men, and that its principles are therefore to be found in the modification of our same human mind' (*New Science*, §331). Historians can understand the ideas and actions of historical agents by virtue of their common humanity. They can know what it is like to scheme, love and fear in a way that they cannot know what it is like to be a salmon swimming upstream. Recapturing the ideas and actions of historical agents is no easy matter, however, as understanding the 'age of poetry', say, requires us to consider myths as literal truths. Five things can limit our chances of achieving historical knowledge. First, Vico warns of making exaggerated claims about the wealth and power of past periods. It is tempting to think of a period as 'the good old days', or a 'golden age'. Such embellishments, however, can lead us to neglect features that contradict these labels.[4] Second, he draws attention to the 'conceit of nations', the opinion that developments in one's own country are of prime concern to all other countries. Here, one falls prey to the belief that one's country has excelled above all others in culture, lifestyle, military achievements and so on. National histories, Vico reminds us, tend not to dwell on failures. Third, Vico identifies the 'conceit of scholars'. Here, historians tend to think of people in the past in the light of their own values and abilities.

Fourth, he highlights what Collingwood calls the 'fallacy of sources'.[5] Here, the historian labours under the false belief that societies must share sources in order to have the same characteristics. Thus if two societies have similar institutions, one must have learned it from the other, or both from another society. This belief, Vico argues, denies the creative power of the human mind. Finally, Vico reminds his readers that they are probably better informed about historical events than those who were present as witnesses. Here, Vico suggests that any statement made by a person in the past must never automatically be accepted for historical truth. Rather, historical truth is to be found in the critical examination of words, myths, traditions and rituals. Etymology (the study of the derivation of terms) is particularly promising, as many of the words that we use bear the traces of their origins in remote times. Furthermore, Vico believes that thought and language are intertwined. It thus follows that the words people use and how they use them offer an excellent indication of the ways in which they thought about the world.

The fact that we have heard of Vico today must be largely credited to nineteenth-century thinkers such as Jules Michelet. Michelet was greatly impressed by Vico's ideas and produced an abridged French translation of *The New Science* in 1827. Through Michelet's efforts, Vico was credited with the discovery of the historical, political and aesthetic ideas that swept Europe at that time. Vico's ideas were later analysed by the Italian philosophers Giovanni Gentile and Benedetto Croce. Croce's analysis of Vico's ideas are even today held with high regard both in the Italian-speaking world and, thanks to R. G. Collingwood's translation of *La filosofia di Giambattista Vico* in 1913, the English-speaking world. Collingwood himself developed many of Vico's ideas in his writings on the principles of history. Because of the impact of Croce's and Collingwood's writings on Vico, it is often difficult to establish who said what. More recently, writers such as Badaloni, Berlin, Burke, Fisch, Haddock, Momgliano, Pompa, Tagliacozzo and Verene have contributed much to our understanding of Vico's thought. The tricentenary of Vico's birth in 1968 was marked by a number of conferences, literary collections and the establishment of two Vico institutes (one in Naples and one in New York).

It is difficult to spell out in detail the extent of Vico's influence on later writers. Numerous scholars assume a 'constructive' view of knowledge and his ideas on the patterns underlying societies bear many similarities to those of Hegel, Herder, Marx, Spengler and Toynbee. It seems fair to conclude, however, that Vico changed existing views of history and knowledge in at least two significant ways. First, Vico showed through his 'new science' how constructive and critical historical thought can be. This 'science' not only allows historians to gain a richer account of societies that have only been seen through written testimonies, but also gives them access to civilisations that left no written documents. For instance, Vico viewed myths not as false statements about reality or fanciful accounts of past events, but as embodiments of early outlooks and beliefs. Second, Vico challenged the then prevalent belief that only mathematics and science could produce certain knowledge. That issues concerning constructivism and the relationship between science and history continue to dominate historiographical discussion today shows that it is worth the effort to recapture what Vico says.

Notes

1   I have described God as a 'he' because Vico did so.
2   Achilles, warrior of the army of Agamemnon in the Trojan War; Aristides, Athenian statesman and general of the fifth century BC; Scipio Africanus (236–184 BC), Roman general, victor over Hannibal; Alexander the Great, King of Macedonia from 336 to 323 BC; Caesar (100–44 BC), Roman general and statesman; Tiberius, Roman emperor from 14 to 37 BC; Caligula, Roman

Emperor from AD 31 to 41; Nero, Roman Emperor from AD 54 to 68; and Domitian, Roman Emperor from AD 81 to 96.
3 R. G. Collingwood, *The Idea of History*, revised edition, W. J. Van der Dussen (ed.) Oxford: Oxford University Press, 1993, p. 67.
4 Ibid., pp. 68–9; C. Miller, *Giambattista Vico: Imagination and Historical Knowledge*, Basingstoke: St Martin's Press, 1993, chaps 1, 7.
5 Collingwood, *The Idea of History*, p. 69.

Vico's major works

Opere di G. B. Vico, 8 vols, ed. F. Nicolini, Bari: Laterza, 1914–41.
On Humanistic Education: Six Inaugural Orations, 1699–1707, trans. G. A. Pinton and A. W. Shippe, Ithaca, NY: Cornell University Press, 1993.
On the Study Methods of our Time, trans. E. Gianturco, Ithaca, NY: Cornell University Press, 1990.
On the Most Ancient Wisdom of the Italians Unearthed from the Origins of the Latin Language, trans. L. M. Palmer, Ithaca, NY: Cornell University Press, 1988.
The Autobiography of Giambattista Vico, trans. M. H. Fisch and T. G. Bergin, Ithaca, NY: Cornell University Press, 1963.
The New Science of Giambattista Vico, trans. M. H. Fisch and T. G. Bergin, 1744 edn, Ithaca, NY: Cornell University Press, 1968, revised edition, 1984.
'On the Heroic Mind', trans. E. Sewell and A. C. Sirignano, in G. Tagliacozzo, M. Mooney and D. P. Verene (eds) *Vico and Contemporary Thought*, Atlantic Highlands, NJ: Humanities Press, 1979, pp. 228–45.
Vico: Selected Writings, ed. and trans. L. Pompa, Cambridge: Cambridge University Press, 1982.

See also

Aristotle (MP), Bacon (MP), Collingwood, Croce, Descartes (MP), Hegel, Marx, Michelet.

Further resources

Adams, H. P., *The Life and Writings of Giambattista Vico*, London: Allen & Unwin, 1935.
Bedani, G., *Vico Revisited*, Oxford: Berg, 1989.
Berlin, I., *Vico and Herder*, London: Hogarth, 1976.
Burke, P., *Vico*, Oxford Past Masters, Oxford: Oxford University Press, 1985.
Collingwood, R. G., *The Idea of History*, revised edition, ed. W. J. Van der Dussen, Oxford: Oxford University Press, 1993.
Croce, B., *The Philosophy of Giambattista Vico*, trans. R. G. Collingwood, London: Howard Latimer, 1913.
Miller, C., *Giambattista Vico: Imagination and Historical Knowledge*, Basingstoke: St Martin's Press, 1993.
Pompa, L., *Vico: a Study of the 'New Science'*, Cambridge: Cambridge University Press, 1990.
Tagliacozzo, G. (ed.) *Vico: Past and Present*, Atlantic Highlands, NJ: Humanities Press, 1981.

Tagliacozzo, G., Mooney, M. and Verene, D. P. (eds) *Vico and Contemporary Thought*, London: Macmillan, 1980.

Tagliacozzo, G. and Verene, D. P. (eds) *Giambattista Vico's Science of Humanity*, Baltimore, MD: Johns Hopkins University Press, 1976.

Tagliacozzo, G., Verene, D. P. and Rumble, V. (eds) *A Bibliography of Vico in English (1884–1984)*, Bowling Green, OH: Philosophy Documentation Center, Bowling Green State University, 1985.

Tagliacozzo, G. and White, H. (eds) *Giambattista Vico: an International Symposium*, Baltimore, MD: Johns Hopkins University Press, 1969.

Verene, D. P., *Vico's Science of Imagination*, Ithaca, NY: Cornell University Press. 1981.

——, *The New Art of Autobiography: an Essay on the 'Life of Giambattista Vico Written by Himself'*, Oxford: Oxford University Press, 1991.

W. H. WALSH 1913–86

'Philosophy of history', W. H. Walsh wrote in 1962, 'has never been a popular subject in Great Britain, whether with philosophers or with historians, and it shows few signs of genuinely gaining in prestige at the present time.' Such a state of affairs fascinated Walsh, and in a number of articles and the work for which he is best known – *An Introduction to Philosophy of History* (1951, third revised edition, 1967) – he tried to stress the importance of problems that arise out of reflections on the nature of history.

William Henry Walsh was born in Leeds on 10 December 1913. After studying at Leeds Grammar School, Walsh went to Merton College, Oxford. He had a strong connection with Merton: after graduating with a first class degree in *Literae Humaniores* (classics and philosophy), he was a junior research fellow and tutor from 1947 to 1960, and after his retirement in 1979 he returned as an emeritus fellow. Between 1960 and 1979, Walsh was professor of logic and metaphysics at the University of Edinburgh. He died on 7 April 1986.

That philosophy of history is 'an object of suspicion, if not of contempt', Walsh believes, is due in no small part to its traditional association with 'metaphysical' speculation. Up until the nineteenth century, what Walsh calls 'speculative philosophy of history' was essentially the only form of philosophy of history. Its aim, he writes,

> was to attain an understanding of the course of history as a whole; to show that, despite the many apparent anomalies and inconsequences it presented, history could be regarded as forming a unity embodying an overall plan, a plan which, if once we grasped it, would both illuminate the detailed course

of events and enable us to view the historical process as, in a special sense, satisfactory to reason.

(*Introduction to Philosophy of History*, p. 13)

Such a search for pattern or meaning in the course of history can be seen in the works of writers like Vico, Herder, Kant, Hegel, Marx, Spengler and Toynbee. The speculative quest for unity, Walsh claims, is 'anathema to the cautious British mind' because its supporters are prone to select and manipulate data to fit in with their ideas (ibid., p. 14). There are grounds for the revival of 'philosophy of history' in Britain, however, because there is another way in which these terms can be understood. Just as the word 'history' may refer to either past human actions or the account of past actions that historians construct, so too 'philosophy of history' may refer to either the study of the course of historical events or to the study of the methods and assumptions of historians. When we reflect on the assumptions or methods of historians, Walsh tells us, we engage in 'critical' or 'analytical' philosophy of history. Walsh's division of philosophy of history into speculative and critical branches is now widely accepted.

Though Walsh's writings focus on various problems of critical philosophy of history, he is especially interested in the status of history as a form of knowledge and its relation to other forms of knowledge. Walsh's interest echoes that of other critical philosophers at the time. Their discussions were dominated by the question of whether historical knowledge was similar to either perceptual or scientific knowledge. This was considered to be a question of prime importance, because an answer would show whether there was any need to reflect separately on the nature of historical knowledge. For example, if historical knowledge was shown to be commensurate with scientific knowledge, then philosophy of history would be a part of philosophy of science.

For those who see a connection between historical and perceptual knowledge, the essential task of historians is to find out and describe 'precisely what happened'. They limit themselves to describing what they perceive in a 'plain narrative of events' (ibid., p. 32). Few historians, Walsh believes, would be satisfied with such a limitation. This is because they wish to understand and explain *why* events happened the way they did. This, in Walsh's view, entails the construction of a 'significant narrative', 'a reconstruction of the past that is both intelligent and intelligible' (ibid., p. 33). So what form do their explanations take? 'Positivists' believe that historical explanations are equivalent to those of natural scientists. They explain events by subsuming them under empirically verified universal laws. This view, Walsh believes, does not match what historians commonly do. To begin with, historians differ from scientists in their view of what warrants inclusion in an explanation. In the sciences an 'instrumental' notion of importance operates: items are judged to be important because of what they bring about. Historians may also use the same criterion; for instance, a historian may say that the Industrial Revolution was an important event in modern history because it brought about far-reaching changes in society. But this is not the sole criterion of selection that operates in history. An event may be thought to be 'intrinsically' important; for example, a historian may write about the Vietnam War because he or she wants to show the brutality of war. So what makes an item worthy of inclusion does not have to be its tendency to bring something else about.

This raises the 'most important and the most baffling' problem in critical philosophy of history: that of historical objectivity (ibid., p. 93). This problem arises because, while historians claim to tell us about what happened in the past, they have no direct access to it. Historians cannot observe their subject-matter as scientists do, and historical evidence 'is not something which is fixed, finished, and uncontroversial in its meanings and implications' ('Truth and Fact in History Reconsidered', p. 54). Evidence has to be authenticated and assessed. This state of affairs has led some writers to ask if value judgement is a necessary part of historical inquiry and whether an independent or real past has any verificatory role to play in historical inquiry at all. Goldstein, for instance, has written: 'To demand of historical descriptions that they conform to such a past is to demand what cannot be realised. Far from overlooking the distinction between facts and the description of facts . . . in history that distinction does not exist.'[1] Walsh disagrees with Goldstein's 'constructivist' arguments on the grounds that 'they admit of no refutation and produce no conviction' and that they go against our long-cherished belief in an actual past (ibid., p. 62). This has led Pompa to argue in response that 'philosophy ought to be constrained not by belief, no matter how deeply ingrained, but by argument, and arguments which admit of no refutation ought to be accepted'.[2] Walsh's and Pompa's assertions thus raise questions about the nature of philosophy itself.

For Walsh, historians also differ from scientists in that they are interested exclusively in the activities of human beings, as Collingwood and other writers stressed (Introduction to Philosophy of History, p, 31; see also 'Colligatory Concepts in History', pp. 129–30). But Walsh is not satisfied with Collingwood's further suggestion that to understand a past human action, the historian must 're-enact' the thought expressed in it in his or her mind. He writes:

It is not true that we grasp and understand the thought of past persons in a single act of intuitive insight. We have to discover what they were thinking, and find out why they thought it, by interpreting the evidence before us, and this process of interpretation is one in which we make at least implicit reference to general truths.

(Ibid., p. 58)

Walsh's difficulty with Collingwood's idea arises, as Dray has suggested, from his assumption that Collingwood was promoting a method for discovering previously unknown historical facts. How, Walsh asks, does a historian who doesn't already know what a past agent's thought was go about discovering it by rethinking it?[3] In his view, historians need some knowledge of the ways in which people act and react in particular situations. Re-enactment is thus not the sole key to the past. Historical interpretation also entails the consideration of general truths. Indeed in practice, historians utilise general truths in the procedure of 'colligation'.

Drawing on William Whewell's *Philosophy of the Inductive Sciences Founded upon their History* (1840), Walsh defines 'colligation' as the procedure of interpreting an event 'by tracing its intrinsic relations to other events and locating it in its historical context' (ibid., p. 59).[4] This concept may be found throughout Walsh's writings, but in later works it is associated with historical interpretation rather than historical explanation; compare, for instance, 'The Intelligibility of History' (1942) with 'Colligatory Concepts in History' (1967). In the procedure of colligation, events are interpreted by being grouped under 'appropriate' general concepts. To do that, Walsh claims, the historian must 'look for certain dominant concepts or leading ideas by which to illuminate his facts, to trace connections between those ideas themselves, and then to show how the detailed facts become intelligible in the light of them by constructing a "significant" narrative of the events of the period in question' (*Introduction to Philosophy of History*, p. 61). In *An Introduction to Philosophy of History*, for instance, Walsh suggests that Hitler's reoccupation of the Rhineland in 1936 can be made intelligible by connecting it to a larger whole, such as the policies of self-assertion and expansion which Hitler pursued from the time of his gaining power (p. 59). Here colligation entails the consideration of some actions and ideas in a wider context. 'Colligation' may also refer to the grouping of actions and ideas under a concept. For instance, Walsh suggests that 'the Romantic movement', 'the Renaissance' and 'the Industrial Revolution' are examples of colligatory conceptions. What makes these colligatory is the similarity of the ideas expressed by the agents (individuals or groups). Drawing on Walsh, McCullagh distinguishes between 'formal' and 'dispositional' colligatory concepts. Concepts such as 'revolution', 'evolution' and 'decay' are formal colligatory concepts because their applicability depends not on the goals and purposes of the agents involved but on the nature of the changes their actions bring about. The applicability of dispositional colligatory concepts, on the other hand, depends on the goals and purposes of the agents involved. For instance, 'revival' indicates a general desire to recapture an earlier style. McCullagh has also argued that colligatory concepts can be both singular and general. For instance, 'French Revolution' refers to actions in the eighteenth century, but the term 'revolution' may also be applied to a general class of actions in a number of different times and places.[5]

Walsh does not equate colligation with historical inquiry; it has, rather, an important part to play. Accordingly, it is worth thinking about the choice of colligatory concepts by historians. We may, for instance, talk of a 'twelfth-century renaissance', but the term 'renaissance' would have had no meaning for people at that time. Walsh recommends that two conditions should govern the choice of colligatory concepts in history. First, the concepts must do justice to the evidence. They cannot be chosen arbitrarily. Second, they must illuminate the facts. 'Here', Walsh writes, 'what we have primarily in mind is the extent to which their use makes the past real and intelligible to us' ('Colligatory Concepts in History', pp. 139–40). Thus it would be appropriate to use the description 'twelfth-century renaissance' if it accords with the evidence and it helps people in the present to understand that time. These conditions are the key to an intelligent and intelligible reconstruction of the past.

Thanks to the efforts of writers like Walsh, many historians and philosophers took an interest in critical philosophy of history in the mid-twentieth century. By the 1970s, however, its popularity declined as a number of criticisms arose. Some scholars complained that critical philosophers, in focusing so much attention on particular concepts, lacked overall views of the nature and aims of historical inquiry. Others claimed that critical philosophy was utterly irrelevant to historical practice. What is the use of a clarified concept of objectivity, say, if one does not make any recommendations for historical practice? Critical philosophers were also accused of analysing relatively trivial concepts and leaving important ones to languish in obscurity, and of ignoring the different cultural and historical understandings of particular concepts. More recently, the critical viewpoint has been subjected to criticism by feminists and those in cultural and ethnic minorities.

For them, the precision and clarity of critical philosophy masks a deep-seated masculine, Anglo-Saxon bias. Such complaints may be true, but we should never lose sight of what Walsh has shown us: the importance of exploring our assumptions and of explaining them clearly to others.

Notes

1 L. J. Goldstein, *Historical Knowing*, Austin, TX: University of Texas Press, 1976, p. xxi; quoted in L. Pompa, 'Truth and Fact in History', in L. Pompa and W. H. Dray (eds) *Substance and Form in History: a Collection of Essays in Philosophy of History*, Edinburgh: University of Edinburgh Press, 1981, p. 172.
2 Pompa, 'Truth and Fact in History', p. 173.
3 For a critical assessment of Walsh's understanding of re-enactment, see W. H. Dray, *History as Re-enactment: R. G. Collingwood's Idea of History*, Oxford: Oxford University Press, 1995, pp. 52–7.
4 On the history of 'colligation', see L. B. Cebik, 'Colligation and the Writing of History', *Monist*, 1969, 53(1): 40–57; C. B. McCullagh, 'Colligation and Classification in History', *History and Theory*, 1978, 17(3): 267–84; and W. H. Dray, 'Colligation under Appropriate Conceptions', in Pompa and Dray (eds) *Substance and Form in History*, pp. 156–70.
5 McCullagh, 'Colligation and Classification in History', pp. 267–84.

Walsh's major works

'The Intelligibility of History', *Philosophy*, 1942, 17(66): 128–43.
'The Character of Historical Explanation', *Proceedings of the Aristotelian Society*, 1947, supplementary vol. 21: 51–68.
An Introduction to Philosophy of History, London: Hutchinson, 1951, third revised edition, 1967. Published in the USA as *Philosophy of History: an Introduction*, New York: Harper & Row, 1960.
'"Plain" and "Significant" Narrative in History', *Journal of Philosophy*, 1958, 55(11): 479–84.
'"Meaning" in History', in P. Gardiner (ed.) *Theories of History*, London: Collier-Macmillan, 1959, pp. 296–308.
'Plato and the Philosophy of History: History and Theory in the *Republic*', *History and Theory*, 1962, 2(1): 3–16.
'History and Theory', *Encounter*, June 1962, 18: 50–4.
'Colligatory Concepts in History', in P. Gardiner (ed.) *The Philosophy of History*, Oxford: Oxford University Press, 1974, pp. 127–44.
'The Notion of an Historical Event', *Proceedings of the Aristotelian Society*, 1969, supplementary vol. 43: 153–64.
'Collingwood and Metaphysical Neutralism', in M. Krausz (ed.) *Critical Essays on the Philosophy of R. G. Collingwood*, Oxford: Oxford University Press, 1972, pp. 134–53.
'History as Science and History as More than Science', *Virginia Quarterly Review*, 1973, 49(1): 196–212.
'The Causation of Ideas', *History and Theory*, 1975, 14(3): 186–99.

'The Logical Status of Vico's Ideal Eternal History', in *Giambattista Vico's Science of Humanity*, eds G. Tagliacozzo and D. P. Verene, Baltimore, MD: Johns Hopkins University Press, 1976, pp. 141–53.
'Truth and Fact in History Reconsidered', *History and Theory*, 1977, 16(4): 53–71.

See also

Collingwood, Hempel, Oakeshott, Vico.

Further resources

Cebik, L. B., 'Colligation and the Writing of History', *Monist*, 1969, 53(1): 40–57.
Goldstein, L. J., *Historical Knowing*, Austin, TX: University of Texas Press, 1977.
History and Theory, 1977, 16(4).
Levich, M., 'Review of *Philosophy and History: a Symposium*', *History and Theory*, 1965, 4(3): 328–49.
McCullagh, C. B., 'Colligation and Classification in History', *History and Theory*, 1978, 17(3): 267–84.
Pompa, L. and Dray, W. H. (eds) *Substance and Form in History: a Collection of Essays on Philosophy of History*, Edinburgh: University of Edinburgh Press, 1981.
Thompson, D., 'Colligation and History Teaching', in W.H. Burston and D. Thompson (eds) *Studies in the Nature and Teaching of History*, London: Routledge & Kegan Paul, 1967, pp. 85–106.
Walsh, B., 'Number Six Merton Street', *Oxford Gazette*, 1997, second week, Michaelmas term, pp. 5–9.
White, M. G., *Foundations of Historical Knowledge*, New York: Harper & Row, 1965.
Williams, D. C., 'Essentials in History', in S. Hook (ed.) *Philosophy and History: a Symposium*, New York: New York University Press, 1963, pp. 37–93.

HAYDEN WHITE 1928–

Many historians, the American literary and historiographical critic Hayden White believes, tend towards what Jean-Paul Sartre called 'bad faith': a refusal to admit to themselves and to others their full freedom.[1] They do so by clinging to other people's views and ignoring options that are open to them. This 'bad faith' allows them to avoid the anxiety of making decisions but it also allows them to deny responsibility for their views and actions. Traditionally, White argues, historians have claimed that history occupies a middle ground between science and art. They are happy to claim the privileges of both as long as it suits their desire to avoid critical self-analysis. In practice this has meant stubbornly clinging to antiquated views of science and art, White believes. For example, they refuse to acknowledge that facts are 'not so much found as constructed by the kinds of questions which the investigator asks of the phenomena before him' and that they might learn something from the literary techniques of writers such as Joyce, Yeats and Ibsen ('The Burden of History', in *The Tropics of History*, p. 43). In order to re-establish the 'dignity of historical studies', historians must stop deceiving themselves. This entails, primarily, realising that their histories cannot correspond exactly to the way things 'really happened'.

Writing history involves selecting evidence and filling in gaps. But more importantly, histories are 'not only about events but also about the possible sets of relationships that those events can be demonstrated to figure' ('Historical Text as Literary Artifact', *Tropics of Discourse*, p. 94). For example, the chronological sequence $a, b, c, d, e, \ldots n$ may be endowed with different meanings, such as:

$A, b, c, d, e, \ldots n$;
$a, B, c, d, e, \ldots n$;
$a, b, C, d, e, \ldots n$;
$a, b, c, D, e, \ldots n$; and
$a, b, c, d, E, \ldots n$

and so on. In these sequences, capital letters indicate the privileging of a certain event or set of events. These sets of relationships, White claims, are not inherent in the events themselves. Rather, they are a part of the language that the historian uses to describe them. Historians, White notes, use the conventions of figurative, not technical, language. Technical languages, such as those used by physicists and chemists, are meaningful only to 'those who have been indoctrinated in their uses and only *of* those sets of events which the practitioners of a discipline have agreed to describe in a uniform terminology' (ibid.). Linguistic conventions are not laws that hold for all times and all places; they are assumptions that are held (consciously or unconsciously) in common by a group and are subject to change ('Introduction', *The Tropics of Discourse*, p. 13). These assumptions do not determine a group's ideas and actions, but *structure* its possibilities.

The number of conventions available to historians is not limitless, White believes, but may be more than the sixteen 'emplotment', 'argumentative', 'ideological' and 'tropic' conventions he presents in *Metahistory*, *The Tropics of Discourse* and *The Content of the Form*. Echoing the literary theorist Northrop Frye, White suggests that the Western literary tradition prescribes four structures of emplotment or ways of fashioning events into a narrative: romance, tragedy, comedy and satire.[2]

Romances tell of the escape of individuals and groups from a particular situation. Satires, on the other hand, are 'dominated by the apprehension that man is ultimately a captive of the world rather than its master' (*Metahistory*, p. 9). Comedies celebrate the triumph of individuals and groups over their situation, and tragedies tell of failures to do so.

There are also four structures of argument: formism, organicism, mechanism and contextualism. Formist writers aim to illuminate the particulars of the various ideas and actions they write about. They, White writes, 'serve the function of magnifying glasses for their readers; when they have finished with their work, the particulars in the field appear clearer to the (mind's) eye' ('Interpretation in History', in *Tropics of Discourse*, p. 64). Contextualists believe that ideas and actions are best explained when they are placed in context or 'colligated', as W. H. Walsh calls it. The things they write about 'still remain *dispersed*, but they are now provisionally integrated with one another as occupants of a shared "context" or, as it is sometimes said, are identified as objects bathed in a common "atmosphere"' (ibid., p. 65).

For the organicist, explanation 'must take the form of a synthesis in which each of the parts of the whole must be shown either to mirror the structure of the totality or to prefigure the form of either the end of the whole process or at least the latest phase of the process' (ibid.). Organicists try to find patterns that underpin all historical events. Finally, mechanistic writers try to identify and match 'causes' and 'effects' (ibid., p. 66).

Tidily enough, there are also four ideological structures: anarchism, conservatism, radicalism and liberalism. Drawing on the writings of the sociologist Karl Mannheim, White argues that ideologies are divided into the 'situationally congruent' (accepting of the status quo) and 'situationally transcendent' (critical of the status quo).[3] Conservatives are socially congruent, while liberals are interested in 'fine tuning' parts of society. Radicals and anarchists, on the other hand, seek the transformation of the status quo, the former in order to rebuild society on new foundations, and the latter in order to abolish society and replace it with 'a "community" of individuals held together by a shared sense of their "humanity"' (*Metahistory*, p. 24).

Whether historians are aware of it or not, they suggest to readers that some kinds of ideas and actions are more legitimate than others (*Metahistory*, p. 21; 'Narrativity in the Representation of Reality', in *The Content of the Form*, pp. 1–25). This leads White to suggest that, inasmuch as the historian

> remains unaware of the extent to which his very language
> determines not only the manner, but also the matter and

meaning of his discourse, he must be adjudged less critically self-conscious and even less 'objective' than the [organicist]. The latter at least tries to control his discourse through the use of a technical terminology which makes his intended meaning clear and open to criticism.

('Historicism, History and the Figurative Imagination',
in *The Tropics of Discourse*, p. 115)

Even more radically, he concludes that 'there are no grounds to be found in the historical record itself for preferring one way of construing its meaning over another'. That judgement is made on the basis of the historian's values ('The Politics of Historical Interpretation', in *The Content of the Form*, p. 75).

In theory, a piece of historical writing may include any combination of these conventions. But in practice, White suggests, we find the following correlations ('Interpretation in History', *The Tropics of Discourse*, p. 70; *Metahistory*, p. 29):

Mode of Emplotment	Mode of Explanation	Mode of Ideology
romance	formist	anarchist
comedy	organicist	conservative
tragedy	mechanistic	radical
satire	contextualist	liberal

The existence of these patterns suggests to White that there are conventions on a deeper level. These structures, he suggests, are 'tropic'. For White, tropes are:

deviations from literal, conventional, or 'proper' language use, swerves in locution sanctioned neither by custom nor logic. Tropes generate figures of speech or thought by their variation from what is 'normally' expected, and by the associations they establish between concepts normally felt not to be related or to be related in ways different from that suggested in the trope used. . . . Thus considered, troping is both a movement *from* one notion of the way things are related *to* another notion, and a connection between things so that they can be expressed in a language that takes account of the possibility of their being expressed otherwise.

('Introduction', *The Tropics of Discourse*, p. 2)

There are no prizes for guessing that there are four tropes: metaphor, metonymy, synecdoche and irony. These four correspond to the 'master tropes' identified by Kenneth Burke in *A Grammar of Motives*.[4] In metaphor, a name or descriptive term is transferred to an object; for example, my dog is a sea-slug. In metonymy, the name of an attribute of a thing is substituted for the name of the whole; for example, 'ten heads' means ten people. With synecdoche an attribute is used to describe a quality thought to belong to the totality; for example, 'he is all thumbs'. Finally, irony refers to a figure of speech in which the intended meaning is the opposite of that expressed by the words used; for example, 'he is all heart' applied to a 'heartless' person (*Metahistory*, pp. 34–6).

Ironists are even metatropological, White suggests, because they are aware that it is easy to misinterpret the meaning of words. They understand 'the potential foolishness of all linguistic characterisations of reality' (ibid., pp. 37–8). An analysis of the dominant modes of historical thinking in nineteenth-century Europe, White believes, shows the movement from metaphorical, through metonymical and synecdochial views of the historical world, to an ironic understanding of all knowledge (*Metahistory*, *passim*; 'Introduction', *The Tropics of Discourse*, pp. 5–6).

In the twentieth century, however, historians have averted their gaze from the ironic. In doing so, they have deceived themselves and their readers. Such deception, White contends, can be dangerous. This is seen clearly in the case of the erasure of the 'sublime'. In White's writings on this subject, especially 'The Politics of Historical Interpretation: Discipline and De-sublimation' (in *The Content of the Form*, pp. 58–82), the theories of the German philosophers Kant and Schiller are especially important. In *The Critique of Judgement* (1790), Kant suggests that our experience of mighty or dangerous phenomena from a position of safety can instigate self-awareness. Mighty phenomena, he claims, can make us aware of our limitations and of the tremendous strength of our rational being.[5] Similarly, for Schiller, encountering the sublime means laying important beliefs about ourselves on the line.[6] Schiller was the last writer to discuss the sublime in such a way. Since then, White claims, historians have refused to recognise the openness, confusion and uncontrollable nature of the past.[7] This has cut them, and their readers, off from an open and emancipatory future. Historians, he writes,

> deprive history of the kind of meaninglessness that alone can goad living human beings to make their lives different for themselves and their children, which is to say, to endow their lives with a meaning for which they alone are fully responsible.

One can never move with any politically effective confidence from an apprehension of 'the way things actually are or have been' to the kind of moral insistence that they 'should be otherwise' without passing through a feeling of repugnance for and negative judgement of the condition that is to be superseded. And precisely insofar as historical reflection is disciplined to understand history in such a way that it can forgive everything or at best to practice a kind of 'disinterested interest'[,] . . . it is removed from any connection with a visionary politics and consigned to a service that will always be antiutopian in nature.

('The Politics of Historical Interpretation', pp. 72–3)

Even Marxism is antiutopian because it assumes that history is fully comprehensible (ibid., p. 73). Nobody is served, White believes, by conventional treatments of the Holocaust and modern Zionist and Palestinian claims. What we require, he tells us, is a historiography in which we are confronted by the horror and the chaos of the past. That will make us determined to make life different for ourselves and future generations (ibid., pp. 76–80). When we do so, White concludes, we will be released from the 'burden of history'.

White's writings are historiographically provocative. As Vann has argued, however, literary theorists seem to have shown more interest in White's works.[8] White could of course argue that the relative neglect of his writings by historians is evidence of their 'bad faith'. This may to some extent be true. But they may also feel that White's views are themselves an expression of 'bad faith'. In White's estimation, historians tend towards 'bad faith' because they stubbornly cling to antiquated views of science and art. Having cast off such views, however, White takes shelter in literary theory, and in doing so, he averts his gaze from a number of other historiographical options. Carroll, for instance, questions the assumption that anything that is not a perfect likeness of the past must be fictive. The inapplicability of the correspondence theory of truth, he argues, should prompt historians to explore other notions of 'truth'.[9] Also, Golob has pointed out that White fails to give sufficient attention to the many historiographical writings on understanding human actions from the 'inside'.[10] Mandelbaum questions whether historical writing is best understood tropically and McCullagh is unconvinced by White's claim that because historians use metaphors their accounts cannot be true or false.[11] It is also open to question whether the distinction between the sciences and non-sciences turns on the possession of a technical terminology and whether being a philosopher simply requires one to hold conscious or unconscious assumptions.

Notes

1 J.-P. Sartre, *Being and Nothingness: an Essay on Phenomenological Ontology*, trans. H. E. Barnes, New York, Philosophical Library, 1956, part 1, chap. 2.
2 N. Frye, *Anatomy of Criticism: Four Essays*, Princeton, NJ: Princeton University Press, 1957.
3 K. Mannheim, *Ideology and Utopia: an Introduction to the Sociology of Knowledge* (1936), trans. L. Wirth and E. Shils, San Diego, CA: Harcourt, Brace Jovanovich, 1985, pp. 180–2, 206–15.
4 K. Burke, *A Grammar of Motives*, Berkeley, CA: University of California Press, pp. 503–17.
5 I. Kant, *The Critique of Judgement*, trans. J. C. Meredith, Oxford: Oxford University Press, 1973.
6 See, for example, *On Naïve and Sentimental Poetry*, trans. J. A. Elias, New York: Ungar, 1966.
7 For an alternative treatment of the sublime by a contemporary writer, see J.-F. Lyotard, *Lessons on the Analytic of the Sublime*, trans. E. Rottenberg, Palo Alto, CA: Stanford University Press, 1994.
8 R. T. Vann, 'The Reception of Hayden White', *History and Theory*, 1998, 37(2): 143–61.
9 N. Carroll, 'Interpretation, History and Narrative', *Monist*, 1990, 73(2): 134–66.
10 E. O. Golob, 'The Irony of Nihilism', *History and Theory*, 1980, 19(4): 55–65.
11 M. Mandelbaum, 'The Presuppositions of *Metahistory*', *History and Theory*, 1980, 19(4): 39–54; and B. McCullagh, 'Metaphor and Truth in History', *Clio*, 1993, 23(1): 23–49.

White's major works

Metahistory: the Historical Imagination in Nineteenth-century Europe, Baltimore, MD: Johns Hopkins University Press, 1973.
Tropics of Discourse: Essays in Cultural Criticism, Baltimore, MD: Johns Hopkins University Press, 1978.
The Content of the Form: Narrative Discourse and Historical Representation, Baltimore, MD: Johns Hopkins University Press, 1989.
'New Historicism: a Comment', in H. A. Veeser (ed.) *The New Historicism*, New York: Routledge, 1989, pp. 293–302.
'Figuring the Nature of the Times Deceased: Literary Theory and Historical Writing', in R. Cohen (ed.) *The Future of Literary Theory*, New York: Columbia University Press, 1989, pp. 19–43.
'Historical Emplotment and the Problem of Truth', in S. Friedlander (ed.) *Probing the Limits of Representation*, Cambridge, MA: Harvard University Press, 1992, pp. 37–53.
'Response to Arthur Marwick', *Journal of Contemporary History*, 1995, 30(2): 233–46.

See also

Croce, Hegel, Kant (MP), Nietzsche (MP and CT), Sartre (MP), Vico, Walsh.

Further resources

Carroll, N., 'Interpretation, History and Narrative', *Monist*, 1990, 73(2): 134–66.
Cohen, S., *Historical Culture: on the Re-coding of an Academic Discipline*, Berkeley, CA: University of California Press, 1987.
Constan, D., 'The Function of Narrative in Hayden White's *Metahistory*', *Clio*, 1981, 11(1): 65–78.
'Hayden White: Twenty-five Years On', *History and Theory*, 1998, 37(2): 143–93.
Jenkins, K., *On "What is History?": from Carr and Elton to Rorty and White*, London: Routledge, 1995.
Journal of Contemporary History, 1996, 31(1): 191–228.
Kansteiner, W., 'Hayden White's Critique of the Writing of History', *History and Theory*, 1993, 32(3): 272–95.
Kellner, H., 'Narrativity in History: Post-structuralism and Since', *History and Theory*, 1987, 26(4): 1–29.
——, *Language and Historical Representation: Getting the Story Crooked*, Madison, WI: University of Wisconsin Press, 1989,
La Capra, D., *Rethinking Intellectual History: Texts, Contexts, Language*, Ithaca, NY: Cornell University Press, 1983.
McCullagh, B., 'Metaphor and Truth in History', *Clio*, 1993, 23(1): 23–49.
Marwick, A., 'Two Approaches to Historical Study: the Metaphysical (including "Postmodernism") and the Historical', *Journal of Contemporary History*, 1995, 30(1): 5–36.
'*Metahistory*: Six Critiques', *History and Theory*, 1980, 19(4).
Momgliano, A., 'The Rhetoric of History and the History of Rhetoric: on Hayden White's Tropes', *Comparative Criticism*, 1981, 3: 259–68.

CARTER G. WOODSON 1875–1950

People like Carter G. Woodson show us that it is possible to change the world with deeds and words. Through a host of publications and activities which he arranged as the director of the Association for the Study of Negro Life and History (ASNLH, now ASALH), Woodson spread the message that it was worth studying the experiences of African-Americans to educational institutions and homes across the United States.[1]

Carter Godwin Woodson was born in New Canton, Virginia, in 1875. Although his parents, James Henry and Anne Eliza Woodson, were illiterate former slaves, they instilled in Woodson and his six siblings a thirst for education and a respect for persons. Woodson later recalled that his father 'taught his children to be polite to everybody but to insist always on recognition as human beings; and if necessary to fight to the limit for it'.[2] When not working on the family farm, Woodson attended a one-room school run by his uncles John Morton and James Buchanan Riddle. After he turned fifteen, Woodson left school and worked as a farm labourer. To make ends meet, he also took a string of odd jobs, including driving a rubbish truck. Frustrated by how little he earned, Woodson followed his brothers to the coal mines in West Virginia. One of the miners, Oliver Jones, employed Woodson to read newspapers and magazines aloud in the tea room he operated out of his home.[3] Reading stirred Woodson's interest in education, and in 1895 he moved to Huntington to attend Frederick Douglass High School. He completed four years of coursework in two years and then pursued further studies at Berea College, Kentucky, and the University of Chicago. After graduating in 1903, he taught at a school for miners' children in Winona, West Virginia, Frederick Douglass High School and in the Philippines. Woodson's experiences in the Philippines, where teachers used American textbooks and took classes in English, led him to reflect critically on the educational experiences of African-Americans. Education, he later argued in *The Mis-education of the Negro* (1933), must be built upon the experiences and needs of students. Furthermore, it must aim to break down the barriers between groups in society. What students needed, he claimed, was to see that the achievements of African-Americans were worth celebrating. For Woodson, that could be best achieved by writing African-Americans into American history.

On his return to the United States in 1907, Woodson enrolled at the University of Chicago. He took undergraduate and graduate courses simultaneously and wrote a master's thesis entitled 'The German Policy of France in the War of Austrian Succession' (1908). After graduating from Chicago, Woodson began reading for a doctorate in history at Harvard. A number of his instructors at Harvard, Woodson believed, either neglected African-Americans or left them out of history altogether. Woodson's complaints about such bias soon led to difficulties with his doctoral supervisors, Albert Bushnell Hart and Edward Channing. Eventually, the celebrated historian of the West, Frederick Jackson Turner, helped Woodson to complete his thesis. That thesis, 'The Disruption of Virginia', incorporates many of Turner's ideas on westward expansion and the formation of American identity. Woodson was the second African-American (the first was W. E. B. DuBois) and first son of slaves to gain a doctorate in history. Not long after, Woodson published what was to be the first of many books: *The Education of the Negro prior to 1861: a History of the Education of the Colored People of the United States from the Beginnings of Slavery to the Civil War* (1910). In this work he argued that fear of social rebellion explained the closure of many plantation schools in the nineteenth century. *The Education of the Negro prior to 1861* was widely and favourably reviewed.[4]

In 1915, Woodson established the ASNLH, which aimed to 'treat the records of the race scientifically and to publish the findings of the world' so as to avoid 'the awful fate of becoming a negligible factor in the thought of the world'.[5] Four months later, he released the first issue of the *Journal of Negro History* (*JNH*) without the knowledge or approval of the executive council. The council were angered by Woodson's lack of consultation but were pleased with the enthusiastic reception that the journal received in scholarly circles. Woodson soon discovered, however, that it was difficult to solicit articles and financial support. In a number of the early issues of *JNH*, Scally has noted, he wrote articles under friends' names or pseudonyms.[6]

In 1918 Woodson published *A Century of Negro Migration*, a work in which he explored where and why African-Americans moved after the Civil War. He was also appointed principal of Armstrong Manual Training High School in order to improve its vocational programme. He was soon disgruntled by staff and funding shortages, however, and resigned to take up a position at Howard University. Woodson greatly expanded the scope and number of history courses offered, but strained relations with the president, J. Stanley Durkee, led to his resignation in 1920. Shortly thereafter he was appointed dean of the college department at the West Virginia Collegiate Institute. While at the Institute, Woodson studied the history of African-American education in West Virginia.[7] He also established the 'Associated Publishers' in order to publish works on African-American history that white firms were reluctant to handle. In addition, he worked hard to keep the ASNLH running. In 1921, grants from the Carnegie Foundation and the Laura Spelman Rockefeller Memorial Fund made it possible for him to work for the ASNLH full-time. He began several research projects, focusing in particular on slavery, African-Americans who owned slaves, the African-American Baptist church and the experiences of African-Americans during 'Reconstruction' (the re-incorporation of seceded states after the Civil War). He also published countless articles in the *JNH* and in a number of African-American newspapers, including Marcus Garvey's *Negro World*. Woodson stopped writing for *Negro World*, however, when he learned that Garvey had met with leaders of the Ku Klux Klan.

Between 1921 and 1930 Woodson wrote fourteen books: *The History of the Negro Church* (1921); *Fifty Years of Negro Citizenship as Qualified by the United States Supreme Court* (1921); *Early Negro Education in West Virginia* (1921); *Free Negro Owners of Slaves in the United States in 1830:*

together with *Absentee Ownership of Slaves in the United States in 1830* (1924); *Free Negro Heads of Families in the United States in 1830: together with a Brief Treatment of the Free Negro* (1925); *Negro Orators and their Orations* (1926); *Ten Years of Collecting and Publishing the Records of the Negro* (1926); *The Mind of the Negro as Reflected in Letters Written during the Crisis, 1800–1860* (1926); *Negro Makers of History* (1928); *African Myths together with Proverbs* (1928); *The Negro in our History* (adapted for primary students as *Negro Makers of our History*, 1928); *The Negro as Businessman* (with J. H. Harmon and A. G. Lindsay, 1929); *The Negro Wage Earner* (with L. J. Greene, 1930); and *The Rural Negro* (1930). Drawing on public records, census information, newspapers, local histories and personal papers, Woodson explored five major themes: slavery as a social system; African-American labour during and after slavery; the importance of western expansion in American history; migration as an expression of resistance against oppression; and the centrality of religion in African–American culture.[8]

The Negro in our History and *Negro Makers of History* were designed to take Woodson's ideas into schools and universities nation-wide. The former went through nineteen editions as Woodson wanted to keep it constantly up to date. It covers such topics as Black civilisations in Africa, the enslavement and transportation of Africans, African-American repatriation schemes after slavery, the role of African-Americans in the Civil War and Reconstruction, and recent claims for social justice. Locke argues that *The Negro in our History* 'belongs to that select class of books that have brought about a revolution of mind'.[9] *Negro Makers of our History* is an adaptation of *The Negro in our History* for primary students. In both works, Woodson encouraged students to reflect on questions such as 'Is the world indebted to Africa for anything of much worth?' and 'Had the Negroes of that day any history to write? Have they any now?' (*Negro Makers of our History*, pp. 20, 231). But Woodson wanted to reach an even wider audience. To that end, he inaugurated Negro History Week in 1926. He wrote of this celebration:

It is not so much a Negro History Week as it is a History Week. We should emphasise not Negro History, but the Negro in History. What we need is not a history of selected races or nations, but the history of the world void of national bias, race hate and religious prejudice.[10]

His idea was well received, and before long people were marking the occasion with parades, breakfasts, banquets, speeches, poetry readings, lectures, exhibits and special presentations. This initiative, plus his contribution to African-American scholarship, earned him the National Association for the Advancement of Colored People's (NAACP) Spingarn Medal in 1926. Negro History Week, now Black History Month, is still celebrated annually in the United States.

Though Woodson began to gain recognition for his efforts, he still found it hard to obtain financial support. With the world-wide depression in the 1930s, that task became even harder.[11] Woodson kept the ASNLH, the *JNH* and Associated Publishers afloat and even began new research projects and ventures such as the *Negro History Bulletin* (*NHB*). The *NHB* was launched in 1937 to supplement the printed materials that the ASNLH produced for schoolchildren and the general public. Woodson used the *NHB* to express his views on American history and to promote values such as tolerance and thrift.[12] However, he was careful to avoid promoting any political line, because he thought it would compromise the credibility of his work and lead to the loss of financial support. Increasingly, the ASNLH functioned as a clearing house, providing research assistance to scholars and to the general public. Woodson had to get more done with less money and he even resorted to taking on janitorial duties at the ASNLH's headquarters. Between 1933 and 1942 he still managed to find time to write six books: *The Mis-education of the Negro* (1933); *The Negro Professional Man and the Community: with Special Emphasis on the Physician and the Lawyer* (1934); *The Story of the Negro Retold* (1935); *The African Background Outlined* (1936); *African Heroes and Heroines* (1939); and *The Works of Francis J. Grimké* (1942).

All of these were well received. His plans for a *Encyclopedia Africana*, on the other hand, generated controversy among African-Americans. During the 1930s, the Phelp Stokes Fund agreed to support the publication of an *Encyclopedia of the Negro* edited by W. E. B. DuBois. Woodson was angry at not being asked to participate in the project and expressed his misgivings about the combination of white funds and African-American research. Woodson even rejected DuBois' offer to combine projects. Woodson died before any of the *Encyclopedia Africana* could be published (April 1950).

Few people read Woodson's writings today. When held up against the works of contemporaries such as W. E. B. DuBois, it is clear that they lack polish and a coherent philosophical foundation. But there is more to Woodson than his words. Woodson's genius lay in his creation of the ASNLH, the Associated Publishers, *Journal of Negro History*, *Negro History Bulletin* and Negro History Week and in his sponsorship of innovative research. Through these deeds, Woodson laid the foundations for the mainstream recognition of African-American history as a legitimate area of study and fostered critical reflection on contemporary views of African-Americans. For these achievements alone, Woodson deserves the title of 'father of African-American history'.

Notes

1 Although 'African-American' is the acceptable term for persons of African ancestry today, in Woodson's time the acceptable term was 'Negro'. ASALH stands for Association for the Study of Afro-American Life and History.

2 'Early History of Negro Education in West Virginia', *Journal of Negro History*, 1922, 7(1): 23–63.

3 On Woodson's early experiences, see 'My Recollections of Veterans of the Civil War', *Negro History Bulletin*, February 1944, 7: 115–16.

4 See, for example, M. W. Jernegan's review in *American Historical Review*, 1916, 21(2): 119–20.

5 See *Journal of Negro History*, 1940, 25(4): 422–3; 1925, 10(4): 600. See also *Journal of Negro History*, 1914, 4(4): 474, and 1924, 9(1): 103–9.

6 M. A. Scally, *Carter G. Woodson: a Bio-bibliography*, Westport, CT: Greenwood Press, 1985, introduction.

7 See *Early Negro Education in West Virginia*.

8 J. Goggin, *Carter G. Woodson: a Life in Black History*, Baton Rouge, LA: University of Louisiana Press, 1993.

9 A. Locke, Review of *The Negro in our History*, in *Journal of Negro History*, 1927, 12(1): 99–101.

10 'The Celebration of Negro History Week 1927', *Journal of Negro History*, 1927, 12(2): 105.

11 For details of the financial history of the ASNLH, see Goggin, *Carter G. Woodson*, pp. 108–39.

12 These values are clearly reflected in the following children's books on Woodson: F. and P. McKissack, *Carter G. Woodson: the Father of Black History*, Hillside, NJ: Enslow, 1991; and T. Bolden and L. Knox, *Through Loona's Door: a Tammy and Owen Adventure*, Oakland, CA: Corporation for Cultural Literacy, 1997.

Woodson's major works

The Education of the Negro prior to 1861: a History of the Education of the Colored People of the United States from the Beginnings of Slavery to the Civil War, New York: G. P. Putnam & Sons, 1915; reprinted by Ayer, 1968.

A Century of Negro Migration, Washington, DC: ASNLH, 1918, reprinted by Russell & Russell, 1969.

The History of the Negro Church, Washington, DC: Associated Publishers, 1921.

The Negro in our History, Washington, DC: Associated Publishers, 1922.

Free Negro Owners of Slaves in the United States in 1830: together with Absentee Ownership of Slaves in the United States in 1830, Washington, DC: ASNLH, 1924.

The Mind of the Negro as Reflected in Letters Written during the Crisis, 1800–1860,

Washington, DC: Associated Publishers, 1926, reprinted by Russell & Russell, 1969.
(with L. J. Greene) *The Negro Wage Earner*, Washington, DC: ASNLH, 1930.
The Mis-education of the Negro, Washington, DC: Associated Publishers, 1969.
The African Background Outlined, Washington, DC: Associated Publishers, 1936.

See also

Diop, Moody, Turner.

Further resources

ASALH homepage: http://www.asalh.org
Durden, R. F., *Carter G. Woodson: Father of African-American History*, Hillside, NJ: Enslow, 1998.
Goggin, J., *Carter G. Woodson: a Life in Black History*, Baton Rouge, LA: Louisiana State University Press, 1993.
Greene, L. J., *Working with Carter G. Woodson, the Father of Black History: a Diary, 1928–1930*, ed. A. E. Strickland, Baton Rouge, LA: Louisiana State University Press, 1989.
——, *Selling Black History for Carter G. Woodson: a Diary, 1930–1933*, ed. A. E. Strickland, Columbia, MO: University of Missouri Press, 1996.
Meier, A. and Rudwick, F., *Black History and the Historical Profession, 1915–1980*, Urbana, IL: University of Illinois Press, 1986.
Scally, M. A., *Carter G. Woodson: a Bio-bibliography*, Westport, CT: Greenwood, 1985.
Stone, E. M., *Dr Carter G. Woodson*, Nashville, TN: Winston Derek, 1996.
Thorpe, E. E., *Black Historians: a Critique*, New York: William Morrow, 1971.